D0411891

SISTER QUEENS

Katherine of Aragon and
Juana, Queen of Castile

➤-<

JULIA FOX

DISCARDED

Weidenfeld & Nicolson
LONDON

First published in Great Britain in 2011
by Weidenfeld & Nicolson

1 3 5 7 9 10 8 6 4 2

© Julia Fox 2011

All rights reserved. No part of this publication may be
reproduced, stored in a retrieval system, or transmitted, in
any form or by any means, electronic, mechanical,
photocopying, recording or otherwise, without the prior
permission of both the copyright owner and the above publisher.

The right of Julia Fox to be identified as the author of
this work has been asserted in accordance with the
Copyright, Designs and Patents Act 1988.

A CIP catalogue record for this book
is available from the British Library.

ISBN- 978 0297 85756 3

Typeset by Input Data Services Ltd, Bridgwater, Somerset

Printed in Great Britain by CPI Mackays, Chatham ME5 8TD

Weidenfeld & Nicolson
The Orion Publishing Group Ltd
Orion House
5 Upper Saint Martin's Lane
London, WC2H 9EA

The Orion Publishing Group's policy is to use papers that
are natural, renewable and recyclable products and made
from wood grown in sustainable forests. The logging and
manufacturing processes are expected to conform to
the environmental regulations of the country of origin.

LIBRARIES NI	
C900235228	
Bertrams	28/02/2012
942.052092	£20.00
LURGRP	

For John

Contents

PART IV *Sister Queens*

PART V *The Sky Darkens*

PART VI *Adversity*

Preface

Over the centuries Katherine of Aragon has become an icon: the Betrayed Wife, the Perfect Queen, the Devoted Mother, a woman callously cast aside by a selfish husband besotted by his strumpet of a mistress. While much of this may be true, it turns a woman into a cardboard caricature. By endowing her with almost saint-like attributes, we not only lose sight of the real Katherine, we strip away her basic humanity and we demean her. Her sister, Juana, is also a woman of myth. She is 'Juana the Mad', the wife so in love with her husband that she could not bear to be parted from him even by death, keeping his coffin with her for year upon year, sometimes opening it to gaze lovingly at his decaying corpse, and driving herself mad in the process. Or so we are told.

When I began this book about three years ago, I wanted to peel back the legends to reveal the flesh and blood women behind them. And I became convinced that the only way to do this was to place them squarely back into their family and Spanish contexts and, crucially, to try to recreate their interior worlds. Only then would I have any chance of getting to know them, of discovering what made them tick and how they gained the values by which they lived and died. And they lived in a turbulent age. It was one of religious warfare, of heroism, of family honour, of vast wealth and grinding poverty, of suffering, of ambition, of romance, of beauty, of ideas, of Machiavellian intrigue. Above all, it was one in which women, especially royal women, were readily sacrificed upon the altar of dynastic politics.

Katherine's downfall as a consort came because she failed in that most basic of female functions, that of bearing a son and heir for her powerful husband. Juana produced children with apparent ease, but that was still not enough to ensure success as a sovereign queen. To rule in her own right, she needed the consent of the men around her; it was her tragedy that in her father, her husband and her son, she faced opponents not allies. She deserves to step forward from their shadows, just as Katherine deserves to step forward from that cast by Henry VIII.

The more I delved into the lives of these two remarkable women, the more I realised that looking at their stories together enriches our understanding of both, even though Juana's long years of incarceration inevitably prevents a totally equal allocation of space within the pages of this book. The sisters complement each other, they epitomise their era. They are linked not only by blood, but by their fight against the forces ranged against them, for they were born female in a male-dominated society. I hope I have done them justice.

As ever, I stand on the shoulders of giants, to all of whom I owe an immense debt. Among them are some I must single out. Although written more than sixty years ago, Garrett Mattingly's biography of Katherine began the process of bringing her back to life. David Starkey's extensive work on Henry VIII and his refreshing re-appraisal of Katherine provide an unrivalled exemplar of the best of thoughtful, insightful modern scholarship. Peggy Liss and Felipe Fernández-Armesto have cast eagle eyes over Isabella of Castile and her family; their studies are indispensable to anyone interested in this amazing dynasty. And in her ground-breaking work on Juana, Bethany Aram has presented a compelling picture of this unfortunate princess.

I would also wish to express my gratitude to so many other people who have helped and encouraged me in the writing of this book. I must thank my agents, Peter Robinson in London and Christy Fletcher in New York, for their unswerving support and confidence. My editors, Alan Samson and Susanna Porter, were generous with their time and advice; I could not have attempted this project without them. Emma Guy's patient, painstaking deciphering of my scribbled handwritten notes has resulted in an impressive family tree. I am very grateful to my former student, Dr Jessica Sharkey, for permission to refer to her unpublished doctoral thesis. I must commend too the staff of the various record offices and at the London Library for their courtesy, professionalism and help. To my dear friend, Glenys Lloyd, whose critical judgment and analysis are second to none, I am extremely grateful. It is through Glenys that I had the good fortune to meet Dr Dafydd Wyn Wiliam, who introduced me to the Welsh poetry and literature of the Tudor age, and who so willingly gave of his time to transcribe and translate the beautiful and relevant examples which grace the pages of this volume. I would also like to give special thanks to Margaret Riley, with whom I spent many a happy hour discussing Katherine and all her activities. And to my other family members and friends, who strove to keep me sane over the past few years, I can only offer my sincerest thanks and appreciation. But, as always, my deepest gratitude and my love must go to my husband who has welcomed Katherine and Juana into our hearts and into our lives. He has read every word of this book and offered invaluable comments and advice. I owe him an immense debt.

October 2010

Genealogical Tables

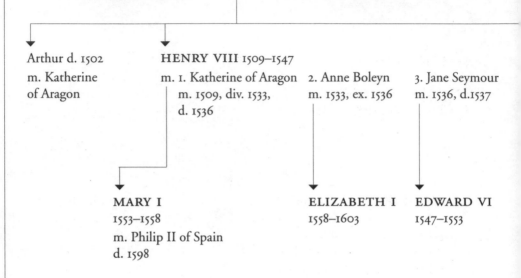

HENRY VII (1485–1509) m. Elizabeth of York (1466–1503)

Arthur d. 1502
m. Katherine
of Aragon

HENRY VIII 1509–1547
m. 1. Katherine of Aragon
    m. 1509, div. 1533,
    d. 1536

2. Anne Boleyn
m. 1533, ex. 1536

3. Jane Seymour
m. 1536, d.1537

MARY I
1553–1558
m. Philip II of Spain
d. 1598

ELIZABETH I
1558–1603

EDWARD VI
1547–1553

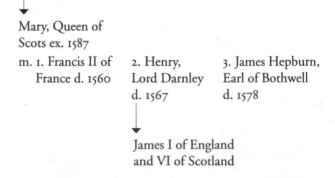

Mary, Queen of
Scots ex. 1587
m. 1. Francis II of
    France d. 1560

2. Henry,
Lord Darnley
d. 1567

3. James Hepburn,
Earl of Bothwell
d. 1578

James I of England
and VI of Scotland

d.   died
diss. dissolved
div. divorced
ex.   executed
m.   married

The Tudor Succession

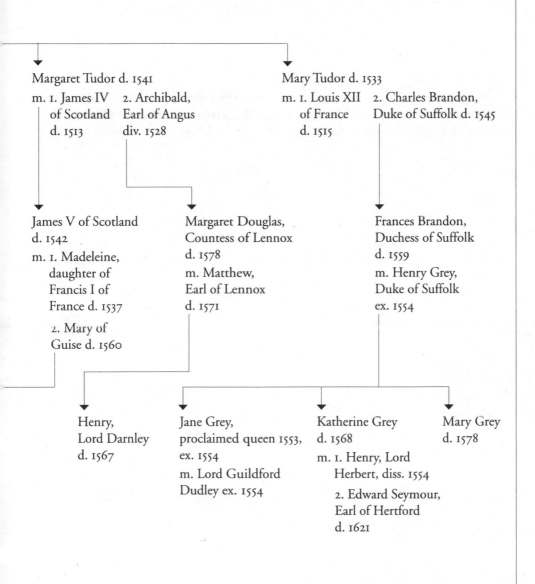

Margaret Tudor d. 1541
m. 1. James IV   2. Archibald,
   of Scotland   Earl of Angus
   d. 1513   div. 1528

Mary Tudor d. 1533
m. 1. Louis XII   2. Charles Brandon,
   of France   Duke of Suffolk d. 1545
   d. 1515

James V of Scotland
d. 1542
m. 1. Madeleine,
   daughter of
   Francis I of
   France d. 1537

   2. Mary of
   Guise d. 1560

Margaret Douglas,
Countess of Lennox
d. 1578
m. Matthew,
Earl of Lennox
d. 1571

Frances Brandon,
Duchess of Suffolk
d. 1559
m. Henry Grey,
Duke of Suffolk
ex. 1554

Henry,
Lord Darnley
d. 1567

Jane Grey,
proclaimed queen 1553,
ex. 1554
m. Lord Guildford
Dudley ex. 1554

Katherine Grey
d. 1568
m. 1. Henry, Lord
   Herbert, diss. 1554

   2. Edward Seymour,
   Earl of Hertford
   d. 1621

Mary Grey
d. 1578

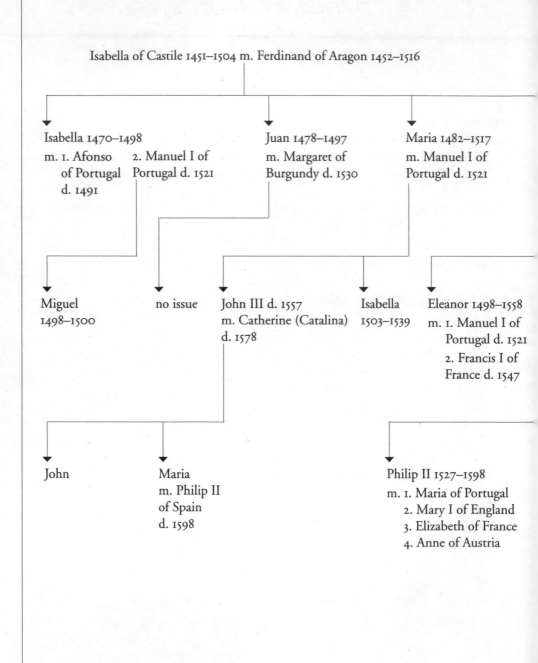

Isabella of Castile 1451–1504 m. Ferdinand of Aragon 1452–1516

Isabella 1470–1498
m. 1. Afonso   2. Manuel I of
of Portugal   Portugal d. 1521
d. 1491

Juan 1478–1497
m. Margaret of
Burgundy d. 1530

Maria 1482–1517
m. Manuel I of
Portugal d. 1521

Miguel
1498–1500

no issue

John III d. 1557
m. Catherine (Catalina)
d. 1578

Isabella
1503–1539

Eleanor 1498–1558
m. 1. Manuel I of
Portugal d. 1521
2. Francis I of
France d. 1547

John

Maria
m. Philip II
of Spain
d. 1598

Philip II 1527–1598
m. 1. Maria of Portugal
2. Mary I of England
3. Elizabeth of France
4. Anne of Austria

The Family of Katherine and Juana

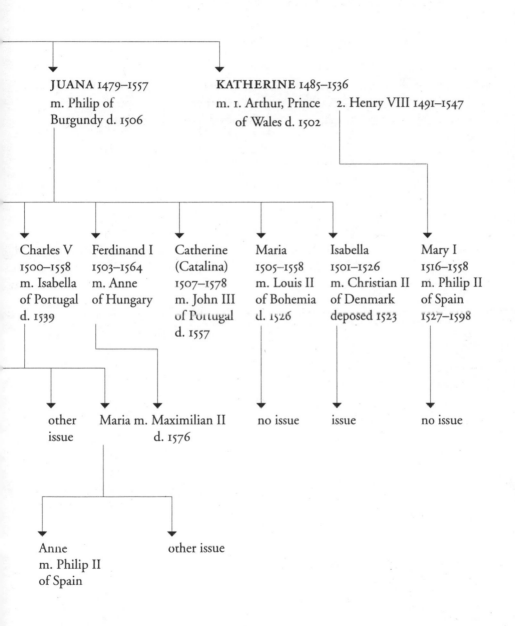

JUANA 1479–1557
m. Philip of
Burgundy d. 1506

KATHERINE 1485–1536
m. 1. Arthur, Prince   2. Henry VIII 1491–1547
    of Wales d. 1502

Charles V
1500–1558
m. Isabella
of Portugal
d. 1539

Ferdinand I
1503–1564
m. Anne
of Hungary

Catherine
(Catalina)
1507–1578
m. John III
of Portugal
d. 1557

Maria
1505–1558
m. Louis II
of Bohemia
d. 1526

Isabella
1501–1526
m. Christian II
of Denmark
deposed 1523

Mary I
1516–1558
m. Philip II
of Spain
1527–1598

other
issue

Maria m. Maximilian II
        d. 1576

no issue

issue

no issue

Anne
m. Philip II
of Spain

other issue

PART I

Isabella's Daughters

A Triumph of Faith

The snow-covered mountains of the Sierra Nevada were clearly visible from the high, castellated red walls of the citadel as the slight figure of Boabdil, the last king of Granada, slipped out of its gates for the final time. Mounted on his mule and accompanied by fifty of his most trusted soldiers, he slowly made his way down the steep, icy paths formally to surrender the keys of the city. Its conquerors, Ferdinand, King of Aragon, and his wife Isabella, Queen of Castile, were waiting with their children by the banks of the Genil River in the fertile valley below. The date was 2 January 1492. To Boabdil, the day marked the loss of a kingdom and the beginnings of humiliation and exile. To Ferdinand and Isabella, on the other hand, it marked a triumph of faith; faith in the destiny of their country, in their dynasty and, above all, faith in the Holy Catholic Church and the God who was the core of their existence.

For Boabdil was a Moor. The Moors were Muslims who had first invaded the Spanish peninsula from North Africa back in the eighth century and who had quickly dominated much of it. Christian Spanish kings had fought against them over the centuries, gradually winning city after city and mile after mile of hotly disputed territory. The Moors had slowly been pushed back so that by the time of Isabella's birth in 1451 they were concentrated only in the south of Spain. But they had never been completely defeated until that cold January day when Boabdil was forced to give up their last stronghold: the city of Granada itself.

The formalities of surrender had been agreed in advance. Resolutely refusing to face further humiliation despite his defeat, Boabdil had already declared that he would not kneel to the victorious monarchs. Isabella was equally determined that he should show due respect to herself and her husband, for this was the day of which she had dreamed since her wars against the Moors had begun ten years earlier. Too much Christian blood had been spilt, and she was very conscious of the malnourished and overworked Christian prisoners languishing in chains in the circular well-like subterranean dungeons of the Alcazaba, the main fortress contained within the walls of the Alhambra, Boabdil's palace and administrative complex. The captives would soon be freed, but their plight, and the sacrifices of the Christian armies, could not go unrecognised; Boabdil would be treated fairly but he could not expect to get away scot-free. Nor would he.

As arranged, Boabdil turned his mule towards Ferdinand and osten-tatiously pretended to dismount and remove his hat. Boabdil, after all, was the supplicant not the victor. Ferdinand, equally ostentatiously, courteously indicated that he should remain in the saddle. Before handing the keys of the city to Ferdinand, Boabdil then rode towards Isabella who, glitteringly dressed and sitting upon a great white horse, also received him graciously. Knowing his wife as he did, Ferdinand immediately passed the keys on to her. Iñigo López de Mendoza, Count of Tendilla, the new governor of the city, and Hernando de Talavera, the gentle, ascetic cleric who had served as the queen's confessor and whom she had appointed its archbishop, then rode up the hill and away from the rejoicing crowds towards the Alhambra itself. The city, complete with its citadel, was now part of Spain. Moorish control was over, and Ferdinand and Isabella's crusade against them concluded, if only for the moment.

Boabdil left behind his lands and his palaces to settle on the estates allowed him by Ferdinand and Isabella in the Alpujerras, an area lying to the south of Granada. He was to stay there for only one year. In 1493, he sailed to Africa, much to Isabella's delight. He died shortly afterwards. Ironically, his half-brothers and his mother, sensibly bowing to reality, were baptised, the young men marrying Castilian noblewomen and settling comfortably into Christian society.

Four days after Boabdil handed them the keys to Granada, Ferdinand and Isabella entered the city for the first time to make their way up the path so recently trodden by Boabdil and then into the amazing world that was the Alhambra. Their royal standards, together with that of St James of Compostella, the patron saint of the enterprise, flew proudly from the battlements of the Alcazaba and the huge silver cross, which had been in the vanguard of the armies since the wars had started, shone out from the Tower of the Winds. The banners would be lovingly preserved and can still be seen today, a little faded but otherwise intact, in the museum of the Royal Chapel of Granada's cathedral, just a stone's throw away from where Ferdinand and his queen now lie.

Those watching the royal cavalcade snake through the narrow streets filled with tiny houses on 6 January 1492 said that the couple appeared 'more than mortal, and as if sent by Heaven for the salvation of Spain'. It was a momentous day, a never-to-be-forgotten day. For the defeated Moors, peering through their latticed windows as their new masters rode by, it was terrifying; the monarchs had promised to allow them to continue their traditional way of life and to practise their religion, but the brutal treatment Ferdinand and Isabella had meted out to the citizens of the Moorish port of Malaga, where most had been enslaved, hardly encouraged confidence in the future. In contrast, Isabella and her husband were ecstatic. Even before Granada's capitulation Ferdinand had been quick to trumpet his exploits against the Moors. Having captured an outlying town, he wrote to Elizabeth of York, Henry VII of England's wife, to let her know because, as he said, his 'victory must interest all the Christian world' so it was only his 'duty to inform' her. With the fall of Granada itself, letters almost flew around European courts announcing it. On receipt of his, Henry VII ordered a special *Te Deum* to be sung in St Paul's Cathedral in London. Another of Ferdinand's letters reached Pope Innocent VIII proclaiming the city 'won to the glory of God, the exaltation of the Holy catholic Faith, and the honour of the Apostolic See'. Innocent died a few months later, but his successor, Alexander VI, gave the title los Reyes Católicos – the Catholic Monarchs – to Ferdinand and his wife.

When they entered Boabdil's palace of the Alhambra, the royal couple were accompanied by their five children: Isabella, Juana, Maria, Katherine and Juan, their only son who, although not yet fourteen, had been knighted by his father before the walls of the city. Theirs had been an itinerant life: during the conflict's many campaigns, the queen had kept her offspring at her side whenever possible so that she could supervise their education and upbringing.

This had not been entirely without risk. One night, as the Christian armies slept peacefully in their camp near to the besieged city of Granada, the queen's tent had suddenly caught fire. Perhaps a candle or lamp had been left too close to the hangings but, whatever the cause, the flames swiftly took hold and spread with alarming speed. Juana, who had been sleeping soundly with her mother, found herself roughly woken up and dragged though the dense, choking smoke to safety. The noise, the shouts and the thick smoke roused the entire camp. Soon soldiers were running everywhere to check if they were under attack, for the besieged defenders had a nasty habit of riding out in sorties to take the offensive. The fire was eventually extinguished, although not before it had caused massive damage and left Juana with an exciting, if frightening, memory. Ferdinand, who had rushed to don armour and join his soldiers to defend the camp, was so alarmed that he ordered the swift building of what went on to become the town of Santa Fe, so that his family could rest within firm walls rather than diaphanous pavilions.

Isabella, scorning danger, had shrugged it off and carried on with her usual activities. A small matter of a fire was not going to stop her. Although never taking part in the fighting, she had frequently ridden with her armies, organising supplies, arranging for medical aid for the wounded and exhorting her troops to deeds of courage and valour for the sake of their God. A retinue of priests accompanied her wherever she went and would join her in praying for victory. Indeed, when the shining silver cross was raised high on the battlements of the Alcazaba, the Spanish armies sank to their knees for a *Te Deum*; Ferdinand and Isabella's monumental undertaking appeared to have come to a magnificent finale. As they explored their new palace, taking in the vibrantly painted and tiled rooms, the intricately carved ceilings, the gently playing fountains of the Court of Myrtles and the Court of Lions, the royal children had every reason to feel proud of their parents. And yet it could all have been so different.

When Isabella had been born deep within Castile at Madrigal de las Altas Torres (Madrigal of the High Towers) in 1451, no one had seriously thought that she would become a reigning queen in her own right, nor that she would be the instrument through which the disparate regions of Spain would become consolidated. For Spain was not then a united country: the Moors dominated the south; Castile, Isabella's homeland, was the largest province, consisting of Castile itself, León, Toledo, Galicia, Murcia, Jaén, Cordoba and Seville, and controlling about two-thirds of the lands we now think of as modern Spain; the kingdom of Aragon, which also comprised Valencia, Mallorca and the principality of Catalonia, controlled the rest.

Isabella, the only daughter of King Juan II of Castile and his second wife, Isabella of Portugal, was third in line to the throne. With two male heirs ahead of her – her half-brother, Henry (Juan's son by his first wife, Maria of Aragon), and her full brother, Prince Alfonso – the young Isabella was to be groomed for marriage not ruling.

Death changed all that. When she was three, her father died and her half-brother, Henry, took over the throne. Although married, King Henry I sired no children; amidst rumours of his impotency, hopes that Alfonso would succeed him seemed well-founded. Or they did until, to the incredulity of the entire court, after seven years of marriage King Henry's queen gave birth to a daughter. Although no one dared say so officially just yet, courtiers gossiped that the little girl was not Henry's at all but was the result of an affair between the queen and a dashingly handsome courtier, Beltrán de la Cueva. The child was even spoken of by the scandal-mongers as 'la Beltraneja' after her supposed father. To this day, we cannot be sure whether or not she really was Henry's child or Beltrán's but the murkiness was a gift to Isabella's brother Alfonso and later to Isabella herself. Neither was prepared to give way to a child they deemed, very conveniently, a bastard.

It was during Henry's reign that Isabella had revealed her remarkable courage and a grittish determination to go to any lengths to achieve her goal, characteristics which were later to be particularly apparent in her daughters Katherine and Juana. Henry, having managed to alienate several key nobles and powerful church figures, found himself facing demands to recognise Alfonso's claim to the throne and disinherit the little daughter he always claimed was his own. Realising the strength of the opposition, Henry did as requested but, a vacillator to his fingertips, changed his mind. The result was civil war. And then, in 1468, probably of plague but suddenly enough to give rise to talk of poison, Alfonso died.

Isabella's position had been radically transformed. She saw herself as heir-apparent. And this was when she played a master-stroke: she married. Rather than let Henry neutralise her by arranging her marriage himself, she took matters into her own hands and became the wife of Ferdinand of Aragon, King of Sicily, the son and heir of King Juan II of Aragon. Just as one day they would negotiate the weddings of their children with clinical practicality, so Isabella and Ferdinand negotiated their own. Undoubtedly a dynastic match, it brought the advantage of mutual support to both participants. In a male-oriented world, Isabella would have a husband who could lead her armies and give her children; Ferdinand, whose family in Aragon were also facing civil war, would have the backing of Castile in any future conflict. And while their marriage treaty did not formally join their lands into one country, mutual cooperation between Castile and Aragon could only strengthen both.

What started as a marriage of convenience quickly became loving and passionate. It was consummated immediately. To a fanfare of trumpets, flutes and kettledrums, the bloodstained bed-sheet was proudly exhibited the following morning. (The failure to do so after King Henry's wedding night had been widely noted.) 'To be well married', Ferdinand was to write to his daughter Katherine, 'is the greatest blessing in the world.' Isabella was eighteen, Ferdinand a year younger. Despite the eulogies of her chroniclers, extant portraits suggest that she was no beauty. Auburn-haired, petite but with a tendency to put on weight, she had a round face, plump cheeks, a small and rather pursed mouth, and eyes which were distant and cold. She also had a very slight double chin. But, as a modern biographer points out, she had a 'youthful freshness' and could certainly be charming and kind when she chose. Ferdinand came to love her, as she did him. Of middling height, he had full, sensual lips, dark hair and a slight cast in one eye. More to the point, he was an accomplished soldier and was soon to prove himself a courageous and resourceful commander.

He had needed to be, for when Isabella claimed the throne immediately after King Henry's death in 1474 and was crowned in Segovia, the couple had been forced to embark on a fierce battle for the throne. Dismissing the claims of Henry's own daughter, whom she insisted on calling la Beltraneja, Isabella went so far as to allege that when the child was born 'certain taps were administered to her on the nose, in order to give it the form of the nose of King Henry IV, and so make her resemble him'. Isabella also had no qualms in repeating hearsay evidence that 'on the same day that the Beltraneja was born, another lady was delivered in the same town of a son'. When 'attempts were made to exchange the Beltraneja', the other mother 'refused to part with her child'. Or so Isabella maintained.

Whatever the truth might have been, it took Ferdinand and Isabella five long years to defeat la Beltraneja and her adherents. In the end, she was immured in the Portuguese convent of Santa Clara in Coimbra, safely out of Castilian territory. She remained a nun until her death in 1530.

The bitter war of succession gave Isabella the opportunity to really prove her mettle. Ferdinand soon discovered that his bride was anything but the submissive stereotype of fifteenth-century womanhood. This was no figurehead but a queen in her own right, and she would rule through that right, proving that the concept of a woman sovereign was no oxymoron. Certain that her cause was just and showing the dogged spirit that her children would witness for themselves as their parents fought the Moors, Isabella not only used spin and propaganda on an epic scale to discredit her rival for the throne but, through sheer personal charisma, energised and inspired her soldiers and shrewdly bargained with her opponents to make them change sides and fight for her rather than against her.

That Ferdinand was with her every step of the way was crucial; she could not have done it without him. Theirs appeared to be a marriage of equals, ostensibly joining their respective lands. In some ways that was true, for both were monarchs rather than monarch and consort, their banners and seals bore both their arms, there were times when they sat together to administer justice. Visitors to Granada today can still see the arms of the Catholic Monarchs, with the arrows of Isabella and the yoke of Ferdinand entwined, firmly placed upon so many doorways, walls and gates to signify their ownership of this once Moorish city. But since Isabella's Castile was far larger, richer and more powerful than Ferdinand's Aragon, he was in a sense the junior partner, and the two kingdoms were never officially joined to make one country. Even the currencies, despite being emblazoned with the heads of both of them, remained stubbornly separate. More importantly still, Ferdinand could not claim Castile for himself any more than his wife could claim Aragon. The union was fragile, depending on the lives of the two individuals concerned. Should either die, Castile and Aragon could break apart again.

But such a prospect was not in the forefront of their minds when they rode into the Alhambra and considered the impact of their victory. The epithet 'The Catholic Monarchs' was well earned. Isabella's Catholic faith was central to her being, and she did all in her power to ensure that the same was true of her children. Although less outwardly pious than his wife, Ferdinand too was devout. It was Isabella, though, who was most determined to convert or rid her lands of those she considered infidels. The true faith must be defended from the enemy within.

And she was quick to take up the challenge. When she appointed Talavera as the archbishop of Granada, it was on the clear understanding that his main task was to persuade his new flock to give up their own religious beliefs and become baptised Christians. As a man who respected the Moors' culture, learning and wisdom, he preferred kindness and example to torture and threats. Isabella, though, was not averse to the use of force in what she believed to be a good cause; in fact, to her, if the cause was good, the means really did justify the end. The establishment of the Holy Office, or the Inquisition, which brought so much fear and distress to those unlucky enough to fall into its hands, was very much the policy of the queen, who applied to Rome for papal permission to set it up in 1478. It would be used against her new subjects in Granada.

It would also be used against the Jews, despite Isabella's assertion at the beginning of her reign that her Jewish subjects were under her protection. Convinced that Jews who had converted to Christianity, the conversos, were being influenced to return to their old faith by those who had not converted, Isabella was incensed that souls were being lost and a mockery made of her church. So, in March 1492, and from Granada, the Catholic Monarchs issued an order expelling all those Jews who refused to become Christian. They were given until July to comply or to leave Spanish shores. Those who remained and were now ostensibly Christian were subject to the pitiless control of the Holy Office.

Isabella had no doubts of the wisdom of her decision. She had made it for God and for the sake of Spanish unity. The lands ruled by herself and Ferdinand would be united under God, the souls of the righteous would be protected, there would be no toleration for infidels. And, as they sat with their parents and their siblings in the rooms and courtyards so recently enjoyed by Boabdil and his court, Katherine and Juana, the two sisters whose fortunes were to be so closely joined, understood that they too were committed to the service of Spain and, even more importantly, to the service of God.

Royal Siblings

With the fall of Granada, Juana and Katherine had settled down with their parents and their siblings at the town of Santa Fe, just outside the city. Ferdinand and Isabella, though elated by Boabdil's departure and surrender, had not moved into his recently vacated palaces immediately. They had wanted to be sure the area was safe and they needed to make some basic repairs. This done, the family slept within the Alhambra's walls for the first time in April 1492.

Juana had been born at Toledo on 6 November 1479. Isabella had not contemplated suckling the infant herself because breastfeeding was commonly believed to delay a mother's ability to conceive. Instead she had entrusted her baby to a wet-nurse, Maria de Santistevan. Soon the child grew into a very lively, pretty and graceful little girl who was to develop into a beautiful woman. She was, the Venetian ambassador would write, 'very handsome'.

Katherine had been born six years later, on 16 December 1485, in the Archbishop of Toledo's castle in Alcalá de Hénares, a town about twenty miles from Madrid, her birth coinciding with a convenient lull in the wars against the Moors. Although known to us as Katherine, a name she was given after Isabella's grandmother, the daughter of the English duke, John of Gaunt, she was always called Catalina within her birth family. She inherited her mother's fair colouring but her features were more sensitive than Isabella's, her lips more yielding, the set of her jaw less pronounced, her 'sweet face' suggesting a submissive, compliant nature. Appearances are often deceptive.

To imagine the Alhambra as Juana and Katherine's childhood home is tempting but fanciful; the truth is that after their initial visit in 1492, the royal family did not return to the city until 1499. In fact, home was where their parents, usually their mother, were at the time and she was rarely anywhere for long. All rulers sometimes travelled throughout their lands to show themselves to their subjects and establish their authority, but the Catholic Monarchs moved around more than most. After the civil wars that Isabella had fought to gain her crown in the first place a public display of majesty and power was politic. Then, during the Reconquista, as the wars against the Moors were always known, the Catholic Monarchs were to be found wherever the fighting happened to be. Isabella wanted her children with her whenever it was practicable, and so the close-knit family had journeyed together from camp to camp, from village to town, from city to city.

But although almost fourteen by the time she saw the golden walls of Granada again, the city was clearly very important to Katherine. When she left her homeland to marry abroad, she had to choose a personal badge. She chose the pomegranate. She never said why. Yet while she probably had many reasons for her choice, we have a clue to one of them: the Spanish word for pomegranate is 'granada'.

It is easy to see why the city and Boabdil's palace retained so special a place in her memory. Even today the Alhambra is magical. With its dramatic backdrop of the Sierra Nevada mountains, the hill on which the main buildings are set dominates the rest of the city. As the young Katherine sat by one of the delicately carved arched or rounded windows, she could gaze down on the maze of tiny houses in the narrow streets below. She could see the great mosque which her parents would turn into a huge cathedral, she could see the Albaicin, the area that housed the metal foundries and the silk works, she could see the Vega, the richly fertile, well-irrigated plain which provided the city's food. She could wander through the shaded arcades where Moorish sultans and their court had so recently sat on cushioned pavements, glowingly coloured hangings adorning the walls behind them as they sheltered from the summer heat listening to music and poetry or discussing matters of state. And she could go into the throne room, with its tiled floor and intricately sculpted ceiling, where Boabdil had met with the Christian negotiators before accepting their terms and yielding his last stronghold. Years later Juana's future son, Charles V, was so enchanted by his visit to the complex that, contemplating Boabdil's capitulation, he was reputed to have said that he would rather have made it his grave than give it up.

It was not that Katherine was unacquainted with such buildings. The Catholic Monarchs and their family were familiar with Islamic art and culture since other former Moorish cities and towns, such as Cordoba and Seville, had already fallen into Christian hands. But the Alhambra was, and still is, different. Many of its rooms were small and intimate, their decoration spectacularly beautiful; its gardens were enticingly cool in the scorching summer sun; its setting was unique; its romance as the venue for the Moors' last stand was beguiling. Isabella and Ferdinand both fell under its spell. They commissioned artists and craftsmen to restore it, albeit with alterations, they frequently held court there and Isabella chose Granada as her burial place. But it was more than a work of art: it was the symbol of Christian success, the city that above all others represented the triumph of their faith over that of the Moors. Katherine shared her mother's joy when the royal mosque was consecrated as a Christian church and a Franciscan monastery founded in what had been a leading Moor's private house. Reverently, the Moors had carved Arabic inscriptions on the palace walls to glorify and praise Allah. 'There is no conqueror but God' could be read everywhere, as it still can today. Neither Ferdinand nor Isabella would have had any quarrel with that sentiment, provided it was their God who was the conqueror. Capturing Granada and assuring the supremacy of Catholicism had been the queen's personal crusade; Katherine and Juana, who would one day have their own crusades to wage, could appreciate that.

While the Alhambra brought them into close contact with Islamic art, learning and wisdom, Juana and Katherine also grew up within the context of the European Renaissance. Keen to ensure that Spain was not a cultural backwater, Ferdinand and Isabella welcomed foreign scholars, endowed chairs in Hebrew and Greek in the University of Salamanca and patronised artists from abroad as well as from within their own realm. Katherine and Juana may well have lived amidst the bustle of a court which was forever on the move, but it was not a court bereft of ornament or exquisite artefacts.

Isabella's art collection contained a number of stunning works. With an eye to posterity, she commissioned portraits of herself and her children, a few by one of her favourite court painters, Michael Sittow. While today many of her pictures, frequently on a religious topic, are scattered through the galleries of Europe, there are also many which remain in Spain, some housed in the museum close to her tomb, a few paces away from the glass cases containing the standards and pennants which once dominated Granada's towers. Thus it is still possible to gaze on pictures that Isabella loved, several of which Katherine and Juana too would have seen.

There is the *Garden of Gethsemane* by Botticelli showing Christ kneeling beneath a comforting angel as He prays for the cup to be taken from Him; the disciples, separated from Christ by a wooden fence, sleep peacefully close by, blissfully unaware of what is to come. There are versions of the Nativity by masters such as Hans Memling, Rogier van der Weyden and Dieric Bouts, all of breathtaking beauty. There are depictions of the Crucifixion which do not shield the viewer from the full agonies of Christ upon the cross or from the harrowing grief suffered by the Virgin at the death of her son. Such images are not for the squeamish. What is interesting, though, is that the type of painting which appealed to the queen, and to which she exposed her children, tended to be conservative and contemplative, with suffering a key theme: the queen bought Botticelli's *Garden of Gethsemane* not his *Birth of Venus*.

A similar emphasis can be seen in the tapestries which Ferdinand and Isabella accumulated over the years. They inherited some, received others as presents, but purchased most themselves, so that Isabella possessed about 370 tapestries by the time she died. Again they were religious or moral in tone, several being used by the queen and her family in their chapels or in their private places of prayer, and again the pain of the Crucifixion is overt. The children would have been left in no doubt that suffering was an inevitable part of life and should be borne with stoicism, even with willing acceptance.

And yet their early lives were not unhappy or filled with care. There was music and dancing, and there were presents. For the Christmas of the year when Granada fell, Ferdinand had taken time off from the Reconquista to choose dolls to delight his daughters. The little girls were even given dolls' clothes in which to dress them. A much-cherished gift for the Catholic Monarchs' son, Juan, was the chess set which he kept in his bathroom. And the children were often allowed the sweetmeats they so clearly relished; they could gorge on rose-flavoured syrup, on quince jelly, on aniseed balls, on lemon blossom candy. And their clothes were splendid too, for upon such matters were royal houses judged. Cloth from Flanders and from England was imported; there were velvets and silks; there were pretty ribbons; there was coral; there were hoops for farthingales; there were hats; there were fur-lined cloaks. Even the mules that they rode were equipped with silk and brocade to adorn saddles and girths. Every luxury that money could buy was lavished upon the children. An awareness of human tribulation and the importance of repentance and redemption did not preclude parental love.

And it certainly did not preclude the need for ostentatious display. Later in her life, the queen was comfortable in the coarse habit of the Franciscans, and indeed asked to be buried wearing one, but this was not how she would have appeared in public. When Roger Machado, one of a group of envoys from Henry VII met her in 1489, he wrote that 'the Queen was all dressed in cloth of gold, she wore a head-dress of gold-thread, and a fine necklace adorned with large pearls, and large and very fine diamonds in the centre'. On another occasion, Machado said that the rubies in her headdress were the 'size of pigeon's eggs'. Isabella knew exactly when it was politic to impress an audience: her simple, much-used bead rosary can still be seen but so can her elegant, regal silver crown. And, as she appeared before her people, so did her children. 'It was a beautiful sight', wrote Machado enthusiastically, 'to see the richness of their dresses.' Yet this was despite Isabella once protesting to her confessor that 'all excess is distasteful to me'.

Even as children, Katherine and Juana had understood that their gender determined their future. It was their brother, Juan, who was destined to govern their parents' kingdoms; their role was to marry foreign princes and bear children, preferably sons. When they became wives, Katherine and Juana were led to believe, they should dedicate their lives to the service of God and act as ambassadors for their homeland. If they were lucky, the man they married might be young, handsome, chivalrous and charming, or he might be as old as their father; marriage could bring them joy or despair. Although Ferdinand and Isabella would never have deliberately prejudiced their daughters' happiness, neither could they afford to take that into account. What mattered was that the girls should cement useful alliances with foreign powers to benefit Spain, for adept and shrewd queen consorts could wield considerable influence over their spouses. It was for such marriages that they were born and it was with this in mind that Isabella planned their upbringing. She wanted to equip her son with the knowledge needed to run his domains and her daughters with the skills and accomplishments that would make them desirable and respected wives and mothers.

Isabella approached this task with characteristic practicality. Acutely aware of her own educational deficiencies, she determined that her children would not suffer from the same limitations. The queen's religious ideals were certainly shaped by the early years she had spent in her mother's highly devout household at Arévalo but, other than that she was instructed in housewifely crafts like spinning, weaving, sewing and baking, we know very little of her education. While she was certainly taught to be literate, a formal classical training was considered unnecessary as no one dreamt that she would one day rule Castile in her own right.

After becoming queen, Isabella had worked to fill the gaps in her own knowledge. While fighting the Moors she found time to study Latin, the international language of diplomacy and culture, soon considering herself sufficiently expert as to correct pronunciation she thought inaccurate, and both she and Ferdinand were keen to promote learning within their dominions. Isabella's championing of educational achievement not only meant giving tacit approval to erudite women such as Doña Lucia Medrano who lectured publicly at Salamanca, it earned fulsome accolades for herself.

Using the works she had inherited from the existing royal library at Segovia as a basis, Isabella built up an extensive collection of books and manuscripts. While most of them were in her native Castilian, she also had several in Latin or in translations from the Latin. With her passionate religious faith, the fact that many were bibles, prayer books, homilies or general religious tracts is unsurprising, but she went very much further than that. There were chronicles of Spanish history; a copy of Caesar's *Commentaries*; there were works on how princes should be educated; there were books on the law; there were volumes of Aristotle and on moral philosophy; there were Virgil's poems and Aesop's Fables; there was Boccaccio's *Decameron*; and there were also works on chivalry and romance such as those about King Arthur. Isabella was indeed the Catholic Monarch, but her interests were more eclectic than that title suggests. And it was not just Juana and Katherine but her other three children who would reap the benefit of the queen's love of learning.

Of all of them, the eldest daughter, another Isabella, was probably the most similar to her mother in her intense piety. The queen's first child, she was born in 1470, just a year after her parents married. She grew into a serious-minded girl, emotionally close to her mother, and always conscious of her duty to Spain and to God. Until her brother Juan was born in Seville seven years later, Princess Isabella was the Catholic Monarchs' only heir. She was given the title of Princess 'of the Asturias', to signify this special status, the title being the Spanish equivalent of 'Prince of Wales' in England or 'Dauphin' in France. Clearly, though, the king and queen yearned for a male heir: the long gap following her first daughter's birth had worried Isabella so much that she had asked her doctors' advice.

The sheer jubilation and delight that greeted Juan's arrival was tangible proof that a boy was always more welcome than a girl. And this was even true for Isabella. Despite being the epitome of successful female monarchy, she knew that it was her duty to produce future kings. It was Juan, whom she called her 'angel', who was her main pride and joy.

The child was baptised when he was ten days old. In an age when infant mortality was common and could strike rich and poor alike, babies needed to be given God's protection very quickly if they were to avoid any risk of a perpetual after-life in limbo, the terrible nothingness awaiting those who died before being received into the Church. Crowds, braving the searing heat, had lined the streets of Seville on 9 July 1477 as the procession wound its way to the cathedral for the baptism, the baby in the arms of his nurse and accompanied by the most important figures of the court and the city. No expense was spared. This was, after all, the first glimpse the people would have of the boy destined for kingship. Isabella did not attend. As was the custom, she would have to wait until being ritually purified of the corruption of childbirth, a ceremony which usually took place about a month later, before returning to normal religious life.

Isabella was to be disappointed in her hopes for a second son. When she gave birth again, in 1482, it was to a third daughter, Maria. Like Juana, her second daughter, Maria was a healthy baby, but her birth was tinged with sadness for Isabella since Maria was one of twins; the other child did not survive. Three years later the queen had Katherine, her last child.

As soon as they were old enough, the children's education began. Most effort, of course, was devoted to Juan, the son and heir, for he needed to be equipped for government, although the Catholic Monarchs had earlier lavished particular care on the upbringing of their eldest daughter, Isabella, going so far as to let her participate on state occasions. Her position, naturally, was transformed by Juan's birth but even then she was kept involved in political affairs, for infant mortality was an ever-present worry. With the succession in the forefront of their minds, Ferdinand and Isabella ensured that doctors saw Juan every day to check on his general health.

The prince's daily routine was carefully programmed. He fitted in fixed periods of study with his tutor, Diego Deza, with ample time for prayers and for the music which he very much enjoyed. Determined that their son should be as cultured as any monarch in Europe, Ferdinand and Isabella arranged for him to have music lessons, gave him instruments, provided him with his own musicians and no doubt listened proudly as he sang in his pleasant tenor voice. In addition, they did their best to prepare him to rule, encouraging him to sit with them as they discussed matters of state, just as they had done with Princess Isabella. It was Deza who supervised Juan's intellectual development. A Dominican friar who lectured in theology at Salamanca, he was himself an outstanding Latin scholar. His orthodoxy was beyond question so the queen was confident that he could instil the basic tenets of the Catholic faith while giving Juan a grounding in the new humanist, classical learning of the Renaissance. It was important to keep up to date.

As for Juana, as soon as she was seven, her parents appointed Andres de Miranda as her first tutor. As with Deza and Juan, it was his task to teach her Latin, a language in which she became proficient, and Catholic doctrine. Records of some of the little girl's possessions have survived so that we know that she was given a special box in which to carry letters, a lavishly decorated book of hours, prayer books and various Latin texts including poetry. She was taught to ride, she was taught music and dancing, she learnt how to behave in public. And, just like her own mother, Juana learnt housewifely tasks like baking, spinning, weaving and sewing.

Her sister Maria was taught alongside her for a while and then it was Katherine's turn. Katherine too was instructed in the female arts like spinning and sewing, skills in which she was particularly talented for later in life she took considerable pride in making and mending her husband's shirts herself. Music and dancing lessons were also arranged for her. Dancing was something that Katherine particularly enjoyed. She did so in the Spanish tradition, which involved women dancing alone or with other women, making it rather like a public performance.

Then, like her sisters, Katherine was nurtured in the classics, her parents engaging two remarkable humanist scholars, Antonio Geraldini and his brother Alessandro (who stepped in when Antonio died) as teachers. Alessandro, who took his duties very seriously, wrote a book on the education of girls. The book has long since disappeared, but it clearly remained in Katherine's memory, for she was to commission a similar work for her own daughter. Perhaps due to Alessandro, Katherine's Latin was excellent. Both she and Juana were able to speak it fluently, a very useful asset. Katherine would also have had access to her mother's extensive library, although her reading was carefully monitored. She was introduced to the Christian poets, to history, to law, to the lives of the saints and to religious works such as the writings of St Augustine, as well as to carefully vetted classical authors like Seneca. Religion and morals were, of course, central to everything with which the girls were allowed to come into contact. Aesop's Fables would have been allowed because they were a perfect way to teach moral precepts and, for yet lighter relief, there were always Isabella's copies of Arthurian romances and chivalric tales.

Ever-mindful of her own experiences, the queen was determined to give her girls the best start available and, by the standards of her time, she did. Her daughters were not the only educated noble women among the European aristocracy but they were certainly better educated than most women of their era. There was one omission, though: the study of foreign languages was largely neglected. Latin might be fine in the diplomatic sphere, but it hardly allowed for spontaneous chatter in the bedroom.

And what happened in the bedroom was crucial because the carefree years of youth were ending: marriage negotiations were under way almost before the sisters could walk, let alone open a book. Katherine and Juana would soon face futures far removed from the gently playing fountains of the Alhambra.

Of Weddings and Funerals

Even as very little girls, Juana and Katherine were aware that one day they would leave Spanish shores permanently to wed for the good of their country and their dynasty. In 1490, when Juana was eleven years old and Katherine almost five, they were given their first taste of what that really meant.

Throughout the spring and summer of that year, Ferdinand and Isabella hosted a series of magnificent celebrations. There was jousting, there was feasting, there were torchlight processions to accompany the every move of the cloth-of-gold-clad queen and her eldest daughter, Princess Isabella, together with the seventy court ladies, themselves shimmering in brocaded dresses and fine jewels, who were constantly at the side of Isabella and the princess.

And, on Easter Sunday, there was a solemn Mass held in the cathedral of the formerly Moorish city of Seville. Surrounded by guards and members of the court, all sporting their very best and most impressive garments, the royal family went in procession through the crowded and decorated streets to the great church where Juan had been baptised over twelve years before. Once inside the cool, candle-lit building, with the scent of incense heavy in the air, the children listened as the Latin words echoed around them. This was no ordinary service: it was a proxy marriage for Katherine and Juana's elder sister, the girl who had been playing such a prominent part in all of the events her parents were organising. Ferdinand and Isabella had agreed that their first born should marry the Portuguese prince Afonso, heir to the throne then occupied by his father, King John II. Only when she arrived in Portugal would the true marriage ceremony take place but it was customary for a proxy service to be held first.

The extended festivities continued for some months. Since this was the first time that the Catholic Monarchs had married off one of their brood, they took every opportunity to flaunt their wealth, success and might to the other nations of Europe. No foreign power could be left in any doubt of the benefits a Spanish match could bring.

The goodbyes could not be postponed for ever, though, and in November 1490 the princess left Spanish territories and entered Portugal. Once she was there, and married in person rather than by proxy, the round of merrymaking started all over again. We know exactly what happened because several of the banquets and entertainments laid on for the young princess were very well documented by the Portuguese chroniclers.

One evening, there was a mummery.* King John started things off by appearing disguised as the Knight of the Swan. To the accompaniment of mock gunfire, trumpets, horns and minstrels, he came into the hall at the head of a fleet of large model ships which were fixed on to cloth painted with waves and foam. The quarterdecks of the ships were made of brocade, with sails in the princess's colours of white and purple; the ships' rigging was of gold and silk and had flags displaying the arms of both the king and Princess Isabella. Challenges for the next day's jousts followed before King John danced with his new daughter-in-law. After yet more dancing and jollities, everyone retired to their chambers to get some sleep before the jousts began.

The chronicler, Garcia de Resende, described two of the special banquets held in honour of the young couple and again, magnificence was the order of the day. At the first banquet, the royal family, sitting at a brocade-draped table, were waited on by the leading nobles' young sons, all elegantly dressed in the richest of fabrics and all conscious of the honour of serving their king and his special guests. Even those seated at other, lesser tables were served by attendants whose liveries were of brocade and silk.

Every major dish was ushered into the hall with elaborate ceremony, much bowing and doffing of caps, and with fanfares from musicians playing trumpets and drums. Indeed, the noise was so loud that it was impossible for people to hear themselves talk. The gourmet food,

---

* A mummery was a court entertainment which often preceded a joust.

although perhaps not to modern taste, was the most expensive and enticing that the palace cooks could provide. Roasted peacocks, complete with their wonderful tails, together with other game birds and poultry, sweetmeats and fruit, were all proudly conveyed to the tables. And it did not stop there. A golden cart, filled with roasted sheep with gilded horns was brought in. The cart had been so skilfully constructed that it looked as if it was being pulled by two roasted whole steers with golden hooves and horns. For sheer theatricality, the banquet was outstanding. And it was but one of many.

Ferdinand and Isabella could have had no reason to complain of the way in which their daughter was welcomed. However, it was only what they expected, and what Juana and Katherine would one day expect too. A precedent had been set.

But if Princess Isabella's wedding was a blueprint to which Juana and Katherine might aspire, what followed was not. In June 1491, King John was swimming in the River Tagus near to the town of Santarem. Afonso, who was riding close by, suddenly challenged one of his companions to a race to see who could reach the banks of the river first. As he hared off with his friends, the prince was thrown by his horse and killed. Princess Isabella, a wife for only seven months, was now a widow. And the much-heralded alliance with Portugal was in tatters.

The princess and Afonso's parents were heartbroken. The banquets were no more, the music stilled, the tilting fields were silent. And Isabella, her hair cut off to show her sorrow and cloaked all in black, the colour worn for mourning by the Portuguese monarchs, returned home to the arms of her mother, arriving in time to be present when the city of Granada fell.

The change in the princess was glaringly obvious to everyone. Before her marriage, Princess Isabella had enjoyed court entertainments and had willingly danced in public. Henry VII of England's envoy, Machado, had remarked on her performances in his journals. The Catholic Monarchs had asked her to dance for Henry's ambassadors and Machado described her partnering a Portuguese girl whom 'she liked best' of all her ladies. On another occasion, he wrote, she took the floor with all of her ladies, effortlessly executing 'a low dance'. With Afonso's death, however, she became the personification of raw misery. Thin, listless, weeping, she 'determined not to marry' ever again. All she wanted was to devote her life to God and never risk another such crushing bereavement. Faced with her daughter's torment, Isabella supported her as best she could, and she did not immediately rush to betroth her again. For once, the queen put politics aside.

But politics could not be put aside for long. Afonso's accident was more than a personal tragedy for Princess Isabella; it meant that the much-heralded alliance with Portugal was in tatters. It was not, however, beyond repair: the solution was glaringly obvious. The new heir to the Portuguese throne, Prince Manuel, was a bachelor who was already acquainted with the widowed princess, and had always liked her. He was only too willing to take her as his wife. The only problem was trying to reconcile the girl to her duty.

Neither Katherine nor Juana was particularly close to their elder sister. The age gap of nine years between Princess Isabella and Juana, and almost fifteen with Katherine, meant that Princess Isabella was virtually out of the schoolroom even before Juana could read. Nonetheless, both had played their part in the wedding celebrations and both witnessed their elder sister's spectacular collapse. Katherine was still much too young really to understand what had happened to change the princess so radically, but Juana, at twelve, saw only too clearly what it could be like to lose a husband. And it was the question of husbands for their daughters and a bride for their son that was very much preoccupying the minds of the siblings' parents.

The crux of the matter was how best to use their offspring to further Spanish interests. Clearly the alliance with Portugal had to be resurrected but the Catholic Monarchs were also considering how to counter a growing threat from the Valois kings of France. Although still developing in strength and expanding its territory, France was fast becoming the key player on the European stage. The trouble was that this brought France and Spain into conflict. Two main areas were in dispute: having seized the Aragonese provinces of Roussillon and Cerdagne in 1463 from Ferdinand's father, the French went on to invade Italy in 1494. Ferdinand was not only resolved to win back his lost provinces but was also hoping to gain Naples to complement his existing Italian lands of Sicily and Sardinia. Because France would not sit back and let Ferdinand do

whatever he wanted to redraw the map of Europe, encircling the French
by marrying off his children to France's enemies might be the solution.
At least Ferdinand would then have allies in useful strategic spots.

So, as Juan played chess in his apartments, he and his sisters were
becoming living pawns on the board of international diplomacy. Gender
would play its part, for the one sibling who would not have to leave
Spain was Juan. 'They do not like to part with their only son, and to
send him to a foreign country', was said to be the reaction of Ferdinand
and Isabella when a match with the teenage Duchess of Brittany was
suggested for him. As their heir, the Catholic Monarchs could demand
that his bride come to him rather than the other way around.

And they selected that bride and the girls' husbands with considerable
care. Maria would be held in reserve, just in case Princess Isabella
continued to decline and refused to marry the new Portuguese heir; to
save one princess for emergencies was prudent. For Katherine, it was to
be an English wedding. Henry VII, who had won the crown from the
Yorkists on the battlefield at Bosworth in 1485, had two sons, Prince
Arthur and Prince Henry. Katherine would marry Arthur, the eldest,
and eventually would become England's queen. The alliance would be
valuable for Spain since England and France had been enemies for
centuries. Then, for Juan and Juana, a brother and sister team was
chosen: Archduchess Margaret and Archduke Philip of Burgundy.

The duchy of Burgundy was rich in trade and culture. It had also
once been huge, originally straddling much of north-eastern France
and most of what we now think of as the Netherlands, Belgium and
Luxembourg. Geography alone had long made Burgundy and France
uneasy neighbours in the 1470s and had brought the Burgundian duke,
Charles the Bold, into direct confrontation with Louis XI of France.
Casting his ever-avaricious eyes on those Burgundian areas which
abutted his own, Louis had taken his chance to grab what he could of
Charles's lands when the duke died in 1477. Charles's heir was his only
daughter, Mary, who had married Maximilian, the son of the Holy
Roman Emperor, Frederick III. The union was happy, Maximilian
finding his wife enchanting. In a letter to a friend, he described her as
tall, slender, 'lovely, good and virtuous'. Although Maximilian had tried
to recover his beauteous wife's conquered lands, he failed. Yet, despite

her losses, the territories Mary still retained were substantial, chiefly comprising the Netherlands or Low Countries, and consolation had come to the young couple in the form of two healthy children, Philip and Margaret. It was these children who Ferdinand and Isabella thought would be suitable partners for Juan and Juana.

Juana counted herself lucky: she could have been married off to the father rather than the son. When Philip was just four years old, Mary of Burgundy died following a hunting accident. Not one to succumb to the sin of excessive mourning, Maximilian contemplated a substitute with almost indecent haste. A Spanish princess he thought (and he was not too particular about which one) might fill the vacant slot. When the Catholic Monarchs demurred at this, he married elsewhere and so Juana was earmarked for Philip.

On paper, it seemed an excellent bargain for both sides. Conveniently sited on France's doorstep, Burgundy was a promising ally for Spain, and Maximilian hoped to count on formidable support should the French attack those (still extensive) lands that remained. True, Juana would be an archduchess rather than a queen, but if Philip became Holy Roman Emperor some time in the future, she might become an empress. She should do well in the personal sphere as well. Just a year older than herself, Philip took after his mother in looks and in a love of sporting pursuits. He was, wrote the Venetian ambassador, 'above the middle stature, of fair proportions, handsome, and of a most pleasing appearance, and most gracious both in manner and language'. No royal princess could ask for more.

And, with Juan marrying Philip's sister, there was an additional reason for satisfaction. A double marriage was financially advantageous: dowries could be dispensed with, and the fleet which took Juana to Burgundy could bring Margaret back to Spain, which meant that yet more money could be saved. That was ideal too.

Once all was decided, there was the matter of Juana's trousseau and travel arrangements. For sixteen-year-old Juana, all was bustle and excitement. Ferdinand and Isabella were determined to send their daughter off in style so Juana and her mother spent hours choosing the jewels, fabrics and clothes she needed to create the right impression once she reached Burgundy. Ample provisions for the voyage were amassed as well. Two hundred cattle, one thousand chickens and four thousand barrels of wine ensured that Juana and the crew would not starve. Juana's household also included Moorish slave girls; after capturing the city, Isabella had allocated some of Malaga's people as living gifts to her own family and privileged nobles. Having the girls in her entourage was comforting for Juana; it meant that she took part of Spain with her as she entered an unfamiliar world.

Knowing that they might never see Juana again, the entire royal family accompanied her to the port of Laredo where she would board the ship that would take her to her new life. For Katherine, it was a taste of what to expect when it was her turn to leave home. Although she had known that such a parting was inevitable, Isabella found the process heartbreaking. As she watched the small fleet gradually sail out of view on 22 August 1496, the battle-hardened queen wept. She treasured every last moment she spent with her daughter. And she worried terribly over the perils of the journey. The French might attack, the seas were dangerous, anything could happen. She sent several letters to Henry VII, begging him to look after Juana and Margaret as though they were his own children should either of them be forced to seek refuge in an English port.

The queen was right to be worried. The French did not attack, but freak winds caused one of Juana's ships to be wrecked off a sandbank within sight of the Burgundian coast. Although unhurt, Juana lost some of her precious baggage along with some of the ship's crew. It was hardly a triumphant start to her marriage. To make matters worse, when the apprehensive princess looked for her betrothed, Philip was nowhere to be seen: he was miles away in Germany. It was to be several days before they met. But Juana had been well schooled: she knew exactly how to behave and set herself to win the hearts of the people who must now become hers.

The ships that took Juana to the Burgundian Netherlands then braved the return voyage, with Margaret on board. Just like Juana, she too had a terrifying journey. Bowing to Isabella's entreaties, Henry VII was quick to offer help to the young archduchess when the Channel became so rough that she was compelled to shelter in Southampton. With his son's marriage to Katherine in his mind, the king was eager to please the Catholic Monarchs in any way he could. So he sent servants to help Margaret, he begged her to take 'all and everything' she wanted and 'to order any service' she required. He even offered to visit her if she stayed long enough in Southampton. She did not.

Katherine first met her new sister-in-law when Margaret landed at Santander in March 1497. It was difficult not to like her. Margaret was seventeen, bubbly, clever, spirited, charming and very attractive. Ferdinand and Isabella were delighted with her. Juan was entranced. Married less than a month after her arrival, the two were inseparable, the physical side of their relationship so intense that his doctors were concerned for Juan's health.

Weddings were very much the order of the day in 1497. As Katherine greeted Margaret, she prepared to bid farewell to Princess Isabella. Patience had paid off. The widowed princess at last agreed to marry Manuel of Portugal. Following the death of King John II, Manuel had become king in his place, so Princess Isabella would become Queen of Portugal. Now that she had made up her mind to do her duty by her homeland and her family, the Catholic Monarchs set off to escort her to the frontier.

As the royal party set off, all seemed well. Only Maria's future was still under discussion. Juan was blissfully happy with Margaret, Juana was secure as Archduchess of Burgundy, and it would not be too long before Katherine left for England. But then Katherine was brought face to face with tragedy. Her first experience of death had been when Prince Afonso, her sister Isabella's husband, had died so unexpectedly, but Katherine had been barely five then and had never met Afonso anyway. What happened now was very different and, at eleven, she was old enough to share the grief which shattered her family.

The disaster came very suddenly. As the royal party progressed happily to the Portuguese border, a messenger reported that Juan had been taken ill. Instead of going with everyone else, he and Margaret had gone to Salamanca to show themselves to their future subjects. It was there that Juan became ill; even today no one can be sure quite what was wrong with him. Perhaps it was an infection, perhaps tuberculosis, it is impossible to say. All anyone knew at the time was that, whatever it was, it was very serious. Ferdinand rushed to his son's bedside, leaving Isabella to complete the journey with their eldest daughter.

When Ferdinand arrived in Salamanca, he found Juan weak from fever but conscious and able to talk. Horrified by Juan's decline, Ferdinand desperately tried to encourage the boy to fight, telling him that the sickness would soon pass. Juan was more fatalistic. Realising he was in the throes of his last illness, the twenty-year-old prince stoically surrendered to God's will as he had been taught that a good Catholic should, bravely spending his last days preparing himself for death. That death came on 4 October 1497. The deep happiness he had shared with Margaret had lasted for only six months.

His mother's response to the loss of her only son was also in good Catholic mode: 'The Lord hath given, and the Lord hath taken away, blessed be His name', she was reported to have said. Yet Juan's death hit the Catholic Monarchs hard, their own misery compounded by fears for the succession. 'Never was there a death which occasioned such deep and general lamentation throughout the land,' wrote an unknown chronicler. Briefly, the focus switched to Margaret; as Juan had lain dying, his baby had been growing in her womb. But, to the family's anguish, Margaret miscarried.

Scarcely had Princess Isabella reached Portugal than she heard of her brother's death. Somehow she had pulled herself together after her widowhood, now she had to do so again. And this time, she had to cope with more than personal sorrow, for Juan's inheritance was now hers. Together with Manuel, she travelled back to Spain so that her claim to her future legacy could be recognised by the various regional parliaments, the Cortes.

It was a sad homecoming. But there was hope that good fortune would return: she was expecting Manuel's child. To universal joy, the child was born safely and was a boy. But death had not yet finished with Katherine and Juana's family. Still reeling from Juan's demise and Margaret's miscarriage, they had another blow to bear: Princess Isabella died shortly after giving birth. The only comfort was that the child, who was baptised Miguel, seemed healthy, and Manuel agreed that his son could be raised in Spain so that he could learn about the lands that one day would be his. Two years later came the unthinkable: the little boy sickened and died, cradled in his grandmother's arms.

For the Spanish royal family, so much had changed so quickly. Mourning the loss of two of their five children and a grandson, Ferdinand and Isabella tried hard to accept God's will. Yet they had little time to grieve, for state business had to carry on, the dynasty had to be secured. Each of their three remaining children would now have to play her part.

If potentially the most glorious, Juana's task was the most challenging. After kissing her mother goodbye at Laredo, she had had to put thoughts of Spain out of her mind. Now she was her parents' heir and would have to return to be acclaimed by the various Cortes, just as her sister had done before her. As the Catholic Monarchs' third child, this was something she had never contemplated.

The placid Maria, providentially unmarried, slipped seamlessly into King Manuel's bed in her dead sister's place; widowed and childless, he needed another wife and she was available. Through her, the alliance between Spain and Portugal could be maintained.

Katherine was the last to leave home. Perhaps Isabella wanted to wait until Arthur had reached at least fourteen, considered a suitable age for marriage; perhaps she wanted to be certain that Henry's grip on his throne was firm enough to risk her youngest child; perhaps, and quite likely, worn down by the stream of deaths within her family, she found comfort in Katherine's company and wanted to keep her remaining child with her for as long as she could. Whatever her reasons for delay, Isabella knew that Henry VII would not wait for ever, and the English match would bring advantages to Spain. It could not be allowed to disintegrate. So, on 8 April 1501, Isabella wrote to Dr de Puebla, her ambassador in London, to say that Katherine would be leaving from Coruna, the port which allowed 'the shortest passage from Spain to England' as soon as practicable. It was now Katherine's turn to serve her country and her family. She had not yet reached her sixteenth birthday.

'Our Illustrious Children'

While Katherine took her final, lingering look as the shoreline of her homeland gradually disappeared from view, Henry Tudor, Henry VII of England, prepared to meet his daughter-in-law and Arthur his bride.

As far as the king was concerned, all was ready. His plans for her reception were in place, and they were detailed. He had tried to think of everything because this moment was one that he had been working to achieve since 1488 when Katherine had been little more than a toddler and himself still a fledgling monarch on a decidedly rocky throne. Always a man to stand on his own dignity, not only would he require the same courtesy for his son's wife, he was shrewd enough to realise that despite Isabella's pleas that the cost of the various ceremonials should be 'moderate', the Spanish queen too would expect every protocol to be observed. When Princess Isabella had married Afonso of Portugal, the Portuguese could not have been more fulsome; Katherine deserved no less. She might be coming, as her mother stated, 'to be the source of all kinds of happiness' not 'the cause of any loss to England', financially, but she was still a princess of distinguished lineage and any 'dem-onstrations of joy' which might erupt spontaneously at her daughter's reception would be 'naturally agreeable' to Isabella.

Demonstrations of joy did indeed erupt when Katherine's fleet at last reached the safety of the English harbour at Plymouth in Devon on 2 October 1501. She could not have been more welcomed, her mother was informed, 'if she had been the Saviour of the world'. After prettily thanking the mayor for greeting her, Katherine's first act was to go to the nearest church to thank God for stepping on to dry land.

Well might she have done so, for her journey could hardly have been much worse. It was definitely protracted. And she had left Spain without the last-minute farewells that her sisters had enjoyed. Ferdinand and

Isabella had intended to go to Coruna with Katherine so that they could see her comfortably installed on her ship and say their final goodbyes. Isabella's letter to de Puebla announcing that Katherine was to leave as soon as possible is dated 8 April 1501 but, because Ferdinand was forced to suppress a sudden Moorish rebellion, he had not reached Granada, where Katherine was staying, until 15 May.

Granada is always at its best in the mild spring sunshine; the earthy red walls of the Alhambra take on a golden hue, blossom scents the air, the trees are laden with the palest of green leaves. Waiting for him within the palace which she knew she would never see again had been so distressing for Katherine that she became ill and had to delay her departure for almost another week. In view of that her parents had changed their minds about taking her to Coruna as they would only slow her up. Thus, of all their children, it was their last-born who had ridden towards the ship that would carry her to her new life with only her household in attendance. But at least she was taking a little part of Granada with her: her chosen pomegranate badge.

Although she left Granada on 21 May, she had not boarded her vessel until late September. It had taken her almost three months struggling along dusty roads in soaring temperatures even to reach the coast. And then she had faced such furious storms in her first attempt to sail to England that she and her entourage had been forced to take refuge in Laredo before trying again on 27 September. When Henry heard this, he sent 'one of his best captains', Stephen Brett, to guide her towards English shores. Even so, the fifteen-year-old girl had faced yet more 'jeopardies from storms and tempests' before she set foot in her new land. While the weather had been good at the start of the six-day trip, it had deteriorated so much that fellow travellers said that 'it was impossible not to be frightened'. Katherine's faith had been surely tested, but neither then nor later would she ever waver in her trust in the ultimate goodness of her God. But taking her first step on English soil cannot have been anything other than a great relief.

As she made her way in easy stages towards London, Katherine had the satisfaction of knowing that, so far at least, she had done all that was expected of her. Her parents were delighted with their bargain. For the Catholic Monarchs, a new ally against France had been purchased, their enemy's encirclement intensified; by marrying Arthur, Henry's eldest son and heir, Katherine knew that she was playing her part in nurturing her family's interests.

What she did not know was just how tight-fisted her parents had been on the matter of her dowry, a matter that had dragged on for years and years and would come to blight her own position later on. Insisting that the sum agreed 'must be as small as possible', the Catholic Monarchs had pressed ambassador de Puebla to persuade Henry to accept part of it 'in ornament and apparel for the person and the household of the infanta'. De Puebla's opening offer was to be that these goods should comprise one half of the total dowry, although he could slip to one quarter if Henry refused to budge. Eventually Henry had reluctantly agreed that the dowry could be paid in instalments but questions of finance dogged letter after letter that trundled its way between the Spanish and the English courts and there was ominous scope for further argument and dispute even as Katherine set sail.

For the young princess herself, unaware of this particular cloud on the horizon, everything in England was new, from the landscape to the people she met. The Devon countryside, still bathed in the mists of autumn, was soft and luxuriant; even the lush vegetation flourishing close to Granada had quickly given way to harsh, arid plains and a rugged mountainous terrain. Southern England, which she saw before the bleakness of winter had a chance to gain hold, was an area of rolling hills, woodland, and green, fertile farmland.

When he knew that she had arrived safely, Henry wrote to her at once. His letter has survived. Alas, it was 'hardly possible' for him to meet her immediately, he wrote, but he begged her to consider him 'henceforward as your good and [loving] father, as familiarly as you would do the king and queen your parents'. On his part, he said, he was 'determined to treat, receive, and favour you like our own daughter, and in no wise more [or less dearly] than any of our own children'. He could not have been more encouraging. And the carefully selected courtiers whom Henry sent to receive her could not have been more welcoming or helpful. That is, after they had overcome a major hurdle.

There had been one development that Henry's schemes had not

foreseen: because of the dreadful weather, Katherine's fleet had docked at Plymouth. Those instructed to welcome her were over one hundred miles away in Southampton, where she had been expected to disembark. Quickly revising the arrangements, Henry ordered Lord Willoughby de Broke, the high steward of his household, to meet Katherine at Exeter. His overtures were shortly followed by those of the Earl of Surrey and the Dowager Duchess of Norfolk, both of whom treated her with considerable respect and courtesy. Language difficulties were smoothed away with the help of an interpreter. All went so well that, as her stately progress continued, Katherine had every reason to feel optimistic about her future. She also had the consolation of being surrounded by familiar faces from her homeland.

Isabella had spent some time deciding on the numbers and personnel of the princess's household, an issue which had occasioned considerable correspondence with Henry VII. Perpetually balancing his naturally parsimonious nature (which rivalled that of the Catholic Monarchs) with the need for public display, and anxious when he heard that she would be bringing 'an incredibly large' retinue, Henry had requested that Katherine's servants should be 'as small a number as possible'. He promised to provide for her within his own court where she would be 'attended and obeyed and loved by the first noblemen and ladies of the kingdom', obviously a cheaper option in the long run. However, he was also keen that Katherine's ladies should be 'of gentle birth and beautiful, or at least that none of them should be ugly'. Creating the right impression mattered just as much to Henry as it did to Ferdinand and Isabella. In a list which is still extant, we can see that Katherine was to be accompanied by over fifty people, including ladies of honour who in turn had two slaves (presumably Moorish girls taken at Malaga) to care for them. The list also includes a laundress, a master of ceremonies, a major domo, a confessor, chaplains, pages, a butler, equerries, keeper of the plate, a cook, a baker, squires – it goes on and on. The most important figure for Katherine, though, was Doña Elvira Manuel, the first lady of the bedchamber. The young princess looked to the older woman for guidance and support in these early days, support and guidance which Doña Elvira was only too happy to offer.

Although she had as yet seen none of them personally, the princess already had a very good idea of the family which she was about to join. Henry VII, like her own mother, had fought for his crown. With only a slight claim through his mother, Margaret Beaufort (who was descended from one of the illegitimate children of John of Gaunt, Edward III's son and the grandfather of Katherine's own mother), it was chance more than anything that had given Henry his opportunity. That chance had come because of the Wars of the Roses, which were fought between the rival houses of York and Lancaster, the white rose and the red. Although bitter antagonisms had remained quietly simmering beneath the surface, the fighting had largely died down when the leading Yorkist, Edward, became King Edward IV. His early death in 1483 had sparked trouble because both his sons were children. It was then that Edward's brother, Richard, had seized the crown for himself, thrusting aside his late brother's sons on disputed charges of illegitimacy. The two young princes had been imprisoned within the grim walls of the Tower of London; their subsequent disappearance making many suspect that Richard had ordered their murder. Henry Tudor, more or less the last Lancastrian left standing, had decided to take over himself. This he duly did by defeating and killing Richard in the short but desperately fought battle at Bosworth near Leicester in August 1485, just three months before Katherine's birth.

Conquering Richard was one thing; hanging on to the crown was another, but Henry was remarkably successful in doing just that. Otherwise, the Catholic Monarchs would never have envisaged entrusting Katherine to him regardless of how advantageous an alliance the marriage would bring; it would have been the waste of a daughter. Since Henry was also a man who thought before he acted, he would not have wasted a child either, particularly not his precious son and heir. The match suited him: not only did it prove that the Tudors had earned their place as one of the major ruling dynasties of Europe, it might ensure support against France or against remaining Yorkist claimants or plots.

The political dimensions of the marriage had been negotiated between Henry and Katherine's parents, sometimes via direct diplomatic correspondence, sometimes through ambassadors. But the personal side of the union was different and much of this had been undertaken by the two central female figures at Henry's court, his mother and his wife, both of whom were as eager to see the young princess as she was to see them.

Margaret Beaufort was of a type that the daughter of Isabella of Castile would recognise: austere, pious, formidable, a woman to be reckoned with. Married around the time of her twelfth birthday to Edmund Tudor, a man twice her age, Margaret gave birth before she was fourteen to the child who would one day become Henry VII. Born two months after his father's early death, Henry was Margaret's only child in spite of two further marriages, and she loved him fiercely. She plotted and schemed like a tigress, sometimes putting herself in danger, to secure his future.

Many of the tender letters between mother and son have survived. While punctiliously showing him the respect that kingship engendered, Margaret speaks to him in terms of endearment, often calling him her 'dear heart', her 'only desired joy in the world', her 'sweet king', her 'worldly joy'. And Henry, who could so often appear cold and clinical, responded similarly. In one letter he begged her to forgive him for not writing 'with myne owne hand' as often as he would wish, because his eyesight was 'nothing so perfitt [perfect] as it has ben'.

Extremely wealthy in her own right, Margaret was made even richer once Henry was king. Despite a favourite establishment at Collyweston in Northamptonshire and a mansion on the banks of the Thames, she was often to be found at her beloved son's side, taking the semi-official title of the 'King's Mother'. She was far from being a merely silent, supportive presence. 'The King is much influenced by his mother ... in affairs of personal interest and in others,' the Spanish ambassador, Pedro de Ayala, informed the Catholic Monarchs. 'Affairs of personal interest' naturally involved the marriages of Margaret's grandchildren. And of those, none would matter more than that of Arthur, Prince of Wales.

Henry's queen, Elizabeth of York, prudently said nothing about what she thought of her mother-in-law's possessiveness, although the same Spanish ambassador told Ferdinand and Isabella that she did 'not like it'. Henry had married her four months after triumphing at Bosworth.

Like everything else he undertook, his marriage was sensible and pragmatic, for Elizabeth was the eldest daughter of Edward IV and the niece
of the defeated Richard III. Marrying her, therefore, ostensibly united
the warring factions of York and Lancaster and neutralised any ambitions
Elizabeth might have had to rule herself. Described by the Venetian
ambassador as 'a very handsome woman and in conduct very able', she
was tall, fair, lovely and with a naturally charming manner. While the
king, it was said by the Spaniard de Ayala in his very full report, was
generally 'disliked' because he imposed such high taxes, the queen was
'beloved'. She and Henry had four living children by the time of
Katherine's arrival: Arthur, Prince of Wales, his younger brother, Henry,
and two daughters, Margaret (probably named after the 'King's Mother')
and Mary.

Although Margaret Beaufort was present at many discussions, and
gave her opinion with some force, the private letters about Arthur
and Katherine had been left to their mothers. Elizabeth, keen to
communicate with the Spanish queen, had encouraged Isabella to
contact her so that they could share news on 'our illustrious children'.
In a letter which is still extant, Elizabeth began by flatteringly
declaring that she had always 'entertained singular love and regard'
for Isabella 'above all other queens in the world', and that love had
been 'increased and accumulated by the accession of the most noble
affinity which has recently been celebrated between the most illustrious
Lord Arthur prince of Wales, our eldest son, and the most illustrious
princess the Lady Katherine, the infanta, your daughter'. Despite all
'cares and cogitations', Elizabeth continued, 'we wish and desire from
our heart that we may often and speedily hear of the health and
safety of your serenity, and of the health and safety of the aforesaid
most illustrious Lady Katherine, whom we think of and esteem as
our own daughter'.

Elizabeth had appeared to receive Isabella's letters with great pleasure,
even if perhaps that pleasure was diplomatically exaggerated. The ambassador, Gutierre Gomez de Fuensalida, once told the Catholic Monarchs
how the English queen was so determined that her replies should be
'just right' that sometimes she had them redone three or four times
before agreeing that they could be dispatched. When, on another occa-

sion, two letters from Isabella and two from Katherine herself were delivered, she had refused to give one to her husband who wanted to 'carry [it] continually about him' because she wanted to keep it herself. She had forwarded the others to Arthur.

One matter which had concerned both Elizabeth and her mother-in-law was how they would converse with Katherine when she came, since they spoke neither Latin nor Spanish. Henry, who had spent some time voluntarily exiled in France during Richard III's reign in fear of assassination, spoke excellent French, Arthur was taught the language, and it was the native tongue of Margaret of Burgundy who had married Katherine's brother Juan. French, therefore, seemed the ideal solution, so the queen and the 'King's Mother' had suggested that Margaret of Burgundy should teach it to Katherine so that communication might be easier. Alas, Margaret's marriage to Juan had proved all too short for that to happen.

As for Katherine and Arthur, they too had corresponded, but in Latin. For both, the match was a matter of royal duty, but that did not preclude a personal rapport, and the letters that have survived suggest that a bond was being nurtured. 'I have read the most sweet letters of your highness lately given to me, from which I have easily perceived your most entire love to me,' he writes. 'Traced by your own hand, [they] have so delighted me, and have rendered me so cheerful and jocund, that I fancied I beheld your highness and conversed with and embraced my dearest wife.' He declared himself very thankful that Katherine had 'so lovingly corresponded' to his 'ardent love'. And, like his betrothed, whose luggage already included an exquisitely worked cloth for a christening robe, the teenage prince knew that royal duty involved procreation. Thus, he pleaded that her 'coming . . . be hastened, that instead of being absent we may be present with each other, and the love conceived between us and the wished-for joys may reap their proper fruit'. He, at least, envisaged no problems on their wedding night.

That wedding night was still some way off as Katherine travelled sedately through the counties of Somerset, Dorset and Hampshire towards London, her arrival in every town causing large, excited crowds to gather in the hope of catching a glimpse of the woman who one day would be their queen. She did not expect to meet the king, the queen, the 'King's Mother' and, most importantly, Arthur, until the day of her wedding. But, as would so often happen in Katherine's life, she was soon to discover that events do not always go according to plan.

Face to Face

From their earliest years, Juana and Katherine understood that because their futures would lie in the lands of their husbands they would have adjustments to make in everything from language to food, from landscape to climate, from clothing to cultural mores. Such was the fate of all princesses used to seal alliances. Practical matters could be expected, even planned for, but at the centre of all diplomacy, negotiations and marriage settlements were the lives of two people. To legislate for how they would relate to each other was impossible. Courtly letters promising enduring love were one thing, sexual chemistry quite another.

Juana was in the Netherlands for over a month before she met Philip. To be fair, no one had been quite sure when she would arrive. Not only was her journey difficult, dangerous and unpredictable but the courier sent ahead to bring news to the Burgundians ended up sailing with Juana's fleet since passing through France was too dangerous. The moment Philip heard that she had landed, though, he set off from a meeting of the imperial diet at Lindau, a small town on Lake Constance in Germany, and rode to meet her.

The intervening weeks gave Juana a chance to see something of her new country. She was not quite seventeen and had never left the Iberian peninsula before so everything was very, very new. The picture of health, youth and innocence, she looked wonderful. Like her mother and her sister, Katherine, she had auburn hair and a fair complexion. Her nose was long and straight, her blue eyes were large, deep and soulful, her mouth was an almost perfect cupid's bow, her lips were full, her fingers slim and delicate. If there was a hint of her intense, passionate, volatile nature, it was well hidden. Confident in her worth as the daughter of Ferdinand and Isabella, and well drilled in how to behave and in what her parents expected, she put herself out to be as engaging as possible to everyone she saw as she travelled through the countryside towards the little town of Lier to wait for Philip.

Everywhere she was a success. In Bergen-op-Zoom she was present at the christening of the daughter of a Burgundian noble family who were particularly pro-Spanish; the child was named Jeanne as a mark of respect to her. In Antwerp, which had already planned a lavish reception, she donned cloth of gold to ride through streets lined with cheering merchants and their families, passing houses draped with brilliantly coloured embroidered hangings, and with her presence announced by trumpeters. The crowds thought her enchanting.

En route to Lier, she met Philip's sister, Margaret, the girl destined to return to Spain to marry Juana's brother, Juan, and it was Margaret who went with her to Lier and remained with her for those final days before Philip, tired, dusty and expectant, rode into the courtyard of the nunnery where she was staying. The wedding was due to take place in the large gothic cathedral of St Gummaruskerk on 20 October 1496 but when Philip turned up at the convent a week before that and took one look at his beautiful bride, he wanted the union celebrated, and therefore consummated, earlier. The physical attraction between Juana and Philip was immediate and electric; it was Juana's misfortune that, for her, that initial spark would never be quite extinguished. Philip of Burgundy, she would discover to her cost, liked women too much to be content with marital fidelity.

When Katherine set off for England to start her own married life, Juana had already been Philip's archduchess for five years. In some ways Katherine's reception was similar to that experienced by her sister. She too, had landed unexpectedly, throwing all the advance preparations into disarray. But Henry had quickly rallied, plans had been altered, and Katherine had found herself escorted towards London with appropriate courtesy and respect. What was very different, though, was Katherine's first face-to-face encounter with her betrothed. Hers, although unexpected, was far more sedate.

It happened when she reached Dogmersfield, a palace in Hampshire which belonged to the Bishop of Bath and Wells. According to Don Pedro de Ayala, one of the Spanish ambassadors, Ferdinand and Isabella had given strict orders that their daughter should not be seen by her bridegroom until the day of her marriage. This was a step too far for Henry VII, who decided otherwise.

But it was not until 4 November 1501, a month or so after she had stepped ashore at Plymouth, that the king left his newly refurbished palace of Richmond just outside London to travel to her side. Arthur, in expectation of Katherine's arrival at Southampton, was already waiting for her at the royal hunting lodge at Easthampstead in Surrey. Delayed by poor weather, Henry did not arrive at Easthampstead until 5 November. After spending the night there, father and son rode on towards Dogmersfield only to be headed off by de Ayala who informed them that there was no way they could see the princess. Since Juana had seen Philip before their wedding, and Philip's sister had been greeted with great affection by the Catholic Monarchs soon after her embarkation at Santander, this seems bizarre; that too was what Henry decided 'after certaine musing on this Mynde of the Kinge of Spaine'.

Quite what he mused the sources do not tell us, although one of Katherine's modern biographers suggests that Henry, equally as crafty and wily as Ferdinand, may well have suspected some sort of trick. Perhaps. In any case, the result was that Henry held an impromptu council meeting 'in the Fieldes' at which his advisers 'concluded and answered' that Katherine was now in England and thus the 'Pleasure and Commandement of her seemed to lye in the Power, Grace, and Disposition' of the 'noble King of England'. That was enough for Henry. Leaving Arthur behind for the moment, he rode straight to Dogmersfield where he told Katherine's outraged attendants, who tried to protest that the princess could not see him because she was resting, that he would see her even if she was in bed. This, stated the king, was 'the Mynde and Intent of his Comminge'.

Katherine, showing wisdom beyond her years, graciously bowed to the inevitable and prospective father-in-law and daughter-in-law saw each other for the very first time. Any suspicions that the king may have had concerning Katherine's appearance were swiftly allayed. She was pretty, petite, auburn haired, with a demure expression, yet well educated, poised and eager to please, surely the ideal wife for Henry's precious eldest son. It was true that she spoke no English, but time and

effort would soon remedy that. The king had no doubts that he had
made a good bargain. England would be linked to one of the most
powerful monarchies in Europe and one which, after Isabella's spon-
soring of Christopher Columbus, had yet more potential wealth in the
New World. The prestige value for his dynasty was immense and,
more pragmatically, he had an ally against France and against possible
pretenders. Of the dangers of the latter, he had already received proof.

In 1493, a young man named Perkin Warbeck, claiming to be the
younger of the two sons of Edward IV who had disappeared, presumed
murdered, in the Tower of London in Richard III's reign, had written
to Isabella asking Spain's help in deposing Henry. In return, he would
ensure that England remained a sound friend to the Catholic Monarchs.
Isabella had given no help to Warbeck, although Margaret of York, the
dowager duchess of Burgundy and Philip's step-mother, said that she
recognised him as her long-lost nephew, and he had received aid from
James IV of Scotland and Charles VIII of France. Although eventually
captured and executed by Henry, Warbeck had posed a serious threat
to the Tudor king for some time. Henry did not want anything of that
sort repeated and, with Katherine married to Henry's heir, the king was
confident that Isabella would never prejudice her daughter's chances of
becoming queen by backing his enemy. If a similar crisis ever arose
again, Henry knew he could count on the Spaniards to be on his side.
With Juana as Archduchess of Burgundy, there was even more reason
for the Catholic Monarchs to support the status quo; they would not
encourage war between their daughters' new lands.

With Katherine passing muster, Henry summoned Arthur to see his
bride. In a letter sent to Katherine while she was still in Spain, Arthur
had said how much he yearned for her presence. 'I cannot tell you what
an earnest desire I feel to see your highness,' he had written. Now he
had his chance. The audience at Dogmersfield was followed by a second
and, at this one, the pair were officially betrothed yet again. They had
already been betrothed by proxy three times before, when the Spanish
ambassador, de Puebla, had played the part of Katherine. This time, the
betrothal was celebrated by Arthur and Katherine in person.

After supper, which the king and Arthur took separately from the
princess, they returned to Katherine's chamber to finish the evening

with music performed by her minstrels and with dancing. Katherine danced with her ladies and Arthur with Lady Guildford, the wife of one of his father's ministers. It would never have done for the betrothed couple to have danced together.

Katherine has left us no clue on her thoughts about Arthur but she had no reason to feel disappointed with her lot, even if he did not have the sheer sexual magnetism that radiated from Juana's Philip. Barely fifteen, nine months younger than Katherine, he was a slender and studious youth, but he seemed strong and healthy. From the very few representations still extant, Arthur appears rather like an early version of his father: both have the long, thin nose of Margaret Beaufort, both have fine hair and a firm chin. Arthur's eyes, though, seem less guarded and suspicious than those of his father and his mouth is more like his mother's; it is smaller than his father's, the lips are slightly thicker and, perhaps because he did not yet have his father's responsibilities, they are less set and determined. In looks at least, Arthur showed promise.

He showed promise in other ways as well. His father hoped the boy was destined for greatness. The very name, 'Arthur', set expectations. He had been born on 19 September 1486 at Winchester, which legend declared to be the site of King Arthur's Camelot, where today's visitors to the Great Hall, the only part of the castle remaining, can still see a Round Table reputed to be the very one used by that king. And that same table was there in Henry VII's time. Just as the mythical, chivalrous Arthur and his knights of the Round Table saga guarded the realm, defeated its enemies, saved maidens from passing dragons while the fabled king still found time to rule wisely over a land flowing with milk and honey, so Henry's own Prince Arthur, it was suggested, would eventually build on his father's achievements, lead England to glory and win the devotion of his people. That Prince Arthur was allegedly born under the stars of Ursa Major was a further link to the Arthurian romances. Many believed that the mythical king was associated with the star, Arcturus; the medieval name for Ursa Major was Arcturus. Everything fitted so neatly.

The less savoury aspects of the Arthurian legends such as the adulterous affair between Arthur's queen, Guinevere, and Sir Lancelot as well as the rivalries and betrayals that caused Arthur's downfall were all conveniently ignored by Tudor propagandists. It was enough to kindle evocations of long-past noble deeds, heroism and honour. That the stories were just that, stories rather than fact, did not matter; Henry was marketing a concept.

But he was far too astute to attempt to rely solely on symbolism and allegory. Allusions to the coming of a new golden age rooted in past triumphs were fine for pageants and public displays of Tudor magnificence, but they were hardly suitable foundations for the day-to-day government that, it was hoped, would one day be Arthur's role. Thus, Henry organised the best possible education and training for his heir, just as the Catholic Monarchs had done for Katherine's brother Juan, who had also been destined for kingship. No expense was spared, only the best was good enough, so Arthur's tutors were hand-picked for their expertise.

Thanks to one of them, Bernard André, who wrote a *Life of Henry VII*, we have first-hand information on at least some aspects of the young boy's education which, like Katherine's, revealed humanist influences, although, as a male heir, Arthur's reading material was more extensive and far-ranging than hers had been. Once the prince was competent in the basic skills, John Rede, a former headmaster of Winchester College who later became Warden of New College, Oxford, undertook the next stage of Arthur's instruction, while at the same time acting as his chaplain. Since previously Rede had been a scholar and then a fellow of New College, which was closely associated with the new learning of the Renaissance, his appointment in Arthur's household suggests that Henry wanted his son to be kept abreast of all the very latest intellectual developments, just as the Catholic Monarchs had selected the Geraldini brothers to do the same for their own family.

Precise details of what Rede taught Arthur are not documented, although probably his task was to equip the child with the rudiments of Latin grammar and lead him towards a mastery of the classics, but André tells us that Arthur was a model pupil who learned effortlessly. André himself, a distinguished, blind Augustinian friar and a renowned court poet, became a tutor to Arthur, most likely working alongside Rede, when the prince was ten years old. 'After some years . . . I brought him not a little help,' explained André, 'and that famous utterance of the Apostle Paul has been proved true of me: "Apollo planted, I watered, God has given the increase".' Increase there was. In André's *Life*, he cited a long list of works with which he maintained Arthur was familiar before his sixteenth birthday.

The list is certainly impressive; Katherine would have a husband whose erudition was more than comparable to her own. Grammar, poetry, oratory and history formed the backbone. The focus was largely on classical authors like Cicero, Homer, Virgil, Ovid, Thucydides, Suetonius, Casear, Pliny and Tacitus, but with fifteenth-century human-ists such as Guarino, Leto and Perotti included. Since Arthur was to be a good Catholic monarch, the writings of Christian authors such as St Augustine, in which Katherine herself was well versed, took a prominent place, although André forgets to mention them. Nor does he tell us whether Arthur was acquainted with Sir Thomas Malory's *Morte d'Art-hur*, although it is very likely that he was. Queen Isabella too had Spanish versions of these tales in her own library, so Katherine probably understood perfectly the imagery associated with her betrothed. Where she could not compete with him, however, was in the crucial area of modern foreign languages: since André was a native French speaker, he must have taught it to Arthur.

Isabella had wanted her daughters to have the academic skills she had been denied but to acquire practical skills as well. Katherine's brother, Juan, had been instructed in the art of government via the institution of his own separate court. Set up when he was eighteen and comprising administrative and financial officials as well as his companions, house-hold staff and servants, the court's existence meant that Juan was given everyday experience of what running a royal court actually meant.

It was this type of practical experience that was provided for Arthur, in his case focusing on the government of Wales. From the moment of their betrothal, Katherine had been encouraged to think of herself as not only a Spanish princess, but also as the Princess of Wales. The country had been conquered in the twelfth century by Edward I, who had tried to reconcile the Welsh to his rule by giving them their own prince in the person of his son whom he had created Prince of Wales. That title had been bestowed upon the heir to the throne ever-afterwards and Henry, whose own grandfather, Owen Tudor, had been of Welsh

stock, made Arthur Prince of Wales when the child was but three years
old. Shortly afterwards a special council with the young prince at its
head was established to run Wales and the border areas known as the
Marches. Because of the boy's age, his headship was of course merely
titular and his uncle, Jasper Tudor, ran it for him. While still in his
cradle Arthur had had a separate household from that of his parents and
he had spent his youth in several different palaces and venues. One of
them was Ludlow Castle in the Marches area, a residence to which he
would one day take his bride.

So, when Katherine and Arthur cast nervous eyes on each other at
Dogmersfield, each could feel satisfied. This was a marriage of convenience, not a love-match or a steamy romance rooted in instant sexual
passion as in Philip and Juana's case – it was something far more
mundane. Katherine would gain a well-educated husband of her own
age and of a sufficiently pleasing appearance, Arthur an accomplished
and attractive wife. The greatly relieved young man wrote letters to her
parents in his own hand saying that he had 'never felt so much joy' in
the whole of his life as when he 'beheld the sweet face of his bride'. 'No
woman in the world could be more agreeable' to him, he protested.

Katherine was still not quite sixteen when she came to England. She
had grown up in a world that could encompass family love, the delicate
beauty of the Alhambra, the screams of those condemned to die in the
fires of the Inquisition and the searing sorrows of personal grief. While
the disasters that had struck her family were bound to be in her mind,
she had no reason to think that her own life would be anything other
than happy and lengthy. She would be a wife and a mother, first Princess
of Wales then queen, just as Ferdinand and Isabella and Arthur's parents
had been planning from the time Machado had accompanied the
English ambassadors to Spain all those years ago. A new life was beckon-
ing: Katherine would enter London, which was now her capital city,
and she would marry her prince in St Paul's. The future looked bright.

PART II

Wives

Wedding Pageantry

London. A vibrant, living community, with sprawling streets and wooden gabled houses clustered companionably together, churches, brothels, taverns, great noblemen riding to their town residences, their retainers bunched around them, merchants edging past stray animals and the detritus of human existence as they made their way to their shops or to their warehouses edging the Thames, the ordinary folk working, laughing, perhaps crying as they coped with whatever life threw at them – this was the city which was about to take a Spanish princess to its heart. And it was to the wealthy members of the trade guilds which gave the capital its energy and life-blood, that Henry VII had entrusted the major responsibility for organising Katherine's wedding processions.

Thus, as dawn rose on Friday 12 November 1501, many an anxious eye in the City turned skywards. Luck was with them, it was dry. London was packed to overflowing. Important court figures, nobles like the Earl of Oxford and the Earl of Derby, foreign visitors, anyone who was anyone wanted to be in town for that special time.

The streets on the route Katherine would take were sanded and gravelled to prevent the horses slipping; colourfully embroidered hangings were fastened from the windows of many of the houses; rails were in place to keep back the ordinary folk thronging to see her and to stop anyone getting hurt in the crush and excitement. Guild members, proudly wearing their silk hoods and liveries, were allowed to stand just inside the barriers to get a better view as her procession passed by. As the morning progressed, people started to take their places. Those concerned with the pageants organised for Katherine's delight got into position as well: last-minute adjustments were made to scenery, musicians practised, actors donned costumes.

For the lord mayor, Sir John Shaa, a wealthy goldsmith, it was vital that all went according to plan; the king expected a magnificent show and it was Shaa's responsibility to make sure that Henry was not displeased. Although the chroniclers tell us that Shaa was 'lytill of stature', something of which he was acutely self-conscious, he had proved himself one of the king's most loyal supporters, fighting fiercely for Henry at the battle of Bosworth and earning himself a knighthood as a result. Now was his chance to prove himself in another sphere. In his crimson robes and with his gold chain about his neck, he would ride from the City to meet Katherine on London Bridge.

She had spent the night at the Bishop of Rochester's palace at Lambeth, towards the west of the City and on the more rural south side of the Thames. After her unexpected meeting with Henry and Arthur at Dogmersfield, the king and the prince had ridden on ahead while she had continued her journey towards London in stately, pre-determined stages. She had been met partway by a delegation including Edward Stafford, 3rd Duke of Buckingham, one of England's premier noblemen, who traced his descent from Edward III and was, therefore, not only closely related to the king but had a distant claim to the throne himself, a fact he never forgot. It had been in Buckingham's company that she had finally arrived at Lambeth where she had a couple of days' rest before the London procession.

As Shaa's servants were helping him to get ready, so Katherine's ladies, under the eagle eye of Doña Elvira, were doing the same for her. The documents do not tell us whether it was Katherine herself or Doña Elvira who decided what the princess would wear and how she would enter London, although one suspects it was likely to have been Doña Elvira. What the sources do tell us, though, is that Katherine did both 'aftir the manour of her co[u]ntre[y]'. She wore Spanish garments in the Spanish fashion; her clothing was 'riche', her long auburn hair flowed freely down her back through a specially designed gap in her headdress. The headdress itself consisted of a wide-brimmed hat rather like that of a cardinal which was held in place by a golden lace. It was certainly different and it certainly provoked comment. Then, instead of using the chariot (carriage) that Henry and his queen had been willing to provide for her, she rode into the City but upon a mule not a horse.

Not only were the animal's trappings Spanish in style, its side-saddle pointed in the opposite direction to those normally ridden by Englishwomen. Katherine's ladies, and Doña Elvira, rode just as Katherine did and wore similar hats and clothes, although in Doña Elvira's case her hair was covered with a black mantilla which, in one chronicler's eyes, made her resemble a nun. He also commented on the strange contrast between Katherine's ladies and the cloth-of-gold-clad English ladies, who were paired with them for the procession and who faced in opposite directions because their saddles did not tally.

Katherine herself was probably too excited to notice. Only with the marriage service at St Paul's would her new life truly begin, but this day, the day of her ceremonial entry into the City, marked a rite of passage. No matter what the weather had in store, her sun was just rising. So it was with a feeling of expectation and of duty about to be fulfilled that she mounted her mule to start the journey. Since she was lodged on the south bank of the river and the major events were to take place on the northern side, she had to travel eastwards to cross London Bridge, then the only bridge over the Thames. With her ladies and her attendants, and with her hat tied firmly to her head, she rode off to St George's Fields where the king's second son, Prince Henry, Duke of York, waited to escort her the rest of the way.

Although still only ten, Prince Henry was self-assured, confident in his abilities and in himself. His father had allocated him a leading role in the day's events and he would not disappoint. Poised and at ease, happy to bask in the admiration of the crowds, he greeted the woman who was about to become his sister-in-law and would eventually become his wife, before setting off for London Bridge. Londoners were very proud of their stone bridge. With tall houses and shops clinging to its edges, and forever swarming with citizens rushing about their daily tasks, it was a marvel of their city. For Katherine, the structure was more than just an impressive feat of engineering, it led towards her destiny.

The northern bank of the river was really the heart of the capital and its suburbs. To the eastern side sat the huge Tower of London, started by William the Conqueror after his victory at Hastings over four centuries before, now almost a town itself with its regal apartments, its prison cells, its storehouses, its mint and its menagerie. Here too was St Paul's, its tall steeple topped by a copper-and-gilt weathercock clearly visible even from the south side of the river; and here was the City of London itself, prosperous and proud. To the western side, beyond Temple Bar and Charing Cross, was St Peter's at Westminster, the great abbey-church begun by Edward the Confessor and the place where Henry VII and Elizabeth of York would eventually be buried; here was Westminster Hall where the judges of the King's bench passed sentence on those unfortunate enough to cower before them. There were buildings on the south side of the Thames too, of course, especially in the suburb of Southwark that was closest to the bridge, but it was as if a different world began once that bridge was crossed.

And it was to that different world that Katherine was travelling. While she had enjoyed the privileges that naturally accrued to a child of Ferdinand and Isabella, and she had been cosseted by the English as soon as she had stepped ashore at Plymouth, never before had she been the centre of such attention. This was her day, a chance for the people to see her and for her to see them as she began her transition from being a daughter to being a wife.

When she reached the bridge, Prince Henry solicitously at her side, and the Duke of Buckingham close by, Katherine was met by Shaa and the City dignitaries, all brimming with courteous greetings. She was scheduled to spend the night at the Bishop of London's palace at St Paul's, the church chosen for her marriage, but there were to be entertainments on the way. Six pageants had been devised for her delectation, each with its own elaborate set, actors and musicians and each with its own message that contributed towards an overall theme. All, we are told, were 'goodly' and 'costlewe' [costly].

The first, which took place on the bridge itself, indicated what the series was about: that through virtue, Katherine, together with her husband Arthur, would attain true honour. The holy state of matrimony, therefore, was a recurrent leitmotif. Since the words were, naturally enough, in English, Katherine did not understand exactly what was said by the no doubt nervous actors. But because much of the symbolism was familiar and the occasional Latin inscription gave an additional clue to the sense of each piece, she grasped the essentials. The first tableau was set inside an open-fronted tower, described by one chronicler as a 'tabernacle', which had back walls painted in blue and red and had two pillars at the front. The pillars were decorated with images Katherine recognised as significant to the Tudors and to Arthur himself. Thus there were red roses for the house of Lancaster, portcullises which were associated with the Beauforts and ostrich feathers representing the Prince of Wales. The tower had two floors. St Catherine, complete with wheel and accompanied by a group of young virgins, sat in the lower floor while St Ursula, and her set of virgins, sat in the upper.

St Catherine spoke first. Reminding Katherine that they shared the same name and that she was her particular saint, she told the princess that she would have two husbands, a heavenly one in Christ and an earthly one in Arthur.

St Ursula addressed Katherine next. Ursula was supposed to have been a British maiden who, accompanied by thousands of innocent girls, went on a pilgrimage to Rome but she and they were all murdered by marauding pagans on the way. The key factor here was that Ursula was British – and Katherine could loosely be thought of as British because of her descent from John of Gaunt. Since he had been Duke of Lancaster, Katherine could have considered that the pageant's painted red roses were meant for her too. Ursula went on to talk about Arthur, linking him to the star constellation of Ursa Major and herself to Ursa Minor. It was now that the pageants' writers, of whose identity or identities we remain ignorant, began to allow their knowledge of mythology, cosmology and symbolism, as well as their imagination, full rein. If Prince Arthur had superseded King Arthur – and Ursula told Katherine that he had – then Katherine herself could become a second Ursula and thus epitomise Ursa Minor to his Ursa Major. The young couple would complement each other.

After Ursula's oration, the royal party crossed the bridge and passed into Gracechurch Street where the actors for the next pageant were waiting. This tableau, the 'Castell with Portculleis', took place in the widest part of Gracechurch Street where there was a water conduit. Using the stone conduit as a base, a castle-like structure was set up. Without hindering the flowing of the water or preventing people passing through arches underneath it, it stretched right across the street and was attached to the houses on either side. The castle was made of wood with a cloth painted to resemble stonework masking the underlying framework. Its centrepiece was a huge portcullis dominated by the red dragon of Wales and the royal arms.

The three actors of this section of the drama represented Policy, Nobleness and Virtue. Each spoke in turn, telling her that honour could not be won without nobleness and virtue, both of which had to be combined with good policy. Katherine, the actors declaimed, was lucky: she would find it easier than many to achieve honour since she would have Arthur to help her.

With the outstanding merits of her betrothed still ringing in her ears, Katherine and her retinue entered Cornhill to attend the third pageant. This, the Pageant of the Moon, again stressed Katherine's fortune in being called to the married state, and to the married state with such a 'parfight' prince. According to one of the chroniclers, this section of the entertainments was truly spectacular, 'ffer [far] excedying the othir In cost & cunnyng of dyvyse [device]'. Katherine would not have seen anything quite like it before. Three pillars, two green and one red, were in the foreground of the stage, a backcloth painted to look like stonework behind them and with various royal emblems attached above it, but the centrepiece was a huge blue sphere or zodiac depicting the planets, the stars, the twelve astrological signs and indicating the waxing and waning of the moon. A check cloth painted in the Tudor colours of white and green covered the sides and top of the entire set.

There were four main actors involved: the angel Raphael, King Alfonso of Castile, Job and the philosopher Boethius. Raphael, complete with feathered and glittering golden wings, spoke first. Angels, he told Katherine, were the intermediaries by whom God's purposes and mysteries could be explained to human beings. It was Raphael's own special task to be the angel in charge of marriage. Marriage, stated Raphael, was a gift of God, established for the procreation of children within a loving and reverent relationship. Such a relationship was in store for Katherine.

The actor portraying King Alfonso was the second speaker. The real King Alfonso, one of Katherine's distant ancestors, was a long-dead medieval Castilian monarch who had been interested in academic study and astronomy in particular. It was foretold in the stars, said the actor, that 'a goodly pryncesse yong and tendre' would come to England to marry 'a noble prince'. Clearly, Katherine was that 'goodly pryncesse'. Moreover, the conjunctions of the stars signified that this marriage would be long and happy. Katherine and Arthur were indeed blessed.

Job, the Old Testament prophet, also looked towards the heavens for assurances that Katherine's marriage was pre-ordained and would be successful, basing his reasons on complicated, intricate imagery which only those well schooled in biblical references and interpretations would have fully appreciated. The essence of his text, though, was plain enough.

Whether the princess actually heard what Boethius had to say is uncertain for one of the chroniclers asserts that she moved on before Boethius had a chance to speak. Perhaps she did, but the lines were pronounced (and recorded) nonetheless; no actor willing to forgo his moment of fame on such a day. Boethius in fact said little new, but reaffirmed that Katherine and Arthur were destined for each other and would reign 'in honour and dignytie'.

Leaving Cornhill, Katherine entered Cheapside for the fourth display, this one held near Soper's Lane, once the street for soap makers. Cheapside, with its shops and business premises a principal thoroughfare of the City and very much at its core, was railed and ready. The crowds behind the barricades, some very merry from drinking the free wine which flowed from the conduit instead of the usual water to celebrate Katherine's arrival, strained and pushed to catch sight of the Spanish princess and to marvel at the Pageant of the Sun.

In this one, Arthur, or an image of him anyway, was a key character. Again there were pillars with Tudor symbols like the Welsh dragon or the lion of England perched on top of them, again there were stars, again there were angels and clouds. There was even a representation of God. The predominant feature, though, was another mechanical wheel with the twelve signs of the zodiac painted on it, but this one revolved, propelled by three boys in their early teens, 'stripelinges' as one of the chroniclers calls them. Then, dressed in the 'spirituell Armour of Justice', an actor playing Arthur came into view. He sat in a chariot in the middle of the wheel like the sun dominating the universe. Once the observers had had long enough to gaze at the stage, an actor turned to Katherine, welcoming her to her new lands and reminding her that God had given her a very special bridegroom, one who was a flower among princes.

The real Arthur was waiting with his father a little further down Cheapside, opposite the Standard, a main water conduit, where the fifth pageant was about to start. One of the London merchants, a haberdasher named William Geffrey, had been asked to put his house at the king's disposal since it just happened to be at precisely the right spot to provide a perfect view of the proceedings. No doubt flattered, but certainly aware that such a request was really a command, Geffrey consented: he, along with so many others on that day, would have plenty to talk about for years to come. Protected by the Yeomen of the Guard, Henry, Arthur and a select group of court nobles, stood by a window to watch everything. The queen and the 'King's Mother', Margaret Beaufort, stood by another window. Neither lady had yet seen Katherine for herself, so they were very interested in what was happening.

The penultimate pageant, that of the Temple of God, resembled the previous ones in pillars and royal beasts, but in this one there was even more emphasis on the divine blessings heaped upon the marriage and of the nature of marriage itself. An enthroned God, surrounded by singing angels, sat amidst golden candlesticks and burning tapers. In an overt comparison between Henry and God, the actors declaimed that while God had bestowed matrimony as a sign of the union between Himself and human beings, Henry had bestowed matrimony on Katherine and Arthur to bring peace and prosperity to the realm.

In full view of the family that was now hers, Katherine and her entourage rode towards the final pageant, this one situated near the Little Conduit at the entrance to St Paul's Churchyard. In the grand finale of the series, the princess was invited to imagine that she and Arthur had reached their goal: honour. The stage was divided into two main levels connected by seven stairs, on each of which stood a figure representing one of the seven cardinal virtues. Of the three thrones standing on the upper tier, only the middle one was occupied, and that by a purple-clad Honour himself. The other two thrones, clearly reserved for the prince and princess, were empty, apart from a crown and sceptre left on each. Language problems not withstanding, Katherine was left in no doubt that, by acquiring virtue, she and Arthur would finally gain honour and that this would benefit England and its people. Their marriage would not just ensure happiness and a righteous future for themselves, it would do the same for the country.

The pageants over, Katherine arrived at St Paul's itself, the church in which she and her Arthur would become man and wife on Sunday. There were still more formalities to go through, gifts and speeches from the mayor, the Archbishop of Canterbury to meet, prayers and offerings to be given but, at last, the ceremonies of the day were ended and everyone could disperse.

As Sir John Shaa's servants helped divest their master of his heavy robes and chain, the mayor could congratulate himself on a job well done. He had ridden at the head of the procession, his sheriffs and aldermen in scarlet not far behind him, and had given his mandatory speech of welcome perfectly. He could sleep easy in his bed that night. William Geffrey's attendants set all to rights again in the merchant's house after the royal party had finally left; like Geffrey himself, they would have much to tell their children and grandchildren.

The royal family were delighted with everything and everyone. Queen Elizabeth had caught her first glimpse of Katherine, and the princess was due to visit her the next day. Arthur now knew just what an asset his bride would be. Despite her mule and odd hat, she had behaved with dignity and grace, charming the crowds who had seen her. She would indeed make an excellent queen. Thomas More, a young lawyer who lived near Cheapside and would one day come to know Katherine well, was enchanted by her. In a letter to his old schoolmaster, John Holt, More scoffed at the ludicrousness of Katherine's Spanish escort, but he enthused over the princess. 'She thrilled the hearts of everyone,' he wrote, little dreaming just how closely his own fate would become entwined with hers.

For Henry, who spent the night at Baynard's Castle, a fairy-tale turreted mansion on the river bank, about a quarter of a mile from St Paul's, the day had been a complete triumph. Even the unpredictable weather had been on his side. He had wanted the City to put on a show and put on a show they had; each and every pageant had been cleverly built to impress, the actors had been thoroughly rehearsed, no detail had escaped the choreographers' attention. Ferdinand and Isabella would have no cause for complaint, their daughter could not have been greeted more splendidly. Henry had proved that neither the Portuguese nor the Burgundians, who had welcomed Katherine's sisters, had a monopoly in magnificence. And, for a king who 'coveted to accumulate treasure' rather than spend it, there was another cause for satisfaction: the City merchants had been liable for much of the cost, collecting 500 marks (£333) intended for gifts to Katherine just four months earlier.

How much of the complex and involved convolutions of imagery and symbolism layering these wedding pageants Katherine, Doña Elvira or the rest of her ladies, now fussing over her at the Bishop of London's residence at St Paul's, would really have understood can never be known. It hardly matters. For Katherine, the day was an unqualified triumph. She could sense that the Londoners had warmed to her, she knew just how proud her parents would have been of their youngest daughter. And she had gleaned enough from the pageants to confirm what she had already been taught: her vocation was to marry the English prince and bear his children. It was written in the stars, it was the will of God, it was what she had been born for. So, if the sun was rising for Arthur, it was rising for her too.

The Estate of Matrimony

On Sunday morning, 14 November 1501, Doña Elvira and the princess's ladies gently woke their mistress for what was to be a momentous day. Within a few short hours, Katherine's status would change from the virgin daughter of Ferdinand and Isabella to that of Arthur's true wife and Princess of Wales. No more proxy marriages with a beaming and simpering de Puebla revelling in every minute as he substituted for his princess. This time the ceremony would be the full and solemn ceremony of matrimony, performed in the sight of God.

The bustle and excitement of Katherine's apartments was mirrored throughout the city. In his lodgings at the Great Wardrobe, one of his father's buildings which was conveniently close to St Paul's, Arthur too was up and about on that November morning. As arranged, he prayed quietly and peacefully inside the church, saying his last prayers as a bachelor, before changing into his wedding outfit in a room set aside for that purpose in the Bishop of London's palace; thus he and Katherine were not very far apart. The king, the queen and, as ever, the 'King's Mother', prepared as well. They were to watch the service from a special box inside the cathedral which gave them a very good view while shielding them from curious onlookers. Prince Henry, who had performed so admirably in the processions, was required by his father to escort Katherine into the church; yet another starring role for the king's spare heir. The Duke of Buckingham, another key figure at Katherine's entry into the City, donned embroidered robes, cloth of gold, and furs of sable, to ride in her procession once more. As for Sir John Shaa, out came his crimson garments and gold chain ready for his role in the proceedings; his mayoralty was nothing if not eventful.

Katherine's gown, like that she had worn on the Friday, was very Spanish in style. It was also white, not then the traditional colour for brides. Since Arthur had chosen white as well, the young couple would complement each other as much in clothing as it was hoped they would in life. Just like another Princess of Wales who, almost five hundred years later, would wed her prince in St Paul's (albeit Wren's cathedral not its medieval predecessor which was familiar to the Tudors) Katherine's dress was full sleeved and full-skirted. Katherine's wide skirts, puffed out by hoops, aroused considerable interest among the chroniclers who have left us their versions of the events of that day. They commented too on her veil, which reached to her waist and was edged with gold, pearls and precious stones.

There had been several days of work behind the scenes to make the great church ready. Originally a Saxon foundation, rebuilt after a disastrous fire by the Normans using stones brought from Caen, the church was huge, a symbol of strength, reverence and pride for the citizens of London. Inside there were wall paintings, there were gilded alabaster statues of saints with glittering haloes, there were jewelled chalices and relics on display, and vibrant wall hangings fastened in the choir. Everywhere glowed with colour in the fragrant incense-laden air. A special platform, covered in rich red cloth, railed at each side and with a round stage at one end, ran from the west door towards the choir so that all could see the prince and princess during the ceremony.

Trumpets sounded as Katherine was led into the church by Prince Henry, her train carried by Lady Cecily Welles, the queen's sister. Katherine was accompanied by her ladies, by the ladies of the court, by the most important nobles and figures like Buckingham and Oxford, and by many of her own countrymen who had come with her from Spain, all dressed in the costliest of fabrics and several with gold chains around their necks. When everyone, including Shaa and the City aldermen, had taken their places in the packed church, Arthur stepped forward to stand next to her. She was on his left, for the Bible taught that women had been formed from a rib taken from the left side of Adam. The ageing Archbishop of Canterbury, Henry Deane, performed the nuptials, uttering the well-loved words so familiar to those gathered in St Paul's on that cold November Sunday. The chroniclers did not trouble to record what those words were, they assumed all would know them. And today we still know, for Missals are extant which tell us. Everyone was there, Deane would have announced, 'to join together two bodies' into 'one body', for that was the purpose of matrimony. Arthur and Katherine exchanged vows of fidelity, promising to care for each other in sickness and in health and for richer or poorer, words of love which resonate with us even now. With the formalities complete, Katherine and Arthur turned to both sides of the congregation to acknowledge their obvious good wishes. Then, hand in hand, and now husband and wife in the sight of God, they walked into the main body of the great church for a solemn Latin Mass. And that, at least for the present, was that: the culmination of more than ten years' diplomacy between the Catholic Monarchs and Henry.

The wedding feast which took place inside the bishop's palace, where tables were laid for over one hundred guests, catered for the most discerning of palates. There were three main courses, each one comprising a series of dishes: twelve in the first, fifteen in the second and a massive eighteen in the final one. Lords and knights, none too arrogant to refuse the honour of serving their future king and queen, delivered the laden dishes to the rowdy cheers of the hungry guests. A goldsmith by profession, Shaa was particularly interested in the gold plate on display in two open cupboards, one in the chamber where the meal was consumed and the other in a room nearby. Golden pots, flagons and cups studded with precious stones were exhibited to Shaa and his brother, who are said to have valued the contents of the second cupboard at £20,000. Henry really was determined to show Ferdinand and Isabella that his country was no poverty-stricken backwater on the edge of Europe.

Marriage, however, consists of more than just words. There is a physical dimension. And that was about to come. Doña Elvira and a select group of ladies left the hall during the meal so that they could prepare the marital bed. This had to be done according to strict protocol, a process that took almost two hours. At last, though, all was ready and it was time for Katherine and Arthur to leave their guests and spend their first night together as man and wife. Just as the ceremonies and services were traditional and public, so too was the putting to bed of the newly married couple.

Arthur's companions joined him for some last-minute ribaldry. There was, one of the chronicles says circumspectly, dancing, pleasure and 'myrthe' to cheer and encourage the studious young prince before the time came for him to be escorted to the bedchamber where he was expected to fulfil his duties. As Arthur gathered his courage, and Doña Elvira cast a last-minute glance around the room to make sure all was in order, Katherine's ladies helped their mistress out of her wedding finery and into her night robe. Custom dictated that the bride should be put to bed first, and so she was. Tucked up among the soft pillows and crisp linen sheets of the flower-strewn bed, she waited for Arthur in the candle-lit room.

Katherine did not have to wait for long. A joking, laughing group of nobles and gentlemen ostentatiously escorted their prince to her chamber door. The Earl of Oxford was there, along with the future Earl of Shrewsbury and the Marquis of Dorset, so too came young Anthony Willoughby whose father, Sir Willoughby de Broke, had welcomed Katherine when she first set foot on English soil. Among the other merrymakers was William Thomas, one of Arthur's privy chamber grooms whose tasks included helping his master to dress and, significantly, to undress. As they gathered to watch Arthur climb into bed beside Katherine, who was lying demurely underneath the covers, little did these young men imagine that in twenty-five years or so they would be questioned intimately on all that they thought they saw and heard that night. Nor did they conceive that their answers, and the circumstances under which they gave them, would be forensically dissected by lawyers, then sceptically assessed again by historians almost five centuries later. We can read those answers in printed Victorian summaries but, safely stored in the British Library, for those who can decipher them, are the original manuscripts, fortunately preserved despite the passage of time. And those documents make gripping reading.

If these statements are to be believed, everything certainly seemed to go according to plan. The Marquis of Dorset said Katherine lay 'under the coverlet' as Arthur climbed in beside her; Sir Anthony Willoughby said that he saw the bridal bed 'wherein the said prince was laid with the princess'; Robert, Viscount Fitzwater, said that he saw Arthur in the bed 'where he believed surely the princess lay'; Mary, Countess of Essex, was to assert that she saw Katherine and Arthur in the same bed after the wedding, a statement echoed by the Duchess of Norfolk, who declared that she saw them 'lie ... in one bed', and that she left them there all night. While not specifically referring to the wedding night, William Thomas remembered helping the prince into his nightgown and taking him 'unto the princess's bedchamber door often and sundry times'. Arthur and Katherine always called each other 'prince and princess, man and wife', Thomas continued.

And it was as man and wife that Katherine and Arthur nestled beneath the covers waiting, not just for the assembled group of nobles to leave them, but for a priest to arrive for a final blessing. When he walked into the room, the priest intoned the prayers heard by many a young Tudor couple. He began by blessing the bed itself, asking God to protect its occupants from 'phantasies and illusions of devils'; there should be no bad dreams as Katherine and Arthur should feel safe and protected. The priest went on to bless the prince and princess themselves. 'May the hand of the Lord be over you,' he prayed, 'and may he send his holy angel to guard and tend you all the days of your life.' After sprinkling them both with holy water, the priest left, his duty done. He was followed by the onlookers. Sir Anthony Willoughby tells us that 'at the departing of the noble men every man said to the prince and princess, God give you joy together'.

Whether or not they did have 'joy together', either then or at any other time in their brief months of marriage, was to become an issue which would later rock the very foundations of Tudor England, giving rise to passionate, often partisan, debate. Only two people really knew the truth: Katherine and Arthur. Once the door closed behind the boisterous revellers, prince and princess were alone; there could be no witnesses to what ensued. Anything said by anyone other than the two people involved would be no more than hearsay.

At the time, it was uncritically assumed that sexual intercourse did take place. After the blessing of the bed, one of the chroniclers writes, 'thise worthy persones concludid and consummat theeffecte and complement of the sacrement of matrimony'. Perhaps. There certainly seemed no reason to suppose otherwise. Though Arthur was just fifteen and Katherine almost sixteen, both were considered old enough to

consummate the wedding; Margaret Beaufort had, after all, given birth
to Henry VII before her own fourteenth birthday. And, while he might
have lacked the ebullience and glaring good health of his brother, Prince
Henry, Arthur was no weakling. He had, said the Marquis of Dorset, a
quarter of a century later, 'a good and sanguine complexion'; 'lusty' was
what Charles Brandon had heard said of the prince.

Nor could there be any doubt of what was expected. Katherine's
knowledge of the precise details of the how procreation occurred was
likely to be vague at best but, like all her sisters, she had been brought
up with the dynastic principle firmly entrenched in her psyche. She had
never been in any doubt that her God-given role in life was that of a
wife and mother; even the pageants she had witnessed on the streets of
London emphasised that. The same was true for Arthur. England had
emerged from a period of civil war; if the Tudor regime was to survive,
progeny was essential and, as the heir, it was up to him to ensure that
progeny ensued. So, as the two young people shyly faced each other
in that darkened bedchamber, both were thoroughly aware of their
responsibilities. But it had been a very long, and a very arduous day.
Maybe they did their best, managed an embarrassed adolescent fumble,
but tiredness and inexperience meant that Arthur did not achieve full
penetration; maybe they quite simply fell asleep. Or perhaps, as so
many 'witnesses' confidently asserted when their king demanded their
responses in a court of law, true consummation did in fact take place
once all had left and Arthur and Katherine were, at long last, by
themselves.

Arthur is alleged to have been full of the joys of marriage next
morning as he joked with his gentlemen. If nothing had occurred to
end his own virgin state, he was certainly not going to risk losing face
among more experienced men of the world by admitting failure. On
being jocularly told that he looked 'well uppon the matter', Arthur had
happily boasted that he looked 'well for one that hath been in the midst
of Spain'. Then, just in case his jest had not been fully appreciated, he
went on to make it even plainer, announcing, 'it is good pastime to have
a wife'. Such comments would appear to decide the matter; the trouble
is that his alleged remarks were not repeated and publicly aired until
Arthur lay cold in his tomb and the times had become dangerous.

Immediately after the wedding night, Katherine herself was suitably silent. This is entirely understandable and in character. While the odd bawdy comment was almost de rigueur for a man, it would have been highly unbecoming and demeaning for any woman, and especially for a princess. Katherine spent the following day quietly resting, closeted with her ladies. One of them, of course, was Doña Elvira. If Katherine needed to share the secrets of her bridal bed, her most likely confidante was this woman, whom Queen Isabella had personally chosen to care for her daughter and who guarded her charge jealously. For the moment, Doña Elvira too kept her own counsel, but it may be significant that there was no ostentatious display of bloodstained bed-sheets as there had been after the wedding of Ferdinand and Isabella.

The brief rest was needed as the exhausting round of celebrations continued for several days following the solemnisation of the marriage in St Paul's. Now Princess of Wales, Katherine took her place at Arthur's side within the court as Henry, still delighted with his daughter-in-law, prolonged the festivities despite the cost or his reputation as a king who 'coveted to accumulate treasure'. Hoard he did, but he also knew just when it was politic to spend, and this was one of those times. And at each joust and banquet the importance of the Spanish alliance, which Katherine embodied, was constantly reiterated.

When the jousts began on the Thursday after her marriage, Katherine joined her husband, the king, the queen, Margaret Beaufort, Prince Henry and Arthur's two sisters, Margaret and Mary, together with leading courtiers in the special box constructed for them at the north end of the tiltyard at Westminster. At the opposite end of the field, Sir John Shaa and the most important of the city dignitaries sat in another box, their round of royal duties far from over. As she watched the contenders going through the various combats, Katherine was left in no doubt of her own role as her country's ambassador. Buckingham, who took a prominent role in the jousts' opening day, not only sported ostrich feathers, the acknowledged symbol for the Prince of Wales, in his helmet, but rode a horse whose blue velvet trappings included four castles to symbolise Castile. And, on the final day, a carriage used for a ceremonial entry by some of the competitors was drawn by beasts (actually men inside animal costumes) including a silver lion and an ibex; the silver lion represented León, one of Queen Isabella's provinces, and the ibex was renowned as a Spanish animal.

That Katherine was the living symbol of the Anglo-Spanish alliance was also hammered home to her in various after-supper entertainments performed in Westminster Hall. Sometimes, the spectacles ended with a carefully choreographed dance performed by the actors, sometimes the audience danced. Katherine danced sedately with one of her ladies; Arthur danced with his aunt, Lady Cecily; and young Henry, throwing off his outer gown in the heat of the moment, danced exuberantly with his sister, Princess Margaret, much to the delight of the onlookers. All seemed so perfect.

And yet, if we are to believe what she would swear twenty-five years later, Katherine nursed a secret, for she knew that all was not as it seemed: her marriage was, so far at least, unconsummated. Perhaps it was this which prompted her sudden lapse into childish temper. She was alleged to be visibly very much out of sorts, 'annoyed and pensive' say the chroniclers, when many of the Spanish grandees who had come with her from Spain returned home. Yet the chroniclers generously attribute her changed mood to homesickness; they may be right, the documents give us no more insight. Or perhaps Katherine was only too aware that she could not fulfil her destiny as a wife and mother, working for the interests of Spain as well as England, until she achieved full intercourse with Arthur. Merely sleeping in the same bed was not enough.

King Henry, ignorant of what went on between Katherine and Arthur in their bridal bed, and assuming that her changed mood was indeed due to homesickness, decided to console her by showing her his extensive library at Richmond and allowing her to choose a jewel from a selection that he produced for her perusal. Henry's strategy seems to have worked and Katherine seemed herself again, in public at least.

But the rounds of entertainments and frivolities could not continue for ever. Affairs of state intervened. As Prince of Wales, Arthur had to return to his principality and to his base at Ludlow Castle on the Welsh borders. And, after much discussion between the king, his council, the Spanish ambassador Don Pedro de Ayala (whose responsibilities were shared, sometimes uncomfortably, with Dr de Puebla) and the princess herself, who dutifully professed herself happy to do whatever was thought best, it was decided that the new Princess of Wales should accompany her husband. Although the king was alleged by the ambassador to have used his son to pressurise Katherine into agreeing to go to Wales, it is extremely unlikely that Henry would have consulted his son in this matter; sons were expected to obey their fathers. De Ayala was very unhappy about the journey, suspecting that it was all a devious ruse by Henry to ensure that Katherine was forced to use some of the plate she had brought with her from Spain and which, if damaged, would no longer be counted as part of her dowry. Knowing Henry, that was an eminently reasonable suspicion. De Ayala's additional concern was that the newly married pair would have far too many opportunities for intercourse, which was popularly believed to be unhealthy for very young men. Indeed, Juana's future son, Charles V, would one day assert that 'an undue indulgence' in 'the pleasures of marriage' at too young an age had caused the untimely death of Prince Juan, the Catholic Monarchs' only male heir.

For Katherine, though, the trip to Wales was probably welcome for the very reason that frightened Ayala: if the wedding night really had not proved eventful, living in close proximity with Arthur, well away from the formalities of Henry's court, might just be the answer. Her God-given destiny was to be a wife and mother, so the sooner she started on her mission the better. Thus, on a cold December morning in 1501, with her husband at her side, Katherine, Princess of Wales, began the long journey to Ludlow Castle on the Welsh borders. She little realised that she would return as a widow.

Marital Harmony

In 1501, as newly wedded Katherine travelled with Arthur to Ludlow, her thoughts filled with anticipation and hope for the future, her sister Juana was also making a journey. Together with her husband, Archduke Philip, Juana was returning to Spain.

When she had gone to Burgundy as a bride in 1496, Juana had expected the Low Countries to be her home. As Archduchess of Burgundy and Philip's empress should he succeed his father as Holy Roman Emperor, there would be no reason for her to set foot on Spanish soil ever again. With one brother and a sister ahead of her in the line of the Spanish succession, the idea that she would become her parents' heir had not occurred to her. Yet, with the series of deaths that so afflicted the Catholic Monarchs, that is what happened. All that was Isabella's would certainly come to Juana when the great queen died and, in all probability, everything that had once belonged to Ferdinand would be hers as well. Juana's life had been suddenly transformed.

Juana was no stranger to change, upheaval and upset. The Juana who returned to Spain was very different from the sixteen-year-old girl who had said goodbye to a weeping Isabella more than five years earlier. Not only had she become a wife and mother, she had discovered that marriage was no guarantee of constant happiness. Almost from her first moments in the Netherlands, Juana had been forced to confront problems no one had anticipated, and for which her mother's carefully devised programme of study had not prepared her.

It had very quickly dawned on her that the welcome she was receiving from many of her new subjects ranged from ecstatic to hostile. Unlike Katherine, who had never doubted that Henry VII and his court wanted her to marry Arthur, the teenage Juana had soon discovered that her situation was nowhere as clear-cut. While Philip's father, Maximilian, had advocated the Spanish match as the best way to protect Burgundian interests, many of Philip's own advisers saw closer ties with France as a better long-term bet, so Juana had been caught in the middle of dip-lomatic factionalism from the moment she had first arrived. For a teenage princess, totally untutored in the murky world of political intrigue, it had been bewildering.

Isabella, anxious about her daughter, had sent her envoy, Friar Tomás de Matienzo, Sub-Prior of the Convent of Santa Cruz, to the Neth-erlands to find out what was happening. His detailed reports bear witness to Philip's systematic campaign to assert his dominance over his inexperienced young wife. Worse, they show just how powerless and demoralised she had started to feel.

For, to her dismay, the Philip with whom she had enjoyed such an electric physical relationship had soon shown his true colours. As her husband, and as Burgundy's duke, he required her complete surrender to all his commands, and that included controlling the personnel and the running of her own household, an area in which, according to royal protocol, she should have been independent. Philip and his councillors did 'not permit her to take part in it', she told Friar Tomás.

Philip had begun by taking over her finances: he did not give her the annual sum supposed to be allocated to her for her household expenditure, despite contracting to do just that in their joint marriage treaty. Instead, the archduke's own appointees administered all the money that should have gone to Juana. This meant, the envoy wrote to Isabella, that 'she [Juana] is so poor that she has not a maradevi to give alms'. She certainly did not have the money to pay her servants, who began to drift away because they could not 'sustain themselves at court'. Within six months of her arrival in Burgundy, eighty of her ninety-eight male servants had left her side. That suited Philip very well. It meant he was able to replace the vast majority of his wife's Spanish officials with his own nominees; even many of those who loyally remained were bribed to support Philip as master rather than Juana as mistress. And, totally out of her depth, she simply did not know how to react to the man she could see was taking over her life but to whom she was still so physically attracted.

Yet she had tried. On at least one occasion, Friar Tomás noticed that Juana had found the courage to protest. When asked to approve payments already made, about which she had known nothing, she signed as she was bid but then said, 'Be it so for this year, but next year I desire that they do not make grants without my consent.' As this flash of spirit did not occur until 'after they [Philip's representatives] had left her' wrote Friar Tomás resignedly, 'I think it will always be the same thing'. The envoy was right; Juana saw no point in protesting again. And after each battle that he won, Philip cruelly and deftly went a stage further.

Turning his attention to his wife's private apartments, Philip had insisted that Madame de Hallewin, once his own governess, should become one of Juana's key ladies-in-waiting. Juana's desire to have Doña Marina Manuel, whom Isabella also trusted, in that post had been ignored. According to Friar Tomás, Madame de Hallewin, together with Philip's councillors, 'have so much intimidated' Juana 'that she dare not raise her head'. If she tried to complain to Philip himself about how she was being treated, Juana confessed to Isabella's messenger, her husband just told his councillors and she 'receives great injury from it'. Friar Tomás does not tell us what that 'injury' was, but he does report on her sadness and her growing realisation that she was so very much alone. Luckily for Juana, a handful of her former attendants, including ten of her women, did choose to remain with her so she retained some links to alleviate her homesickness. And homesickness was a problem for her in those early years. 'She could never think of how far she was from your Highness', the envoy wrote to Isabella, 'without feeling the desire to cry, because she was so far from your Highness for ever.'

If Juana cried, she did so privately. In public, she was the gracious archduchess, just as Philip was every inch the affable archduke. Any friction within the marriage was well hidden. On state occasions Juana and Philip dined publicly together, the embodiment of marital harmony. Juana was well dressed and bejewelled, Philip saw to that. Appearances mattered, status had to be upheld. He presented Juana with diamonds and pearls that had once graced the delicate neck of his mother, Mary of Burgundy; he made sure that her horses were impressively saddled; he gave her pictures; he gave her religious items such as an image of St

Margaret, possibly because St Margaret was the patron saint of women in childbirth.

In the latter area, the couple certainly did their duty by the state. Juana produced healthy babies with an ease that Katherine would envy. Clearly disappointed that their first child was a girl, Eleanor, Philip expected Juana to pay herself for the infant's nursemaids and attendants. 'The Archduchess may provide for the places in the household of this child because it is a daughter,' Philip asserted. 'When God grants us a son I shall provide for his household.' God did grant them a son. Juana gave birth to Charles in March 1500, much to Philip's joy: fireworks raced across the sky, church bells rang, and Philip gave Juana a magnificent and costly emerald as a reward. Their third child, prudently named Isabella after Juana's mother, was born in July 1501. Because Juana was pregnant with Isabella when news of Prince Miguel's death and her subsequent inheritance reached her, she and Philip were unable to start for Spain until the autumn of 1501, a couple of months before her twenty-second birthday.

If Juana had not anticipated inheriting her parents' kingdoms, the possibility had certainly crossed Philip's mind. And it had done so from the moment that Isabella's 'angel', Prince Juan, died. In a move unlikely to endear him to his in-laws, Philip had begun calling himself 'Prince of the Asturias', and behaving as though the Spanish dominions and their wealth would one day belong to him, even though Princess Isabella, then Queen of Portugal, was at that time ahead of Juana by virtue of seniority. With the deaths of the Queen of Portugal and of Prince Miguel, Philip's fantasy became reality. The fact that the heir was Juana and not himself was a mere detail; as her husband, what was hers was his. Thus, he was overjoyed at the prospect of accompanying Juana to Spain for the acclamation of the Cortes: by recognising Juana's future title, the Cortes was also recognising his. And he yearned to be a king rather than an archduke.

In the light of all of this, the visit was unlikely to be an unmitigated success. As far as the Catholic Monarchs were concerned, it even began badly. In a move which could not fail to annoy Ferdinand and Isabella, who wanted Juana and her husband to come by sea, Philip decided to take the land route, which meant going through France, Spain's enemy, and meeting the French king, Louis XII, face to face. To make matters worse, Louis and Philip agreed that baby Charles should one day marry Louis's daughter. Juana, of course, was not consulted about the betrothal, and nor were Ferdinand and Isabella, even though Charles was, after Juana, their heir.

But Juana was not entirely suppressed. Although forced to accede to her husband's decision to travel through France, which she knew would upset and worry her parents, Juana deliberately emphasised her birth by ostentatiously wearing Spanish dress. Her refusal to acknowledge Louis's queen, Anne of Brittany, as anything other than an equal also almost caused a diplomatic incident. And while Juana was excluded from the discussions of her son's betrothal, she did arrange that her daughter Isabella should one day marry the heir to Navarre, a kingdom on Spain's northern borders which Ferdinand coveted. Spanish Juana was still alive and defiant, despite Philip.

Inevitably, encounters between Juana and Philip and Ferdinand and Isabella were often strained. Philip was not the obedient son-in-law that the Catholic Monarchs anticipated, eager to earn their approval and happy to pursue a foreign policy in line with their aims. He could be charming when it suited him, and his sporting prowess aroused admiration, but if the Catholic Monarchs had hoped that he would be the Ferdinand to Juana's Isabella, they were in for a major dis-appointment. He was personally ambitious, greedy and vehemently pro-French, none of which boded well for a future king of Spain. For that was what he would become. In theory, he was to be Juana's consort, accepted as such by the Cortes; in practice, he had already resolved to rule himself when the moment came. Juana would need to be strong if she was to assert her authority. And whether Juana really was strong enough to do that certainly troubled her mother.

Feeling disturbed about Juana was nothing new to Isabella. She had been concerned about her daughter's welfare almost from Juana's first months in Burgundy, when disconcerting rumours of Juana's conduct had led her to believe that the girl had abandoned her heritage in favour of a frivolous, unholy way of life. Hence her decision to send Friar Tomás to report on the situation. And Friar Tomás's early reports had only heightened the queen's anxiety. Juana, he wrote in August 1498, 'did not confess on the day of the Assumption' and had no interest in anyone in Spain. However, by January 1499 Friar Tomás had become more reassuring. He had spoken to Juana, he said, after 'she had been to mass', and he stated that 'in her house there is as much religion as in a strict convent'. 'She has the qualities of a good Christian,' he asserted. Anything other than complete religious orthodoxy was something Isabella could not overlook; suspicion and denunciations were the basis for many an investigation by the Inquisition, and God's enemies could not be allowed to flourish, no matter who those enemies were.

Juana's subservience to Philip added to Isabella's sense of foreboding. Once Juana had realised that her mother had not dispatched Friar Tomás to Burgundy exclusively to spy on her, she had begun to confide in him. But her accounts of the household and financial restraints she must endure, and of her homesickness, revealed the extent to which she was manipulated by Philip. While this was upsetting to the forthright Isabella, she had to accept that Juana was, after all, only a consort in Burgundy. In Spain, however, Juana would become a queen in her own right; it would be Philip who would be the consort. Yet even before she met him, Isabella had heard enough of Philip's conduct to think he would never willingly take second place to his wife. Isabella knew it would take all her skill to turn her daughter and errant son-in-law into the responsible rulers that Spain would need after her own death.

So, when at last the couple arrived in Spain for the Cortes' acclamations, Isabella thought that the best course of action was to persuade both Philip and (particularly) Juana to stay in Spain for the foreseeable future. Then the queen could teach them how to rule the lands that would be theirs. Both started with handicaps: in Philip's case, he knew nothing of Spain, and Juana, whose training had been geared towards marriage, knew nothing about governing. If the couple stayed in Spain under Isabella's guidance, those handicaps could be addressed. In the process, Juana would be exposed to the strict rituals of the Church, be kept under her mother's keen eye and might even realise the sacred burden of monarchy. The image of Christ standing alone in the Garden of Gethsemane was one that Isabella understood.

But Philip had other ideas. Once the various Cortes had recognised Juana's claims, Philip saw no reason to waste his time in Spain. He had no intention of learning Spanish ways and customs, he did not want to speak the language and he could not wait to go back to Burgundy. And he made this all too clear. Finally, he announced his departure, leaving without Juana who was pregnant with their fourth child and unfit to travel. Neither the pleas of his wife nor those of his mother-in-law that he at least wait until Juana was safely delivered had any effect.

With Philip gone, though, the stage was cleared for Isabella. She would have liked to have Charles, the grandson who should one day take over everything from his own parents and from Ferdinand and Isabella herself, in Spain under her control, but he remained in Burgundy with the queen's former daughter-in-law, Margaret. Still, she had Juana and, from March 1503, she had another grandson, for Juana's new baby was a boy, named Ferdinand to please his grandfather. All Isabella needed to do now was to persuade Juana to remain.

Pulled in two directions, Juana could not please both her mother and her husband. Philip, uneasy about the pressure Isabella was exerting, wanted Juana with him and well away from Spanish influence; Isabella, equally troubled by Philip's mastery over her daughter, wanted the complete opposite. So, for the first time in her life, Juana had a choice, a crucial one.

Until now, she had been subject to the will of others. Her parents had planned her education and negotiated her marriage, her husband had then treated her as a chattel and made his own position as head of the family and head of state abundantly plain. If she obeyed Philip's summons to return to Burgundy, she would place herself in his power once more. She may have asserted herself somewhat in France but, by allowing him to reduce her role within her own household to little more than a cipher, she had already shown Philip that she would give way to him. He was the dominant partner in their relationship, and he knew it. That she would become a ruler herself when her mother died merely made her a more valuable commodity in his eyes.

Yet yielding to her mother's entreaties would not necessarily allow the archduchess to determine her own destiny either. The Isabella who had fought the Moors and ignored the screams of the Inquisition's victims was not about to give free rein to her own daughter. But Isabella was over fifty. Age, the pressures of state affairs and her own personal griefs were all beginning to tell and, although she tended to make light of her physical ills, Isabella was unwell. There was a strong possibility that Juana might succeed to Isabella's thrones sooner rather than later.

When that happened, Juana would have the opportunity to prove herself her mother's daughter and not just Philip's subservient wife. But to do so, she needed to stay in Spain. If Juana's emotional dependence on Philip decreased (and with two sons and a daughter, she certainly did not need him in the marital bed any longer), if she was resident within the Spanish court, and if she worked to earn the respect and reverence of the Spanish people, her chances of emulating her mother as a sovereign queen who made her own decisions and answered only to God would be dramatically increased.

In a contest between pragmatism and passion, the head and the heart, everything rested on just how much Juana really cared for Philip. Contemporary sources conflict, some telling us that she adored him, others that she was perfectly content without him. But her action surely reveals to us her true feelings. When offered a chance to escape his clutches, she opted for Philip and not her mother, and she opted for him in a spectacular fashion. The queen, although ill, did her utmost to cajole Juana into staying in Spain. She failed. While willing to leave Prince Ferdinand in her mother's care because he was too young to travel, Juana was obdurate. She was leaving and that was that. Facing her daughter's intransigence, Isabella tried another stratagem, that of proposing a delay, citing the current war with France as an excuse for postponing what, at the best of times, was a dangerous voyage.

Guessing that her mother was trying every trick she could think of to keep her, Juana abandoned pleading and talking. Instead she exhibited an astonishing display of histrionic, virtually hysterical, behaviour, indulging in tactics she would employ for the rest of her life whenever she was thwarted or powerless. She refused to eat, to talk or to sleep, she attempted to force a ship's captain to prepare to sail, she stood in the driving rain and would not take shelter for hours. Even a personal visit from Isabella would not move her. She wanted to go to the country she now thought of as home, and to the husband she still loved, and she wanted to go immediately.

In the end her tantrums worked. By May 1504, she was in Burgundy.

But the cost was considerable, for her startling antics had alarmed all who witnessed them, including Isabella. Her subsequent demeanour in the Burgundian court caused yet more apprehension. Her longed-for reunion with Philip was a sour disappointment. Finding his ardour directed elsewhere, Juana, feeling desperately unhappy and betrayed, followed the same blueprint that had seen off her mother. Philip, however, was made of even sterner stuff than Isabella. When her carefully calculated displays of tears and temper failed to move him, Juana resorted to a more drastic approach: she physically attacked the woman she believed was her rival. The result was, understandably, a growing reputation for instability. Unwittingly, Juana was providing ammunition that her enemies could use against her in the future if the stakes were high enough.

Once Isabella died, those stakes would become very high indeed. And, in a strange twist of fate, the queen's death not only changed Juana's life completely but brought Juana and Katherine together one last time.

Isabella of Castile, Juana and Katherine's mother. With a finger in a book of hours possibly at the page for the office for the day, she presents an image of the virtuous, pious and dedicated ruler.

Ferdinand of Aragon, Isabella's husband, was Juana and Katherine's father. Crafty, devious, yet able, he was a model for Machiavelli's 'Prince'.

Spain, from a contemporary map of 1582.

The Alhambra and the city of Granada, 1582. Boabdil's palace and the gardens of the Generalife are on the left, labelled numbers 9 and 5.

The Court of Myrtles, the Alhambra, Granada.

The gardens of the Generalife, the Alhambra, Granada.

A Catholic Antiphonary from Castile of the sort familiar to Isabella and her daughters. An antiphon was a verse from the Bible often sung before or after a psalm.

While the identity of the sitter remains unproven, the letter 'K' in the necklace adds weight to the belief that it is indeed Katherine of Aragon.

Juana, Archduchess of Burgundy and Queen of Castile. There is a suggestion that this may be a portrait of Katherine, although the consensus favours the sitter as being Juana. The similarities of facial features between the two women are marked.

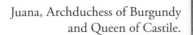

Juana, Archduchess of Burgundy and Queen of Castile.

The Holy Roman Emperor Maximilian I, Juana's father-in-law, a wily, shrewd ruler who could easily match Ferdinand of Aragon in duplicity and deceit.

Philip, Archduke of Burgundy, Juana's husband, a portrait that suggests his sensual, hedonistic nature.

Henry VII, King of England. With his pursed lips and deeply hooded eyes, Henry personifies political calculation and chicanery.

Death of a Prince

When Arthur and Katherine set off for Ludlow a few weeks after their spectacular wedding in St Paul's, both seemed in good health and with a glowing future before them. Katherine's first glimpse of Ludlow was not very different from the one that greets visitors now. Overlooking the steep hills and deep valleys of the Welsh borders, the town is still dominated by its castle, albeit now in ruins, and by the church of St Lawrence where there is a Victorian stained-glass window depicting a youthful and handsome Prince Arthur, the Arthur that Katherine knew. The narrow, winding streets and the market square in front of the fortress are much as she would have seen them.

But there the comparisons stop. Today a quiet, peaceful place, the stone-walled Ludlow of Katherine's day was a thriving market town with an economy based largely on the woollen trade, and was the centre of English government for Wales. Lawyers jostled with merchants in the crowded alleyways, drawn by the legal cases heard when the Council of the Marches met in session, which it did even if irregularly. Farmers and tradesmen did brisk business in the market place. And amidst the busy townsfolk were keen, and highly talented, Welsh poets hoping to find wealthy patrons among the throng that surrounded their prince and his princess, people to whom they could dedicate their intricate, lyrically beautiful, verses. To the Welsh, Arthur was one of their own. After all, his great-grandfather, Owen Tudor, had been Welsh through and through, and many of those who had fought so ferociously for Arthur's father at Bosworth Field came from proud Welsh stock. Much was hoped for from Katherine's husband.

The castle itself was formidable. Originally built in Norman times, it had undergone many changes depending on the politics of the time and the fortunes of its owners. And it had been crucial in the history of the Tudor family: once it had offered shelter to Queen Elizabeth's father, Edward IV, during the turbulence of the Wars of the Roses; and it was from here that the queen's young brother, Edward, had set off on his fateful journey to London on his accession, a journey that was to end in the young boy's death in the Tower of London.

Now it was the turn of Henry's son and daughter-in-law to take up residence. In the depths of winter, Katherine and Arthur rode through the imposing main gatehouse of the castle into the open area known as the outer bailey. This is huge, comprising almost four acres. Today the area is simply laid to grass; then it was a hub of people, activity, noise, for it was the working heart of the fortress. As the royal entourage made its way to the main citadel, they passed by stables housing whinnying horses, the fires of the blacksmiths, outbuildings where the castle servants and garrisons could sleep and eat, storerooms filled to the brim with supplies.

The inner bailey, the oldest part of the castle, was where the main living quarters were situated. In the north-eastern part of the complex, protected by yet another thick limestone wall, the bailey was entered via a small gatehouse next to the ancient Norman keep. Arthur's private apartments were on the extreme left of a long connected range of buildings, which included the great hall. Arthur's suite of rooms, which are still known as 'Prince Arthur's Chamber', were on the first floor and could be reached by a staircase from the ground-floor rooms or through a private entrance in the great hall. The apartments were L-shaped, with one wall flanking the great hall and the other facing the bailey. In the corner were stairs leading to a tower room with unparalleled views of the rivers Corve and Teme and the undulating countryside of the borders, views slightly reminiscent of the slopes and mountains visible from the battlements of Granada.

The sources do not tell us how long it took the couple to travel the 160 or so miles from London to Ludlow, nor the exact date on which they arrived, but they probably reached the castle in the middle of January 1502. By then, the bare trees would have been hung with frost, the wind biting and the weather piercingly cold, so the fire burning in the wide fireplace on the eastern side of Arthur's rooms was no doubt very welcome. What is striking is just how small these rooms actually are. Although the complete range, of which they were part, is an impressive edifice containing a large great hall, its individual chambers are cosy and intimate. Arthur's are about fourteen paces by sixteen paces for the entire floor space, with another ten or so for the tower room.

If Katherine hoped that time and close proximity to her husband would bring about the consummation of their marriage, the arrangements at Ludlow could not have been bettered. And, if the later depositions in court of the prince's gentleman, William Thomas, are to be believed, she and Arthur probably did spend some nights together in those small and private castle rooms. Thomas, who went with his master and Katherine to Ludlow, then deposed that 'they of his knowledge continued together as man and wife, prince and princess of Wales by the space of 5 months or therebouts as well in London and therebouts as in Ludlow in the marches of Wales'. The couple were 'together in household until the death of the said Prince Arthur', he said, an assertion he made 'of his knowledge'. Moreover, he remembered conducting Arthur 'in his nightgown unto the princess's bedchamber ... whereupon he [Arthur] entered and there continued all night'. Thomas then 'received him at the said doors' in the morning. But, as after the wedding night in London, only Katherine and Arthur really could have known what went on between them before Thomas returned to escort Arthur back to his own rooms to prepare him for the business of the day.

As Prince and Princess of Wales, and the future rulers of England, Arthur and Katherine were accompanied by a full entourage. In the prince's case, he needed both his privy chamber gentlemen and political advisers. One of the most important political appointments was that of Sir Richard Pole, who, as lord chamberlain, controlled much of what happened in the prince's household and who, because of his previous and extensive experience in Welsh affairs, played his part in the overall administration of the principality.

Henry VII completely trusted Sir Richard, to whom he was even slightly related as Pole's mother was a half-sister of Margaret Beaufort. Within a month of the battle of Bosworth, he had selected Pole as an esquire of the body, a key attendant, and given him various strategic offices in Wales. As the years passed and Sir Richard continued to prove his worth and gained yet more offices, the king appointed him to

Arthur's service; it was in fact Sir Richard who had officiated at a proxy marriage between Arthur and Katherine in 1499. Thus, when the prince and princess arrived at Ludlow, Sir Richard was with them.

So, probably, was Sir Richard's wife, Margaret. Married to Sir Richard when she was fourteen and he was twenty-eight, Margaret had royal blood. And that blood was very royal indeed, for she was Elizabeth of York's first cousin. The queen's father, Edward IV, had had two brothers. The youngest, Richard, usurped the throne on Edward's death, becoming Richard III; the other was George, Duke of Clarence. By the time Henry VII defeated Richard at Bosworth, George was already dead, but he had left two children. One was Margaret Pole. The other was her brother, the Earl of Warwick, who many felt had a better claim to the throne than Henry himself. Taking no chances, Henry imprisoned the boy immediately after Bosworth and executed him just before Katherine set sail from Spain, a move which undoubtedly put at rest the minds of Ferdinand and Isabella, if causing uneasiness to Katherine when she heard about it. Unwilling to imprison Margaret, Henry had done the next best thing and married her off to one of his closest allies; as such, she was given a place at court as one of Katherine's ladies. And, while we have no direct proof that Margaret accompanied her new mistress in the winter of 1502, it is very likely that she did. If so, it was during those months at Ludlow that a friendship was formed which would last for the rest of the two women's lives.

But Margaret was not Katherine's only attendant, for most members of the princess's existing household went with her on that long journey from London. Among them were her chaplain, Alessandro Geraldini, and Doña Elvira, no doubt zealous as ever and keeping a very close watch over her charge. If anyone other than the young couple themselves was aware of the true state of Katherine's marriage, it was Doña Elvira. In Ludlow as in London, very little escaped her.

Certainly for a few brief months, all seemed well. The castle was in a constant state of activity. For Arthur, there were council meetings; he was ruling, so the chronicler tells us, with 'moost and rightuous ordre and wisdam ... uppholdyng and defendyng the pore' and 'repressyng malice'. He was certainly busy every time he went to Wales: many documents with his seal fixed firmly are extant. For Katherine, there was time to sit peacefully with her ladies, sewing, chatting, laughing. At night, the great hall sprang into life as servants brought dishes to the table, courtiers discussed the day's events over the steaming plates of food and goblets of wine, minstrels played softly in the background. There were prayers and services on Sundays and holy days, most likely within the tiny chapel of St Mary Magdalene with its round nave and rectangular chancel and its corbels carved in the shape of heads. Perhaps there was hunting as winter began to give way to spring. We cannot know, no record of all the day-to-day happenings has survived.

What we do know is that this brief, almost idyllic, period of calm ended abruptly when Arthur was stricken with a 'moost petifull disease and sikeness' and on 2 April 1502, within a week of falling ill, he died. Katherine was now a widow. Quite what it was that carried off the young boy so brutally is unknown. Chances are that it was the sweating sickness, a virulent influenza-type virus which could kill even the strongest within a day; certainly there was a sickness of some sort prevalent in the area at the time. There is also a suggestion that Arthur succumbed to testicular cancer – which is certainly possible since the chronicler describes his illness as 'dryven in the singuler partise of him inward'– or maybe it was tuberculosis. We can never be sure.

When the prince died, the machinery of the state swung into action. While the embalmers began their grisly tasks, Sir Richard Pole dispatched messengers to London. They rode with desperate speed, reaching Greenwich in just over two days. As Katherine herself would one day discover, there is no easy way to tell a parent that their child is dead, or for them to put aside their grief and accept the will of God. But Henry and Elizabeth were no ordinary parents. Like Ferdinand and Isabella in similar circumstances, their concern was also for their dynasty. Elizabeth did her utmost to comfort her husband, reminding him that the succession was secure as they had another son as well as two daughters. Besides which, she said, they were both young enough to have other children. In the privacy of her own apartments, however, the usually stalwart Elizabeth gave way to her 'great losse', becoming so distraught that the king rushed to console her.

The news of Arthur's tragic end aroused genuine sadness, even anguish, beyond his immediate family circle. His very name had conjured up hopes of future glories rooted in a long-lost legendary time of heroism, chivalry, self-sacrifice, duty and romantic love: the sordid and bloody in-fighting of the Wars of the Roses would be superseded by the just rule of this young, well-educated man and his pretty bride. Now that was not to be.

Nowhere was the sorrow deeper than in Arthur's own principality where so many had seen in him the resurgence of their own heroes, the rebirth of their own history. And, because Wales was a land of poetry and song, Welsh poets expressed their despair in their own unique fashion. One particular ode, by Rhys Nanmor, a man who had composed a poem of praise to Henry VII in happier times as well, sums up this feeling of unfulfilled dreams and lost promise with heart-rending beauty. The poem, in its original Welsh, is still extant. Within its 126 lines, which conform to stringent rules on metre, rhyme and syllable length, its author describes the effects of the death of Arthur, his 'coronetted leader', on the lands and peoples of Wales:

> *The proud steeds of the beautiful warriors will no more tread*
> *the land,*
> *Nor will flocks of birds fly,*
> *They will not sound their call in the hills, wild and sane,*
> *Throughout, the land cannot but lament.*
> *No more a kind bud, where the English traverse,*
> *Nor an heir for an island as long as they desire,*
> *Arthur, of the golden wound, will they cherish, Arthur,*
> *Arthur of the azure sword they buried . . .*

The tears that flowed, said the poet, were 'a tide of water, spoiling the whole island'.

But, tears flowing as well they may have been, Henry VII had a son to bury. It was not then the custom for the royal family to attend the funerals of even their closest relatives, so Henry entrusted the arrangements to Arthur's gentlemen and council. The noble selected by his king to be chief mourner was the Earl of Surrey, a man who had loyally fought for Richard III at Bosworth but who had earned Henry's forgiveness and his confidence as the years had passed. Together with the Earls of Kent and Shrewsbury, and the Bishops of Lincoln, Salisbury and Chester, Surrey rode as fast as his horses could take him for the elaborate funeral obsequies. And they were indeed elaborate. With his internal organs carefully removed and the cavities filled with spices and herbs, Arthur's body lay in state for three weeks in the great hall at Ludlow, his casket covered in cloth of gold, tapers burning day and night, a group of poor men praying continually at its side. Then, on Saturday 23 April, draped in cloth of gold and with holy banners raised at each corner, the coffin was taken in procession into the parish church of St Lawrence, a stone's throw from the castle, for the first of several services. Everywhere was black: the official mourners wore black, the paupers who accompanied the prince wore black, the prince's household wore black, black cloth hung in the choir where the body lay. And there Arthur remained over the weekend, as the bishops intoned the dirges and the Masses so necessary for the repose of his soul. The comfort of the living was not neglected, however: every day, the bishops and the principal lords went up to the castle for dinner, a meal then served towards noon.

The king decided not to bring his son back to London. Instead he ordered that Arthur should be buried in Worcester Cathedral, the abbey-church of an ancient Benedictine monastic foundation situated in the prosperous market town on the River Severn. Therefore, on Monday 25 April, the prince's funeral cortège wound its way through the twisting streets of Ludlow to begin the final journey. His coffin, covered in black cloth of gold, rested on a hearse draped in black velvet and drawn by six horses with black trappings. Black-clad mourners and torch-bearers walked or rode beside the hearse through the driving rain (the chronicler tells us that he had never seen such bad weather). The aim was to reach Worcester, which was about thirty miles from Ludlow, via the little town of Bewdley. Sited at more or less a halfway point along the journey, Bewdley was the perfect place for everyone to rest while last-minute preparations were made in Worcester itself. Even the fourteen or so miles to Bewdley were difficult; sometimes oxen had to be used to drag the hearse along the muddy roads, and the thick black overmantle thoughtfully provided to protect the hearse and its precious cargo from the elements proved very useful.

For the people of Worcester, Arthur's funeral was something to remember for the rest of their days. Following precise instructions given them by members of the prince's household who had ridden on ahead, the city officials made sure all was ready. When the procession reached the outskirts of Worcester where waiting friars censed the body, fresh torches were lit, and Arthur's mourners walked two by two through the silent streets which were lined on both sides by the city dignitaries and other 'honest men'. Once all were in the great church itself, the various services could begin again. The chroniclers describe the events in minute detail but, for us, as for them, two incidents sum up the poignancy of a life lost at such a tender age. The first is when Lord Garrard, acting as the prince's Man of Arms, rode Arthur's own horse into the choir as an offering to the abbey. Those who did not weep at the sight of the magnificent beast bereft of its owner, wrote the chronicler, had a 'herd hert'. But the second incident is perhaps yet more moving, particularly as it remains a custom at some royal funerals today: key figures in Arthur's household, such as Sir William Uvedale and Sir Richard Croft, broke their staves of office over their own heads and then threw them into the grave where the body now lay. They no longer needed them: with their master dead, his household was no more.

So, with the last echoes of the services fading away, and the mourners leaving the church, Arthur was left in the care of the monks. His tomb, and the chantry chapel built around it, still stands. Just south of the high altar and close to the sepulchre of the medieval King John, the tomb is grand and impressive. On the tracery around it there are intricate carvings of Tudor roses, of Katherine's beloved Spanish pomegranates, of his own Prince of Wales feathers – nothing was too splendid for a sixteen-year-old boy of whom so much had been expected.

While all of the pageantry ran its course, Katherine lay in her bed-chamber at Ludlow cared for tenderly by her ladies, for she too was ill, perhaps suffering from the same disease that might have killed Arthur. Ferdinand and Isabella were so concerned that they wrote to their ambassador, Dr de Puebla, expressing their 'profound sorrow' at hearing of their son-in-law's death and demanding that he arrange for Katherine to be moved 'without loss of time, from the unhealthy place where she now is'. No doubt the Catholic Monarchs were genuinely anxious for

Katherine, but they were also looking to salvage their alliance with England. They had, after all, been in exactly the same situation once before when their eldest daughter, Isabella, had been widowed so very soon after her marriage to Prince Afonso, the heir to the Portuguese throne. And, just as had happened then, when Princess Isabella had married King Manuel, thus saving the Portuguese link, there was a possible way forward: Henry had a second son, Prince Henry, who was as yet unmarried.

Katherine, very much a dutiful daughter of Spain, would be guided by her parents. Then, too, as a dutiful daughter of the Catholic Church, she accepted that she must overcome her natural sadness for her young husband, regarding his death as the will of God. Suffering was an inevitable part of normal life; so she had been taught and so many of her mother's pictures had emphasised. And, supported by her faith and with a naturally strong personality, sixteen-year-old Katherine coped well with her loss. Aside from one slight lapse shortly after her wedding when she had allowed her temper to surface and Henry had wisely distracted her with a visit to his library, Katherine's behaviour in her adopted country had been exemplary. From early childhood she had known that she was to marry in England and become its queen. This was what the Catholic Monarchs wanted because it was in Spanish interests; it was her destiny. The London pageants had confirmed it. So if her first attempt had failed because Divine Providence willed it so, then that same Divine Providence would ensure that her second would succeed.

To Be a Wife

In March 1503, royal officials settled some outstanding bills. Among them we can find one of five shillings for John Cope, a London tailor. His task, entrusted to him by Queen Elizabeth, had been to line and cover a litter with black cloth and to edge it with black ribbons and a black fringe. It had been designed for a sombre purpose.

When she lost her eldest son so tragically at Ludlow, the queen had played no part in arranging his burial. Her task was with the living, and the living was her daughter-in-law, Katherine. Once the widowed princess was strong enough to travel, Doña Elvira and her ladies gently helped her into the litter so thoughtfully sent by her mother-in-law, and Katherine journeyed slowly towards London. It was spring, that loveliest of English seasons, a time when the burgeoning leaves are still a soft yellow, blossom is beginning to emerge from bud, and the fresh, pure air promises rebirth and hope. Enveloped inside her litter, shielded from the prying populace, Katherine saw little of the beauties of the countryside. Her thoughts had to be more pragmatic.

Those of her parents certainly were. 'The news of the death of Prince Arthur', they wrote to de Puebla, still one of their London ambassadors, caused them 'profound sorrow', reviving 'the affliction caused by all their former losses'. Nonetheless, continued these most devout of monarchs, 'the will of God must be obeyed'. Condolences expressed, they applied themselves to practicalities, aiming to maintain the alliance with England at all costs. The international situation, uneasily calm for a while, was becoming increasingly ugly. 'The King of France wishes to attack us, and to make war upon us and our kingdom, with all his forces, without cause or reason,' they told another of their London ambassadors, the Duke of Estrada. Should fighting break out, Henry would be useful, especially since he could seize the chance to make war on the French himself so that Louis XII would be committed on two fronts. There was, therefore, only one course of action open to Ferdinand and Isabella: 'to conclude with Henry ... a marriage between their daughter Katherine and his son Henry, Prince of Wales'. That was the instruction given to Estrada. 'In order ... to have this affair of the betrothal concluded, use all the eloquence that you may see to be requisite,' they ordered him, 'not omitting anything which may prove advantageous to it.'

Unfortunately, their control over what might prove disadvantageous was limited. One area, in particular, was central: had the marriage been consummated or not? With Arthur decaying in his tomb, only Katherine really knew the answer, and she told neither Henry and Elizabeth nor the Catholic Monarchs. Despite later rumours, the latter did not receive blood-spattered sheets smuggled aboard a Spanish ship for only them to see.

As her parents attempted to discover the truth and frantically schemed to get her installed in Prince Henry's bed, Katherine quietly recuperated at Durham House, the London palace of the Bishop of Durham. The house was splendid. Sited close to the Strand, near Charing Cross and Covent Garden, the three-hundred-year-old mansion boasted a huge hall supported by impressive marble pillars, and had well-tended gardens stretching down to the banks of the River Thames. If Katherine was destined to become a queen, she could have asked for no better a residence.

Yet perhaps she was to become a mother instead. Cases of widows giving birth after their husband's death were far from uncommon, and were indeed very close to home. Henry himself had been born almost three months after his father, Edmund Tudor, died from plague and Katherine's sister-in-law, Margaret of Burgundy, had had a miscarriage shortly after Prince Juan's death. Interestingly, contrary to Ferdinand and Isabella's letter dated 10 May 1502 addressing him as the Prince of Wales, young Prince Henry was not given the title immediately. This pause suggests that Henry VII and Elizabeth believed that the marriage of Katherine and Arthur had been consummated and that they were waiting to see if Katherine menstruated. Clearly she did, because Prince

Henry was recognised as Prince of Wales at the end of June and given
the title officially eighteen months later.

The question of consummation was important because the Pope's
consent in the form of a dispensation was needed if Katherine was to
marry Prince Henry. This was because, according to the Church, she
had become related to him 'in the first degree of affinity' by marrying
his brother Arthur. The Catholic Monarchs were old hands at getting a
thorny problem like this sorted out; after all, they had successfully
obtained a dispensation for their third daughter, Maria, to marry Manuel
of Portugal on the death of their eldest daughter, Manuel's first wife. The
Arthur–Henry difficulty was surely a mirror-image of the Portuguese
situation, and since the pope had proved accommodating then there
was no reason to suppose the current pope would be any less helpful
now. A dispensation could be issued whether or not consummation had
taken place; it was just that the wording would be different in each case.
And it was vital that the dispensation was precise and correct to head
off potential repercussions some time in the future.

So it mattered very much whether Katherine and Arthur had done
more than merely sleep in the same bed. Her former tutor, now her
chaplain, Alessandro Geraldini, obviously believed that more had indeed
been done, and hinted as much to de Puebla. Katherine herself wrote
letters to her parents but obviously drew a modest veil over the intimate
secrets of her nights with Arthur because, two days after mentioning
that they had received her missives, Ferdinand told Estrada 'to get at
the truth as regards the fact whether the Prince and Princess of Wales
consummated the marriage, since nobody has told us about it'. Shortly
afterwards, someone did tell them, but that someone was Doña Elvira,
furious that Alessandro had confided what he thought he knew to de
Puebla. She wrote a personal letter to Isabella telling her that Katherine
was definitely still a virgin. Although Doña Elvira's original letter has
long since disappeared, we know of its existence because the queen
referred to it when writing to Estrada. 'It is already known for a certainty
that the said Princess of Wales, our daughter, remains as she was here,
for so Doña Elvira has written to us,' Isabella declared. Doña Elvira's
word was good enough for the queen. Negotiations with the pope,
however, dragged on.

And so did the other question that vexed the Catholic Monarchs, that of money. On the same day as she had married Arthur, the first half of Katherine's dowry had been handed over, in cash. The other half was due in two further instalments, the first within six months of the marriage and the remainder, to be paid partly in cash and partly from the jewels and plate that Katherine had brought from Spain, within twelve months of the marriage. Unfortunately Arthur had died five months after the ceremony. So, Ferdinand and Isabella were adamant not only that they would not pay the second half of the dowry but they expected Henry to return the first half. They also thought he should grant Katherine her jointure rights, the allowance made to a widow from her deceased husband's estates.

Although warned by their ambassador, de Ayala, that 'if gold coin once enters his [Henry's] strong boxes, it never comes out again', Ferdinand and Isabella pressed their demands. Repeatedly. And they got nowhere.

In fact, they were getting nowhere over the entire marriage project for, unlike when he was almost begging for Katherine's marriage to Arthur, Henry was taking his time over her marrying Prince Henry. By now, the king had been on the throne for more than sixteen years. His grasp on power was firmer; he was richer; he had fought off rebellions, he had executed plotters; he had beheaded Warbeck and Margaret Pole's brother, the Earl of Warwick. True, one key rival, Warwick's cousin, Edmund de la Pole, Earl of Suffolk, was still at large, protected by Maximilian and Philip, but perhaps an agreement with Philip might be brokered one day. All in all, there was no need to rush into a match for his only son and heir; he would take his time, consider all options.

Katherine, the subject of these negotiations, played no part in them. She grew steadily stronger at Durham House, surrounded by familiar servants and her ladies, leading a comfortable, tranquil, if boring existence. While her parents painted a poignant picture of their daughter's plight as a widow 'overwhelmed by grief', there is no evidence that she was anything of the kind. It is impossible to say how deeply her emotions were affected by Arthur's death. While her marriage had been political and had lasted for less than six months, the pair had been closeted together at Ludlow and she was bound to feel a natural sadness at a life cut short. However, she had not given way. She had certainly been ill, as she often was in her early years in England, but she coped with Arthur's sudden death with a stoicism of which her mother would have been proud. Katherine's eldest sister, the Queen of Portugal, had almost collapsed under the weight of her sorrow when her first husband, Prince Afonso, was fatally injured. 'No other Princess ever endured more grief . . . or led such a sad and bitter life,' Isabella had written to Estrada at the time. Not so Katherine. Made of sterner stuff than her elder sister, Katherine was her mother's daughter in this regard as well as in so many others.

And, as Henry dawdled and the pope deliberated, Isabella was busily scheming to finalise her daughter's next marriage. Katherine was a royal princess with plenty of child-bearing years ahead of her and royal princesses were meant to be wives and serve their countries; that was what Isabella was set on achieving. The queen's methods reveal much of her inner character, a character so similar to Katherine's own.

Committed Catholic though she was, Isabella had the lucky gift of sometimes convincing herself that what she believed was good for Spain was also good for God. In a letter concerning war against France which she sent to de Puebla in 1495, part of which is so obscured by water stains as to be undecipherable, she writes, 'Though this business is the business of God and of the Church, to defend which all we Christian Princes are obliged, there might be mixed in it something of [here it is unreadable] our own interest.' In other words, while defending God, there was no reason why she could not defend her own interests as well. To her mind, politics and religion could work in tandem.

And she was quite prepared to lie in what she felt was a just cause, as she had done in 1496 when the King of Scotland had asked to marry one of her daughters. If Katherine married Arthur, the queen wanted to prevent skirmishes on the Scottish border so, knowing perfectly well that all her daughters were spoken for, she had instructed de Puebla not to stress these prior commitments. Instead, she said: 'We must not deprive the King of Scots of his hope of having our daughter. On the contrary we must amuse him as long as possible.' She had been perfectly happy to deceive the Scottish monarch if that was the way to achieve her ends. As her letters reveal, she tried the same approach with Henry VII.

It might be better, she pretended, for Katherine to return home rather than stay in England. 'You shall say to the King of England', she told Estrada, 'that we cannot endure that a daughter whom we love should be so far from us when she is in affliction, and that she should not have us at hand to console her.' Besides, she said, Katherine would feel more at liberty to express her sorrow in Spain than in England: 'The Princess of Wales can show the sense she entertains of her loss better here, and give freer vent to her grief because the customs of this country better permit it than do those of England.'

In a move clearly calculated to bounce Henry into agreeing to the new marriage, the ambassadors were frequently told to make ostentatious preparations for Katherine's departure. Yet, the queen reiterated to her ambassador, 'the one object ... is to bring the betrothal to a conclusion as soon as you are able'. Whether she remembered to tell Katherine of her machinations or whether the princess thought that she really was about to go home is unknown.

Still the English king took his time. With nothing concrete from the pope as yet, he felt no urgency. And he anticipated a personal joy: Queen Elizabeth was pregnant. Towards the end of January 1503, she moved into her private apartments within the Tower of London to prepare for the birth of her baby. The child, a daughter rather than the longed-for son, was born 'suddenly' (presumably prematurely) on 2 February. She was named Katherine in honour of one of the queen's sisters. Sadly, the child was sickly and Elizabeth herself soon became dangerously ill. Henry, worried about the woman who had been his wife for seventeen years, sent urgently to Kent for one of his most trusted physicians, Dr Aylesworth. Even he could not save the queen, who died eleven days later on the morning of her thirty-seventh birthday, her baby lasting but a few days longer.

Coming so soon after the death of Arthur, the news was devastating for the royal family. We have no record of Katherine's response, she was perhaps too young to voice independent condolences, and she did not attend the queen's funeral. Ferdinand and Isabella said that the 'tidings have, of a truth, caused us much grief'. Arthur's former tutor, Bernard

André, summed up the feelings of many who had known the queen when he wrote: 'She exhibited from her very cradle, towards God an admirable fear and service; towards her parents a wonderful obedience; towards her brothers and sisters an almost incredible love; towards the poor, and the ministers of Christ, a revered and singular affection.'

The most affected were, of course, Elizabeth's children and her husband. Now almost twelve, her remaining son, Prince Henry, found her death very difficult to bear. 'News of the death of my dearest mother' was 'hateful intelligence', he would write a few years afterwards.

The normally taciturn, self-controlled King Henry kept sufficient hold upon his emotions to give the necessary orders for his wife's funeral and then 'departed to a solitary place to pass his sorrow, and would no man should resort to him but those whom he had appointed', his action offering us a rare glimpse into the personal feelings of this most private of kings.

Elizabeth's funeral was as elaborate as that of Arthur. Her body was embalmed and enclosed in a lead coffin. She lay in state within the Tower, her ladies and attendants keeping watch over her both day and night as prayers were said and Masses were sung. She rested in the Tower for the next eleven days before she was taken to her grave. In the solemn funeral procession the silent streets of the City of London were lined with people carrying lighted torches and candles as her coffin, placed on a chariot draped with black velvet, drawn by six horses also draped in black, travelled slowly towards St Peter's, Westminster. Finally the casket was lowered into a hastily prepared vault within the great abbey-church to await the day when it would be moved into the specially constructed marvel that is now Henry VII's Chapel, where she lies to this day. Maybe coins did not flow readily from his treasure chests, but Henry was not parsimonious in matters of state; his wife's funeral expenses totalled £2800.

Elizabeth's demise impacted on Katherine in an unexpected fashion. The succession to Henry VII's hard-won throne now depended on just one son and two daughters. At forty-six, the king was perfectly capable of fathering more children, he just needed a new wife. With Elizabeth barely cold, he began to cast his eyes around for a suitable bride. What appears to us as indecent haste was, by the standards of the age, simply common sense. Death came swiftly then, indiscriminately striking down rich and poor, old and young, male and female with terrifying ease; Elizabeth was not the first queen to die in childbed, nor would she be the last. And a spare heir was always advisable, as Henry had discovered from bitter experience.

So, far from condemning him for indecent haste and callousness, the Catholic Monarchs, and Katherine, sympathised with Henry's plight. They drew the line, however, at any suggestion that Katherine should replace Elizabeth as Henry's next queen. When de Puebla informed Isabella that such a union was 'spoken of in England', she was quick to put a stop to it. Such a thing, she wrote, 'would be a very evil thing – one never before seen, and the mere mention of which offends the ears – we would not for anything in the world that it should take place'. Whether Henry himself really had suggested the match, or whether de Puebla merely repeated unfounded gossip, is uncertain. In any case, Katherine was too marketable a property for Isabella to waste her on the ageing king; Isabella and Ferdinand wanted Katherine to be a queen-consort for as long as possible. Even the new Prince of Wales, they said prophetically, was not as well suited to their daughter as Arthur had been 'on account of her age'. He was, after all, six years younger than she. Still, he was the only English prince available, so they stepped up their efforts.

Finally it seemed as if they were getting somewhere because Henry, having weighed up the alternatives, concluded that Katherine was, after all, a suitable wife for his beloved son and a tentative treaty was signed in June 1503. The couple would wed, it was stated, once Prince Henry was fifteen, which he would be in two years. But the treaty, so welcome in Spain and in Durham House, contained glaring pitfalls.

One was the wording of the clause referring to the knotty question of consummation, and the need for both Henry and the Catholic Monarchs to 'employ all their influence with the Court of Rome' to secure a papal dispensation. Instead of affirming Katherine's virgin status, the clause confirmed that her marriage to Arthur 'was solemnised according to the rites of the Catholic Church, and afterwards consummated'. Surprisingly, the usually shrewd Ferdinand seemed disinclined to haggle. In a letter to his ambassador in Rome he said:

In a clause of the treaty which mentions the dispensation of the Pope, it is stated that the princess Katherine consummated her marriage with Prince Arthur. The fact, however, is, that although they were wedded, Prince Arthur and Princess Katherine never consummated the marriage. It is well known in England that the Princess is still a virgin. But as the English are much disposed to cavil, it has seemed to be more prudent to provide for the case as though the marriage had been consummated . . .

Evidently, the Catholic Monarchs did not let the issue rest, however. By December 1503, the dispensation had been obtained and its wording changed to 'perhaps' consummated. There things stood. Katherine, living in a state of uncertainty while her future was being thrashed out by her elders, was as relieved as her parents that at least a dispensation was granted, but the ambiguity concerning the question of consummation would eventually come to haunt her.

In comparison to this, the financial part of the treaty appeared almost tame. Ostensibly, all was straightforward. Her parents conceded that the first part of the dowry for her original wedding, which Henry had safely locked away in his treasure chests, would form the first part of her new dowry. The second half would be paid just as had been authorised previously. Ferdinand and Isabella concurred with Henry that their daughter should give up the widow's jointure which she had been owed on Arthur's death providing Prince Henry settled the same sums upon her when they married. Unfortunately, despite everything appearing to be settled, the financial details were to become yet another cause of anguish for the young princess over the next few years.

With the final treaty having been duly signed, and a betrothal ceremony performed, Katherine emerged from Durham House affianced. Providence, and her parents, had decreed that her duty was to be Queen of England; so be it. Henry treated her kindly; even allowing her to see the papal dispensation for added reassurance, and he brought her to court. In the brief period before Arthur's death, she had visited some royal residences; now she did so once more. She stayed at Richmond, the palace of which the king was most proud because of the major improvements he had instituted there, and at Windsor she went hunting in the park and in the forest, a pastime she loved. She met her future husband again, and formed an enduring friendship with the king's youngest daughter, Princess Mary.

But the strain was all too much for her. She found it hard to adjust to the English climate and that, combined with the heady round of gaiety, to which she was unaccustomed, and the relief of the betrothal, all took their toll. She became ill with 'ague and derangement of the stomach' and, after seeming to recover, suffered a relapse that left her more prostrate than before. A solicitous Henry had her conveyed back to Durham House to recuperate. He enquired after her every day, sent messages of comfort to her, offered to visit her, and was eager to send doctors to tend her; he could not have done more. Katherine's own physicians resorted to the traditional remedies of purging and bleeding, not entirely successfully as on two occasions 'no blood came'. She looked pale, she lost her appetite, and she suffered every day 'from cold and heat'. Yet Katherine had a natural resilience and an inner strength; within a few weeks she was much better. And the episode served a useful purpose in helping her to develop her relationship with the king. He 'rejoices to hear that she is recovered', he wrote to her, and 'is glad that she wishes to hear from him so greatly'. Katherine was, at this stage, the perfect daughter-in-law to be.

But her happiness would be short-lived once more. Before 1504 was out, news came from Spain that would change her sister's life irrevocably and would bring Katherine nothing but misery.

'The Greatest Affliction'

On 26 November 1504, in Medina del Campo, with the steadfastness, courage and calm resignation only to be expected of her, Isabella, 'by the grace of God Queen of Castile, of León, of Aragon, of Sicily, of Granada, of Toledo, of Valencia, of Galicia, of the Mallorcas, of Sevilla, of Sardinia, Cordova, Corsica, Murcia, Jahen, of the Algarves, Algeziras, Gibraltar, and the islands of Canaria, Countess of Barcelona, Sovereign Lady of Biscaya and Molina, Duchess of Athens and Neopatria, Countess of Roussillon and Cerdena, Marchioness of Oristan and Goziano', took her last breath and went to meet her God.

She had asked to be buried, wearing the rough habit of a Franciscan, in the Franciscan monastery that she had founded in a house within the Alhambra, in the city whose conquest she had always seen as one of her greatest triumphs. Her casket was slowly escorted to the Alhambra from Medina del Campo, a journey covering almost two-thirds the entire length of Spain. Finally, it was carried up the same steep track that Boabdil had used twelve years before. The queen wanted a tomb that was simple and low. And so it was until, in the reign of her grandson, her body was reverently transferred to the specially constructed Royal Chapel in the cathedral at Granada. There she now rests, Ferdinand at her side, beneath a splendid sepulchre that is neither simple nor low. However, visitors to the Alhambra today can still see the tiny chapel, with a plaque on its floor marking the spot where her body lay for just over fifteen years, and where she would have much preferred to stay.

Katherine was taken by surprise when she heard of her mother's death. Knowing that both of her parents had been ill, she had just written to them. These letters are in her own hand and in her native Spanish. In her note to her father, she said that she was 'anxious to hear' from him as she had been told that his health was 'suffering' and she had received no letter from him for 'the whole of last year'. In fact, Ferdinand had been ill at the same time as Isabella but had recovered within a few weeks. Katherine sounds less worried about her mother. Although she told Isabella that she could not be 'satisfied or cheerful' until she heard back from her, the princess said that she had heard from Juana, with whom she was in occasional contact, that 'the daily attacks of ague, and the fever which followed upon the ague had disappeared'. Believing Isabella to be improving, the rest of Katherine's letter, the last one she would ever write to her mother, concerns a domestic matter, the marriage of one of her ladies. The queen never saw her daughter's missive; sadly, both letters are dated 26 November, the very day that Isabella died.

Sorrowful though she was, Katherine overcame her grief just as she had for Arthur. Somehow Isabella had coped with the deaths of her own mother, her only son, her eldest daughter and her grandson. If her mother could survive under such a burden, Katherine could survive a lesser one. What she did not realise was the effect that the queen's death would have upon her own prospects and value in the marriage market. As a daughter of the powerful Catholic Monarchs who together ruled over such vast dominions, Katherine was a prize, the living symbol of a useful alliance. With her mother's death, though, there was every danger that Spain would disintegrate. If that happened, and there was every indication that it might, then Katherine was far less significant. And Henry, with just one son left, would bestow that son with considerable care and acumen; Katherine might no longer be good enough.

Ferdinand certainly appreciated the impact that Isabella's death would have upon him. After a marriage of thirty-five years, and despite his numerous infidelities and illegitimate children, Ferdinand had been genuinely fond of his wife. Theirs had been an enviable partnership personally as well as politically. On the day she died, he wrote to tell Henry VII the news. Isabella's death was, he confided, 'the greatest affliction that could have befallen him' because he had lost 'the best and most excellent wife that king ever had'. 'The grief for her pierces his heart,' he went on. Yet he knew that 'she died as holy and catholic as she lived'. He hoped, therefore, that she would be 'in glory'. As for himself, he must 'conform' to the will of God. But Ferdinand had lost more than a wife: he had lost all her lands. He was King of Aragon yet, but had only ever been King of Castile by virtue of his match with its queen. Now that she was dead, Ferdinand's hold on Castile had, technically at any rate, died with her. All belonged to Juana. Or it would do unless Ferdinand could somehow keep hold of it. And Juana's temperamental, exhibitionist behaviour just might help.

After those heady early days of physical passion, Juana's marriage to Philip had gone from bad to worse. They had quarrelled so much and so often after her return to Burgundy from Spain that gossip said they had even come to blows, Philip's easy affability fast slipping into domestic tyranny. He had locked Juana in her room, he had sent her favourite Moorish slave girls back to Spain, he had dismissed some of her ladies, he had tried to keep her incommunicado. And he had made sure that Ferdinand and Isabella heard how difficult a time he was having with their headstrong daughter, a woman who he was insinuating was unbalanced.

Isabella had heard, and had listened. Cocooned inside her room at Medina del Campo, a chamber hung with religious tapestries for her contemplation and comfort, she had turned her mind to the unthinkable: what would happen to her lands if left to a daughter who could indulge in hysterical tantrums and was dominated by a son-in-law who was ambitious and cruel? Her own rule in Castile had succeeded because she and Ferdinand had worked together; her husband had not tried to take over her territories for himself, he had supported her not sidelined her. Such mutual respect and cooperation between husband and wife would not be the case with Juana and Philip. Isabella's solution, hardly likely to please Philip, lay in the clauses of her will and the last-minute codicils she added to it. Everything, of course, belonged to Juana, but the queen acknowledged that there might be problems:

> It may chance that, at the time when our Lord shall call me from this life, the Princess Doña Juana, Archduchess of Austria, Duchess of Burgundy, my very dear and beloved firstborn daughter, heiress and lawful successor to my kingdoms, lands, and signories, may be absent from them, or, after having come to them and stayed in them for some time, may be obliged to leave them again, or that,

although being present, she might not like or might be unable to reign and govern. If such were the case, it would be necessary to provide that the government should be nevertheless carried on . . .

Despite being in the throes of her last illness, Isabella was nothing if not shrewd so this clause, stating as it does that Juana 'might not like or might be unable to reign and govern' deserves close attention because the inference is that the queen was trying to pave the way for her daughter's exclusion.

An obvious interpretation is that, after witnessing the histrionics employed by Juana in her determination to return to Burgundy in 1504, and hearing from Philip that she had behaved just as worryingly with him, Isabella really did fear that Juana had inherited the mental instability the queen had witnessed in her own mother. In that case, Juana would be 'unable to reign and govern', or might 'not like' to govern, preferring to live quietly in seclusion. The queen was definitely anxious about her daughter's health, even asking Philip to treat her kindly. Yet Isabella cannot but have noticed that Juana became irrational only in matters concerning Philip.

Gustav Bergenroth, the great nineteenth-century historian who transcribed and translated so many Spanish royal documents, offered another explanation for the key clause in her will. He suggests that Isabella was considering barring her daughter on religious grounds: that the queen found Juana's religious views so suspect that she was unwilling to trust her with the strict Catholic state that she herself had been so intent on forming and defending. This is credible, but Isabella's ambassadors had been at pains to set her mind at rest on this issue even before Juana had journeyed to Spain with Philip to meet the Cortes after Miguel's death. Her daughter's religious observances were entirely satisfactory, the queen had been told; she had also become involved with Franciscan nuns and had visited convents of the sisters of St Clare. And, when back in Spain, her religious attendances had been as orthodox as her mother could have wished; she had also visited the Franciscan monastery at Toledo and the nuns at Rejas, even staying overnight at the convent.

A more recent theory is that Isabella's main concern was Philip.

Having assessed Philip's character for herself, and seen how tightly he controlled her daughter, the queen could see that Juana would have no capacity for independent action. Castile then, and Aragon too if that passed to Juana on Ferdinand's death, would be ruled not by the rightful queen but by Philip, a man whose Burgundian outlook and pro-French predilections were alarming. The clause in Isabella's will certainly fits that situation admirably: Juana 'might not be able' to govern because Philip would not let her, or she 'might not like' to govern because it would involve her in quarrels and confrontations with him. The carefully worded phrase also provides for the possible absence of Philip and Juana, should he decide that they would go back to Burgundy once 'his' inheritance had been secured.

Whatever Isabella's motives for the insertion of those few but vital words, in her mind there was only one person equipped to carry on her government in these dire circumstances, a man of 'greatness ... excellence ... nobility ... eminent virtues' who already had 'great experience of the government of the said kingdoms':

> I have directed and ordained in my testimonial and will that in each of the aforementioned cases, the ... King my lord shall reign, govern and administer the said kingdoms, lands, and dominions, and have the government and administration of them instead of and in the name of the Princess our daughter, until my grandson, the Infante Don Carlos, first born son and heir of the said Princess and her husband Prince Philip, has attained the age required by law for governing and reigning in these kingdoms, and has at least accomplished his twentieth year.

'Don Carlos', then four, was being brought up in Burgundy. That had disappointed Isabella, who had yearned for him to spend his formative years in Spain, where he could learn to speak Spanish and to understand the lands that would one day be his. In fact, Isabella never even saw Charles.

In an additional clause of her will, inserted in a move intended to restrict Juana and Philip even should they decide, and be able, to rule, Isabella decreed that they should obey Ferdinand in all things as 'good and obedient children' and listen to his advice on all matters pertaining to government. So, as she said goodbye to this world, Isabella hoped that she had thought of everything.

At first it looked as though she had. Ostensibly the good, upright parent, Ferdinand publicly acknowledged Juana's rights even as Isabella's corpse grew cold. He went on 'the very day on which Queen Isabella died to the marketplace of Medina del Campo', where he 'ascended a platform' and renounced his title as King of Castile in favour of Juana and Philip. He wrote to them at once, asking them 'to come to Spain, in order to take upon themselves the government of Castile'. So, as he would self-righteously protest, he had played fair. In fact, he was pre-pared to do whatever was necessary, be it devious or treacherous, to maintain his tenure of Castile. If he had to abandon his daughter in the process, then so be it.

As she attended requiem Masses for the repose of her mother's soul, Juana had no conception of the snake-pit which had opened before her, or the forces which opposed her. At twenty-six, she had no experience of statecraft; to her, the poisonous intrigues of Spanish politics were a closed book. Nonetheless, all should have been straightforward; the worrying catch-all clause of Isabella's will should be unnecessary. As Ferdinand had acknowledged, Juana was her mother's heir and she should go back to Spain and govern in Isabella's place, with her husband Philip as her loyal consort. If that occurred, her father must step aside and restrict himself to offering advice. But the crux of Juana's predicament was that the two men who should have been her most devoted of supporters were in fact her most deadly opponents. Both wanted what was, by right, hers. Philip even sent a letter, supposedly signed by Juana, to Ferdinand's ambassador in Burgundy, saying that she wanted her husband to rule in her place. That was the last thing she wanted; her 'signature' has recently been proved a forgery. But the odds against her seizing her birthright were overwhelming.

When she heard that her mother had died, Juana was in Burgundy where all the cards were held by Philip. Like Ferdinand, he was an established ruler. His ministers were accountable to him; ambassadors visited him and reported to him; foreign kings, such as Henry VII, treated with him in international affairs. True, Henry did sometimes write to Juana to get her help but he did not expect her to act independently of her husband. Gender ensured that it was Philip who made the decisions. Juana was largely isolated; she had no power in Burgundy and no influential supporters. Once she reached her homeland, it might be different. Then it would be she who was on home ground and she would have the opportunity to show that God had spoken and she was a worthy successor to Isabella the Catholic. Perhaps. But making arrangements for the journey to Spain was a slow business, and in the meantime she remained in Philip's power. And he was saying she was out of her wits.

However, despite the rumours Philip was assiduously circulating about her mental state, she continued to behave perfectly on public occasions, casting doubt on her husband's claims. She could be composed, dignified and regal, as she was when her father-in-law, Maximilian, visited Brussels in 1505. After an audience with her in her chamber on this occasion, the Venetian ambassador reported that she looked 'very well ... her bearing being that of a sensible and discreet woman'. She listened to his address and 'made a loving reply'. The ambassador gave no indication that she was anything other than normal. He did remark on a 'late illness' she had had, but went on to say that she looked 'very well'. And she was well enough to watch a torchlight joust in which Philip, happy to bask in any available admiration, competed alongside Maximilian. The joust, which went on until four in the morning, was followed by a 'sumptuous banquet' so that 'well nigh the whole night' was 'passed in dancing and other amusements'. Juana sat through it all, the gracious archduchess and queen.

Yet she could still play right into Philip's hands. Though their marriage was unhappy and tempestuous, the couple were still sleeping together and sharing him was still anathema to her. She could not bring herself to accept Philip's infidelities and ignore them, as her mother largely had with those of Ferdinand and as most queens managed to do. Despite being bullied and ill treated, Juana was jealous of any woman upon whom his mere glance might fall. Rashly, she surrendered to her emotions again, making a huge fuss just as she and Philip prepared for their voyage to Spain to claim the throne: she ordered a ship with women attendants on board not to sail with her because she suspected that Philip would bed them. Her actions were noted and repeated to the Venetian ambassador, who then of course repeated them himself – wonderful ammunition for Philip's propaganda. Unfortunately for Juana, it was ammunition for her father too.

By the time Juana and Philip eventually did set sail for Spain, more than fifteen months had elapsed since Isabella had been lowered into the earth of her beloved Alhambra. No one had been idle, however. Juana, largely isolated from events in Spain, had given birth to her fifth child, a daughter, whom she called Maria. The widowed Henry VII had spent the time scouring Europe for a new bride for himself; he had also considered whether he might find a more suitable one for his son than Katherine, and wondered whether he could procure the capture of the Earl of Suffolk, that leftover Yorkist claimant from the Wars of the Roses, who had taken refuge in the lands of Maximilian and Philip. And the betrayal of Juana had begun.

Ferdinand clinically started the process of disinheriting his daughter. At the Council of Toro in 1505, he secured what amounted to a regency over Castilian lands. To do so, he presented evidence to the councillors that Juana was unfit to govern herself, thus invoking Isabella's will. Having deliberated, they played right into Ferdinand's hands by affirming that because of Juana's 'infirmity' they considered that 'by right as well as according to the laws of these kingdoms the lawful guardianship and administration of these kingdoms and dominions is due and belong to the said Lord, King Ferdinand'. The honest, if duped, councillors drew a polite veil over the precise nature of Juana's 'infirmity', except to say that they had been 'privately informed' of it and they agreed that it was 'notorious that the said infirmity' rendered it impossible for her to rule herself.

It was a promising beginning for Ferdinand. Juana's 'infirmity' was now well publicised and he had authority within Castile again, authority which had lapsed when Isabella died. For all that he was wily and shrewd, the perfect model for Machiavelli's *The Prince*, Ferdinand did care about the security and prosperity of his realms. Since his marriage to Isabella he had worked to forge a unity of sorts within their joint dominions. Perhaps he genuinely saw Juana, and especially Philip, as threatening all that he had achieved and likely to bring 'affliction' to Spain and its peoples; perhaps he considered himself to be simply keeping an eye on Castile as his wife had wished; or, more probably, he could not bear the thought of relinquishing the power that he had so enjoyed wielding. Whatever his motivation, Ferdinand was clearly determined to remain at the centre of Spanish politics.

Ever a realist, he understood that his gains at Toro could prove only temporary. Philip and Juana might yet oust him, for he was not popular within Castile. Castilian grandees might prefer the possibly malleable Philip, eager to win their favour and ready to make concessions, to a skilful, efficient monarch like himself. Therefore Ferdinand did the unthinkable: he allied with France and was betrothed to Louis XII's niece, Germaine de Foix. That would muddy the waters nicely. If Germaine had a child, at the very least Aragon was safe from Philip's clutches because that child would inherit it instead of Juana; and there was always a chance that a child who brought Aragon back into a union could be very attractive to Castilian interests. Possibly. But, to cover all bases, Ferdinand was ready to negotiate with Philip as well. Perfidy became them both.

For Philip, too, had been busy in the lull between hearing of Isabella's death and sailing to Spain. He finished off a minor war, negotiated with the French himself, corresponded with Henry VII and, more importantly, built up his support in Castile, mainly on the simple premise that he was not Ferdinand. He even managed to embroil Katherine in his squalid machinations, abusing her genuine desire to see her sister. And more treacherously, he schemed to betray his wife, not in dalliance in the bedroom with his latest amour, but far more insidiously and cruelly: as a first step towards assuming total power himself, he strove to ally himself with Ferdinand so that ultimately he could declare Juana insane and incarcerate her for ever. By the time his ship left port, Philip had gone partway to achieving his goal. He had haggled with Ferdinand until they reached agreement that the government of Castile should be undertaken by Juana, Ferdinand and Philip in a tripartite system.

Thus, before she had put one foot on Spanish soil again, the rights that should have been Juana's alone were now shared with her husband and her father. And neither Ferdinand nor Philip would willingly surrender them.

'A Happiness Rare'

'A happiness rare for princes', wrote Lord Herbert of Cherbury in the seventeenth century, 'was to see one another after they had been once dispos'd of abroad.' None of the Catholic Monarchs' daughters really supposed that they would ever see each other after being 'dispos'd of abroad' themselves. True, Princess Isabella had returned to Spain when she was widowed and again when she became heiress to all of her parents' lands, and Juana too had been home when the prospect of that inheritance first fell to her, but those journeys were matters of pure chance and Juana had seen only the Catholic Monarchs, not her sisters. The final farewells, for daughters anyway, were usually just that.

Within less than a year after her mother's death, however, Katherine hoped that 'a rare happiness' would be hers and that Juana and Philip would meet Henry VII near Calais, then an English possession. Practical reasons certainly existed to make this a sensible idea. Beset by furious merchants complaining of poor treatment by the Spanish authorities and angered by his failure to pay the next instalment of Katherine's dowry, Henry was fast becoming disenchanted with Ferdinand. An agreement with Philip and Juana, perhaps with trading concessions and the return of the troublesome Earl of Suffolk, was worth considering. Yet no meeting was planned by Henry VII. Instead, Katherine, in what was to be her first hands-on experience of the murky world of international diplomacy, was inveigled into suggesting it.

The culprits in what was really rather a shady enterprise which played on the young, naive princess, were Doña Elvira and her brother, Don Juan Manuel, the Spanish ambassador in Burgundy. Don Manuel, a proud Castilian, had been happy to serve Isabella as his queen. In his eyes, her death had changed things; he would prefer Philip and Juana ruling his precious Castile rather than Ferdinand who was, after all,

Aragonese not Castilian and who was not easily manipulated as Philip might well be. And, reasoned Juan Manuel, Henry VII's support for Philip would be useful should Ferdinand fight to keep control of Castile, a distinct possibility. All that was necessary to ensure amity was to engineer a meeting between Philip and Henry. And that was where Katherine came in: Juan Manuel's sister, Doña Elvira, could persuade her to write to Henry to bring it about. Where Philip went so did Juana, and because of her longing to see her sister once more, Katherine was easily manipulated.

We can be sure that the initiative was not hers because Doña Elvira ruled the princess and those about her with a ferocious hand. On the few occasions after Arthur's death when Katherine had attempted to assert herself, Doña Elvira had quickly squashed any incipient signs of rebellion: she made sure that the princess did not squander money that Henry gave her; she kept the young widow in the strict seclusion that Spanish custom demanded; she supervised Katherine's maids, even considering one of them as a bride for her son. In all of this, Doña Elvira had been supported by Katherine's parents, by Henry VII himself and ambassador de Puebla. In one of his reports, de Puebla recounts a telling episode of 1504 in which he made sure that Katherine was put firmly in her place in order to 'increase her [Doña Elvira's] authority':

> I took her [Doña Elvira] a head-dress from the King [Henry VII], a St Peter in gold, which the King never sends excepting to her Highness the Princess, or to her Highness his mother, or to his daughter the Queen of Scotland, or to such like personages. This head-dress was not given her in secret, but in presence of the Princess and her ladies, in order to invest her with as much authority as I could.

De Puebla wanted to deal with a compliant princess, not an awkward one.

But just after Isabella's death Ferdinand began to suspect that Doña Elvira was no longer an ally. Writing to de Puebla, the king instructed his ambassador to warn Henry to 'confide nothing to Doña Elvira Manuel, sister to Juan Manuel, because he cannot be trusted'. Ferdinand's suspicions were correct, for brother and sister were indeed working together and plotting to use his daughter against him.

Again we have the indefatigable de Puebla to thank for the entire story, all of which we can read in his dispatches to Ferdinand. Telling the king that 'the ambassadors from Flanders have of late been very often to kiss the hand of the Princess of Wales', the ambassador also explained why and how this was happening:

> Doña Elvira Manuel, influenced by her brother Don Juan Manuel, procures them these frequent opportunities of seeing the Princess, who has been won over by them to such an extent as to propose an interview between the King of England, the King Archduke and the Queen Archduchess. The Princess hopes to accompany the King of England to this meeting, and in this way to see her sister.

Letters were soon going to and fro between England and Burgundy, de Puebla reported: 'Doña Elvira had taken great pains, and persuaded the Princess of Wales to send one of her servants to the King Archduke, the Queen Archduchess, and Don Juan Manuel, with a message concerning this interview.' Happy to oblige his sister-in-law, Philip proposed that if Henry went to Calais, he and Juana would go to Saint Omer, just a few miles away, and then a meeting could be organised.

Not realising she had been duped, a delighted Katherine sent for de Puebla. She showed him Philip's letter 'with the greatest joy' and said that she would write to Henry 'without losing an hour's time'. Thinking on his feet, de Puebla offered to take the letter for her. Then he 'would have taken care to bring the whole affair to nothing'. Loyal to Ferdinand, the ambassador appreciated that such a letter would not only drag Katherine into the acrimonious disputes between Ferdinand and Philip, it could threaten Spanish interests, perhaps helping to foment civil war. When the princess refused to entrust him with her note, the ambassador tried to reason with Doña Elvira herself. Pretending to give way, she promised to stop Katherine writing to Henry.

A much relieved de Puebla went home, intending to settle down to dinner. It was a meal he was destined not to consume. Just as he was about to start eating, one of his servants rushed into the room to tell him that Doña Elvira 'had betrayed him' and that the damaging letter was already on its way to Henry. Poor de Puebla, now unable 'to swallow a mouthful', rushed back to see Katherine. Making her take an oath not to reveal what he was about to say to Doña Elvira or anyone else, he told her the truth: 'the interview was the work of Don Juan Manuel and Doña Elvira, who intended to do injury to her royal father, and to the Queen her sister by it'. Katherine believed him. And she did exactly what de Puebla told her to do: she wrote a second letter to Henry but this time 'according to his [de Puebla's] dictation'. She abjectly apologised to Henry, telling him that while she 'had proposed an interview with the King Archduke', she now realised that Ferdinand 'would be very sorry if such an interview were really to take place'.

Because of de Puebla's swift action, the affair, at this stage anyway, did indeed come 'to nothing'. Yet the episode marks the first stage in Katherine's political education. Doña Elvira's treachery made the princess realise that even those closest to her could betray her. She did not forgive that, and she no longer wanted Doña Elvira anywhere near her: we hear that Doña Elvira suddenly travelled to Burgundy 'to get cured' from a condition which had caused her to lose vision in one of her eyes.

And Katherine grasped another crucial lesson, one that her mother had always understood: she learned how to dissemble. De Puebla told her not to say anything about what had really happened. Instead she should 'keep up an appearance in public, of desiring the interview now, more than ever'. That would be the best way to protect Ferdinand: 'such dissimulation, by which the secret would be safely guarded, would be of greater service to her father than two thousand men-at arms,' wrote the ambassador to his king. Katherine would not forget her induction into the mechanics of statecraft.

Ironically, all of de Puebla's frenzied activity was fruitless: the meeting between Henry and Philip and Katherine and Juana did in fact take place, albeit entirely due to storms and tempests in the English Channel.

Philip and Juana's much-talked-of journey to Spain to claim Castile began at last when they set sail in January 1506 accompanied by over two thousand nobles and a fleet of ships. At first, all augured well. They passed Calais with a display of strength, guns firing, torches blazing, the sounds of music drifting towards the shore. Then the weather changed dramatically. Soon, the fleet was engulfed in a desperate fight for survival. The winds increased, the waves grew mountainous and the tiny ships were tossed backwards and forwards in pitch darkness. It was every boat for itself, none could aid its neighbour. In most cases they could not even see the other vessels for 'such was the darkness that not an object could be distinguished one span ahead', wrote the Venetian ambassador, Vincenzo Quirini, who has left us a first-hand account of just what it was like to be a passenger on one of those ships as the seas heaved and the sailors desperately battled for their lives. They were all caught up, he tells us, in a hurricane 'of which the oldest mariners in the fleet say they have not experienced the like within the last half century'.

According to Quirini, Juana 'evinced intrepidity throughout', as would be expected of one almost raised on a battlefield. Philip, ever the man of action, was the personification of bravery when their ship caught fire three times, almost capsized and was in such peril that 'the crew were utterly bewildered and had given themselves up for lost'. After a further battering from the storm, he and his companions embraced each other in a final gesture of farewell before awaiting 'death, without any hope of escape'. Yet escape they did, for Philip and Juana's ship, blown completely off course, managed to reach the shore at Weymouth in Dorset. Several other vessels, including Quirini's, also struggled towards English soil, at various points along the south coast.

Once Henry heard that Philip and Juana had landed, he ordered servants to rush to their aid with horses and supplies, and suggested just what de Puebla had fought so hard to prevent – a meeting. Leaving Juana behind for the moment, Philip and his entourage rode towards Windsor where Henry was waiting. The two men pussy-footed around elegantly, each treating the other with ostentatious courtesy, but there was no doubt that Henry was the person in charge. Over the following weeks, the king entertained his guests lavishly with bear baiting, jousting, hunting, and even tennis. When the tennis started, Philip, true to form, rushed to take part; Henry, equally true to form, remained 'looking on'. Philip became a member of the Order of the Garter; Prince Henry, Katherine's presumed betrothed, was given the Order of the Golden Fleece. It was all very jolly, very elaborate and went very much

Henry's way. The various discussions he held with Philip gave him just what he wanted: trading concessions for English merchants, an agreed surrender of the Earl of Suffolk (whom, it was assumed, Henry would treat fairly and never execute), support for a possible new marriage for Henry with Philip's sister, Margaret, and the possibility of a match between Philip and Juana's eldest son, Charles, and Henry's youngest daughter, Mary.

When she heard the news of her sister's arrival, Katherine was in London. Henry arranged for her to come to Windsor on Saturday 31 January 1506, the same day that Philip arrived there. Katherine met him on Sunday when he was invited by Henry to watch the ladies dancing. She danced 'two or three dances' with 'a Spanish lady', presumably one of her attendants, her performance being followed by that of Henry's daughter, Mary, with an English lady as her partner. Yet, for once, Philip did not throw himself into the spirit of the occasion: when Katherine asked him to dance, he refused, saying he was a 'mariner'. 'And yet', Philip went on, 'ye would cause me to dance!' Perhaps Philip simply wanted to continue chatting to Henry, but the words are intriguing. One recent historian's interpretation of them, though, rings true: Philip had sailed to England, and was on his way to Spain, despite Katherine's earlier attempts to stop him. Publicly snubbed, Katherine sat quietly to one side, to be joined by Mary who had smoothed away the embarrassment by dancing again herself.

But the one face Katherine yearned to see was not there. When Philip's ship had limped ashore, he had ridden on ahead to meet Henry himself, leaving his wife to follow in his wake at a much slower pace. She did not arrive at Windsor until Tuesday 10 February, over a week after her husband. Then, after all her hopes, Katherine was destined to see her sister for only a few short hours; it was as if they were deliberately being kept apart.

Although accompanied part of the way by some of Henry's gentlemen, Juana's welcome was far more low-key than that given to Philip. While Katherine waited impatiently, Juana entered 'secretly ... by the backside of the castle unto the king's new tower'. It was here that Henry greeted her 'and kissed and embraced her', crossing Philip who clearly had not wanted Henry even to see her. Philip had, we read, 'divers times before desired the king's highness for to have remained in his own lodging, and not to have taken the pains to have gone so far'. Did Philip want to emphasise his own status as King of Castile by talking to Henry man to man? Or, eager to spread rumours of Juana's instability, did he fear that seeing Juana face to face might make Henry suspicious? The evidence does not tell us, but we do know that Juana created a favourable impression on the English king, one that he would later remember.

Only after seeing Henry was Juana taken to see Katherine. They had not met since Juana had sailed for Burgundy almost ten years earlier, since when so much had happened to transform both of their lives. Tantalisingly, we have no account of what the sisters said to each other in those precious hours. All we hear is that Katherine and Mary, 'having many ladies and gentlewomen attending upon them welcomed her [Juana]; and so all together went up into the king of Castile's lodgings'. And that is it. The following day, Wednesday, Katherine and Mary left Windsor for Richmond, Henry following on Thursday to make all ready for Philip to come there as well. Most likely, Katherine assumed that Juana would join Philip in Henry's show-case palace. If she did, she was disappointed, for although Philip did indeed come to Richmond, where the round of entertainments and talks started all over again, he came only with his councillors and gentlemen not with his wife. Juana, by easy stages, was taken back to their ship. And always, we wonder why this was so.

Perhaps Philip thought Katherine might mention the Manuels' scheming, but his main concern was probably Juana herself. The more often she was seen in public, and the longer she spent with her sister, the harder it would be for him to maintain that she was so unbalanced that he had no choice but to rule for her once they reached Spain. Most of all, he did not want Katherine to encourage his wife to attempt to oust him and take over her lands for herself. She might well have done just that: like Queen Isabella, Katherine was determined, courageous, stubborn, a woman who would doggedly fight a crusade to the bitter end if she believed the cause to be just. And, as Isabella had discovered when she had tried to keep her daughter in Castile, Juana could be wilful and unpredictable. Far better, then, for Philip to keep the sisters apart. And he managed to do that for the next three months, for he and Juana did not leave the country until April.

Yet it was cruel. In a letter that Katherine wrote to her sister just over a year later, she briefly but poignantly described her anguish that their time together had been so short: 'I have to express the very great pleasure it gave me to see you in this kingdom, and the distress which filled my heart, a few hours afterwards, on account of your sudden and hasty departure.'

They were never to meet again, their happiness was indeed 'rare'. Juana sailed to Spain with Philip; Katherine stayed in England, the negotiations for her marriage to the Prince of Wales dragging interminably on and on.

PART III

Widows

A Sea of Troubles

As Juana's ship sailed closer towards Spanish shores, Katherine settled back into her normal routine. And her normal routine involved worrying about if and when her marriage to Prince Henry would take place and how to manage her finances in the meantime.

No matter how many hours she spent in prayer, or how determined she felt about fulfilling her destiny by marrying Arthur's brother, Katherine was in a state of limbo. Henry VII would neither commit himself to the marriage nor officially end it and send her back to Spain. According to the 1503 treaty, the marriage should have taken place once the prince 'completed the fourteenth year of his age', which was the minimum legal requirement for a male under church law unless an additional papal dispensation was obtained. Since Henry was fifteen on 28 June 1505, Katherine should have become a bride again shortly after that. Indeed, when she met Juana at Windsor, she should have been Prince Henry's wife. She was not.

On the day before the crucial birthday, the prince had issued a protestation against the match, as church law entitled him to do, declaring that because it had been arranged 'during his minority', it was 'null and void'. Clearly this was a ruse organised by the king to keep his options open: just because the original betrothal was 'null and void' did not mean that the entire affair was off, just that it was no longer so definite. A wedding could still take place, with the boy's consent, some time in the future. Katherine, taught to see England as the country her parents and indeed God had chosen for her, was in despair. She wanted the marriage, she believed in it, she would do everything she could to bring it about, but persuading the king to finally agree and set a firm date was another matter entirely. He was in no hurry, for he had it all ways: his son was not bound because the betrothal had not been binding on his side, whereas Katherine remained affianced because she had been well above the minimum age of consent for a woman when the treaty was signed. She found herself trapped in an impossible situation.

And money was a terrible problem too. The question of whether Henry or her parents should pay for her keep had surfaced quite soon after Arthur's death. Sometimes Henry gave her money, mostly he did not. Her parents had been of little use. She should 'accept whatever she can get' from Henry she was told firmly. Since Henry was almost on first-name terms with every coin in his treasury, that was expecting much. So she had borrowed. When her parents remonstrated that for a princess of Spain to borrow was 'a thing unheard of', she retorted that she had not 'contracted debts for luxuries' but because 'otherwise she would have had nothing to eat'. Histrionics apart, and they were an area in which she quickly became as adept as Juana, the daily struggle to make ends meet sometimes overwhelmed her.

What she was really dreading was that she might be compelled to sell, or pawn, some of the plate and jewels which she had brought with her from Spain. That, she knew, was the road to disaster for these items were to form about one-third of the final amount outstanding on her dowry. If she let any of her 'treasures' go, she would end up with a massive shortfall and she knew Henry well enough to fear his reaction to that. Even finding the second instalment of her dowry was such a problem to Ferdinand, particularly after Isabella's death left him short of funds himself, that he was constantly begging Henry for post-ponements. So even assuming that Henry finally consented to the wedding, the nuptials could be jeopardised because her dowry was not fully paid. It was a nightmare.

Yet, with Juana and Philip in control of Castile, and in control of Castilian finances, perhaps things might improve. If Katherine really did hope for that, and certainly Ferdinand encouraged her to believe that Philip might take on the dowry debts, she was to be disappointed. Too keen to get his hands on Castilian funds for himself and his rapacious councillors, many of whom had flocked to Spain with him, Philip was unlikely to lose sleep over Katherine's dowry. He could hardly have cared less about Katherine's troubles. His focus was on preventing Juana trying to assert herself once she was on home soil.

If the Venetian ambassador, Vincenzo Quirini, is to be believed, Philip's disquiet was well-founded. 'It is evident', Quirini reported back to the Doge, 'that on reaching Spain, the Queen [Juana] will choose to govern and be mistress.' She and Philip reached Spain on 26 April 1506 when their ship docked at Coruna.

However, if Juana really did intend to seize control, she would need allies and information. She had neither. In fact, she was more marginalised than her sister. Katherine, aiming for the more lowly role of consort, albeit one of influence, was not isolated. Sometimes she went to court; she talked with King Henry; she wrote and received letters; while not always convinced that every one of her ladies was faithful to her, she had some, like Maria de Salinas, to whom she was devoted; even if she never liked him, the Spanish ambassador, de Puebla, brought her news, letters and advice. Still a novice on the stage of international politics, Katherine was beginning to learn how the world worked; she could not have done that without knowing at least a little of what was happening outside the walls of her palace.

Juana, although now a queen regnant, had few such channels of information. The women around her – she had at last conceded that there should be some – were chosen by Philip, her household officials were bribed by her husband, she had few visitors, and she was fed misinformation whenever it suited him. And he was particularly eager to sow distrust between Juana and her father. The Spanish ambassador reported a conversation he had had with her in a meeting grudgingly allowed by Philip after keeping him waiting for 'many days'. She asked the ambassador 'very tenderly' about her father, 'six months having elapsed since she had received news of him'. She enquired fearfully 'whether he [Ferdinand] wished her as much harm as she was told he did'. The ambassador was in no doubt over why she had been led to believe that, reporting that he knew

for certain that Philip's councillors had given the Queen to understand that her father bears her ill will, and would fain not see her in Spain, in order that on going thither with this impression, she might, at their first meeting, treat him unbecomingly; whilst King Ferdinand, being informed in like manner, that his daughter loved

him not, and was such as they described her, would the more
readily consent to deprive her of the government.

However, while keen to disabuse her of this notion and perfectly well
aware of how the land lay, the ambassador was careful not to foster
dissension between husband and wife. 'Her father loved her and her
husband as his very dear children, and had no greater wish in the world
than to see them,' he assured her.

Pinning her hopes on her father and trusting that he really did love
her as much as the ambassador affirmed, she was anxious not to do or
say anything to upset him. Thus, she refused to confirm the local
privileges previously enjoyed by the people of Coruna, simply because
she wanted to make sure that her father thought this the correct way to
proceed. She would commit herself to nothing. Again, Quirini noticed
what was happening:

> Queen Juana continues to lead the same life of seclusion as in
> Flanders, nor has she received the visits of any of the envoys, and
> it is said, persists in not allowing herself to be spoken to, until she
> sees her father; nor is she visible to any man, save a few servants.

Unfortunately her policy of waiting for her father suited Philip only too
well. The less she did on her own initiative, the more time he had to
consolidate his own hold on power and, if he wanted to portray her as
unstable, it was better that she saw as few people as possible because she
behaved so normally in public that his lies would quickly be exposed.
For Juana, as Bergenroth in the nineteenth century and historians such
as Chrimes and Loades in the twentieth century have realised, was not
the hopelessly deranged woman of legend.

Philip continued to try to control her in the best way he knew
how: there were 'those nights when he sleeps with her', or so Quirini
informs us. Juana had adored Philip when they were first married,
revelling in the physical side of their relationship as much as he did.
Clearly, she still cared about him despite his infidelities and his
bullying or she would not have been so jealous of other women. But,
if Quirini is right, and she wanted to govern and rule as a sovereign

queen, which is quite likely to have been the case, she knew she could face confrontation with her husband. Then anything could happen: an agreement with him might be possible; he might return to Burgundy and leave her to govern Castile; he might change and become a support rather than a hindrance; more probably, he would try to bully and dominate her just as he always had done. In any case, she knew that she was as yet in no position to stand up to him. Thus, while making love to Philip might seem proof that Juana remained his puppet, it is also possible that, like her sister, she was learning the value of dissimulation.

Yet she could do nothing to drive a wedge between her father and her husband. True, they viewed each other with hearty dislike and mistrust, but both saw their best chance of power was to ignore her. And this they did. Knowing that he had insufficient resources to defeat Philip in battle, Ferdinand chose to continue the accommodation he had already made with his son-in-law rather than treat with his daughter and risk war with her husband. Indeed, to her distress, he did not even meet her.

Instead, on 27 June 1506, he met Philip at Villafáfila to iron out an agreement. Neither thought to complicate matters by inviting Juana. From now onwards, Philip and Ferdinand concurred, 'the most intimate friendship and alliance' would prevail between them, Ferdinand leaving the government of Castile in the capable hands of Philip, who was, Ferdinand hypocritically announced, his 'very dear and much beloved son'. With expressions of loving regret, the pair excluded Juana. 'For the sake of honesty and out of respect', they said, they could not explain their reasons. While paying lip-service to 'honesty and respect', they used the alliance to destroy Juana's credibility. Unfortunately, said Philip and Ferdinand, lying through their teeth, she was 'not inclined, on any condition, to occupy herself in the despatch of any business concerning the royal prerogatives and government'. If she did want to interfere, father and husband continued, 'it would be to the total destruction and perdition of these kingdoms'. Much better, then, to leave it all to the men.

It got worse. Wary that she might somehow evade their efforts and drum up support, they tried to counter that danger too:

Considering her infirmities and sufferings, which for the sake of her honour are not expressed ... and being desirous to remedy and prevent the evils and inconveniences which would be the consequences thereof, it has been concerted and concluded between us [Ferdinand] and the most serene King, our son, that in case the ... most serene Queen ..., either from her own choice or from being persuaded by other persons ... should attempt, or that they should attempt, to meddle in the government, or to confound and oppose the said treaty; neither we, nor the said most serene King, our son, shall suffer it, but on the contrary shall be unanimous in preventing it.

Juana's hands appeared effectively tied, her betrayal complete.

But that was to reckon without Ferdinand's talent for duplicity. On the very same day that he had given everything to his 'much beloved son', he denounced the whole treaty as being obtained under duress. He had gone to meet Philip, Ferdinand said, 'with that good faith which ought to subsist between a father and son', only to find that Philip had such a 'powerful and strong army' that Ferdinand's 'royal person' was 'in notorious and manifest danger'. If he was in peril, he felt, so were his kingdoms 'considering what is going on in these times'. Thus, he had consented to all that was demanded purely to save his own life.

Philip, maintained Ferdinand, was 'determined to usurp ... the administration of these kingdoms' which in fact belonged 'by right' to Ferdinand himself. Not content with that, Philip had sunk to 'depriving the most Serene Queen, Doña Juana, his wife and my daughter, of her liberty and all that belongs to her as heiress and proprietress of these kingdoms'. Had he been 'at full liberty', Ferdinand protested, he would never have agreed to 'such enormous injustice'. As soon as he was in a position to do so, he promised, he would restore Juana's freedom and her throne, in the process recovering 'the government again which for many reasons belongs to me'.

Reluctant to make too public a denunciation in case it led to 'dangers, fear and apprehension' – or so he said – Ferdinand swore all of this before the Public Notary, who happened to be his secretary, and some of the members of his council. At a single stroke, Ferdinand effectively muddied the waters and gave himself every chance to interfere in Castilian affairs from then onwards. Philip was on the receiving end of a political masterclass.

The real loser was Juana. However, deciding that Ferdinand, of whom she had spoken 'very tenderly', cared for her more than her husband did and could provide a refuge and succour, she determined to talk to him. This meant taking independent action for the first time since she had arrived back in Castile. She used the pretence of a gentle ride in the park of the castle of Benavente, where she had been staying with her husband, to spur her horse and ride furiously to meet her father. She failed miserably. Pursued by Philip's soldiers, she was cornered in a humble bakery; she did not escape again.

Unaware of her daring bid for freedom, or possibly preferring not to know of it, Ferdinand made no attempt to visit her himself. All he did was to justify his actions to Henry VII, stating piously that he desired only peace and tranquillity in his lands and with his children, so that he could think about going on a crusade to North Africa to fight the Moors. Thus, he told the English king, he had come to an additional agreement with Philip that he himself would rule Castile should Philip and Juana be absent. Then, after advising Philip to 'cultivate a better understanding with the Queen, his wife' whose health depended 'upon gentle measures being used', but still without setting eyes on her, Ferdinand left Castile and left Spain not, in fact, for his much-heralded crusade but to deal with more prosaic concerns in Italy. He did make it clear to Philip that he would not stand for Juana being incarcerated in a 'strong fortress' but that was as far as he went in condemning the way in which his daughter was being treated.

Perhaps because her pleading letters had touched him after all or, more probably, because he was eager not to lose the prized English alliance, Ferdinand did remember Katherine. Close to his departure, Ferdinand reminded Philip that money was still owed on Katherine's dowry. This had become Philip's responsibility; the debt was Castile's, not Ferdinand's. Katherine would be 'well married' if the money was sent to England, 'lost' if it was not, so Philip should send it as quickly as possible. And, knowing Henry, Ferdinand advised Philip to make sure he got a receipt.

Ferdinand may have made a token effort on Katherine's behalf, but he had left Juana on her own. Philip seemed to have won. Contemptuous of his father-in-law's strictures on how Juana should be treated, he did his utmost to propagate notions of her insanity, but found himself thwarted in his efforts to imprison her by members of the Cortes who insisted on seeing her for themselves before countenancing such a plan. When they did see her, she behaved so normally that they refused to sanction Philip's request. Yet, their support was limited: they also accepted Philip as their king. Juana's position remained dire.

She was saved by a totally unexpected event. In September 1506, the couple travelled to the city of Burgos. Within days, Philip became violently ill, allegedly because he over-indulged in various banquets and festivities. Inevitably, because everything happened so swiftly, rumours of poison surfaced. In fact, his high temperature and fever give little clue as to what was wrong with him; in the days before antibiotics, the slightest of infections could become life-threatening in a matter of hours. And sickness was rampant in Castile that autumn.

Juana's feelings for Philip were always a turmoil of emotions. Cruel and heartless though he often was, he was her husband and the father of her children. As the daughter of Isabella the Catholic, the concept of marriage as a sacrament had been well instilled in Juana. So, faced with his dreadful illness and vulnerability, she found it within herself to become the exemplar of the devoted and dutiful wife again, if only for one last time. Showing no signs of instability and brushing aside concern for her own health – she was five months pregnant at the time – she nursed him selflessly, never leaving his side, doing all she possibly could to save him, and always believing that he would recover. It was to no avail. Six days later, on 25 September 1506, Philip died. He was just twenty-eight years old.

Juana was now at a crossroads. With Philip a lifeless corpse and Ferdinand safely in Italy, her chance to rule as Castile's 'proprietary ruler' had arrived. This was the moment for her to show what she was made of. And she tried to do just that.

The odds were stacked against her. In the eyes of her mother's former confessor, the strict, austere, pitiless Cisneros, Archbishop of Toledo, a staunch upholder of the Inquisition, she had become a deadly enemy. Perhaps alarmed by the tactics she had once employed to force her mother to allow her to return to Burgundy, perhaps harbouring doubts about her religious probity, perhaps viewing government as a male preserve, he convinced himself that Juana was incapable of ruling. And he stepped in swiftly. On the day before Philip's death, he set himself up as the leader of a Regency Council and requested Ferdinand to return to Castile. Juana and her lands, he proclaimed, needed her father. That, though, was not what Juana had in mind. To work with Ferdinand to curb Philip's excess ambition and assert her own, and her children's entitlements, was quite a different matter to asking her father to rule in her place. And, with Philip dead, the situation had changed.

For the newly widowed queen to overcome such a powerful and determined adversary as Cisneros, she needed supporters, a healthy treasury and luck. Instead, she faced depleted finances, a divided Cortes, a people ravaged by hunger, drought, poor harvests and disease. And two opposing factions (one led by the archbishop and the other, consisting of Philip's erstwhile adherents, led by Doña Elvira's scheming brother Juan Manuel) competed to influence her. She had loyal supporters in her secretary, Juan Lopez, a man who had once served her mother and earned the trust of both Catholic Monarchs, and in her treasurer, Ochoa de Landa, but they wielded little power compared to the forces ranged against their mistress.

In those early days as Philip's corpse was embalmed, Juana was exhausted and emotionally drained. Yet, like her mother and her sister, she had courage, determination and an inner strength. It was fortunate that she did, for she knew what she wanted to do: she wanted to rule and, in particular, she wanted to safeguard her eldest son's inheritance. When she and Philip had sailed to Spain to claim Castile, Juana had been forced to leave Charles and his sisters with Margaret, her former sister-in-law. Margaret was lovingly caring for the boy, who was now six years old, but he was being brought up in Burgundian not Spanish traditions, with French not Spanish as his native language. And, to Charles, his mother was a distant figure who had spent so many years in Spain after his birth that he barely knew her. Yet Juana's sense of family and dynasty was inbred: she would fight her own crusade to ensure that, one day, her eldest son would gain everything that she and Philip had possessed. Provided Ferdinand did not have a male heir with his new wife, Queen Germaine, Charles would gain Aragon as well. Combined with a chance of becoming Holy Roman Emperor when his grandfather, Maximilian, died, his legacy would indeed be huge. And in his mother he had a noble champion, one whose faith in him never wavered.

However, in the aftermath of Philip's death, she did nothing. She would sign nothing, she would see no one. It was bound to take her some weeks to recover from the shock and to adjust to her own dramatically altered circumstances, but she also needed time to think and to plan. Only if she was at the mercy of others did she rush into tantrums and exhibitionist behaviour; in her current situation, with her own and her children's futures at stake, she needed a cool head. Then, when she did decide to act, she did so decisively. On 18 December she cancelled all the grants and offices with which Philip had shamelessly rewarded his followers, all of which, she said, had been handed out without her permission and to the detriment of both herself and of the state. Now she was ready to sign whatever documents were necessary for the government of her realms. Next, she tried to gather men around her to re-form a council similar to that of her mother, a council which reported to her and acted only upon her authority. If these measures worked, she would be well on the way to achieving her goal: time would tell.

Then, just before Christmas and in the depths of a bitterly cold winter, she made what proved to be a fateful move, one which would fuel a myth that has lasted to the present day. She ordered that Philip's coffin should be escorted in a slow and solemn procession from the Monastery of Miraflores, just outside of Burgos, where it then was, to Granada so that he could rest close to Queen Isabella. Philip had wanted that, and Juana wanted it for him. But she wanted it for herself and for Charles too. A symbol of the triumph of Christian Spain against the infidel, Granada had iconic status. If Philip lay close to the great Catholic herself, his place within Spanish history was assured. It was politic for Juana, the sorrowful widow, to accede him the honours due to a great king, a rightful king – and a king with a strong, if young, male heir.

Already Juana strove to enhance Charles's position. No matter what the provocation, and there would be much, she would never do anything to the boy's detriment. Then again, as she well understood, the journey to Granada was in her own interests too, for the grandees of Andalusia, hoping for a more malleable monarch than Ferdinand, could form her power base. And Philip's Burgundians were more likely to drift back home than ride to an area where even they could see they would be unwelcome.

Thus it was that, accompanied by the prayers of monks, Philip's candle-lit cortège left the confines of the monastery for its last journey. Juana, now eight months pregnant, was at her husband's side but she could not go far. Within three days, she had to stop or risk losing her baby. In January 1507, in the town of Torquemada, Juana went into labour. The birth was difficult but the child lived. Juana called her Catalina, presumably after her own sister, whom Juana had so recently seen in England. Although debilitated and weak, Juana was then itching to resume her interrupted journey.

With hindsight, her insistence that Philip be buried only in Granada was the pivotal moment of her entire life, the one decision upon which she has been judged ever since. She played directly into her enemies' hands. The legend started, and the legend spread, that she was a woman driven mad by grief, so distraught that she could not bear to be parted from Philip even by death, and therefore would not allow his body to be laid into the pitiless earth at all but wanted it with her for ever. It was said that she opened the coffin, that she kissed Philip's decaying feet, that she allowed no woman except herself anywhere near the corpse. The stories just grew and grew. She was a woman who was 'crazy from love'. She was 'Juana the Mad', an epithet by which she is still known in Spain to this day.

The tales were certainly music to Ferdinand's ears, and his supporters were assiduous in repeating them, but are they true? To those with an open mind, Juana's actions speak for themselves, indicating sanity not madness. To bury Philip in her mother's chosen city was shrewd politicking, to act against his avaricious advisers shows decisive statesmanship, to try to glean support wherever she could reveals the sort of common sense that Isabella herself possessed. And, as a recent biographer of Juana points out, Pedro Mártir, the chronicler who was with Juana on her gruesome journey with Philip's remains and was not the queen's noted partisan, made no mention of the alleged coffin-opening at all. In the highly unlikely event that Juana had opened the coffin, a possible cause might have been to be certain that the corpse was indeed Philip's. He had wanted his heart taken back to Burgundy. Knowing his followers as she did, Juana might have steeled herself to check that they had not taken the entire cadaver. As for the exclusion of women from the immediate vicinity of Philip's casket, that was in accordance with the monks' rules; the only women allowed on monastic premises were royal. The nineteenth-century Italian composer, Giuseppe Verdi, was familiar with such a proviso: in the second act of his opera, *Don Carlo*, one of the Queen of Spain's ladies tells the audience that they are waiting outside a monastery for their mistress since, as commoners, they cannot enter.

It seems prudent, then, to remain sceptical of the various horror stories about Juana's alleged obsession over her husband's body. Those who knew her best tended to view her as rational and reasonable. Frequently in her presence, and thus able to observe her on a day-to-day basis, her faithful secretary Juan Lopez never doubted her, maintaining to the last that she was 'more sane than her mother' no matter what others might say.

Yet, with so much and so many ranged against her, Juana could not win. Even the elements conspired against her, as if set on proving that God was not with her. Plague ravaged Castilian cities, starvation was rife, lawlessness abounded, Juana's council did not obey her, her revocations of Philip's wasteful grants went unheeded. Never could she overcome the traditional stereotype of gender: a woman, even a queen such as Isabella, needed male help, or so it was believed. With Philip gone, that left only her father. How fortuitous, then, that Ferdinand was at hand, ready to sacrifice himself to help his beleaguered daughter.

Respect for truth never had been one of Ferdinand's traits. Ostensibly responding to the pleas of his 'beloved daughter' and those of her councillors, he prepared to leave Italy to save Castile from the tumult flourishing within it. Writing to Katherine, he vowed:

I am determined, with the help of God, to go to Castile during this spring, because the Queen, my daughter and your sister, continually sends and begs me very pressingly to do so, and all write to me that, after God, there is no other means to preserve those kingdoms from ruin and destruction except my return to them . . . As they beg me very earnestly to go, and as the happiness of the most serene Queen, my daughter and your sister, and of those kingdoms greatly depend upon it, I have decided to give up my own comfort and to undergo all the labour of assisting her and her kingdoms.

He lied: Juana, while happy to see her father, had not urged him to take up the reins of her government at all.

No matter. She was a woman in a man's world. Ferdinand's machinations had worked. He had Castile in his grasp once more, and Juana would shortly exchange one gaoler for another.

The Art of Politics

Anxiously waiting for Ferdinand's return, Juana knew that her chance of governing as a queen in her own right was slipping inexorably from her grasp. She did not give up: she brought her second son, three-year-old Prince Ferdinand, whom she had seen so infrequently, to her side so that he could not be used as a hostage against her; she signed decrees; she kept trying to reform her council; she continued a few miles further towards Granada with Philip's corpse. Once Ferdinand was back, she knew that it would be to him that most eyes would turn.

For Juana, 1506 had been pivotal – but not in the ways she had hoped. The year had seen her return to Spain, but instead of independence it had brought her widowhood and a sharp lesson in the realities of power and the limitations of gender. With Ferdinand waiting impatiently for the weather to improve so that he could board his ship, 1507 boded no better.

Aside from the rare happiness of seeing her sister, albeit for such a short time, 1506 had brought Katherine no joy either. Her wedding to Prince Henry seemed as far away at the end of the year as it had been at the beginning. Her personal situation, dependent on Henry's occasional handouts, had failed to improve. Yet it was in the years between Arthur's death and her own eventual remarriage that so much of Katherine's character formed and crystallised. As a fifteen-year-old, she had come from Spain with firmly fixed ideas that would never change until her dying day: marriage mattered; family mattered; dynasty mattered; religion underpinned everything and must be defended at all costs; life brought suffering and struggle as well as joy and happiness. But she had known nothing of the nature of power or that success in her world required pragmatism, scheming, even downright deceit and mendacity. Juana had learned that lesson in Burgundy, she was experiencing it all too painfully in Spain. Only after the incident with Doña Elvira did Katherine start to realise the skills she needed to function effectively in a male-dominated society: she became a student of the art of politics. Once perfected, it was a craft she would never lose, and one for which she developed an abiding passion – her mother's daughter indeed.

In Ferdinand and in Henry VII, both highly polished tacticians, Katherine had superb tutors. In Dr Roderigo Gonzalvo de Puebla, she had another. An expert in canon and civil law and a former royal administrator in Andalusia, de Puebla first came to England in 1487 or 1488 to negotiate Katherine's marriage to Arthur. He returned in 1494 and remained for the next twenty years. Though there were a succession of additional ambassadors – including Don Pedro de Ayala; Ferdinand, Duke of Estrada; and the Knight Commander of Membrilla, Gutierre Gomez de Fuensalida – none stayed as long as de Puebla, and none could match him in his understanding of England, its peoples and above all its king.

Fiercely loyal to the Catholic Monarchs, he supported their daughter through the many trials of her widowhood with commendable tolerance, tact and, at times, sheer genius. Her battles were his battles. All was at considerable cost to himself, for though Ferdinand and Isabella demanded almost body and soul dedication to their causes from their ambassador, they berated him soundly if things went wrong and paid him his meagre salary only sporadically. Tucked on to the end of many a dispatch to his monarchs, we read his ever-respectful requests for payment. In one, he begs them to send him 'enough to have always something to eat'; in another, he says that his salary 'is only half as great as that of other Spanish ambassadors' and begs for money to be sent; in another, he wrote that he had 'sold all his property, and been obliged to incur debts', for which he lived 'in fear of being sent to prison'. His penchant for eating at the royal palace whenever he could, supposedly to save money, made him the butt of jokes which brought a rare smile to the austere features of Margaret Beaufort and made Henry VII laugh out loud.

The one person who could empathise with Katherine's financial predicament was de Puebla. And yet she never liked him and spent hours writing to her father demanding that the ambassador be recalled; if the princess disliked anyone, she did so in spades. De Puebla, she told Ferdinand waspishly, was 'a most faithful servant' but 'to the King of England'; he was more a 'vassal of the King of England' than a servant of her father's; the ambassador was 'the cause' of all her troubles; his letters were likely to be 'full of calumny and lies', particularly if they were about her or her conduct. Sometimes she was still more explicit:

> I beg your Highness that nothing which he [de Puebla] may say or write to you may be credited, excepting in so far as it shall agree with what I say. For if what I say be contrary to what he reports, your Highness may be assured that what he writes is also contrary to the interests of your Highness.

She took pride in her ability to 'dissimulate' with de Puebla, using against him the very technique he had been at pains to instil in her over the Doña Elvira affair. As for why she was not married, that, too, was the fault of poor de Puebla who, she continued, 'puts more difficulties than ever in the way of my marriage being concluded'. The only thing to do, she repeatedly told her father, was to send a better, more accomplished, ambassador who would serve both Ferdinand and herself with the steadfast commitment that they undoubtedly deserved. Only when it was too late did the rash princess come to respect the fidelity and sheer expertise of the man she had derided and whose qualities she had been so quick to dismiss.

Fortunately for de Puebla, he was not the only envoy Katherine so casually castigated. Though the king might profess to love her the most, preferring her 'to all his other children' and assuring her that he 'loved her more than ever a father loved his daughter', he understood that her outbursts were born of frustration at her limbo-like status. Katherine could be charming, virtuous, gracious, sweet and kind, but she was also impatient, stubborn, quick to express her feelings and quick to judge. Her view of the world was still monochromatic. Given time, she would learn to ponder, to hold back, to appreciate the good qualities of those around her but, until she did, her father knew how to handle her. Thus, he could soothe her ruffled feathers by declaring that he placed 'as implicit faith in her communications as in the Gospel', while simultaneously allaying his ambassadors' disquiet.

Writing to Fuensalida, the ambassador he sent to assist de Puebla in response to Katherine's repeated demands, only for the princess to rapidly transfer her fire from de Puebla to the new envoy, the king said that he was 'very sorry to hear what had passed' but appealed to Fuensalida 'to forget what has happened'. Knowing that appeasement tended to disarm Katherine, Ferdinand recommended Fuensalida practise it when coping with her tempers and moods, even suggesting that the ambassador should 'beg the princess to forgive' him. In any case, warned Ferdinand, nothing about her views or her treatment of the affronted ambassador should leak out to the English, even if Fuensalida suffered 'injustice' as a result. It was far better that Henry saw only her submissive, docile side; he would not want a headstrong bride for his only son.

Yes, Ferdinand certainly knew his daughter. And he also realised that, if treated carefully, she could become a valuable tool in attaining the marriage that Ferdinand was deeply convinced would benefit Spain, and of which she was the living symbol. Now in her early twenties, she was of an age to show her worth. If her role in life was to represent her country's interests, it was time she started doing that more vigorously.

From 1502 onwards, but especially after Doña Elvira departed in disgrace to Burgundy, Katherine embarked upon a period of apprenticeship in which she learnt the mechanics of diplomacy. The major topic upon which she honed her craft was that which was of paramount importance to her sex: marriage. She certainly had plenty of material, for she had seen several matches. While still a girl in Spain she had witnessed her sisters Isabella, Juana and Maria used as agents of foreign policy; indeed, that was what she was herself. Then, in the summer of 1503, she watched Henry VII's eldest daughter, thirteen-year-old Princess Margaret, used in a similar fashion when Margaret left Richmond for Scotland to marry King James IV. By then far more worldly wise than the young girl who had come to marry Arthur, Katherine was beginning to perceive the complex negotiation, delicate bargaining and consummate skill needed to effect royal marriages.

In very few marriages, however, did the bride herself play much part in the behind-the-scenes manoeuvrings which would so determine the shape of her life: Katherine was an exception. She worked to bring about her match with Prince Henry and she worked tirelessly because, to her, this union was her God-given destiny. The match was important, it could not be allowed to slip away.

Ferdinand had encouraged her to believe that her marriage to Prince Henry was already a fact and was accepted as such by God. In 1507, advising her to 'try to win the good will' of Henry VII, he reminded his daughter always to speak of her marriage 'as a thing beyond doubt'. Such advice fell on highly receptive ears; to the princess, her marriage was indeed 'a thing beyond doubt'. The only question was how to persuade Henry and his son of that. In pursuing her goal, Katherine was to discover that few policy objectives could be viewed in isolation, each was but one strand among many. For Ferdinand, upon these strands depended the security of Spain; Katherine, obsessed with her own match, began to appreciate how that slotted into the wider European picture and why she must strive to bring it about. As she tried her best to do so, she began to understand how the machinery of politics actually worked; she was learning lessons she would never forget.

Ferdinand began his tutelage by explaining to her just why he had decided to return to Spain and take up the burden of ruling Castile. Katherine had seen Juana before Philip's death. Then, she had not considered her sister deranged. Indeed, the two had corresponded since Juana's return to Castile. In a letter dated 17 October 1506, and once erroneously believed to be addressed to Ferdinand's second wife, Germaine de Foix, Katherine put her sister's mind at rest on the state of her own health. 'Since I wrote the other day', Katherine said, 'I had more attacks of fever, but they have left me, as you desire, so that, thanks to God, I am somewhat better now, and in better spirits.' Her note gives no hint that Katherine thought her sister anything but rational.

Rationality, of course, was not what Ferdinand wanted associated with Juana. And, when writing to Katherine, he was quick to act as his own propagandist: he wanted to ensure that Katherine did not support her sister against him. Thus, he was at pains to tell her that he was only going back to Castile because everyone, including Juana herself, was entreating him to do so. Having heard these pleas, Ferdinand, a devoted father and responsible monarch, could never desert his daughter or her people in their hour of need. Or so he said. What he did not say, of course, was that those who so earnestly begged him to return were in fact his own supporters, men like Archbishop Cisneros.

Katherine, however, believed her father. She responded as he had known she would:

> I am so glad your Highness is returning to Castile ... The advantages are very great. Not to speak of the comfort and consolation of the Queen [Juana], although that is also of great importance. I rejoice to think that the kingdom to which the Queen my lady [Isabella] succeeded is to remain in the hands of your Highness, and will lose nothing of the prosperity and security in which she left it.

Even at this juncture, though, Katherine did not forget her own predicament, for she continued: 'Besides, I hope that, by staying in that kingdom, your Highness will be in a better position to remedy all that concerns me.' Since her father had blamed Philip for the non-payment of her dowry, she had very neatly hoisted Ferdinand by his own petard. Now that Ferdinand was in control again, perhaps he would sort things out and procure the requisite funds so that a date could be set for her wedding. Katherine was nothing if not single-minded and perseverant.

Ferdinand's story was that Juana could not rule herself because she was too devastated by Philip's demise to do anything. She had suffered a blow which caused her 'unspeakable affliction', rendering her incapable of action. She was in retirement, seclusion, despair, her country going to rack and ruin around her. And he assiduously spread the stories of Juana's worryingly unhealthy devotion to her husband's corpse as manifested by her refusal to sanction its burial. In a later letter to de Puebla, Ferdinand craftily gave voice to his counterfeit concern:

> The said Queen, my daughter, still carries about with her the corpse of King Philip, her late husband. Before I arrived they could never persuade her to bury him, and since my arrival she has declared that she does not wish the said corpse to be buried. On

account of her health, and in order to content her, I do not
contradict her in anything ... but I shall endeavour to persuade
her by degrees to permit the corpse to be buried.

What the king would not tell Katherine was that he was just as determined that Philip would not be buried in Granada as Juana was determined that he would be. Juana's true reason for pushing for the Granada
interment, that it was better for her children's inheritance prospects, was
better left unexplained; the fiction of a distraught Juana maintained.

Fighting a lone and punishing battle, Juana could not look to Katherine for help, for she too was on Ferdinand's side. So, almost certainly,
was Juana's third sister, Maria. Since travelling to Portugal to marry
King Manuel more than six years previously, she had settled down to
contented domesticity with alacrity. She bore child after child, most of
whom survived, giving way to her husband in all things. Manuel supported Ferdinand and had done so since 1504 when forced to choose
between him and Philip. 'He loveth and favoureth most the King of
Arragon,' Henry VII had been informed by the envoys he had instructed
to investigate the matter. And Manuel was hardly likely now to switch
his support from Ferdinand to Juana, the woman who was so weighed
down by grief that she could not bear to part with her husband's coffin.
Thus, neither of her sisters would help Juana; they had no reason to
question Ferdinand's statements that she was unfit to govern.

Katherine, moreover, was starting to enjoy becoming so involved in
Ferdinand's schemes and strategies. Sitting within her apartments, she
penned letter after letter to him in her own hand, even managing to
write in cipher, although she said that her father and his secretary would
laugh if they could see her. She pored over Ferdinand's replies and,
slowly, she began to act as his ambassador herself. She could not instigate
events or change her father's decisions – nor did she try to, particularly
because father and daughter were at one over the question of her remarriage. Yet, if policy formation could never be within her remit,
steering through what her father determined, and perhaps venturing to
give advice, was a different matter, and those were the areas in which
the princess found her vocation. She was learning to be a political
animal.

To think of Katherine as a passive, submissive woman, akin to the legendary Patience sitting on her monument, is romantic but very wrong. She might whine and wail to Ferdinand that she could no longer endure what she had gone through after Arthur's death, or that 'no woman, of whatever station in life can have suffered more' but, in what to her was a just cause, a godly cause, she would fight to the bitter end. And it was as a widow that she developed the skills that one day would be her lifeline, skills which enabled her to fight a form of crusade which to her was every bit as important as that once fought by her mother.

A Knife's Edge

On a hot July day in 1507, a ship docked at the port of Valencia, a town on Spain's Mediterranean coast. Ferdinand was back on his home soil. It was very much his home soil, for Valencia is in Aragon. He made his way slowly into Castile, leaving his wife, Queen Germaine, safely behind within his own realm. This was not the time to introduce her to his daughter.

From now on, all would be well in Juana's lands, or so Ferdinand and his supporters maintained. His letters to Katherine describe how, from the moment of his arrival, he was besieged by well-wishers; 'the prelates and chief persons of the kingdom' had written expressing their 'joy' at his return; there were deputations who rushed to say the same thing; there were 'demonstrations of rejoicing' from crowds who met him at the Castilian border. 'All tumults and disturbances' ended because of the 'measures' he had taken. As for Juana, she could hardly have been more delighted to see her father. Their first meeting 'had given them both equal pleasure', he enthused. He went on to say that, following a series of discussions, Juana had agreed that he should do whatever he thought necessary 'for the peace and security of the kingdom'. Order, stability, happiness and trade would revive; he would look after everything.

A telling comment by an anonymous chronicler sums up the political reality with chilling shrewdness. Chronicles should not be taken at face value. If they are official – and Isabella had realised the value of those – they can simply act as vehicles for propaganda, giving details which may be total truth or spin; if they are unofficial, the accounts must be compiled using information gleaned from all manner of sources, not all of them reliable or accurate. But in this instance the unknown chronicler voiced the accepted view of women in a patriarchal society. With

Ferdinand at the helm, he recorded, Castile returned to its 'previous happy prosperity, because, as the sacred scripture reads: "choose a man to govern the republic, and the people will live in peace".' When even the plague died away, as though Ferdinand had waved a magic wand that worked only for men, Juana's attempt at personal rule was doomed indeed.

And she knew it. Unwilling to confront her father's authority, she had no choice but to sink back into the role of dutiful daughter once more. As the months passed, she had less and less say in what happened. Ferdinand took over her finances, he reorganised her household; it was as if Philip was back. She was being ignored. She signed nothing. She would never sign anything again; proclamations and instructions issued in her name were in fact signed by her father. He even insisted that Prince Ferdinand should be with him rather than with her. And it was her father who plotted Juana's future.

Katherine knew only what Ferdinand reported, and she trusted her father. She had to, for she saw in him her only hope of marrying Prince Henry. Her situation in England was unenviable. Following Doña Elvira's departure, Henry VII had suggested that Katherine and her entourage should live at court. But, sensible though this seemed, she found herself part of the court, yet apart from it, rather like a nineteenth-century governess who was neither a servant nor a member of the family. And while the king once wrote that she could live wherever she wanted, her reduced circumstances meant that she had little choice but to go where he placed her; and her apartments were often the most inferior in his palaces.

Since he rarely paid her expenses, trying to make ends meet was still the root cause of so many of her problems. Henry's handouts remained irregular, her debts multiplied, demands upon her from her household never stopped. Feeding, clothing and safeguarding her attendants had been a worry for years, more or less since Arthur's death, and she took her responsibilities seriously.

Caring for those who served her was a duty, and duty was always a concept close to her heart. Thus, while pressing for her own dowry payments, she frequently begged for money to help her ladies find theirs. Other than the cloister, marriage was the one respectable career open to females; Katherine, ever a woman of her age, did not want to condemn her ladies to the shame of a lifetime of dependent spinsterhood. As early as 1504, she had begged her father to assist these loyal women, especially six who had come with her from Spain:

> Some of them were with the queen my lady (who have the holy joy), and they served her a long time; and for that it is reason that they should marry, and I have nothing for to give to them and to help them. I beseech your highness for to do me a grace, and that you will command to give unto their marriages, and that you will please for to write unto me the sum that your grace shall be pleased and served for to give them, for that I may make answer unto them that shall move of marriages unto them.

Unfortunately, since Ferdinand was finding it hard to assist even his own daughter, helping her attendants was low on his list of priorities. Katherine's financial straits became so dire that one of her ladies, Francesca de Caceres, eloped to marry an elderly, but very rich, banker, Francisco de Grimaldi, much to the princess's chagrin.

Yet Katherine was a demanding mistress whom it was not always easy to please. Even before Queen Isabella's death, she had asked Henry VII to help her deal with squabbles in her household. The king had refused, telling her that although he was 'sorry that the few servants' she had could not 'live in peace with each other', the individuals were not under his jurisdiction and she should appeal to her parents if things did not improve. Dr de Puebla and Fuensalida both felt the full force of her scorn and so, sometimes, did her own personal attendants. Francesca de Caceres only eloped after the princess 'sent her away' because of the 'annoyance' de Caceres had caused her. And, while trying to protect her household as best she could, Katherine also pointed out to Ferdinand that 'not all' had served her 'as they ought'. If only she had more money, she continued in the same letter, she could pay those who were decent and trustworthy while sending away those who gave her 'great annoyance'.

One person who caused 'annoyance' to others but never to herself was her confessor, Friar Diego Fernandez. This young friar became her rock. Ladies like Maria de Salinas did their best to comfort Katherine and keep up her spirits as she wandered through her rooms, fumed against her poverty, waited for her father's letters or looked for visits from his ambassadors who would tell her what was going on in Spain and what her father wanted her to do in England. But, lonely and worried, she gained the most support from Friar Diego. Her dependence on him led her to indulge in conduct verging on the indiscreet.

Blind to any faults the young man had, Katherine wrote to tell her father that she considered Friar Diego 'the best [confessor] that ever woman of my position had, with respect to his life, as well as to his holy doctrine and proficiency in letters'. He served her 'with such labour and fatigue as no one else would have undergone', being 'faithful in his office' as well as 'giving good advice and good example'. If only she could reward him as he deserved, she would feel less afflicted and grieved. She could not understand why others failed to spot in Diego the same selfless qualities that so enraptured her; Fuensalida behaved 'badly' towards him, she reported in astonishment. Katherine, who had learnt so much from de Puebla and who was acting as her father's ambassador, becoming heavily involved in diplomacy in the process, could still behave with endearing, if surprising naivety.

To Fuensalida, the friar was not only a possible rival, he was dangerous. The ambassador may well have had a point. Diego got above himself, overstepping the mark. That Katherine mentions the friar giving her 'good advice' speaks volumes: clearly she was listening to the strictures of her spiritual adviser in a political as well as a religious sphere. Neither a councillor nor an accredited envoy, Diego was intervening in areas that should not have been within his remit. One incident illustrates this perfectly.

It happened after Katherine suddenly felt ill and vomited, sadly not an unusual occurrence for her. That same evening, Henry VII sent a message telling her to get ready so that she, and Princess Mary, could travel together to Richmond the next day. Katherine, eager to be with the king again, was ready at the appointed time, as was Princess Mary. Suddenly Diego interfered. Katherine, he said, should not go. 'I am well; I do not wish to stay here alone,' protested the princess, but to no avail. Diego was adamant, using his office to exert his authority: 'I tell you upon pain of mortal sin you do not go to-day.' Faced with Diego's shameless threat to her soul, Katherine dared not go, pleading illness to Princess Mary, who had waited patiently for her for more than two hours. Few believed Katherine was really sick because her 'illness' had not prevented her attending Mass or eating heartily. The king 'was very much vexed', but Diego had his way, and Katherine had to set off on the following day instead.

Fuensalida reported the event venomously to Ferdinand. The ambassador was genuinely anxious, scenting an ominous whiff of scandal which might even scupper Katherine's projected marriage. The friar, he wrote, was 'young, and light, and haughty', he 'governed' the princess's household, she was 'so submissive' that she obeyed him when he made her 'do a great many things which it would be better not to do'. In a further epistle, this time to Ferdinand's secretary, Almazan, the same man to whom Ferdinand had sworn that he had only come to an agreement with Philip because his own life was in peril, Fuensalida drove the point home:

> I wrote to your Lordship about a friar who is here as confessor to the Princess, who would to God he were in his monastery, and not here, because he neither brings nor has brought any good, and if he is here much longer, he will bring greater injury on her Highness … may God destroy me if I see in the friar anything for which she should have so much affection, for he has neither learning, nor appearance, nor manners, nor competency, nor credit …

And the Katherine who could sob that she had barely enough cash to clothe herself, and who professed that she had 'suffered martyrdom' for her country and her family, managed to secure sufficient resources to spend on books for her beloved confessor. She also berated her chamberlain for trying to stop her selling plate 'to satisfy the follies of the friar', as Fuensalida put it.

Worse still, the friar seemed to know how he was compromising the princess. When taxed by Fuensalida about the gossip he said casually, 'in this house there are evil tongues, and they have slandered me, and not with the lowest in the house, but with the highest'. It was as if he was boasting that his name could be linked to that of the princess. He would have left, he exclaimed, except that there was 'no disgrace' in him and only by staying could he prove his worthiness. Fuensalida was so outraged he told Ferdinand that he came 'almost beyond power of restraint from laying hands on him'.

No matter what Fuensalida said, Katherine would have none of it. She needed the friar, she dreaded him leaving her. In a letter to her father berating the ambassador, she entreated Ferdinand to write himself to the friar 'commanding him to continue and not to forsake' her. 'For the greatest comfort in my troubles is the consolation and the support he gives me,' she wrote wretchedly. She seems to have had no conception that her devotion to the friar, even if it were justified, could be construed as going beyond the accepted norms of courtly demeanour; and Henry VII did not preside over a court notorious for scandal.

Fuensalida appreciated the potential fallout only too well. After the episode in which Katherine did not go to Richmond on the day Henry ordained, the king did not see her for almost three weeks and did not check to see how she was after she had become ill again. That, and the fact that Henry did not bother to intervene when tales of the young friar reached the royal ears, seemed ominous to the ambassador. Negotiations for the princess's marriage were forever delicate: giving Henry free ammunition to call off the match was foolhardy. Despite Fuensalida's best efforts, though, Ferdinand did not recall Diego. Perhaps he did not want to upset his daughter any further. So the young friar remained firmly ensconced for some time.

If the friar really was Katherine's 'greatest comfort', she certainly had need of him for the diplomatic intrigues and bargaining in which she was becoming involved were incredibly complex. Her marriage to Prince Henry, though the core issue to her, became intermingled with other unions and with the European situation as a whole. And in that mix, her sister Juana would also be a player, albeit a silent one.

Still reeling from Arthur's death in April 1502, Henry VII had been dealt an additional blow when Queen Elizabeth had died after childbirth less than a year later. With only one son and two daughters left, he had very quickly turned his thoughts towards remarriage, having his portrait painted to show he was still a fine figure of a man. Whether or not he seriously considered Katherine as a contender, he was soon scouring Europe for a new wife, bringing his usual perspicacity and thoroughness to bear. When Ferdinand and Isabella had suggested Ferdinand's niece, the widowed Queen Joanna of Naples, Henry had been eager to find out just what she looked like. In addition to having poor de Puebla request that the Catholic Monarchs send a picture 'portraying her figure and the features of her face', Henry sent out his own envoys to discover how old she was, her height, what her face was like in shape, expression and complexion. He also wanted to know about her hands and fingers, her breasts, whether she had hair on her lips, whether her breath was sweet, and if she had 'any sickness of her nativity, blemish or deformity'. Clearly, Henry was not about to waste himself on a woman he found repulsive. In fact, once he had established that the queen had no lands or wealth to offer, his interest, despite her sweet breath and 'somewhat great and full' breasts, evaporated remarkably fast.

Soon Henry was searching elsewhere. And one of the front runners was Katherine's sister Juana, who most of all was a queen and whom the king had already met during her brief visit to Windsor. Since he appears to have broached the subject with Katherine first, he obviously saw how useful she could be as a go-between for himself and her father, especially after a proud Katherine delivered a 'letter of credence' to him proving that Ferdinand regarded her as one of his accredited ambassadors. For the next couple of years, Katherine promoted her own interests, her father's interests and a potential union with Juana assiduously and vociferously. For if Henry married Juana, the Spanish alliance would be finally secure, and her own marriage with Prince Henry much more certain.

Katherine threw herself into the project wholeheartedly. Once she had established that Ferdinand was interested in the proposal, she took up her pen to write to her sister urging it. In an intriguing letter, which treats Juana as quite sane, she began by assuring her sister that Henry had felt just as disappointed at seeing her for so short a time at Windsor as Katherine herself had been. Had the king not been advised by his council 'not to interfere between husband and wife', he would have kept her at court longer. As it was, Juana's abrupt departure had 'weighed much upon his heart'. And, despite her own complaints about how badly Henry had treated her since Arthur's death, she launched into a eulogy of his excellent character. He was endowed, she said, 'with the greatest virtues'; he was 'feared and esteemed . . . by all Christendom, as being very wise and possessed of immense treasures', as well as 'having at his command powerful bodies of excellent troops'. And her sister should not forget, Katherine continued, how beneficial the marriage would be to Castile, and how it would 'double the affection' existing between Henry and Ferdinand. Playing next on Juana's maternal feelings, she vowed that the match would be useful to her son Charles, too. Katherine even pressed the religious button: should the marriage take place, Ferdinand would be able to go on a crusade against the Moors of North Africa which would bring the entire continent under Christian rule.

It was all very persuasive; every base was covered, although she did not tell Juana how it might hasten her own wedding with Prince Henry. For Katherine, everything she wrote to encourage her sister to marry Henry VII was true. And, over the coming months, she continued to do all she could to make it happen. She wrote to her father frequently, she talked to Henry, she acted as intermediary between the two kings, she had meetings with de Puebla and with Fuensalida. And, using all the skills she was so rapidly acquiring, she acted on her own initiative, venturing, diffidently, to proffer advice to her own father. When Henry, growing impatient with the lack of progress, asked her to write to Cisneros on his behalf, she did just that, although she assured Ferdinand that she wrote only in general terms. Then, growing in confidence, she recommended that her father should only give the archbishop the letter if Cisneros was 'very much devoted' to Ferdinand's service. She really was learning; de Puebla could be gratified with his student.

But she had not graduated yet, she was still outclassed by her father. Just because Katherine believed in the match did not mean that either Juana or Ferdinand was as committed as she was. Juana's views were not considered important so we cannot really know what she thought but, for the rest of her life, she made sure that she never did anything that might risk her son Charles's inheritance. Another child by another husband might just do that. On the one occasion when her father risked allowing the English envoy, John Stile, to visit her, she refused to be drawn on the marriage, adopting her usual practice of promising nothing.

As for Ferdinand, the current situation, with himself in full control and Juana excluded, suited him admirably. Giving Henry an excuse to interfere in Castilian affairs might be most unwise. It would be exchanging Philip for a much shrewder and craftier opponent. No, probably better to leave things as they were, but there was no need to spell it out to Henry or Katherine: the prudent course was to leave the door open in case things changed. Ferdinand always was a man who liked to run with the fox and hunt with the hounds.

Unfortunately, as Katherine became uncomfortably aware, her marriage to Prince Henry was more than ever on a knife's edge because it now seemed to depend on Henry's marriage to Juana. In a dispatch so typical of the wily Spanish monarch, therefore, Fuensalida was told to keep dangling the prospect of the latter, but without giving a formal pledge, while at the same time pushing for Katherine. 'It would be well' if the ambassador did not 'hold out a certain prospect of effecting his [Henry's] marriage with the Queen', but he 'should not deprive him of all hope whatever'. Complex intrigue and double-dealing was second nature to Ferdinand. If Katherine thought herself an expert dissembler, she was but a novice compared to her father.

At length Ferdinand came to a decision: Katherine's marriage mattered enough to give way to Henry, not over Juana but over something that was even closer to Henry's heart – money. For years, Katherine had begged, badgered, wept, over the outstanding sums on her dowry; for just as long, Ferdinand had procrastinated, fretting over how much her plate would be worth, whether the English goldsmiths would undervalue it, how he was to find the coin to make up the difference as well as for the agreed cash payment, entreating Henry for postponement after postponement. By the middle of 1508, Ferdinand had made up his mind. If it secured the actual ceremonies, he would give way. Fuensalida was ordered to tell Henry that Ferdinand would settle the remaining amount in cash, removing Katherine's plate from the equation. The banker, Grimaldi, the very one who married one of the princess's ladies, would be able to sort out the sum required.

It was a massive concession, but Ferdinand was increasingly worried that there would be no wedding for his daughter no matter what he did. Perhaps Henry might take the rumours about Friar Diego seriously; perhaps he might arrange for Prince Henry to marry a different bride; perhaps he would betroth him to a French princess. Anything could happen.

Katherine clung on to her hopes. Despite all her complaints, despite all that had happened to her, her belief that she would triumph one day is apparent in virtually every letter she wrote. Just once, in 1509, as she defended her friar, sent diatribes against the ineptitude of Fuensalida, and worried herself almost to the point of illness over whether Prince Henry might wed another, she indulged in uncharacteristic defeatism and begged Ferdinand to either help her or bring her home so that she could spend her 'few remaining days in serving God'.

The person with 'few remaining days', however, was not the princess. Towards the end of April 1509, just a month after Katherine's despairing letter, Henry VII lay dying at his favourite palace of Richmond. Katherine's future would now lie in the hands of his seventeen-year-old son.

The Triumph of Hope

On 11 June 1509, at the royal palace of Greenwich on the banks of the Thames, Katherine's dreams came true as she heard the words for which she had waited for so long:

> Most Illustrious Prince, is it your will to fulfil the treaty of marriage concluded by your father, the late King of England, and the parents of the Princess of Wales, the King and Queen of Spain; and, as the Pope has dispensed with this marriage, to take the Princess who is here present for your lawful wife?

The king's answer, 'I will', was echoed by her own response as the corresponding words were put to her.

At last. All the years of hoping, of planning, of praying, of dogged belief that one day all would be well, were over. She had married her prince. And what a prince. At seventeen years and ten months old, Henry stood six feet two inches tall, his red-gold hair glistened in the sun by day or in the candlelight at night. His body, as lean and honed as that of an athlete, was perfectly proportioned and lithe. A keen sportsman, he also had an enquiring mind, he was cultured, he loved learning and respected scholars, he adored dancing and music, he sang, he wrote songs. He was religious, hearing at least three Masses a day, and he appeared to be virtuous. In a public relations move which earned him instant popularity, he invited all who had suffered injustice to come forward and ordered the arrest of Richard Empson and Edmund Dudley, the most hated councillors and tax gatherers employed by his dead father. To all who looked only on the surface, it seemed that it was a paragon who had chosen Katherine as his bride.

No one seemed to worry that Empson and Dudley, who were executed after spending sixteen wretched months in the Tower, were but scape-goats, nor that those who revealed alleged injustices found their complaints ignored once the king's initial burst of generous enthusiasm dwindled. For those with eyes to see, the signs of Henry's true character were there.

But, in those early years, all who came into contact with this magnificent prince marvelled. Superlatives abounded. He was 'much handsomer than any other Sovereign in Christendom', wrote the Venetian ambassador, Sebastian Giustinian, who also indulged his talent for hyperbole after watching Henry play tennis. This game 'was the prettiest thing in the world to see him play, his fair skin glowing through a shirt of the finest texture', said an enraptured Giustinian. Not only did Henry look the part, he was so wonderful in every respect that his people were incredibly fortunate to have him at the helm, or so declared a papal representative just a few years later, having found himself surprisingly impressed by England and its king:

> In short, wealth and civilisation of the world are here; and those who call the English barbarians appear to me to render themselves such. I here perceive very elegant manners, extreme decorum, and very great politeness; and amongst all other things there is this most invincible King, whose acquaintance and qualities are so many and excellent that I consider him to excel all who ever wore a crown; and blessed and happy may this country call itself in having as its lord so worthy and eminent a sovereign.

Henry's 'blessed and happy' subjects could only agree. The chronicler Edward Hall, always a loyal supporter of his king, uncharacteristically found himself almost lost for words when, after a eulogistic description of the young Henry, he confessed 'that for lacke of cunnyng, I cannot expresse the giftes of grace and of nature, that God hath endowed hym with all'. The whole country 'is in ecstasies', enthused Lord Mountjoy, later Katherine's chamberlain, in a letter to Erasmus, urging him to return to England; the revered scholar could be sure of a warm welcome from a king who had said that it was impossible 'to live without' learned men.

Katherine was indeed fortunate, her destiny fulfilled. With such a husband at her side, it seemed she could not fail. Everything had happened so fast. Though Henry VII had died on 21 April, his death was kept secret for a couple of days to ensure a smooth transition of power. The various funeral obsequies and formalities took a few weeks. Then, once the late king was finally buried at Westminster after a funeral oration preached by Lady Margaret Beaufort's favoured cleric, John Fisher, Bishop of Rochester, Prince Henry, now King Henry VIII, King of England and France (for he still claimed the French lands of his ancestors) and lord of Ireland, could begin to put his stamp on his own reign.

Marrying Katherine had been a swift, perhaps surprising, decision. Ferdinand, hearing the news of Henry VII's death, feared that Katherine would be repudiated; he hardly dared even hope that she would become Henry's wife. Letters, instructions, orders, flowed to and fro as Fuensalida struggled to master the sudden turn of events. We can never be sure why Henry decided to marry the princess and so soon. The new king told Margaret, Katherine's former sister-in-law, who was still running Burgundy and caring for Juana's children, that he did so because it was his father's dying wish. Perhaps it was. Spain would be a useful ally against France, the traditional enemy; and the new king rather fancied emulating the glories of his ancestor and namesake, Henry V. Maybe Henry's council wanted him safely married to ensure the succession. Or perhaps Henry himself chose Katherine: he knew her, she was still young and pretty, she was born to the role, she was loyal and dedicated, she knew about England by now and, because she was a little older than he, she could be his confidante as well as his soul-mate. It seemed to be a marriage made in heaven.

Yet while Katherine's brow remained unfurrowed there were those who worried that her status as Henry's former sister-in-law could bode ill. A month or so before the nuptials were celebrated Ferdinand, uncomfortably aware of this, sent specific guidelines to Fuensalida. The ambassador was to remind any critics that the pope had issued the requisite dispensation so all was 'perfectly lawful'. And he was to go one stage further, drawing attention to another, highly relevant marriage that had already taken place in Katherine's family: her sister, Maria, had married

King Manuel of Portugal even though his first wife had been the Catholic Monarchs' eldest daughter Princess Isabella. Thus, just as Katherine had married two brothers, so Manuel had married two sisters. And the marriage was 'flourishing', the couple being 'blessed with a numerous offspring'. Referring to this union should reassure anyone anxious about the legality of Henry marrying Katherine. Or so Ferdinand hoped. Yet Hall, ever wise after the event and always quick to exonerate Henry, pointed out in his chronicle that right from the start, 'this mariage of the brother's wyfe was muche murmured against'.

Murmured against or not, Katherine's marriage took place. Ferdinand, as delighted and relieved as his daughter, ordered festivals and celebrations held in Spain, in at least one of which he played an active part himself. True, the wedding had been a much more private, more subdued, affair than the St Paul's extravaganza of her wedding to Arthur, but the court was hardly out of mourning for Henry VII. There had been just a handful of witnesses at the ceremony, one of whom was William Thomas, Arthur's former gentleman, who had slipped seamlessly into Henry's service. Possibly, though, the event's intimacy made it more distinctive, more loving; after all, this time the bridegroom had been personally involved in selecting his bride. And there was more to come, for Katherine and Henry were due to be crowned at Westminster with the full and very public rituals that Church and tradition demanded. Henry revelled in that attention; so did Katherine.

Saturday 23 June 1509 was the day designated for Londoners to welcome their new king and his Spanish queen. In the narrow streets of the city, servants had been busy for hours cooking, hanging silks, velvets or tapestries from windows, clearing rubbish, laying down sand to stop the horses from slipping, erecting rails to keep back over-curious onlookers. No one wanted a stampede. Many of the city's tailors worked almost round the clock to make the costly, beautifully decorated costumes for the officials, courtiers and gentry who were taking part in the various processions and who would witness the moment the crown was placed upon Henry's head. Even the horses were to be bedecked in the finest trappings that the master craftsmen could devise. No expense was spared to make these few days ones that spectators, as well as the participants, would remember for the rest of their lives. For the 160 men whose job would be to carry 'tipped staves' in the coronation, hardly the most central of roles, the bill for cloth alone was almost five thousand pounds.

It was not the first time that Katherine had been greeted by the city because she had been received there for her wedding to Arthur, but this was different: her ladies dressed her as the queen she was about to become, not as Princess of Wales. She was the first lady of the land now, not the wife of the heir. There was no Doña Elvira to scurry the attendants and determine what her mistress would wear and how she would wear it. Yet that did not mean that her costume was entirely her own choice; the so-called Royal Book, a collection of rules regulating royal life, dictated its form.

At about four in the afternoon on that special Saturday, the celebrations began. The guildsmen lined the streets of their city; the lord mayor, Stephen Jennings, himself a merchant-tailor, stood erect, his gold chain of office shining as the light caught it; the aldermen in their scarlet stood resplendent close by. The procession started at the Tower, where Henry and Katherine had spent the previous night, and progressed along thoroughfares like Gracechurch Street, Cornhill, Cheapside, all of which are still there today, and which were familiar to Katherine from the pageants that had marked her marriage to Arthur. The cavalcade was endless. There were the newly dubbed Knights of the Bath in their blue gowns and hoods, among them Henry's companion Sir Thomas Boleyn; there were bishops; there were priests whose task was to cense the king and queen as they passed by; there were heralds; there were gentlemen; there were courtiers.

And, beneath a canopy, a cloth of estate which signalled his royal status, there was the king himself. Dressed in a crimson robe trimmed with ermine and a golden coat whose front was studded with precious gems, a glittering collar around his neck, he was mounted upon a huge horse, itself draped in golden fabric. Goggle-eyed spectators would have remembered one other figure from the king's section of the procession: the Duke of Buckingham. Proudly astride his great white horse, the diamonds in his coat of gold and silver thread flashing in the afternoon sun, the duke almost rivalled his king, especially since his position,

Constable of England, meant that he rode in front of Henry as if the king was only there on his say-so.

Katherine followed her husband at a distance. Surrounded by her own entourage, all lavishly dressed, she wore only white, in accordance with protocol and tradition. Everything about her was white, from her white cloth-of-gold-covered litter, borne by white horses, to her white satin, exquisitely embroidered garments. Her hair, 'bewtefull and goodly to behold', hung long and loose and was crowned with a sparkling pearl-studded circlet. Her ladies, including those who had stayed with her during the lean years, followed, some riding, some in chariots, all in cloth of gold, cloth of silver, velvet, ermine. The memories of when Katherine's wardrobe had been embarrassingly sparse and she had begged her father for money to buy new clothes were fading fast.

Just one thing marred the day. It rained very suddenly and very heavily. Katherine, drenched, took shelter until the shower stopped. Then, ignoring her discomfort, she continued on her way as radiant and smiling as ever. She did not want to disappoint the crowds who had waited so patiently to see her. But she lived in a superstitious age; omens came in all shapes and sizes, and to have rain was not an auspicious sign.

Katherine herself was too happy and busy to indulge such thoughts, for the following day, Sunday 24 June, marked the climax of her new life: she was to be crowned England's queen. Isabella's faith had triumphed over the Moors; Katherine's hope and faith had triumphed over the tragedy of early widowhood and the trials of those terrible years in a marital wilderness.

Early on that Sunday morning, she and Henry walked across the cloth-strewn path to the abbey at Westminster for the solemn anointing and crowning. The primate of all England, the Archbishop of Canterbury, William Warham, conducted proceedings. Before the altar, close to the sumptuously rich shrine housing the bones of St Edward the Confessor, the founder of the abbey, stood St Edward's chair, the coronation chair, the seat of kings. A smaller throne awaited Katherine. The abbey was ablaze with colour: light of every hue and shade flowed through the lofty stained-glass windows, the gilded and jewelled statues

glowed in the light of the hundreds of flickering candles, precious stones
glimmered on people's clothes.

Anyone who was anyone was there inside the abbey on that day.
Lists of those involved still survive. Among the great and the good,
Henry had included his childhood nurse, Anne Luke, while Katherine
would have spotted Margaret Pole, one of her most important ladies
from Ludlow, Buckingham's sister, Lady Elizabeth Stafford, her own
attendants Maria de Salinas and Agnes de Vanegas (now the wife of
Lord Mountjoy) and, perhaps most satisfactorily of all, Friar Diego,
her confessor. The new queen had had her way over his retention,
and few would dare to contradict her now. One face, sadly, was not
there: de Puebla, who had striven so selflessly and tirelessly to bring
about this triumphant day did not live to see it; one of his sons,
though, did.

With all assembled, Warham began the age-old ceremony which
linked the king to his people through the oaths that he and the key
figures of the country would take. The king promised to respect the
laws of the land, his nobles swore to be loyal and faithful to him in a
ceremony of homage still performed at English coronations now. The
religious part of the ritual was equally important for the coronation set
the king apart, just as Christ was visibly apart from the disciples in
Queen Isabella's painting that Katherine had seen as a child. Katherine
watched as the archbishop anointed her husband with holy oil; now
Henry too was special, apart from ordinary men. After that, the moment
of crowning was almost an anti-climax but, as Warham placed St
Edward's crown gently but firmly on the new king's red-gold hair, Henry
was king indeed. Then it was Katherine's turn as the crowning and the
anointing was repeated for her. She, too, therefore was special, different
from other women.

So it was done. Henry and Katherine processed back through the
west door of St Peter's into the nearby Westminster Hall, followed by
their nobles, their courtiers, their judges, all those entitled to dine, for
the very first time, with the man and woman who now truly were their
king and queen. Beneath the spectacular wooden vaulted roof crafted
over one hundred years earlier in Richard II's reign, Henry and his
queen settled down to a banquet of what Hall considered 'sumptuous

fine, and delicate meates' and 'many deintie dishes'. The serious part of the day over, the festivities could begin.

No food was served until the Duke of Buckingham had made his entrance, with the flourish everyone expected. To the fanfare of trumpets, dressed in cloth of gold and mounted on a magnificent charger, the great duke rode into the hall to herald the arrival of the first course. When the second course was served, there was another distraction. This time it was Sir Richard Dimmock, the king's champion, in full armour, with a plume of ostrich feathers on his helmet, his horse trapped in cloth of gold embroidered with the arms of England and France. Looking fiercely at the elegantly dressed diners, Dimmock ordered his herald to challenge anyone who dared to deny that Henry was their rightful ruler to come forward and fight. Satisfied that no one would and that his king was safe, Dimmock cried for drink to be brought him. It was, in a gold cup complete with a gold lid. After drinking, Dimmock left the hall, but he took the cup and its cover with him as a perquisite. Always supposing that no one would dare step forward, Dimmock had a very profitable role because the armour he wore and the horse he rode, the second best ones in the king's armoury and stables, were also his to keep. Traditions had to be upheld.

Another tradition was very much in the lord mayor's interest. Jennings really was having the time of his life. Immediately before Buckingham had made his grand entrance, the master-tailor knelt at Henry's feet as the king gently dubbed him a knight: when he rose, plain Stephen Jennings was Sir Stephen Jennings. His good fortune did not stop there for it was his duty to hand the king a final drink of spiced wines as the last remnants of the meal were finished. Once the king had drunk, Jennings was allowed to keep the king's cup, in this case a stunningly wrought gold one which came complete with a cover.

Eventually, though, Katherine and Henry could leave the hall and retire to their own private apartments within the palace of Westminster. By now, Katherine was Henry's wife in every sense of that word. We know that this marriage, unlike what Katherine maintained about her previous match, was consummated and consummated quickly. From the first moment of their marriage, she felt that Henry loved her. He even said so. Six weeks or so after her wedding, Ferdinand received a letter from the man who was now his son-in-law. After reminding the Spanish king that he had chosen Katherine 'having rejected all other ladies in the world that have been offered to us', Henry went on to praise his wife with endearing, youthful exuberance: 'And, as regards that sincere love, which we have to the most serene queen our consort, her eminent virtues daily more and more shine forth, blossom, and increase so much, that, if we were still free, her we would yet choose for our wife before all other.'

The following weeks were idyllic for the king and queen. Released from his father's stern clutches, Henry also escaped those of his serious, uncompromising grandmother for Margaret Beaufort followed her beloved only son to the grave just five days after the coronation. Katherine was therefore spared the attentions of the black-clad figure whom one historian, when discussing the formidable matriarch's relationship with Queen Elizabeth, called the 'mother-in-law from hell'. And Henry could set about enjoying himself, delighting in a round of merrymaking and, probably, love-making.

He began as he meant to go on, with a two-day tournament, more exciting and enterprising than anything anyone had seen before. With her husband, Katherine took her place in a stand cleverly turned into a mock castle decorated with Tudor roses, with her own pomegranate emblem, with her mother's device of a sheaf of arrows and, very prominently, with the letters K and H picked out in gold to remind everyone in whose honour the tournament was held. From inside this amazing contraption, she watched as the gorgeously apparelled gentlemen cavorted in front of her, enacting scenes and combats with classical motifs. Pallas Athene the goddess of wisdom was represented, so was Diana; there were men dressed as Athene's scholars; there were men who said they would fight for 'love of ladies'; there was a hunt as deer were killed by greyhounds, the carcasses given as trophies to Katherine and her ladies; there were golden spears; there were imitation mountains, forests, a park. Imagination and spectacle went hand in hand: there was no Henry VII to count the cost.

The new king loved every minute. He could not resist telling Ferdinand what a superb time he was having. He was diverting himself, he wrote, 'with jousts, birding, hunting, and other innocent pastimes', also in visiting different parts of the kingdom, where he wanted to show himself and his pretty bride to his people. Despite all this jollity, however, Henry was quick to reassure Ferdinand that he did not 'neglect affairs of state'; he was a king capable of living life to the full and ruling at the same time. England was lucky indeed!

And so was Katherine. She now had everything she had always wanted. Mindful of her duty, she thanked her father for the love he had constantly shown her and for ensuring that she was 'so well married'. Like Henry, she was carried away by the delights on offer. 'Our time is ever passed in continual feasts,' she reported. But she was not too carried away to forget why Ferdinand had married her so well:

> As to the king my lord, amongst the reasons that oblige me to love him much more than myself, the one most strong, although he is my husband, is his being the true son of your highness, with desire of greater obedience and love to serve you than ever son had to his father. I have performed the office of ambassador as your highness sent to command, as was known by the king my lord, who is, and places himself entirely in the hands of your highness, as of so entire a father and lord ... The news from here is that those kingdoms of your highness are in great peace, and entertain much love towards the king my lord and to me.

She might be England's queen, she was still a Spanish princess.

Among the congratulations on her marriage came one from another Spanish princess, her sister Juana. Ferdinand wrote to Henry mentioning that when he had told Juana about Katherine's 'good fortune', she asked 'to be recommended' to the English king. Juana herself had no such 'good fortune'. Before the news of Henry VII's death had reached Spain, John Stile had settled down in Valladolid to write a dispatch to his master which is dated 26 April 1509. In the letter, the envoy reported that Juana had been escorted, with Philip's body, and her toddler daughter, to Tordesillas, a small town on the Duero River, about fifteen miles from Valladolid itself. Together with her attendants and household officials, all carefully vetted by Ferdinand, Juana was lodged securely within the castle while Philip's coffin was entrusted to the nuns at the convent of St Clare which nestled beside its walls.

Thus, as the world was opening up for a blissful Katherine, the gates of a fortress had clanged shut upon her sister. Juana was now a prisoner; the father whom Katherine loved and trusted had become his own child's gaoler.

PART IV

Sister Queens

To Be a Queen

In September 1509, John Stile, now in Henry VIII's service, sent a long dispatch from Valladolid, meticulously written in cipher, bringing the king up to date on Spanish events and diplomacy. Among the nuggets he imparted was a reference to Katherine's sister. Rumours had reached Stile of Juana's pitiful state and odd behaviour. She had no more 'wisdom' than that of a 'young child' and was 'very feeble', he reported sorrowfully. Sometimes she refused to eat or drink for two or three days at a time and, the horrified man continued, would not countenance hearing Mass for eight days, 'minding it not, but as a child having no order'. Stile heard that Ferdinand was so worried that he visited her every two months.

Naturally Ferdinand was worried on a personal level. But there was an added dimension: should Juana die, her thrones would pass to her nine-year-old son, Charles. The boy's other grandfather, Emperor Maximilian, Ferdinand's equal in mendacity and duplicity, might then seize the opportunity constantly to interfere in Castile on the pretext of protecting his grandson's rights until the boy reached an age to govern himself. Ferdinand needed his daughter alive. In fact, Juana's behaviour, if indeed it was as Stile reported, was entirely true to form. Tantrums, self-starvation and even what appeared to be religious indifference were all stratagems she had tried throughout the years to get her own way. If her aim was to leave Tordesillas, perhaps in order to accompany Philip's corpse to Granada, it did not work. Having persuaded her to go there, her father was determined that there she would remain; his concern for her welfare only went so far.

Yet Ferdinand at least ensured that her surroundings were not uncomfortable. Isolated, among hills, and some miles from the nearest important towns, the castle was certainly secure but it had always been a favourite retreat for the queens of Castile and had a certain rugged beauty. Juana's main chamber overlooked the river, and she was surrounded by many of her treasured possessions, including several sets of tapestries that once she had given to her mother and which were returned to her when Isabella died. During his short life, Philip had keenly supported the tapestry makers' art, going so far as to take his royal tapissier, Pieter van Aelst, to Spain with him in 1506, and, like Isabella, Juana had always appreciated the intricate craftsmanship and artistic skill that produced these glowing works of art.

Among those tapestries that we know she took with her to Tordesillas was a magnificent four-piece set which still survives, the *Veneration of the Virgin*, sometimes called 'the golden hangings' because of the cloth of gold and gilded thread used in its construction. The tranquillity of the Virgin, the delicacy of the angels' feathered wings, the vibrancy of the colours and the shimmering threads combine to make the set a visual delight. Another tapestry which graced the castle walls for Juana was one of which Isabella had been particularly fond, depicting the Mass of Saint Gregory, a Mass at which, it was said, Christ Himself appeared. Juana may not have wanted to hear services as frequently as her devout attendants might have wished, but simply gazing at these wonderful, inspirational hangings would surely bring her closer to her God. It is also highly possible that while in the Netherlands she may have begun to practise the contemplative spirituality then fashionable with some of the aristocratic women of her acquaintance, such as Philip's step-grandmother, Margaret of York. If so, such inner piety could bring her strength, peace and consolation during the long days at Tordesillas.

She had another consolation in her daughter, Catalina, who was allowed to stay with her. Of her other children, Charles, Eleanor, Isabella and Maria were growing up in Burgundy, while Ferdinand had taken his namesake, Prince Ferdinand, into his own keeping. Ever a dynast and now with time on her hands, Juana therefore lavished all her care upon little Catalina, the only one of her children in whose upbringing she could play much part, and whom she came to love with a fierce intensity.

Juana's situation was the last thing on Henry VIII's mind. He barely knew her. Her brief appearance at Windsor following the storms of 1506 went unnoticed; he probably never even saw her because she spent her time with his sister, Mary, and with Katherine. In any case, he had been much more impressed by Juana's glamorous husband who jousted and played sports and was every inch the sort of prince he fancied becoming himself; he would not have given Juana a second thought. And, in 1509, he was still euphoric about being king. Queenship had brought nothing but disaster for Juana, kingship had brought nothing but delight to Henry.

Like her husband, Katherine was wrapped up with the pleasures and the responsibilities of her new position. She had not seen Juana since the afternoon they had spent together three years earlier. Clearly, she had not then thought her sister deranged, and she had chosen to write to her as though Juana was perfectly sane when Henry VII was considering her as a bride, but she trusted her father. Neither she, nor any of Juana's other relatives, had any reason to doubt his word that Philip's death had distressed her so much that she had become unbalanced to the point that she was incapable of governing, and needed seclusion and rest in the hope that her mental state might improve. After all, as Katherine herself had once witnessed, her eldest sister had also buckled under the pressure of premature widowhood.

So, oblivious of her father's perfidy, Katherine could attend to her duties with a clear conscience. And she had much to do. In addition to her public role, which her mother's training enabled her to fulfil to perfection, she had lands to administer and a household to organise. During these first months of her marriage, Katherine was learning how to be a queen.

Her marriage brought her lands, known as her dower or her jointure, from which she would draw rents, profits from such things as mills and mines and the 'draggyng of mussels', and various administrative fees paid by her many tenants. She had forests and she had castles, one of them Fotheringhay, a strong fortress in a remote Northamptonshire village that one day would be suggested as a possible home for herself and was to achieve notoriety in 1587 when Mary Queen of Scots, Henry's great-niece, was beheaded in its great hall. The total revenues from Katherine's landholdings were used towards much of the running cost of her household as queen, but were also intended to keep her in style should Henry pre-decease her. Henry, who exuded youthful vigour and energy, looked extremely unlikely to do so but, as Margaret Beaufort had so tellingly warned in the preamble to her will, 'ev're creatur here lyving is mortall, and the tyme and place of deth to ev're creatur uncerteyn'. It was merely provident to be prepared, and a land settlement was the norm in noble as well as in royal families.

Katherine's dower was extensive, with tenancies in most of the counties across the country. The rents on some properties were enormous. Almost £103 annually (more than five times the yearly wage of one of Katherine's ladies) came from a farm in Bristol, £20 for one in Bedford. A few amounts due were modest by comparison: a mere 108 shillings and 4 pence (between five and six pounds) was charged for some farms in Buckinghamshire. Some lands involved religious institutions, such as the £40 payable by the abbey of Bury St Edmunds 'for the custody of the abbey and its temporalities'; others were linked to key nobles such as the £500 for which the heirs of Michael de la Pole, Earl of Suffolk were liable. Most queens ended up with at least £4000 annually from their lands. Katherine was no exception, for the value of the 'lands assigned by the King to the Queen's grace for her jointure' totalled £4129 and a couple of shillings.

She was also given two residences, Baynard's Castle in London and one at Havering in Essex. Ironically, Baynard's Castle, which had been rebuilt by Henry VII, had a special place in Katherine's history for it was here that Henry VII and Queen Elizabeth had stayed when Katherine had married Arthur, and one of the craftsmen whom Henry had paid to modernise the building was the goldsmith, Sir John Shaa, the lord mayor of London who had played such a prominent part in those marriage festivities. With its Thames-side setting, its turrets, its towers and its beautiful gardens, it looked like a fairy-tale palace which had sprung magically from the pages of a medieval romance. And Katherine had her own barge, fitted with soft cushioned seats and decorated with her own heraldic arms and badges, so she could approach her new property from the river and mount the steps which ran from the water's edge to the palace itself. As for its associations with Arthur, Katherine was too pragmatic, and too religious, to allow herself to indulge in nostalgia. Havering, essentially a stone-built, sprawling medieval dwelling, was far less imposing, stolid in comparison to the beauty of Baynard's Castle, but Katherine still valued it as a useful retreat. And it was at Havering that Katherine once happily entertained her new husband to a sumptuous banquet.

Taking everything, from lands to houses to woods to farms to fines to rents, Katherine was ostensibly a wealthy woman. But, like so many things in her life, there was a catch: the demands upon her purse were colossal, and they began with maintaining her household. Among Henry VII's funeral records, which are safely stored in the National Archives, there is a list of thirty-two members of Katherine's staff entitled to special mourning cloth; if we look at a similar list of names, this time connected with her coronation, there are more than five times that number. Simply paying her employees' salaries, providing food for some of them, clothes for others, and buying household items, would eat into her £4000. Then Katherine found herself faced with giving alms to the poor, making offerings in church or when she went on pilgrimage, sorting out the expenses of her stables, her kitchens, her bargemen, paying for medicines and potions, presenting gifts at New Year and perhaps at christenings, as well as keeping Baynard's Castle and Havering in a good state of repair. And she needed specialist embroiderers, silk workers, tailors, skinners, shoemakers, goldsmiths, many artisans whose names we still know. As queen, Katherine had to find the money for a myriad of purposes, and it was not always easy, so a bequest of items like jewels and furs valued at over £200 from Margaret Beaufort was particularly welcome. She remembered that her deceased mother-in-law, Queen Elizabeth, had sometimes been so stretched that she had been forced to ask Henry VII for a temporary loan. He had obliged but, true to type, only after she had pledged her personal plate as security.

Fortunately, Henry VIII, in love with life, love, marriage and his queen, was ever happy to give presents, often of sumptuous fabrics and clothes, to his 'beloved wife'. Conscious that a king's power and importance was revealed by his appearance and surroundings, he made sure he looked stunning, with his velvets, his cloth of gold, his silks, his satins, his jewels all on display. Even Margaret Beaufort, austere though she had been, had always dressed with care and had spectacles made of gold. Almost all of her gowns had been black but they were hardly the rough habits of a nun. Made of rich materials, they were worn over scarlet petticoats and were usually lined or edged with fur; in any case, true black was not only fashionable, it was very expensive to achieve. Katherine too liked black, but she also loved purple and crimson, and enjoyed wearing the most costly of cloth. Like her mother before her, she never underestimated the propaganda effect of a dazzling, regal appearance. Over the years, her wardrobe became filled with gowns made from cloth of gold, of silver, of tissue (silk cloth interwoven with threads of silver or gold), of velvet, of damask and of satin, many of the materials ordered for her by her doting husband.

But her time was not just spent in trying on clothes and choosing jewels. Katherine had to learn about the practical side of queenship, for her lands and her household had to be properly administered. Again, the names of many of those who served her, men whom Katherine met frequently, have come down to us. Her Lord Chamberlain, whose task it was to make sure that her household operated efficiently, was originally the Earl of Ormond, a relative of the up and coming Thomas Boleyn. By 1512 William Blount, Lord Mountjoy, a loyal supporter of the Tudor dynasty, a patron of Erasmus, and a friend of Thomas More, had taken over. Katherine came to know Mountjoy very well; not only was he with her for about twenty years, he courted and married Agnes de Vanegas, one of Katherine's ladies who had stayed loyally at her mistress's side throughout the lean years of the queen's widowhood. Then there was Katherine's almoner, Richard Bekynsall, a Cambridge connection of Bishop John Fisher and, like him, linked to Margaret Beaufort, for Bekynsall had also served as almoner to that formidable but charitable woman who had left legacies to fund Christ's College and to found St John's.

It was the job of Richard Decons, Katherine's secretary, to act as the receiver of her revenues and the surveyor of her lands, a post also filled by Sir Robert Poyntz. There was much to be done and, after all those years of comparative penury, Katherine took a keen interest in the sources of her income and in overseeing what went on in her estates. Since medieval times, queens had been equipped with a Queen's Council to deal with all of this and to sort out problems that could not be dealt with via the various manorial courts which functioned locally. Any major issues were referred to Katherine's own Queen's Council and she sometimes presided over its meetings herself. One case, that of Richard Staverton, would later worry her so much that she reported him to Henry's councillors. Staverton, Thomas More's brother-in-law, very much the 'family's black sheep', had so terrorised his niece that she had agreed to hand over her lands in Berkshire to him and promised not to marry without his permission. If she did so, she vowed to pay him £300 in compensation. Katherine, who happened to be the lord of the manor of Bray where the unfortunate woman's lands were situated, heard about the case when Staverton, daring to consider himself the wronged party, not only sued his niece when she disobeyed him and married anyway, but went on to try to take over her lands when she died. Katherine was having none of it.

With so much going on, and with so much to learn, Katherine had little time to think about her sister. Even Katherine's surroundings were new to her. English royal residences comprised both public rooms, which she could share with Henry, and private ones for each of them individually. The major public areas were the great hall, largely the preserve of menials and minor officials, and the watching chamber, which was occupied by guards and ushers who kept an eye on who was coming and going, as well as pages who made sure that the rooms were just as their royal masters expected them to be, with space enough for household staff to eat and, in some cases, sleep.

The king and queen had their own presence chambers, in which there was a cloth of estate above the throne to mark royal prominence, one of Katherine's being of 'crimson cloth of tissue, embroidered with the arms of England and Spain'. These were grand public rooms where both king and queen could dine in state, where ambassadors could be granted audience, and where public ceremonies such as the giving and receiving of gifts at New Year took place. Lists of what Katherine was given and what she gave are still extant, showing just how seriously she took this part of her duties, and how frugal she could be: sometimes she did as many do today with Christmas presents, passing unwanted gifts on to others. Thus when the Earl of Devonshire gave her a 'gold pomander, enamelled with the passion of Christ', which for some reason was not to her taste, Katherine ceremonially handed it on to Lady Fitzwilliam. And Henry's sister, Princess Mary, found herself the possessor of a diamond ring set with rubies, an unwanted present originally given to Katherine by the Bishop of Carlisle. Henry VII was not the only one who liked to save money.

Beyond each of their presence chambers lay Henry and Katherine's privy chambers, the private suites where king and queen could unwind with favoured attendants, for only the chosen few were allowed to walk through the gallery which separated the presence chamber from these inner sanctums. In these early years, while her apartments may have lacked the loud, boisterous banter of her husband's male preserve, Katherine's privy chamber was a pleasant, restful place to be, a place for gentle enjoyment and light-hearted chatter.

Behind these closed doors, where she was not on display, we catch glimpses of the woman behind the stiff, familiar portraits. Here, divested of her queenly garments, she could don a nightgown, a loose informal robe worn in the day not at night, and just relax. It was here that she would sit companionably with her female attendants. Sometimes, her mother's emphasis on housewifery never forgotten, she stitched shirts for her husband, or embroidered altar cloths and vestments, for she was an excellent needlewoman; at Coughton Court in Warwickshire there are elaborate church vestments said to be her work. She could happily spend a few hours reading, for she never lost her thirst for learning. Erasmus, the internationally renowned scholar, was to say in 1513 that she had 'sought to attach him to her as teacher'. With her ladies around her, she could listen to music, for she had her own musicians, or while away the time playing chess using one of the ivory chess sets she owned, or perhaps laugh at the antics of her fool. Here too, when not dining privately with the king or at his side for a state banquet, she ate the meals prepared specially for her by the staff of her own privy kitchen, headed by John Case, her master cook.

Among those Katherine most trusted, and who had right of entry to her privy apartments, were stalwarts like Maria de Salinas, Agnes de Vanegas or Margaret Pole, ladies like Elizabeth Boleyn, Sir Thomas's wife, and Buckingham's sisters, Elizabeth and Anne. Then there were her many gentlewomen who, as the years passed, included Anne Boleyn's sister, Mary Boleyn, who married William Carey, a favourite of the king's, Anne herself, Jane Parker, who was to marry Mary and Anne's only brother, George Boleyn, and Jane Seymour, who arrived at court fresh from her family's country seat of Wolf Hall. One woman whom Katherine never envisaged reinstating was Francesca de Caceres. By deserting Katherine to marry her banker, Francisco Grimaldi, Francesca had made a permanent enemy of her former mistress. She had, said the queen, 'cast herself away'. Therefore, when Francesca, now widowed, sought to enter the service of another royal lady, perhaps that of Katherine's sister, Queen Maria of Portugal, or Margaret of the Netherlands, Katherine put down her tiny, expensively shod foot. While 'for very pity' Francesca should be helped to return to Spain, the queen thought she was too 'perilous a woman' to enter royal service again. The only safe place for the treacherous Francesca, Katherine thundered, was in a nunnery. As other historians have pointed out, once Katherine deemed herself betrayed, the offender was unlikely ever to be forgiven.

Alessandro Geraldini, her former tutor, who had accompanied her to England when she had come as Arthur's betrothed, certainly felt the full force of Katherine's implacable wrath. Due to Margaret of Burgundy's influence, Geraldini had been appointed as Bishop of San Domingo, but when he needed another benefice, Katherine spurned him. Pope Leo X asked her to help the man. Margaret wrote to her saying that it was 'reasonable' for Katherine to 'do something' for him. But, as Geraldini himself said, the queen was 'now angry' with him. She was indeed, for she bitterly remembered that it had been he who had hinted to de Puebla all those years ago that her marriage to Arthur had been consummated. Her anger remained forever unabated: Geraldini would have to look elsewhere for assistance.

One visitor whom she always welcomed, though, and for whom she would do anything, was her husband. Sometimes they would dine together in her presence chamber or, more intimately, within one of the other, smaller rooms contained within her suite. And, since they did not routinely share a bedchamber, when the young and lusty king desired her, which he often did, they would retire to her bedroom to make love. For Katherine, as for Henry, the birth of a child was paramount. With six healthy children living, including her two sons, the heir and the spare, Juana had fulfilled her duty to perfection; so, as her ever-filling nursery proved, had Katherine's sister, Maria. There seemed to be no reason why Katherine, blessed with a young, devoted and energetic spouse, would not emulate her siblings.

And, in November 1509, just five months after Henry had made her his wife, the king wrote to Ferdinand to tell him the joyous news. Katherine, wrote an ecstatic Henry, was pregnant, 'and the child in her womb is alive'. Ferdinand, equally thrilled, wrote to her immediately. Her pregnancy, he said, was 'a great blessing'. Yet, perhaps recollecting that his eldest daughter, Isabella, had died shortly after her son Prince Miguel was born, the king prayed that God would 'give her [Katherine] a good delivery', and went on to beg her to take great care of herself. 'With the first child', Ferdinand pronounced knowledgeably, 'it is requisite for women to take more care of themselves than is necessary in subsequent pregnancies.'

As the child grew, Henry made his plans, issuing orders for materials for his wife's lying-in chamber and 'for the use of our nursery, God willing'. Katherine would be able to rest in a chair 'covered with crimson tissue of cloth of gold', the baby's crib was to be lined with crimson cloth of gold too, and there would be mounds of pillows, sheets, swaddling bands. Surely God would be 'willing', Katherine would gaze down at her child's face and Henry would have the son he deserved. Nothing could go wrong. Could it?

Motherhood

Katherine's first pregnancy was disastrous. We know exactly what happened because her notorious confessor, Friar Diego, and the new Spanish ambassador, Don Luis Caroz, wrote to Ferdinand giving him all the salacious details. Even the story of their letters is worth recounting. When, in the mid nineteenth century, the historian Gustav Bergenroth began the mammoth task of collating and transcribing the thousands of original documents stored within the Spanish archives 'at Simancas and elsewhere', the authorities kept some back. The ones they retained largely concerned more private, and less flattering, information about the royal family than it was considered respectful to make public. It transpired that some were about Juana's treatment at Tordesillas, but others were about Katherine. Following six years of dogged negotiations with the Director General of Public Instruction in Madrid, Bergenroth was finally granted access to these letters and dispatches. When he transcribed and translated them, their content made him re-consider his views on Katherine and on Juana; they do the same for us. And the letters from his new ambassador and his daughter's confessor, which Ferdinand opened in the spring of 1510, crucially reveal the real Katherine in a way that very few other documents can do.

The pregnancy obviously began well. The prospects of a secure succession sent a sigh of relief through Henry's council. Katherine was radiantly happy. Ferdinand felt just as pleased although he did not dismiss the dangers, especially when his own wife, Germaine de Foix, gave birth to a son which lived but a few hours. Henry was overjoyed. Yet, like Ferdinand, he knew that pregnancy was risky: he could not have forgotten that his own beloved mother had died in childbirth, nor that the child she gave her life to bring into the world followed her from it so quickly.

Trouble started on 30 January 1510 when Katherine complained of a pain in her knee, or so Diego tells us. Katherine's gynaecological understanding may indeed have been scanty, but even she would not have associated an aching knee with the tragedy that awaited her the next morning when she 'brought forth prematurely a daughter'. As a weakened Katherine lay in her bedchamber mourning her loss, only two Spanish women whose identities we do not know, the king, her physician and Father Diego, his ego correspondingly boosted, knew that she had miscarried. No one at court was informed, and Ferdinand heard nothing either.

As she did her best to cope with her grief and disappointment, Katherine's physician gave her astonishing news: she had been carrying twins, and one was still alive. She was still pregnant. Clearly sceptical, Katherine did not immediately rush to Henry with the glad tidings. She had, according to Diego, 'some doubts'. As the weeks passed, though, and her stomach continued to swell, Katherine's hopes, and Henry's, revived; it was then that Henry placed his order for the cradle, the swaddling cloths and various items for the queen's lying-in chamber. There was just one problem: Katherine was menstruating. It is true that in some rare cases women can continue to bleed, although they are not actually menstruating and the blood usually indicates a gynaecological difficulty, often with the position of the placenta. With no such knowledge at their disposal, Katherine's ladies busied themselves making ready her apartments for the great event. Today, alarm bells would be ringing out.

Katherine, desperate for a child, clung to the hope that God had answered her prayers. Though a poised young woman in her twenties who had already faced personal misfortunes, Katherine's vulnerability and insecurity are painfully apparent as she went along with what was, in truth, a charade. Quite why her stomach enlarged is unknown. The modern historian David Starkey suggests that it might have been 'the result of an infection'; he may well be right, or perhaps it was simply a phantom pregnancy.

Whatever the truth of the matter, Henry remained convinced that she was still pregnant, his yearning for a child as deep and sincere as her own. Thus it was that she did as queens always did: a few weeks before she thought the child was due, she took to her carefully prepared chamber to rest before the onslaught of labour, her ladies around her to encourage and entertain her, perhaps preparing the best herbs and potions to ease the pain. Roses, cyclamen and columbine were thought to be particularly comforting. Childbirth was very much a female affair, dealt with by midwives and other women. Male servants would bring supplies to the door of her privy apartments when necessary but they were never admitted; the doors stayed tightly closed on this mysterious female world. Even Henry stayed away, trying to curb his impatience as he waited to hear that he was a father.

But a father he was not. As an ever despairing Katherine sat, maybe in the wonderful crimson velvet chair he had ordered specially for her, willing the labour pains to start, it became clear that this was a pregnancy like no other, for nothing happened at all. There was no labour because there was no child. Diego expressed it with an outrageous insouciance. 'It has pleased our Lord to be her physician,' he declared, so her stomach had gone down again.

Eventually even Katherine had to acknowledge the truth, though she had to draw on all her courage to face the court after so public a withdrawing, a seclusion which the ambassador Caroz believed to have been a decided error. While sympathetic to Katherine, Caroz was more anxious about 'the account which was to be given to all the world'. Henry's councillors, wrote the ambassador to Ferdinand, were 'very vexed and angry at this mistake'. They must have been if they stooped low enough to say so to Caroz. 'From courtesy', Caroz said, they blamed Katherine's ladies for misleading her but he also picked up dangerous rumours that the privy councillors 'and other persons' were 'mummering' [murmuring] that the queen might not be able to bear children at all. A barren queen was useless. Indeed, Louis XII of France had found a way to have his marriage to his queen, Jeanne, annulled in order to make a more promising match with Anne of Brittany.

And while she had been sitting in her darkened apartments (for fresh air and too much light were considered perilous for expectant mothers and their offspring) Katherine had endured yet another emotional trauma: Henry looked, or maybe more than looked, at another woman. The woman in question was the Duke of Buckingham's younger sister,

Anne, Lady Hastings. Katherine was on good terms with Anne and with her elder sister, Elizabeth, Lady Fitzwalter, both of whose names are recorded as being her 'ladies' in the list of those who attended the coronation, and both of whom lived in the palace so were in frequent contact with her.

Probably Katherine only heard of the episode when Henry angrily insisted that Elizabeth Fitzwalter should be sent away from court. According to Caroz, who lost no time in writing to Ferdinand's secretary about the issue, Elizabeth told Buckingham that their sister's honour was in jeopardy. She thought the man responsible was Henry's Groom of the Stool, William Compton. The Groom of the Stool had the unenviable task of being in charge of the king's commode, but his duties were more extensive and far-reaching than that alone. As the chief gentleman of the king's privy chamber, the Groom of the Stool had virtually unlimited access to Henry and, as such, was one of the king's closest confidants.

Caroz's reports give a full account of the entire incident. According to him, Henry chose to use Compton as an intermediary in his pursuit of Lady Hastings, with the result that the imperious Buckingham, wrongly believing that Compton had dared to importune his sister for himself, 'severely reproached' him 'in many and very hard words'. After that everything escalated remarkably quickly. Henry 'reprimanded the Duke angrily'; Buckingham 'left the palace, and did not enter or return there for some days'; Anne's husband 'carried her off, and placed her in a convent sixty miles' away 'that no one may see her'; and Elizabeth got the blame for telling Buckingham in the first place. She was then 'turned out of the palace, and her husband with her'. This, of course, annoyed Katherine because Elizabeth was her 'favourite'.

Priding himself on 'being a married man, and having often treated with married people in similar matters', Caroz fumed because he had not been told anything in time to advise Katherine on how to react. This was a delicate situation. Caroz did not want her 'to behave ill in this ado', and antagonise her husband. In fact, she was already doing precisely that by making her 'ill will' very plain to poor Compton. Caroz would obviously have preferred that Katherine practised a little of that dissembling in which she was now usually adept. Unfortunately, she allowed her feelings to surface so visibly that 'almost all the court knew that the Queen had been vexed with the King, and the King with her, and thus this storm went on between them'. While typical of Juana's instinctive response to Philip's infidelities, a display of petulance was no more likely to impress Henry than it had Philip. Isabella had learnt to tolerate Ferdinand's affairs, even his illegitimate offspring. As the dust settled, Katherine quickly realised that she would be wise to follow her mother's lead rather than her sister's in future.

She may not have dissembled with Henry but she did with her own father. So did Henry. And there was much to dissemble about. On 27 May 1510, the same day that Caroz was penning his account of all recent proceedings, the king and queen settled down to write to Ferdinand themselves. Ferdinand was bound to be wondering if Katherine's baby had been delivered; indeed he was, for he sent a very blunt note to Caroz demanding an up-to-date briefing. Henry, anxious about what snippets of gossip might have reached his father-in-law's sharp ears about the muddles over Katherine's pregnancy or about his own extra-marital adventure, took the easy way out. He mentioned neither. He had not written lately, he said, because there had been 'no news'; he was only writing now because the Spanish ambassador was returning to Spain so, presumably, would be a valuable courier. Henry could not let 'this occasion pass without telling him [Ferdinand] that he and his Queen are perfectly happy, and that his kingdom enjoys undisturbed tranquillity'. Ferdinand should rest assured that Henry regarded him as his 'true father', a man he held in 'high esteem', and to whom he would be 'a dutiful and obedient son'. That, thought Henry, should suffice.

Katherine's handwritten letter (Henry had only signed his) was more difficult to compose. To tell the truth about her false pregnancy was so humiliating and distressing that she evaded it. She was writing, she said, because she was 'persuaded that he wishes to hear from her'. 'Some days before', she continued, she had been 'delivered of a daughter'. She had not been able to bring herself to tell her father about it sooner, she said, because the infant had been stillborn, which was 'considered to be a misfortune in England'. She said that she had not let anyone else write to Ferdinand about it either. She begged Ferdinand 'not to be angry' with her, as it had been 'the will of God'. No one, least of all the Catholic King, could argue with the will of God.

The letter was one which Ferdinand himself, a master of spin, could not have bettered. Katherine told him nothing about her sore knee or the fact that her 'delivery' had actually been the miscarriage she had suffered at the end of January. Nor did she tell him anything about her months of false hopes afterwards. Instead, she neatly compressed both occurrences into one. When it suited her, and it suited her now, Katherine was quite capable of doctoring facts. As one of her recent biographers points out, she had indeed, 'lied to her father', even if from comprehensible motives. Suspecting that Ferdinand was about to hear the whole story anyway, she decided to put her own gloss on things first. Like Henry, her gloss involved silence on Buckingham's sister. Just as Henry asserted how happy he and Katherine were, so did she. She and Henry were 'cheerful', she told her father. She thanked God, and Ferdinand, that she had 'such a husband as the King of England'. Maybe she did, for no more was heard of Buckingham's sister or any other woman, for a while anyway.

And fortune smiled on the queen. Confounding those who had whispered that she would not conceive, she was pregnant again. With the child developing, she could rest more easily. She was doing her duty. She was doing her duty in another area too.

When she had left Granada all those years ago, journeying to the ship that would bring her to England, she had accepted that her role was to be a mother, but she had always known that she was to act in Spanish interests at the same time. As a widow, more or less her father's ambassador, she had done her best to do just that. As queen, she was in a position to do even more. Six years her junior, inexperienced in government and feeling constrained by the sober, cautious elder statesmen who dominated his council, Henry looked to his pretty wife as his supporter, his adviser and his friend as well as his lover; that would not last, but it was exhilarating for Katherine while it did.

Compared to her, Henry was indeed a novice. For him, brought up on tales of heroic English victories against France in the Hundred Years War, of Poitiers, of Crécy, of Henry V and Agincourt, matters were one-sided: he wanted to fight because that was what kings did, and he wanted to fight France because that was what English kings did. Katherine knew better. International diplomacy was exceedingly complex, subject to what at first glance seem incomprehensible shifts in policy; sometimes alliances were made with one country or state so that war could be made upon a third, at other times those same alliances were turned on their heads. Ferdinand, while wary of French expansion, especially in Italy, could join with France one minute only to attack it the next. That was how international politics worked. A master in the art of deception and counter-deception, Ferdinand practised his art with aplomb; it was in Katherine's blood to do the same.

For the first years of her marriage, she was the true Spanish representative in England, just as Ferdinand had intended. When he sent her his congratulations on her marriage back in 1509, his message came with an enclosure: 'another letter with further details containing political matters' which he begged her 'to communicate' to Henry. In other letters, Ferdinand explained his aims and strategies very, very fully to his daughter, trusting her to convey them to her husband in her own way. He went on to use her to teach Henry, currently far too open and ingenuous, not to show his hand but to conceal his underlying motives. Thus, under Ferdinand and Katherine's tutelage, Henry was enticed to ally with the French while really preparing for a Spanish alliance and war with France at a time of Ferdinand's choosing. It was all heady stuff and Henry loved it, providing the negotiations did not impede too much on his hunting, his jousting or his general merrymaking. The king 'does not like to occupy himself much with business', assessed Caroz shrewdly. Fortunately, Ferdinand could, and did, count on his daughter to occupy herself with as much business as Spanish interests demanded. In the unlikely event of her weakening, her crafty father had an alternative plan: should she refuse to persuade Henry to act against France, Ferdinand ordered his ambassador to go to Father Diego and use him to persuade her.

As the months of 1510 progressed, Katherine's pregnancy became more and more pronounced and she tried to rest and gather strength. With winter approaching, she progressed slowly to Richmond, she and her entourage entering through the stone gateway flanked by its brightly painted statues of heralds placed there to welcome the guests. She passed into the marble-floored inner court with its fountain, along paved galleries embellished with the roses of the Tudors and Margaret Beaufort's emblem, the portcullis, and made her way into her own privy apartments. It would soon be time to take to her chamber again but, before that, Henry could not resist trying to please her, and impress representatives from Maximilian and Ferdinand, with some final extravagant entertainments.

Katherine, happily carrying Henry's child within her, watched indulgently as the king cavorted in front of her wearing fantastic costumes, accompanied by fifteen of his gentlemen, all of whom were equally splendidly attired. In jackets of crimson and purple, with white velvet bonnets draped in golden damask and topped with white plumes, they performed their dances to universal applause and admiration. Then, as they exited, soft music could be heard as six minstrels entered. With them were other gentlemen, clad in yellow satin and carrying flaming torches which threw shafts of flickering light on to the tapestry-hung walls of Katherine's chamber. No sooner were they there, than six more men came in, again in flamboyant clothes and with bonnets of cloth of silver, their faces covered so that no one knew who they were. Katherine, like everyone else caught up in the spirit of the game, pretended not to realise that the tallest of them all, towering above most of the others, was bound to be the king himself. Ladies in crimson satin, their gowns embroidered with pomegranates made of cloth of gold, danced with six of the gentlemen before finally removing their partners' masks, 'whereby they were knowen'. It was all light-hearted fun, ending only when Katherine and the rest of the audience 'muche praysed the kynge'. Henry liked praise.

Just before Christmas, Katherine adjourned with her ladies to her lying-in chamber to await the birth of her child, everyone praying that this child would be born without incident. It was. On New Year's Day 1511, Katherine was safely delivered of her baby. To her joy and relief, and to the king's ecstatic delight, the baby was a healthy boy. Exhausted but exultant, Katherine lay back watching as her ladies cared for her son. They tenderly washed him in warm water, gently rubbing his navel with a powder made from aloes and frankincense, wrapped him in swaddling clothes and then lowered him into his wonderful cradle.

Once Katherine felt well enough, other attendants raised her head and gave her a light nourishing drink or perhaps some thin broth to help her recover after her ordeal. They did not change her clothing or soiled bedding yet, that would wait until she felt able to sit up. Only after forty days would she leave her apartments to go to church where the prayers of the priest would solemnly rid her of the uncleanliness that childbirth entailed. In the meantime, she had time to rest.

So Henry and Katherine had their heir. The country celebrated. Wine was handed out liberally in the streets of London, there were bonfires, there were processions, there were prayers of thanks, it was an occasion to be remembered. Henry was so grateful at the successful outcome that he rushed off to the shrine of Our Lady at Walsingham in Norfolk, about a hundred miles away, to thank God for giving him the son he wanted so very much. The stillborn daughter, the false pregnancy, Buckingham's sister, were but fleeting memories.

The child now needed to be received within the Church as quickly as possible, baptism his protection against the horrors of Limbo. Lusty and strong like his father though he seemed, it was provident to take precautions to safeguard the prince's soul. Thus it was that five days later, wrapped up carefully against the cold, the tiny child was carried in his nurse's arms along the wide walkway leading from Richmond to the Church of the Observant Friars alongside the palace. Chattering, excited servants had worked hard to lay fresh gravel and rushes so that no one would slip, barriers at each side kept back smiling onlookers. Vibrantly coloured hangings draped the way to the candle-lit and decorated church where the congregation, comprising the major figures at court and ambassadors from France, Spain, Venice and the pope, waited quietly. The baby, named Henry after his father and grandfather, had illustrious godparents: Warham, Archbishop of Canterbury, Louis XII who thought he was on reasonable terms with England, and Margaret, Katherine's childhood friend, the competent regent of the Netherlands and informal guardian of Juana's children. Neither Louis nor Margaret could attend in person so the Bishop of Winchester and the Countess of Surrey deputised for them. Henry, by custom, was not present. Nor was Katherine, although the ambassadors visited her within her privy chamber afterwards to congratulate her.

Once Katherine was churched, she and Henry left their prince at Richmond with his nurse while they moved on to Westminster, Henry taking the opportunity to hold a splendid tournament in honour of his wife and his heir. The king, calling himself Loyal Heart, was in his element. Just like a chivalrous knight of old, and backed by three comrades, he issued a challenge to all and sundry to try their luck against his valiant band. As Katherine sat in state in a gleaming cloth-of-gold-lined enclosure, a huge pageant cart appeared. Designed to look like a magical forest with trees, herbs and flowers made from velvet, silk and satin, and with a golden castle at its centre, the cart was pulled on to the tiltyard by two huge 'animals', each led by a group of 'wilde men'. One 'animal' was a lion covered in gold damask, the other an antelope covered in silver damask and with golden horns. As everyone marvelled at this amazing contraption, its sides suddenly opened and, with trumpets sounding, the four brave knights, one of them Loyal Heart, rode out on great golden-trapped chargers, ready to take on all comers. Henry was having a wonderful time.

The second day of the jousts was just as breathtaking. This time Henry and his companions entered the field beneath canopies of cloth of gold and purple velvet, embroidered with the letters H and K in gold, the king's canopy topped with a golden imperial crown, the others with a gold letter K. Several of the king's gentlemen and courtiers also took part in the proceedings, often wearing strange disguises which they could then throw off dramatically before the fighting began.

After the jousts came a banquet, then dancing, minstrels, music, then another pageant. This one, within the palace of Westminster itself, featured lords and ladies beautifully attired in white satin, purple satin and cloth of gold, their garments glittering with gold Ks and Hs, letters which were thrown to many of the poorer folk nearby. At first this was good-humoured, but soon there was such a scrum as people rushed to grab what they could of the largesse, even filching parts of the king's own clothing, that the king's guard had to hold them back. Nevertheless, one enterprising Londoner, no doubt one of many, sold the golden letters he had caught for over four pounds, far more than the man probably earned in a whole year.

Even if things did get a little out of hand, Henry had welcomed his son in his own ebullient, energetic style. Brash, colourful, noisy, fabulously expensive though they were, the festivities were also cleverly devised and enchanting to see, the equal of any laid on in Burgundy, France or any Italian city, and illustrating to the cosmopolitan ambassadors that England was no cultural backwater immune to the images and imagery of the Renaissance. Henry wanted his England to shine, to be in the forefront of European affairs, a worthy prize to bequeath to his baby son.

Katherine wanted no less. She could not have been happier. Henry, her own 'Loyal Heart', was devoted to her, he and her father were as one, and she had just given birth to a beautiful son. We cannot know how often, if at all, she thought about Juana; if she did, she could be forgiven for assuming that her sister's confinement, while regrettable, was necessary and that she was receiving loving care from devoted attendants, meticulously selected by the father whom both sisters continued to trust. The possibility that Juana's seclusion was really imprisonment, or that she was leading a miserable existence, would never have occurred to her. Nor, despite the political talents she thought she had, would she have conceived that she and her sister were still pawns on Ferdinand's chessboard. As yet, there was no reason why she should.

A Taste of Power

Ten days after Katherine had presented the prizes to the victors of the spectacular jousts marking her son's birth, came terrible news. The infant prince, the Tudor heir, suddenly sickened and died at Richmond. He had lived only fifty-two days. The reason for his demise remains unknown; he may have succumbed to an infection, or perhaps it was what we think of as a cot death, one for which there is no easy explanation. Whatever the cause, the grief and shock for his parents was unimaginable. Henry, we are told, played the man. He took the calamity 'wonderous wysely', selflessly hiding his pain in order to console his wife.

Katherine was heartbroken. She had endured so much already. Her brother and her elder sister had died very young, her nephew never lived to grow up, her mother was dead, her sister Juana was supposed to have been driven insane by grief, her own first husband had died within six months of her marriage, she had suffered a miscarriage and a false pregnancy. Now, with everything appearing to go right for her, her destiny in England fulfilled, her beautiful, seemingly healthy child lay in his coffin. Thus, the chronicler, Edward Hall, tells us, 'lyke a naturall woman' she 'made muche lamentacion', her sorrow eased only gradually by the king's 'good persuasion and behaviour'. When Archbishop Warham's niece had lost her husband, Warham had done his best to comfort her but warned that excessive mourning was a sin; those who indulged in it therefore bore two griefs, one for the deceased and one for the sin of angering God. As a devout daughter of the Church, Katherine did not want to anger God. She knew that her tears must cease.

The only thing that Henry and Katherine could do for their lost child, which was perfectly acceptable to God, was to ensure that the baby was buried with all the honours due to a prince. Protocol dictated that neither king nor queen could attend in person; this was a task they must entrust to others. The tiny coffin was gently carried from Richmond Palace to the Thames where three black-draped barges were waiting for the voyage along the river to the abbey-church of St Peter's at Westminster, where Henry and Katherine had been crowned little more than a year before. Everyone who came with the little boy on his final journey, including the official mourners such as the Marquis of Dorset and the Earl of Essex, the courtiers like Sir Thomas Boleyn who helped to carry the coffin, the six knights who held religious and regal banners, the royal servants such as Anthony Leigh and John Cony who worked in the royal kitchen, and the one hundred and eighty paupers who were paid to pray for the little boy's soul, were garbed in black, albeit the quality of the cloth varying according to the rank of the wearer. Wax candle-like torches lit the way, prayers were chanted and sung, all was done with solemnity and reverence as the entourage reached the abbey itself where the monks waited to receive the mortal remains of the baby prince. There, in the beautiful church with its brightly coloured wall paintings, its golden statues gleaming with jewels and, on that sad day, with its choir and nave draped in black, the child was laid to rest. The site of his grave was chosen with touching care: he lies to the left-hand side of the altar, close to the tomb of Edmund Crouchback, Henry III's youngest son, and near to the shrine of the abbey founder, St Edward the Confessor. If he could not be a king in life, at least in death the baby could rest among kings. He lies there still.

Losing the child upon whom they had pinned so many hopes was a cruel blow, yet Henry was only twenty and Katherine twenty-six so there was still plenty of time left for more children. After all, Katherine had shown that she was not barren and was capable both of conceiving and of carrying a child full term, and Henry had no doubts about his own virility for he had already proved it. Perhaps next time luck would be with them. They would try again. In the meantime, there was a country to be governed and, annoyed and frustrated by the cautious advice proffered by his councillors and by their attempts to restrain what they saw as his extravagance and impetuosity Henry relied upon Katherine's support, her wisdom and her experience. The couple were still as one, united despite their failure as yet to produce the heir the king and the country needed.

So Katherine was in her element. A loyal Spanish princess, she knew where her duty lay. So, unfortunately, did her wily father. A man who had shut one daughter away because he wanted to retain power was unlikely to baulk at using another to further his own ambitions and, true to type, Ferdinand proceeded to use the unsuspecting Katherine to dupe her innocent husband while the going was good. He started as early as 1511, luring his son-in-law into supporting him in a conflict against the French, a conflict whose real, but well-hidden, purpose was to enable Ferdinand to gain Navarre. For the English, the entire episode was a disaster. Abandoned in mid-stream by Ferdinand, their supposed ally, and ravaged by disease, the exhausted and starving English soldiers mutinied. Henry, humiliated by their behaviour, naively accepted the blame when Ferdinand had the effrontery to complain that further victories had been prevented because English unreliability had forced him into a truce with the French. Really, Ferdinand mendaciously asserted, all he wanted was to fight the French with dependable allies; the English had let him down. Believing him, and blissfully unaware of just how shamelessly they had been used, Henry and especially Katherine were ready to risk war on a grand scale when the conflict started again.

Katherine, who tended to take most things seriously anyway, threw herself wholeheartedly into planning for war. Her mother had fought the Moors; she was ready to fight the French, whom she described as 'the foes of the Church' in a long letter she wrote to Cardinal Bainbridge, the English ambassador in Rome. The Scots, too, were perfidious, she told Bainbridge, so much so that an English army would 'annihilate the kingdom of Scotland, according to the fashion in which the Catholic King treated the King of Navarre'.

Far from being the tender-hearted queen content to stay in the background with her sewing and her prayers, which is how myth so frequently portrays her, the real Katherine was heavily involved in political affairs whenever the chance arose. A couple of years after Prince Henry's death, that chance was there as, urged on by Ferdinand, war with France loomed again. The Venetian ambassador, Andrea Badoer, was left in no doubt just how important and influential she was as plans took shape, for she even asked him the monthly cost of Venetian galleys. Shrewdly assessing the likelihood of outright war against France, Badoer reported that the king was 'bent on war', the Council was 'averse to it', but 'the Queen wills it'. Badoer leaves us in no doubt as to who would get their way.

Get her way she did, although Henry, keen to reveal himself as a great warrior in the tradition of Henry V, was just as eager and determined as she was. But he had some unfinished business to deal with first. Edmund de la Pole, Earl of Suffolk, a Yorkist claimant to the throne, had languished in the Tower since Juana's husband, Philip, had grudgingly handed him back to Henry VII in 1506. Henry VII had agreed not to execute de la Pole, but his son, never one to feel bound by a promise, especially if it was his father's, ordered the earl's beheading in the spring of 1513. The deed made him feel safer, as the executions of his father's servants Empson and Dudley had made him feel more just and popular. Katherine, who as a queen could beg her husband to spare prisoners' lives, chose not to interfere with any of these dubious, unscrupulous decisions; in this she showed wisdom, for Henry was adamant that death was the only answer to those he saw as traitors.

In any case, she was as distracted by the idea of war as was her husband. Yet war was more than merely donning new armour, mounting huge chargers and waving farewell to weeping wives and mistresses. The sheer logistics behind the undertaking were huge. An army had to be mustered, for Henry had no forces to speak of himself, which meant that the nobility, gentry, even churchmen, would have to be organised to recruit forces from among their tenants and retainers; then horses had to be procured, bought or requisitioned; provisions had to be ordered, stored and shipped to Calais, which in turn meant that there had to be sufficient ships to transport men and equipment. And it was in these various areas that one man stood out: Thomas Wolsey, the king's almoner.

Born a butcher's son in Ipswich and Oxford educated, Wolsey's phenomenal industry and his sheer naked ability had so impressed the equally pragmatic, unsentimental and hard-working Henry VII that he had made him his chaplain and entrusted him with sensitive diplomatic missions. For Henry VIII, ever reluctant to spend time on business in good hunting weather or when other more attractive pastimes beckoned, Wolsey was the answer to a prayer, or a particularly coveted New Year's Gift.

We know just how Wolsey came to manage his master because his servant, his gentleman-usher, George Cavendish, wrote a biography that has been a treasure trove to historians for centuries. In brief, Cavendish tells us that Wolsey manipulated the youthful and gullible Henry by taking over the daily grind of state affairs for him, encouraging the king to immerse himself in a round of pleasure while leaving all the boring chores to his dependable almoner. In a very short time Wolsey dominated the government and soon the Church too. Had the queen but realised it, this man who was so very useful in arranging all that was needed for the war against France was eroding her influence; Katherine's days of being Henry's major solace and adviser were drawing to a close.

But that was still to come. In the meantime, there was a war to fight. Allied to such devious old hands as Ferdinand and Maximilian, Henry was very much the new boy on the block, but his excitement and commitment were palpably obvious. He set off for Dover to take ship for Calais towards the end of June 1513. With him went the ever-present Wolsey, the cream of his nobility and his very best friends from among the gentlemen of the court. The Duke of Buckingham was there, so was Charles Brandon, so were William Compton, Sir Thomas Boleyn, Sir John Seymour, Lord Willoughby – all the names are recorded in what reads like a Who's Who of Henry's England. Some were already in France before the king set off, one of them being the Welshman, Sir Rhys ap Thomas, whom Katherine had come to know because he had served Arthur at Ludlow all those years ago and was still ferociously active in the service of his king.

Katherine accompanied Henry to the port and watched as his ships set sail for France. This promised to be the longest time they had spent apart since their wedding, and it was also the most dangerous. Many a king had died in battle, even within Katherine's lifetime; royalty was no protection against a stray arrow, a sudden charge, even disease. She could not help worrying, nor could she prevent herself expressing her fears. Although we cannot be sure, she may have had an additional reason for her anxiety: uncorroborated ambassadors' reports indicate a possibility that she was again with child. The prospect of losing Henry as abruptly as she had lost Arthur was terrifying. So she wrote to her former sister-in-law, Maximilian's daughter, Margaret of the Netherlands, entreating her to send a physician to be at Henry's side. And she wrote to Wolsey, begging him to send her news of her husband for, she said, she could never be 'in rest' until receiving his reassurance. Wolsey, not yet so secure that he dared neglect Henry's wife, did write, and he did so very frequently, much to Katherine's relief. She responded, thanking him for the 'payne' he took in 'remembering to write' to her 'so often'.

Katherine's main job was to protect England while Henry was away, a task she relished, and one entrusted to her when the king formally appointed her as regent in his absence. On paper, this gave her huge responsibilities: she could summon troops, she could appoint sheriffs, she could sign warrants, she even had some powers within the Church, and she could demand money from Henry's Treasurer of the Chamber, John Heron, 'for payment of such sums as she may require'. She could not do all this alone, of course: Archbishop Warham led a small council left to help her and, just in case James IV of Scotland took the opportunity offered by Henry's absence to attack England, the veteran campaigner the Earl of Surrey was there to command whatever army could be raised.

Predictably, James IV, ignoring any family loyalty engendered because of his marriage to Henry's sister, Margaret, did indeed take his chance and advanced towards the border. It was just a matter of time before he crossed into English territory. He had even sold his gold chains and plate to raise money for his armies and was reduced to eating off pewter, or so the Venetian ambassador had heard. The Scottish menace was definitely not going to go away. So, as Henry was absorbed in skirmishing with the French, besieging and even managing to capture two towns, Tournai and Thérouanne, before happily setting off to visit Margaret, Katherine was engulfed in a far more threatening drama at home.

Surrey, who had fought for Richard III at Bosworth but had then changed sides and become a stalwart supporter of the victorious Tudor dynasty, rushed north to defend the borders and the rest of the country, gathering men where he could. For her part, Katherine knew just what she had to do. With a shrewd nod in the direction of the traditional male view of women, she declared that she was 'horribly busy making standards, banners and badges', professing herself only too happy to be dealing with the Scots as a way of passing the time while Henry was in France. In reality, she and her council were frantically preparing, planning and organising English defences in the brief lull before any major battles actually occurred.

Needing to check on resources, she demanded information on 'men and harness', soundly castigating officials in any town whose replies were tardy; the mayor and sheriffs of Gloucester who had ignored requests for data were commanded to provide it within fifteen days since 'writings and news from the Borders show that the King of Scots means war'. Levies were to be raised in Nottingham, Derby, Warwick, Leicester, Stafford, Rutland, Northampton, Lincoln 'and the neighbouring counties'; anyone who dared to 'obstruct' such action was to be punished. She signed an order to the Great Wardrobe (the department of the royal household which dealt with the provision and storage of much of Henry's property) to deliver certain specified banners and standards, including two with the lion 'crowned imperial', two with the arms of England, two with those of England and Spain and two with the cross of St George, all of which she obviously meant to use to inspire the armies. Isabella had used flags and standards to unite and exhort her forces against the Moors; her daughter would do the same against the Scots.

And she prepared to lead an army herself, leaving London for Buckingham. 'Our Queen took to the field,' wrote an enthusiastic Venetian ambassador. Indeed, as the chronicler Pedro Mártir so vividly, if sycophantically, wrote, Katherine was behaving just as Isabella had done before her, making 'a splendid oration to the English captains' in which she reminded them 'that the Lord smiled upon those who stood in defence of their own' and that 'English courage excelled that of all other nations'. Tempting though it is to imagine Katherine defiantly uttering such words – and they do sound characteristic of her – Mártir was in Valladolid when he put pen to paper so had no way of knowing what Katherine had or had not done.

Lady Margaret Beaufort, the 'King's Mother', the pious and austere matriarch who was such a formidable presence in her son Henry VII's court.

Prince Arthur, from a nineteenth-century stained-glass window at the parish church of St Lawrence, Ludlow, the church in which his coffin rested until its final journey to Worcester Cathedral.

The gatehouse at Ludlow Castle. Katherine and Prince Arthur passed through the gatehouse when they arrived at Ludlow in 1502.

The round chapel at Ludlow Castle. A stone's throw from Prince Arthur's apartments, this tiny chapel may be where he and Katherine worshipped.

Prince Arthur's tomb, Worcester Cathedral.

Prince Arthur's Tudor rose and Katherine's pomegranate emblem from the carved tracery around Arthur's tomb in Worcester Cathedral.

King Henry VIII by Hans Holbein the Younger, a portrait of the middle-aged Henry that hints at the merciless, gross figure that he would soon become.

Jousters on horseback.

EGES PLVRIBVS DELECTATI
onibus gaudent: Aliis victo
ria plus placet: Aliis regimē
populorum per'excibitionem
legum: Aliis plus magnorum
operum construcho: Aliis côes
satio: Aliis ueneris delectatio. Aliis thesaurorum
congregatio: Aliis benefitiorum excibitio: Aliis
ludorum & festuuitatum ordinatio: Aliis plus
uirtum & scientiarum acquisitio: Aliis uenatio:
Aliis alia: Ex omnibus uenatio uidetur'magis cô
ueniens regibus & magis propria: Fere autem oés
reges ceteriq; magnates hanc preceteris appetunt

A miniature from a treatise on falconry dedicated to Katherine's father, Ferdinand, and which he may well have owned. Like her father, Katherine revelled in the sport of falconry.

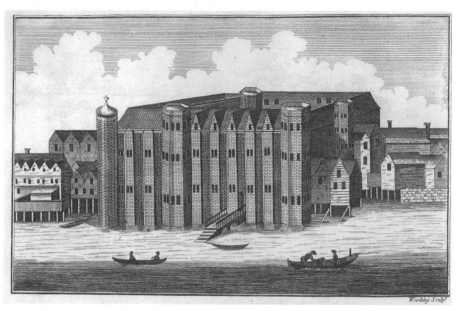

Baynard's Castle, London, which became part of Katherine's dowry when she married Henry VIII.

The children of Philip and Juana. Princes Charles and Ferdinand are on the left, their sisters, Eleanor, Isabella, Maria and Catalina are on the right.

St George's Chapel, Windsor Castle. It was at Windsor, in 1506, that Katherine and Juana met for the last time.

Edward Stafford, Duke of Buckingham, executed for treason in 1521.

Waramus Arch Bᴾ: Cant:

William Warham, Archbishop of Canterbury: an engraving after Hans Holbein the Younger.

Once James, having issued a declaration of war, sent a force into English territory on 13 August 1513, the situation became critical. It got worse. The first Scottish troops were defeated but James himself led his main army into England on 22 August, quickly capturing Norham Castle, which belonged to Thomas Ruthal, Bishop of Durham. Ruthal, who had accompanied the king to France, was devastated when he heard his castle had fallen. The news, he told Wolsey, 'touched me so near with inward sorrow that I had lever to have been out of the world than in it'; in contrast, Henry, when relating the event to the Duke of Milan, put a brave face on it, dismissing the castle as 'a little old town that was almost tumbling down of itself, unfortified and practically deserted'. But then, it was not a royal possession.

To Katherine, Norham and the other spoils which fell to James were far from 'little old' towns. James had to be stopped before he marched further south. Surrey and his sons, Edmund and Thomas Howard, were in position by the beginning of September; their army gathered near Newcastle ready to march towards the enemy. Sir Thomas Lovell had another army at Nottingham; Katherine and her council had gathered a third in the south just in case the worst happened and James somehow got through the other two.

James did not. As Katherine, worried but resolute, reached Buckingham with her troops, Surrey and his sons faced the might of the Scottish army at Flodden, about fifteen miles south-west of the border town of Berwick-upon-Tweed. The fighting, which began in the afternoon of 9 September, was ferocious. Courageous men on both sides fell in bloody hand-to-hand combat in which they knew that a careless move would cost them their lives, but gradually the tide turned away from the Scots to leave the English in control of the field. Many of the Scots, so we read (in English accounts), were so 'vengeable and cruel in their fighting' that their opponents preferred to kill them rather than capture them alive, contemptuously leaving the corpses stripped and naked on the ground. Among the dead was the king: James struggled like a man possessed only to fall within a few feet of the great Surrey himself. The flower of the nobility died with him, so did the Archbishop of St Andrews, two bishops and two abbots (it is always an error to see every sixteenth-century churchman as a gentle, peaceful soul) and perhaps another eleven thousand or so of the more humble. English losses are estimated to have numbered about one thousand. Whatever the correct statistics might be, the day was an unmitigated disaster for Scotland, one forever to be lamented in the annals, the legends and the poetry of that nation.

For the English and for Katherine, in a position to take the credit, it was a triumph, a decisive victory. It was 'the most happy that can be remembered', wrote Ruthal to Wolsey, one practical man of the Church to another. Although no one would have dared to say so, Henry's exploits, which were not inconsiderable, appeared shallow in comparison. To his credit, he had captured two towns, led a successful cavalry charge in which the French retreated so quickly that the skirmish became known as the Battle of the Spurs, and attended some diplomatic meetings with Maximilian and with Margaret, all of which he much enjoyed. He revelled in an especially gratifying welcome from Margaret in Lille: the houses were hung with tapestries, burning torches lined the route to the royal palace, little pageants and entertainments were laid on to please him as he passed by, cheering crowds lined the streets, 'young girls offered crowns, sceptres, and garlands' and 'outlaws and malefactors with white rods in their hands besought pardon'. All was wonderful, and no more than he probably thought he deserved.

Katherine understood Henry and his desire for glory. Even while engaged in the Scottish campaign, she never forgot fulsomely to congratulate him on all that he did. In a letter to Wolsey, shortly after the surrender of Thérouanne, she declared that 'the victorye hath been soo grete that I think noon suche hath been seen befor'. 'All England', she continued in the same vein, 'hath cause to thanke God of it.' Little matter that one of Wolsey's servants later called Henry's trophies 'ungracious dogholes', and that one of them had been flattened by his artillery bombardments. Likewise, when Henry decided to send his wife a captured French duke, the urbane and charming Duke of Longueville, she spent much valuable time in deciding with her council where he could be housed, eventually determining that the Tower of London would be the most suitable place.

To send his wife a French duke was a coup but, after Flodden, Katherine could go one better: she could send Henry the coat of the defeated Scottish king. Henry could use it for his banners. As a young girl Katherine had been with her mother when Isabella had travelled from one battlefield to another, so she was not one to feel unduly squeamish. Had it been up to her, she wrote, she would have liked to send James's battered body to Henry, 'but our Englishmen's hearts would not suffer it'. With a mixture of wifely humility and experienced statesmanship, she vowed that all praise for Flodden was due to God, the victory being 'to your Grace and all your reame [realm] the grettest honor that coude be', an honour made even greater by Henry's magnificent success in France. If Katherine flattered, she did so in spades.

Interestingly, foreign ambassadors sniffed out and possibly exaggerated what they believed to be her true sentiments. The Milanese ambassador thought she boasted that 'she has shown no less promise than he in fighting the Scots' and that 'with regard to the gift of the duke, which is a truly great gift, she hopes to surpass the king ... and instead of a duke, she hopes to send him a king'. 'A certain English lady has captured three Scottish horsemen', the ambassador thought she had told Henry, clearly a hint that women could be just as valiant as men. The Duke of Ferrara heard a similar version of this incident: on receiving the duke, Katherine was alleged to have 'sent him [Henry] back three Scotsmen of note, saying it was not a marvel for one man of war to take another man of war, such as that Frenchman sent to her by the King, to whom she sent back these three Scotsmen taken by a woman alone'.

Her period of regency gave Katherine a tantalising taste of real power and responsibility. Appointments are mentioned as being 'by the Queen's grace', she signed orders with a flourish as 'Katherine the Queen', warrants were marked as 'Teste [witnessed] Katharina'. Yet, many such documents, such as that authorising the release of various banners for the army, were also countersigned by councillors, including Warham, so her position was still somewhat circumscribed. She did not even dare to order the burial of James's corpse without Henry's agreement. And, while she might indeed have addressed the army captains, even ridden with them, she could never really have led them as her husband did; gender produced its own conventional restrictions. Juana, a sovereign monarch eking out her days at Tordesillas, was only too aware of this, her own role so limited by the men around her. Ferdinand visited her occasionally, perhaps keeping her up to date about what was going on in the world outside her rooms, but, while scrupulously referring to her in official documents, he ensured that any decisions or policies were his and his alone.

Although proud of the Scottish defeat and her own performance as regent, Katherine wanted Henry home. There would be 'noo joye' here without him, she confided. There could be no child either. We cannot know whether those ambassadors who stated that she gave birth in the autumn of 1513 were right, but it is doubtful. Certainly no baby or miscarriage is mentioned in her correspondence and it seems unlikely that she would have risked a much-wanted child by accompanying the army from London.

Henry was in no great hurry to come back. He was having too good a time. There were services of thanksgiving to attend, meetings to be held, promises given to his allies of future action against the French, and last, but far from least, several very enjoyable jousts laid on for his participation. By October 1513, though, he was back at the helm in England.

Yet subtle changes had taken place. Wolsey, at Henry's side throughout the French campaign, was now indispensable, firmly ensconced in the position of pre-eminence that Katherine had once held, for his influence with Henry had become personal as well as political. Charles Brandon, one of the king's friends, a man of action after the king's own heart, was created Duke of Suffolk, and Henry's other companions and councillors hovered around as much as ever, but everyone could see that the person to be reckoned with within the government was Wolsey. Henry, too, was different. He had grown up, he had seen war, he had seen death, he had been treated as the important figure on the international stage he believed himself to be.

What was crucial for Katherine was that, while Henry was still very fond of her, she would never again have quite such a hold on him, especially since she had not yet given him the heir for which he yearned. Worse was to come. Having comprehensively betrayed Juana, Ferdinand the puppet-master was about to betray Katherine as well, forcing her into choosing between her new country and her old, between her father and her husband.

Happy Families

At the beginning of 1514, Henry's court was buzzing with gossip and anticipation. Everywhere there was talk about the next royal marriage. And because of it, Katherine anticipated another of the many farewells that had so punctuated her life. But this was to be a happy farewell: in a clear reaffirmation of the Anglo-Spanish family compact, Henry's eighteen-year-old sister, Mary, was to marry Juana's son, Charles, who was four years her junior. Henry was taking the preparations very seriously. Keen to make a good impression with the cultured, worldly-wise Burgundians, he gave detailed instructions to his ambassadors so that Calais, where he would take Mary for her first meeting with her intended, was ready to host the splendid event. But he went further. He was adamant that Mary would present an image of European chic. Therefore the ambassadors were to show different materials to the Archduchess Margaret so that she could 'choose in what manner they shall be made' because the king intended that Mary's 'apparel' should be 'after the fashion of those parts'.

The general fervour peaked on 13 August 1514, the day selected for Mary to enter the holy estate of matrimony. On that Sunday, Katherine's ladies dressed her in a gown of ash-coloured satin. They lowered gold chains around her neck, dotted jewels on her clothes and placed a cap made from cloth of gold upon her still lustrous hair. They did all this with tender care for the queen was pregnant. She was also going to her sister-in-law's wedding.

Within the princess's apartments, all was bustle and laughter as her attendants took extra care that their mistress should appear at her most beautiful. Dressed in a chequered gown of purple satin and cloth of gold, with a cloth-of-gold cap, gleaming jewels and golden chains just like Katherine's, and with a petticoat of the same colour and material as

Katherine's, Mary looked as radiant as every bride should upon this her special day.

Archbishop Warham began proceedings with a Latin sermon. Together with the other members of the congregation, who included the Dukes of Suffolk and Buckingham and Thomas Wolsey, shortly to become Archbishop of York, Katherine and Henry watched as Mary and her bridegroom repeated the words which made them man and wife. Once the gold ring was on Mary's finger and the various marriage contracts signed, everyone walked in solemn procession to Mass, a service followed by a banquet and dancing. It was a joyous, exultant occasion.

But it was not the one that Katherine and Mary had envisaged. The bridegroom was not Charles, as everyone had anticipated at the beginning of the year, and the setting was not Calais but Greenwich by the banks of the Thames. More crucially, the man who had said the vital words to Mary and placed the ring upon her finger, was the Duke of Longueville who had helped in the delicate negotiations and who was acting as proxy for the true bridegroom, King Louis XII of France. To Katherine's despair, Henry's relationship with her father had collapsed and he had switched from fighting the French to allying with them. Mary's marriage symbolised this spectacular diplomatic volte-face. Henry was smugly delighted with his new alliance; his sister was condemned to marrying a decrepit man more than thirty years her senior.

It was partly Maximilian's fault. As ambitious and slippery as ever, the emperor had begun to wonder whether he might procure a more valuable wife than Mary for his grandson. After all, Charles's inheritance, which would include Spain, Spanish dominions in the New World, Navarre, parts of Italy, the Netherlands and vast lands within the empire, made him the most eligible bachelor in Europe. England was hardly the most prosperous and influential of nations, so Maximilian had begun to ponder the worth of a French bride, or perhaps a Hungarian one to increase the boy's already considerable chances of one day taking over as emperor. While not going so far as to directly repudiate the English match, Maximilian put out feelers elsewhere. And unsettling rumours of his machinations reached England.

Yet, as far as the English were concerned, the chief villain was Ferdinand, who had let his English allies down once too often. When Henry had returned home from France so triumphantly, genuinely thrilled with the Battle of the Spurs and with the capture of Tournai and Thérouanne, he was raring for more. He wanted to attack France again and defeat them even more conclusively. He wanted to revive the English successes of the Hundred Years War. And he was led to believe that that was what Ferdinand wanted too.

It was not. What mattered to Ferdinand was not whether Henry gained more land in France, it was French designs on Italy and his own ability to retain Navarre. Ferdinand had merely wanted Henry to divert the French so that he could pursue his own line in Italy and elsewhere. The Catholic King could always make sweeping promises to assist the English and then find a reason to blame someone else as to why such help failed to materialise. He had pulled that stunt before. But when Henry demanded something more concrete, Ferdinand was less than enthusiastic. He wanted peace while he plotted his next moves. He had no intention of allowing Spain to get dragged into a war to enrich Henry. So, protesting that, 'by a miracle' he had discovered a dastardly 'conspiracy' of the Italian princes, on the outbreak of the war with France, to deprive himself and Maximilian of their Italian possessions, Ferdinand stated that the only thing to do was to have peace with France for a year while everything was sorted out. Maximilian, he said, agreed with him and both were very happy to include Henry in the peace treaty.

Even Henry was not that credulous; nor was Katherine. He felt completely betrayed and by someone he had trusted, the man who he had once said was like a father to him. He 'lamented such an opportunity had been lost for crippling the pride of France'. The only thing for a man of honour, like himself, to do was to spite Ferdinand by allying with France himself and breaking off Mary's former betrothal to Charles. Thus it was that he sacrificed his sister on that late summer's day at Greenwich.

If Mary epitomised his new friendship with France, Katherine was in the invidious position of epitomising the old discredited alliance with Spain. Even more distressing for her was that she had to choose between her father and her husband. While her Spanish heritage was in her blood, what mattered to her, as it always would, was to maintain her marriage, the marriage she had fought tooth and nail to achieve, and which she was convinced was not just good for her, but good for Spain and good for God too. What was called for, then, was a cool head; after all, eventually the dust might settle, relations between Henry and Ferdinand might improve and Henry might become disenchanted with the French. There had to be a breathing space for time to work its magic.

So Katherine chose to support Henry. And she did not put a foot wrong. She did not attempt to dissuade him from his pro-French policy, she did not argue that there must have been some misunderstanding and that Ferdinand was somehow in the right. When the Spanish ambassador, Caroz, tried to talk to her about Spain's interests, he found her polite but implacable. She was not going to argue Ferdinand's cause, and that was that.

In any case, she had her unborn child to think of. As with Katherine's previous pregnancies, there was procedure and a protocol to be followed so that the queen's chamber would be ready for her and her much-wanted baby. On 4 October 1514, with Mary safely embarked on her new life in France, various materials, some in blue, were ordered for Katherine's beds (she would have a day bed besides one for her confinement and for sleeping). On the very same day, furniture was requested 'for the use of our nursery, God willing'; the items included 'a cradle covered with scarlet'. All the medical signs seemed good. Louis XII was happy to accede to Henry's request that he become godfather should the child be a boy. Since the French king had ridden out to meet Mary 'like a gay bridegroom ... licking his lips and gulping his spittle' and was described as 'very joyous' on the morning after his wedding, such a gesture was the least he could offer to the brother-in-law who had provided him with such a stunning wife, even if one of Henry's motives had been to spite Ferdinand.

As the weeks passed and winter closed in, Katherine could only hope that this time God would be 'willing' and that the child she carried would survive. Cruelly, disaster struck again. In December, the Venetian ambassador reported that she was 'delivered of a stillborn male child of

8 months to the very great grief of the entire court'. Pedro Mártir had no doubt about the cause of Katherine's latest disappointment. He wrote sadly that her miscarriage had come about 'through grief, as it is said, for the misunderstanding between her father and her husband'. Mártir went on to assert that Henry 'had reproached her with her father's ill faith'. Possibly he had, but Henry wanted the child so badly that he is more likely to have kept his temper in check. Whether Henry had blamed her to her face or not, it was Katherine, physically and emotionally drained, who suffered the most.

Yet, stalwart as always, her public demeanour could not be faulted. Duty, and her pride, demanded that. As she took her usual place at Henry's side in the various Christmas and New Year festivities, she could only hope that the following year would bring her better fortune. Even the revels themselves, though, carried mixed messages. On the one hand, she could convince herself that all was well between Henry and herself – the letters H and K sewn on to the costumes of gentlemen taking part in an elaborate pageant appeared to reaffirm the unity between husband and wife – yet she was very conscious of the constant presence of Elizabeth Blount, a major participant in the mummeries. Elizabeth, one of Katherine's ladies, had family links to Sir Richard Croft, Arthur's steward from the old Ludlow days, and was related to Lord Mountjoy, Katherine's chamberlain and Agnes de Vanegas's husband, but Mistress Blount was not one to let such loyalties deter her from seizing any personal opportunities that turned up. Pretty, graceful, vivacious, and with a talent for music and dancing that brought her many a prominent role in court entertainments, Elizabeth soon attracted the attention of the king.

Katherine, perhaps remembering her outbursts over Buckingham's sister, maintained a dignified silence over Henry's burgeoning relationship with the enchanting Elizabeth, but the issue was further proof that her own dominance over her husband had diminished and could never be quite the same again. However, she could still have a very successful marriage; all hinged on producing an heir. It seems that within weeks of losing the baby just before Christmas 1514, she became pregnant again. She told her father about it in October 1515. While she and Henry were 'in good health', she said, she had given birth 'to a child after Candlemas' (2 February). Maybe she was merely telling him about her previous miscarriage but had given a different date, as she had done once before, but it seems more probable that she had experienced yet another of the miscarriages that were dogging her life.

What she did not tell Ferdinand in that October letter was that by then she was definitely pregnant once more. In January 1516, at Greenwich, she went through the customary ceremony of taking to her lying-in chamber. Thus, with the outer door closing upon the world of the court, Katherine settled to await the birth, a numbingly familiar experience for her. Nothing had been left to chance: the warm, darkened rooms were luxuriously furnished, rich carpets lay on the floor, her favourite tapestries were on the walls, her beds invitingly made up with soft pillows. But the empty cradle waiting for its occupant told its own story.

As she sat with her ladies, whiling away the hours of her confinement and straining every nerve for the onset of labour, there was one area in which Katherine's mind was at peace. She was no longer torn between her husband and her father as she had been when she had last miscarried. The world had suddenly righted itself again: Henry had patched up the quarrel with Ferdinand, signing a treaty with him a couple of months before she had taken to her chamber. Katherine had told her father that the agreement had come about because he had sent Henry 'splendid presents' (a jewelled collar, two horses with ornate trappings, and a wonderful sword) which were considered the most 'magnificent' offerings that had ever come to England. Wolsey, while himself impressed by the costly gifts, felt that his king had 'deserved it for all that he had done for Spain'. Certainly Henry had been delighted with his new toys. 'No one could send such presents who is not animated by the most sincere and tender love' towards him, he had written to his father-in-law. In fact, he went on, he loved Ferdinand 'as much and as sincerely' as before, magnanimously forgiving and forgetting 'all the disagreeable things' that had passed between them.

Such words were music to Katherine's ears, especially because the true cause of the reconciliation was that Henry's animosity had switched back to France. Louis XII, worn out by his lascivious exertions in keeping pace with his lovely bride, had died less than three months after the wedding. His successor, Francis I, was very different from the crotchety Louis. At over six feet tall, considered handsome, a skilled jouster and with a reputation as a poet and musician, Francis cut just as dashing a figure as did his English counterpart. He was also three years younger and ruled a country that was far bigger, richer and more populous than Henry's. When Francis marked his arrival on the European stage by calmly proceeding to send an army to Italy, Henry was only too ready to patch up his relationship with Ferdinand.

Although concerned about developments in Italy, Katherine could not have hoped for a better outcome to her pragmatic policy of supporting Henry and trusting in the passage of time. There was even a bonus, for Mary, now the widowed Queen of France, had shocked the political establishment and escaped any future elderly or repulsive husbands by marrying Charles Brandon, Duke of Suffolk, the man sent by Henry to escort her home and for whom she declared she had 'always been of a good mind'. Such a union was incredibly risky since Henry's fury at losing a marriageable sister might result in the ruin or imprisonment of the errant couple. But Mary had taken out insurance. She had made her brother promise that if she accepted Louis XII without fuss, she could choose her next spouse for herself. For his part, Suffolk pleaded that 'the Queen would never let me [be] in rest till I had granted her to be married'. Eventually, after Mary and Suffolk took the sensible step of enlisting Wolsey's aid and making sure that Henry received valuable tokens of their affection, among which was a 'diamond with a great pearl', and having pledged to pay him over £24,000 in yearly instalments to reimburse him for her dowry, the king welcomed his favourite sister back to England. Since she and Mary had been friends for many years, it was good for Katherine to have her home again, particularly with the prospect of childbirth ahead.

Then, on 18 February 1516, came a miracle. The child was born and the child lived. The cradle was empty no longer. Just one thing prevented unalloyed euphoria: the child was a girl, whom the royal couple named Mary, possibly after Henry's sister. For Katherine simply to be a mother again brought great happiness; her love for her daughter was deep, intense and unwavering. While it was assumed that it would have been better for the country and for Henry had the infant who nestled contentedly in Katherine's arms been a boy, at least the baby was healthy and looked likely to live, and it was that the king seized upon. When congratulated by the Venetian ambassador who tactlessly added that no doubt everyone 'would have been yet more pleased had the child been a son', Henry pointed out that there was still plenty of time for that. 'We are both young,' he said. 'If it was a daughter this time, by the grace of God the sons will follow.' Even within Katherine's family, there were precedents: Queen Isabella's first child had been a daughter as had Juana's, and both women had gone on to produce male offspring (two in Juana's case). Katherine could well do the same.

However, with memories of Prince Henry's unexpected and unexplained death still raw, it was prudent to baptise and confirm the new baby quickly to protect her soul. Although a girl, Mary was the king's daughter and, as things stood, heir to everything her father possessed, so all was done in style. Just a couple of days old, Mary was carried in procession along the enclosed gallery which linked the palace to the adjacent Church of the Observant Friars. Once officially christened at the church door, little Mary was carried by the Countess of Surrey into the main body of the church, an interior which was lit by hundreds of flickering candles and which was decorated in the baby's honour with 'cloth of needlework garnished with precious stones and pearls'. Four grandees of Henry's court, including Sir Thomas Boleyn, held the special canopy aloft over Mary's head; the Duke of Norfolk walked in front of her, the Duke of Suffolk behind, for this was just as much a political occasion as it was a church service. Therefore, although the aristocratic Duchess of Norfolk and Elizabeth of York's sister were two of Mary's godmothers, her godfather was none other than Thomas Wolsey, son of a butcher but now Cardinal Wolsey, a prince of the Church, a man whose meteoric rise seemed unstoppable.

Wolsey had pride of place, raised above the old nobility, his prominence in Henry's affections and trust glaringly apparent, but other leading figures also played their part in Mary's first real entry into the universal church that was to become the central core of her existence. The Marquis of Dorset carried the salt, which was sprinkled at the appropriate moment to safeguard the child from evil; the Earl of Surrey sported a huge taper; the superbly crafted basin for the font was borne by the Earl of Devonshire, assisted by Lord Herbert. Katherine's friend, Margaret Pole, now Countess of Salisbury, was there too. She is described in the documents as 'godmother at the bishopping' (the confirmation). Finally, after a triumphant *Te Deum* sung by the choir, the procession wound its way back along the gravelled walkway into the palace and little Mary could be returned to the nursery.

So, as she gazed tenderly upon her child, the new Princess Mary (for Henry's sister, despite Louis XII's death and her second marriage to the Duke of Suffolk, was always known in court circles, and in official documents, as Mary, 'the French Queen'), Katherine could be forgiven for thinking that her fortunes were changing. She had carried this latest baby full term, maybe the sons really would follow, and the diplomatic pattern had changed back to what she always wanted it to be. But grief was soon knocking at the door yet again. As soon as she was judged sufficiently recovered after the birth, Katherine was given terrible news, news that had been deliberately withheld from her because it had reached England 'on the eve of her delivery': Ferdinand, her father, was dead.

The ever-faithful John Stile had sent Henry a full report from Spain. Enjoying himself to the last, indulging in his favourite pastimes of hunting and hawking, spurning the advice of his doctors to take more rest, Ferdinand was travelling towards Seville when he became ill. He died on 23 January 1516 in the small town of Madrigalejo. He had suffered periodic bouts of ill health for the past three or four years but this final illness had caught his court, as well as himself, unawares. With few of his nobles present, but with Queen Germaine at his side, Ferdinand signed his will. It was uncontroversial. His body was to be taken to Granada to lie next to that of Isabella; he left lands in Naples as well as money to Juana's second son, his namesake, Prince Ferdinand; there were various bequests to Germaine and others. But it was to Juana that he bequeathed all his lands. Since, though, she was 'defecte of wysdom', the governor of all her realms was to be her eldest son, Charles.

Suddenly there was a new player on the international stage, completing a triumvirate of ambitious rival young monarchs. At sixteen, he was the youngest of the three. Tall, thin, gawky and with the pronounced

Habsburg lower jaw, his appearance was not immediately appealing. Yet he was fond of sport, just as accomplished and adept a jouster and hunter as his counterparts, Francis and Henry. Studious, and imbued with the chivalric and religious values of the Order of the Golden Fleece, he was to become a formidable opponent in peace and war.

Described by the Spanish Bishop of Badajoz as having 'good parts' but 'kept too much isolated from the world', Charles himself was largely unknown. Henry had met him briefly when indulging in the French wars. Juana had not seen him for ten years; Katherine had never seen him at all. His upbringing, his education and his tastes were Burgundian; indeed, he had barely left Burgundian soil. Spain, for him, was a faraway country; he did not even speak the language. Nevertheless, he was Juana's heir and the new ruler of Ferdinand's Aragon. And, with his mother's incarceration and Ferdinand's death, he became Katherine's key human link to her homeland and her heritage.

Ferdinand, in view of his grandson's 'tender age', and the fact that Charles was still in the Netherlands, used the vehicle of his last testament to appoint Cardinal Cisneros to rule Castile and the Archbishop of Saragossa to rule Aragon until things were sorted out. Charles was indeed of 'tender age', but there is a telling, if apocryphal, story in the Venetian archives which, if true, gives us a clue as to what the person who would have such an influence upon Europe and, on a more personal note, upon Katherine and Juana, was really like.

Upon hearing of Henry's sister's marriage with Louis XII, we read, Charles had stormed into his council chamber to question, and berate, his advisers. Angered that the woman to whom he was himself betrothed should slip away from him, he had demanded explanations. The councillors had tried to console him by saying that he was still young and that because Louis was 'the first King in Christendom ... it rests with him to take for his queen any woman he pleases'. This conciliatory but condescending reply served only to infuriate Charles, who had immediately ordered his servants to buy a young hawk he had seen from his window. Charles then took the bird into the council room and started picking out the feathers from its breast. When the horrified advisers asked him what he was doing, his reply speaks volumes:

Thou askest me why I plucked this hawk; he is young, you see, and has not yet been trained, and because he is young he is held in small account, and because he is young he squeaked not when I plucked him. Thus you have done by me: I am young, you have plucked me at your good pleasure; and because I was young I knew not how to complain; but bear in mind that for the future I shall pluck you.

Indeed he would. On coming of age in January 1515, he had changed the personnel of his council and his household and, while he retained his love for his aunt Margaret, her days as Regent of the Netherlands were, for the moment anyway, over.

Initially, however, it was his mother whom he 'plucked'. Stories of Juana's incapacity had been allowed to circulate periodically. John Stile had heard them, and so had the Venetians. In one dispatch back to Venice, the ambassador had written that Juana was 'considered mad and the king [Ferdinand] says so'. Ferdinand had said so for some years; it was only because of her alleged madness that he had been able to rule Castile in her name. The Venetians had been treated to a very full account of just how mad poor Juana was. 'She expects her husband to come to life again,' continued the ambassador, 'and carries his body about with her in a coffin.' It got worse: 'she says that this resurrection will take place at the end of ten years'. But the king who had said she was unbalanced was dead. Juana's future now lay in her son's hands.

So, as Katherine grieved for her father, her nephew was deciding the fate of her sister. If Katherine, in her sorrow, tried to write to Juana in an effort to bring mutual consolation – and there is no proof that she did – it would have been to no avail. As young brides far from home, they had communicated, occasionally simply with notes about their own health, but such personal sisterly correspondence had dwindled after Philip's death; when Katherine had written to her sister after that, it had been to urge marriage with Henry VII. Sometimes Ferdinand had told Juana what was going on outside the castle walls at Tordesillas, as he had early on in Katherine's marriage to Henry, and he had always scrupulously included Juana's name in official treaties and documents, but he was never inclined to allow Juana to write to people, even her own sisters, herself. Indeed, once she was imprisoned in Tordesillas, there are no records of her ever writing anything again. And this precedent was one which Charles intended to continue.

For upon one thing Charles was determined: he, not Juana, would rule Spain. At the solemn funeral requiem held for Ferdinand in Brussels, he accepted the acclamations for 'Queen Juana and King Charles' but there could be no doubt where the true power would lie. This was to be no equal partnership. Juana, friendless and helpless, deliberately left ignorant of Ferdinand's death in case it made her more truculent, was to find that losing her father merely meant that her son would take over the role of gaoler that he had vacated. The true irony is that in the man who could imprison his own mother, Katherine would one day gain the most supportive and powerful of protectors.

The Twisting Path

While Katherine enjoyed motherhood, cherishing every minute she could spend with her baby daughter, her nephew Charles was beginning to plan for the future. Scarcely had he officially come of age within the Netherlands than his responsibilities had spiralled with the news of Ferdinand's death. Obviously he would have to travel to Spain to take up his kingship, but that could not happen before detailed arrangements had been put in place for his journey. In the meantime, his inheritance included a duty towards the mother he had been brought up to believe was mentally deranged. Duty mattered to Charles just as much as it did to his aunt, Katherine; as a boy his tutors, including Adrian of Utrecht, had inculcated a clear sense of his obligations towards God and towards the realms which God had entrusted to his care.

Until he could meet his mother again, and see her condition for himself, he relied on Cardinal Cisneros to maintain the status quo in Castile, although Charles sent Adrian of Utrecht to act as a second regent.

By then Juana was thirty-seven. She had spent the last seven years at Tordesillas, in the charge of her late father's appointee, Mosen Ferrer. As a Spanish princess, she had travelled with her mother throughout the royal domains; she had been present when Granada had fallen; she had lived at the Burgundian court as a young wife and mother; she had attended jousts, banquets, masques; she had been fêted in processions; she had been to France, to England. Now her world had shrunk to only two rooms: a large chamber overlooking the river and a smaller one close to it. Very, very occasionally, Ferrer had allowed her to visit the neighbouring convent for prayers with the sisters of St Clare. The nuns' proximity gave her comfort and peace and she remained interested in the convent's affairs for many years. Sometimes Ferdinand had come to see her; sometimes he had sent her 'an object of gold or some jewellery to gladden her heart', as her gaoler explained to Charles. Otherwise, one day was very much like another for her. She could sit, she could talk to her daughter, Catalina, she could sleep, she could read.

An inventory of her possessions shows us that at Tordesillas she had over a hundred books, mostly religious in nature, among which were Books of Hours, missals and treatises on suffering or contemplation. Queen Isabella, no stranger to suffering herself, would have been gratified by her daughter's choice of reading material. Sometimes, however, Juana could bear her situation no longer. Then, when no one took any notice of her complaints or demands, sheer frustration drove her to try her usual tactics of emotional blackmail: refusing sleep or food, even attacking the women set to guard her. When that happened, Ferrer had found his own methods of controlling her.

As the months had turned to years, rumours that he was mishandling his royal prisoner had started to spread within the town. Things had come to a head when news of Ferdinand's death reached the townsfolk. What had been subdued murmurings turned into a torrent of concern; there were riots, local people turned Ferrer out of the castle, priests were brought in to 'heal' the queen. If the events were perplexing to Juana, Charles found them infuriating. Disorder was not something he would tolerate; neither would Cisneros.

Dispatched by the cardinal to quell disturbances and restore equilibrium, the Bishop of Mallorca was horrified at what he heard about Ferrer. Upon reading the bishop's report, Cisneros, not a man noted for sentimentality, was equally horrified. On his orders, Ferrer was no longer allowed anywhere near the queen, Cisneros appointing Hernan, Duke of Estrada in his place and sending details of what had been going on to Charles.

That the information uncovered by the good bishop was disturbing is substantiated by Ferrer's own grovelling letter to Cisneros pleading for his old post back. He whined that those who spoke against him did so only from 'malice and envy'. His enemies were pretending that it was because of him that Juana had not been 'restored to health' and that she had been kept 'a prisoner', he said. In reality, he went on, her 'condition and infirmity' were 'well-known'; it was nothing to do with him. Indeed, he protested self-righteously, during his years in control, Juana's household had been 'governed like a monastery'. He had 'never been in fault or committed any error towards her'; Ferdinand 'would never have shown ... such confidence' in him had he really been 'so bad'; he had only acted upon Ferdinand's orders. His excuses and whining self-pity went on and on. The truth was that Ferrer had treated Juana abominably.

While Charles had been growing up in Burgundy, and Katherine settling down to widowhood and then remarriage in England, Juana was being systematically ill-treated. There is a telling section in Ferrer's letter which proves it:

> ... if God created her such as she is, it is impossible to effect more than His Divine Majesty [Ferdinand] permits and vouchsafes, and the King her father could never do more until, to prevent her from destroying herself by abstinence from food, as often as her will was not done, he had to order that she was to be put to the rack to preserve her life. Was that my fault?

In fact, it is more likely that Juana was beaten rather than racked in the traditional sense, but there can be little doubt that she was physically abused, and with Ferdinand's knowledge and consent – for even Ferrer would never have dared to lay hands upon his queen entirely of his own volition.

Charles, despite all his professions of honour and chivalry, did not rush to his mother's rescue, or try to find out why she had gone on hunger strike. Instead, his response to Cisneros is clinical in tone. He was, he regretted, very 'occupied' with many 'great affairs'. Nevertheless he had 'come to a conclusion' on the three matters which he felt stood 'in the greatest need to be decided at once'. One of those was 'the custody of the Queen my lady, which on account of the difference of opinions is very necessary'. Interestingly, he did not elaborate on whether the 'difference of opinions' was about whether Juana really was deranged, or whether it was simply that opinions differed on her care; he was more likely to be bothered about the latter. When time permitted, he would choose a suitable person to run his mother's establishment, he said, but until then he 'must beg and command' that Cisneros should make various arrangements himself. Charles outlined somewhat circuitously what those arrangements should be.

The cardinal was to ensure that 'whilst she is to be treated well, she be so well guarded and watched that if any persons should endeavour to counteract my good intentions, they shall be prevented from doing so. In this respect great vigilance is necessary.' In other words, Juana was to be kept in continued seclusion, well away from possible sympathisers; and Charles made it plain that anyone who interfered would incur his wrath: 'Since it belongs to nobody more than to myself to take care of the honour, contentment, and consolation of the Queen my lady, those who endeavour to meddle [in this affair] cannot have any good intentions.' And when Cisneros, unflinching and fearless, asked his envoy, Lopez de Ayala, to tell Charles about 'the health of the Queen', Ayala was warned off by two of Charles's closest advisers. They were 'of the opinion', said Ayala, that 'I should not speak about it to the King. So I did not.' Ayala confided that many about Charles discussed Juana's health but, he said, it was 'not because they wish it'. For him to try to fulfil Cisneros's request and talk to Charles about his mother again, he thought, would be risky: 'They are very dangerous people, and one must hold one's tongue here.' Ayala held his tongue. And Juana remained confined at Tordesillas.

Katherine, of course, knew nothing. Other than their brief reunion at Windsor ten years previously, the sisters had enjoyed little personal contact apart from Katherine's attempts to persuade the widowed Juana to marry Henry VII. Just as Katherine had then accepted her father's account of Juana's state of mind, she would now accept Charles's version. Her life revolved around being Henry's wife, Mary's mother and England's queen; she could surely trust Charles to look after his mother without further interference.

As time passed, Katherine's own life saw changes, some personal, some political, some concerning the people around her. Maria de Salinas was with her less frequently and Friar Diego was not with her at all. Maria had married Lord Willoughby, which meant she was often away from court. Katherine did her best for her former attendant and friend: on the document which details Maria's jointure lands, there is evidence of the involvement of Katherine and her council, suggesting that the queen was determined to ensure that Maria received a fair financial settlement. In matters of money, Katherine could be highly practical. Whereas Maria's exit had been happy and voluntary, Diego left unwillingly and in disgrace after being accused and convicted of fornication. Fuensalida, the former Spanish ambassador, would have been overjoyed at such an outcome for the man he considered a malign influence upon Katherine; she was dismayed.

Katherine's relationship with Henry had also undergone important changes. While good, it was no longer what it had once been. Elizabeth Blount was still very much in Henry's affections, and so was Wolsey. The cardinal's presence was constant and highly visible. At one time, ambassadors had rushed to see the queen, but now it was Wolsey who was their first target, for it is Wolsey, the Venetian ambassador confides, 'who really seems to rule all England'. A year or so later, the ambassador went further, insisting that 'the King pays the Cardinal such respect that he speaks only through his [Wolsey's] mouth'. The days when Katherine had been Henry's sole confidante had ended, but she comforted herself with the knowledge that she was his wife, and that no one could part those whom God had joined. And she had not given up hope of further conception; the longed-for son might yet come.

In the meantime, she had her queenly duties to perform. One of those was to speak up for the imprisoned and condemned. In early May 1517, London was suddenly gripped by riots that came to be known as 'Evil May Day'. The cause of the unrest lay in the citizens' distrust of foreigners, whom they believed to be under-cutting them in trade, taking the bread from the mouths of their children, seducing their women. So many salacious stories, rumours and scandals about the hated incomers spread that riots broke out in the streets. Many of the malcontents were young apprentices fearful for their livelihood, others came into the city and its suburbs from neighbouring areas to join in the demonstrations. The scale of the disturbances grew frightening. The Portuguese ambassador was considered lucky to have escaped with his life after being viciously attacked, Wolsey had his dwelling protected by cannon and troops, houses were sacked, people threatened, prisoners freed.

Henry, then at Richmond, was furious. He would not countenance lawlessness on such a scale, especially if it jeopardised trade. The mayor struggled to control the situation, but it took troops finally to quell the troubles. Punishment was swift and brutal, with several of the rioters being hung, drawn and quartered. Not all were executed, however. About three hundred, including eleven women, were captured and imprisoned, their lives in the balance.

It was up to Henry to decide whether they would live or die. Katherine accompanied Henry, Wolsey and leading members of the court to Westminster Hall, where he would decree the prisoners' fate. The huge and ancient hall, with its towering wooden roof and angel buttresses, was draped with shimmering tapestries and hangings of cloth of gold and brocade. When the bound, pitiful captives were led in, dressed only in their shirts and with ropes around their necks to signify their likely end, they were left in no doubt as to the awesome power and majesty that was Henry's. Seated on a throne beneath his cloth of estate, Henry watched impassively as the frightened horde knelt before him begging for mercy. It was then that Katherine, 'with tears in her eyes and on her bended knees', begged alongside them. So did Wolsey, so did many of the lords, but it was Katherine's entreaties that most impressed the papal nuncio who witnessed the affecting scene. She was, he said, 'our most serene and compassionate Queen'. Henry, who had carefully stage-managed the proceedings to display to the world his magnanimity and mercy and so bolster his reputation for justice, allowed himself to be moved by these pleas. He spared the prisoners' lives, an action 'so much to the popular satisfaction, that everybody wept for joy'.

Katherine's tears, though, may also have been shed for an additional reason: she had just heard that her sister, Maria, Queen of Portugal, had died. Now only Katherine and Juana were left of the Catholic Monarchs' five children. No one observing her gracious, regal and gentle demeanour as she knelt at her husband's feet in Westminster Hall would have guessed at her own grief; she knew that personal feelings must never interfere with how she behaved in public. The mask must always remain in place.

When Katherine missed a period some months later, any tears were those of joy. Both she and the king almost held their breath, neither daring to proclaim the glad tidings publicly. The Venetian ambassador,

Giustinian, always a man with an ear to the ground, heard court gossip in June 1518 which, he said, was 'confirmed to him by a trustworthy person'. For once, he was a trifle late off the mark, for Richard Pace, Henry's secretary and Wolsey's confidant, had written to the cardinal about the rumours in April. 'It is secretly said', Pace reported, 'that the Queen is with child', adding that he prayed 'heartily that it may be a prince to the surety and universal comfort of the realm'.

No one could have prayed for that more earnestly than Katherine and Henry. Now thirty-two years old, there was no guarantee that she would become pregnant after this. So Henry treated her tenderly, saying nothing to his court or to the assortment of ambassadors eager to glean up-to-date information to send back to their governments. Katherine said nothing to anyone either, unless to God through her prayers. But Henry did confide in someone: Wolsey.

Henry hated writing, finding the process 'tedious and painful'. Only if the matter was highly sensitive would he put pen to paper himself. In 1518, he settled down at his ornate writing desk, possibly even at the glorious gilded and painted leather-covered walnut desk which is decorated with classical gods, the royal arms, his own and Katherine's initials and the pomegranate of Granada, and which we can still see. In his note to Wolsey we glimpse the vulnerable, human side of the king that Katherine knew in the early days of their marriage. In this letter, Henry told his favourite minister that

> two things there be which be so secret that they cause me at this time to write to you myself; the one is that I trust the queen my wife be with child; the other is chief cause why I am sloth to repair to London ward, by cause about this time is partly of her dangerous times, and by cause of that, I would remove her as little as I may now. My lord, I write thus unto you, not as an ensured thing, but as a thing wherein I have great hope and likelihood ...

His 'great hope and likelihood' were fulfilled in early July when he met a radiant Katherine at Woodstock near Oxford. Pace gave the news to Wolsey: 'the Queen welcomed him with a good belly'. Now the world would know, as a jubilant *Te Deum* was sung in St Paul's, the church where Katherine had married Arthur sixteen years previously.

Katherine had a wonderful summer. Her daughter, Princess Mary, continued to thrive and her own stomach grew larger and larger. Henry hunted, although never too far from where his wife was, and she even risked hunting herself in the middle of July. The only cloud on the horizon was a return of the dreaded sweating sickness, a terrible disease that could strike and kill within hours. Henry, always pathologically afraid of illness, made sure he and Katherine were as far away from it as possible as they moved gradually towards Greenwich where Katherine was due to give birth. When one of Princess Mary's servants became ill with 'a hot ague', the princess was moved on Henry's orders from one palace to another; as his only heir, so far, the king was taking no more chances with his daughter than he was with his wife even though the servant later recovered completely.

Once back at Greenwich, Katherine could begin to rest, to prepare herself for the ordeal and the risks of childbirth. As usual, her apartments were made ready, her bed draped with a purple tissue covering edged with ermine, a wide pillow of similar material at its head, and with a crimson cloth of estate above it. Every comfort was provided but, at the beginning of November 1518, Giustinian sent a report back to Venice. His bald statement tells us what had happened: 'In the past night the Queen had been delivered of a daughter, to the vexation of everybody. Never had the kingdom so anxiously desired anything as it did a prince.'

The baby was either stillborn or died within days of her birth. Katherine, weak and anguished, knew she had failed yet again. We have no extant comment from Henry. He had ordered the font from Canterbury Cathedral brought to the palace to be ready for his son's christening; it had to be returned ignominiously, transport alone costing £4. The bed coverings were taken back to Katherine's London residence of Baynard's Castle where they fell into decay; the fur ripped out, the sumptuous cloth allowed to perish.

Yet Katherine still hoped and hoped that her prayers would be answered. Her mother's struggle for the throne, the fight to capture Granada, her own determination to marry Henry after Arthur's death – there were so many instances in her own experience that showed how triumph could be snatched from disaster. At almost thirty-three years old, her child-bearing years were drawing to a close but there was still some time left. So she went on pilgrimages, she attended Mass after Mass, and she prayed for hour upon hour within the confines of her own rooms. And, as she glanced about her, she could take comfort from familiar items that always came with her as she travelled from palace to palace.

Tapestries of Hercules and Jason adorned the walls, and there were hangings intricately embroidered with the arms of England and Spain, a crown imperial, roses, fleur-de-lys, her beloved pomegranates. There was a small portrait of herself with Henry. There was a picture of St Francis; one of the martyrdom of St Katherine; several of the Virgin Mary, some with Mary's mother, St Anne, others in which Mary held her son in her arms; another of Mary and Joseph. There was a wonderful ivory diptych with Mary and Christ on one side and with (unspecified) religious images on the other. And there was one picture to inspire Katherine: a picture 'of a Quene making peticion to Oure Ladye and Saynte Elizabethe'. St Elizabeth, a god-fearing and righteous woman, together with her equally upright husband, Zaccharius, loved God all their lives but yearned for a child. God answered their entreaties. Though Elizabeth was past the menopause, she became the mother of John the Baptist. Miracles could happen.

As time passed with no miracle for her, Katherine lavished her love and her attention on the one child she had, Princess Mary. The queen had not been able to suckle her daughter herself, bowing to the popular belief that such an activity would hinder further pregnancy – and Katherine's existence was so much geared towards promoting yet another pregnancy. Nor could Katherine have day-to-day care of her child. Instead Mary had a wet-nurse and her own small household, with Elizabeth Denton in charge of the nursery at first, followed by Margaret, Lady Brian, who was herself replaced, if spasmodically, by Katherine's dear friend, Margaret Pole, Countess of Salisbury. And, as Henry's only child, Mary was very much a darling of the court. At New Year, she was given gifts as expensive and elaborate as many presented to her parents; showing respect to such an important infant was only prudent. In 1518, Mary, 'the French Queen', now Duchess of Suffolk with a little girl of her own, sent her niece a 'pomander of gold', Wolsey gave a golden cup, while two smocks were the practical present sent by Lady Morley, the woman whose daughter would one day marry Anne Boleyn's only brother, George.

To Katherine's delight, Mary was very often with her parents in these early years. Whatever happened in the future, whether her prayers for a son were answered or not, this little gem of a daughter was nurtured and educated to become a queen. She might, after all, be Henry's only heir.

Both Katherine and Henry genuinely respected learning. Their court was once described by Erasmus as 'more a university than a court' because so many men of letters found employment or patronage through the king or queen. It was 'an example to the rest of Christendom for learning and piety', asserted the oily-tongued scholar with the thick slice of flattery characteristic of a man always looking for someone to put food on his plate and money in his purse; in the same letter (which was, incidentally, written to the king himself) he thanks Henry for his present, saying that it was 'very agreeable to him'. Nevertheless, Erasmus did have a valid point. Lord Mountjoy, Katherine's chamberlain, was himself a keen and generous patron of the wise and of the brilliant; Thomas More, renowned for his erudition and his deep personal integrity, and now one of Henry's secretaries, was fast becoming a fixture within the king's orbit; Thomas Linacre, a man who had once unsuccessfully aspired to tutor Prince Arthur, was one of Henry's physicians; Richard Pace, also a man of distinction, was among Henry's secretaries. As for Katherine herself, she was 'not only a miracle of learning, but is not less pious than learned', Erasmus enthused; since the letter in which he wrote of the queen is a more private one, his admiration for her is likely to be genuine.

We will never know for sure the names of those chosen to educate Mary. Possibly her chaplain or Lady Brian gave her the rudiments of letters, maybe using the primer given to her as a toddler by the Duchess of Norfolk. Some historians think that Katherine herself taught her daughter in the early years. One letter she sent to Mary appears to suggest that she did. 'As for your writing in Lattine', she wrote, 'I am glad that you chaunge frome me to Maister Federston, for that shall doo you moche good, to learn by him to write right.'

In 1523, though, Katherine definitely took a very proactive part in planning Mary's future. She commissioned a treatise on female education, *De Institutione Feminae Christianae* ('The Education of a Christian Woman') from her fellow-Spaniard Juan Luis Vives. He went on to pen various tracts, listing works the young princess should study, such as those by classical authors like Seneca, Plato and Cicero as well as More's *Utopia*; he also noted works from which she should be protected, such as tales of romance. Vives considered Latin and Greek vital components of a student's education; religion and religious authors like St Augustine were, naturally, central as well. And since housewifely skills also had merit, everything was reminiscent of Katherine's own upbringing under Isabella's keen eye. Katherine had done well for her daughter.

Despite her disappointment over her latest stillbirth, Katherine's life settled into a calm routine as she fulfilled the duties of wife, mother and queen. She had her prayers, she had her pilgrimages, she had her daughter. Her relationship with Henry would never be as it was in the early days of their marriage when he had been her Loyal Heart and she his friend and adviser as well as his wife, but they enjoyed a companionable existence, even if both still yearned for the son that would mean so much. Although only a consort, Katherine enjoyed a more productive, more interesting and more contented life than her sister. But, perhaps when Charles finally saw the mother who had sailed away from him before his sixth birthday, Juana's fortunes would change for the better. Maybe she would even leave Tordesillas and take her place in the world again. It all depended on Charles.

PART V

The Sky Darkens

The Man of the Moment

As Katherine performed her usual round of royal duties, Juana received visitors. On a bitterly cold November day in 1517, a small retinue arrived at Tordesillas. Charles, accompanied by his elder sister, Eleanor, had come to see their mother. The last time they had all met was when Juana and Philip had left the Netherlands to take up the throne of Castile upon Isabella's death. Then, Eleanor had been a little girl of almost eight, her brother two years younger. Now, Charles was a king in his own right, and Eleanor about to become a queen. She was to replace Juana's sister, Maria, as Queen of Portugal. Manuel II, having already married two sisters, was quite happy to marry his niece.

Brother and sister had left the Burgundian Netherlands, the land of their birth, early in November, but the seas were stormy and their fleet of forty ships was soon battered and bruised by the howling gales and tossing waves. Somehow, after a horrendous journey of ten days, they had arrived on Spanish soil and travelled in easy stages to Tordesillas for their first glimpse of the mother they could barely remember and their sister, Catalina, whom they had never seen before. Soon they would also meet their other sibling, Prince Ferdinand, although Charles, recognising a potential rival, was swift to endow his younger brother with some of his Habsburg estates, intending eventually to dispatch him to Germany.

Juana's remaining two children, Maria and Isabella, had already begun new lives when Charles and Eleanor dismounted at Tordesillas. When she was eight, Maria had been sent off to join her grandfather, Maximilian, in the Habsburg lands of the Holy Roman Empire, eventually becoming Queen of Hungary; Isabella was married to King Christian II of Denmark, a union destined to bring the young bride nothing but constant misery.

Still, Juana did at least have Charles and Eleanor. Yet both connived in keeping her ignorant of what was going on in the world outside the walls of Tordesillas. Charles, she was told, had come to Spain entirely for her sake: he intended to 'see that satisfaction be given to her' regarding any complaints she might have about her treatment. Thus, Charles's first meeting with her was based upon a lie, one in which he willingly connived, for he did not tell her that he was really there to claim her crowns for himself because Ferdinand was dead. For that was indeed why Charles had come. Just as she and Philip had needed the acclamations of the various Cortes upon their accession, so did he. And it was politic that it did at least look as if his mother had given him her blessing and that she was happy for him to take up the cares of state with which she could not be burdened. It was also politic for Charles to give the appearance of being devoted to his mother's welfare, a feat he managed to perfection. Katherine, in England, never thought to question her nephew's concern for her sister; she had no inkling that she should.

Quite how Charles and Eleanor expected their mother to behave as they went into her room on that November day is unrecorded. If they expected to view a deranged woman, that did not happen. She did not always dress as a queen, she ate erratically and was often reluctant to hear Mass (a trait which worried her devout son just as much as, if not more than, her physical state), but she was far from 'the wretched brain-sick Queen' mournfully described by one of Charles's most thorough but sympathetic biographers. We will never know what she said to her son but, since she did not know that her own father had died over a year before, she could hardly surrender authority to Charles when she believed that Ferdinand was exercising it on her behalf.

That did not stop Charles claiming it, although he found the Cortes more reluctant to acknowledge his rule than he had anticipated, especially since some grandees were suspicious of Juana's true mental condition. Some, too, disliked the concept of a foreign monarch who knew nothing about Spain and its customs, whose native language was not Spanish, and whose advisers were rapacious Burgundians. Indeed, many would have preferred Charles's brother, who had spent his entire life in

Spain; sending Prince Ferdinand out of the country was a wise move. Nevertheless, over the coming months, despite simmering if underlying discontent, Charles gained the authorisations he required. He could now turn his attention to how to treat his mother. He began by pensioning off Cisneros's choice of 'governor' (i.e. gaoler), Hernan, Duke of Estrada, replacing him with the Marquis of Denia and his wife, Francisca, both former servants of Ferdinand and Isabella, and both firm supporters of Charles's cause. As a consequence, Juana's everyday life was about to get worse, restrictions tighter and isolation greater.

Katherine, about to confront troubles of her own, had no conception of those plaguing her sister. There was still no correspondence between the two. Even had Katherine sent letters, Juana's 'guardians' are unlikely to have allowed her to receive them, unless heavily censored. Keeping her in seclusion, in total ignorance of major events, made her easier to control. As Denia confirmed in one of his letters to Charles, that was why she had not been told of Ferdinand's death:

I have told the Queen our lady that the King my lord, her father, is alive, because whenever anything that is done displeases her Highness, I say that the King orders and commands it so; for the love she bears him makes it easier to her to endure it than it would be if she knew that he is dead.

As Denia let slip, he knew that she had much 'to endure'.

Yet, Juana's respect for her father was not so deep-rooted, nor her spirit so quelled, that she never questioned what she had done to justify her imprisonment. She wanted to return to the world, even perhaps to play a part in government. Again, Denia left Charles in no doubt about what his mother was feeling:

She ordered me to write to the King, her lord [Ferdinand] telling him that she can no longer bear the life she leads, that it is so long a time that he has kept her locked up and a prisoner, and that being his daughter, he ought to treat her in a better manner; that she wished to live where she could know what was going on, and see the nobles of the kingdom.

As always, her pleas were ignored.

In fact, the regime instituted by Charles's choice of gaoler was worse than that she had suffered under Ferrer. When he had been in charge, Juana had been allowed to visit the convent occasionally. Such outings stopped almost entirely once Denia took the helm, though Juana frequently demanded them. 'She desires much to go out', usually to the nearby convent on holy days such as the 'day of All Saints', he informed his master. Once she 'ordered that her dresses be cleaned' so that they were ready for her; once she 'dressed and put her hood over her head' so that she could leave the castle. And, as determined as she always had been to get her own way, she continued to pester him. In every case, Denia found reasons to thwart her. 'It was not convenient,' he said, or there was disease around. 'I intend to prevent her by all means from going out,' he told Charles, but if that proved 'impossible' it would be done 'in such a way that, with the help of God, no inconvenience will be the consequence'.

Denia and Charles knew only too well what such 'inconvenience' meant: if she was seen in public, the elaborate fiction that she was completely and utterly insane would unravel. Her conversations with Denia, all of which he meticulously reported to her son, showed just how sane she actually was. She asked about her family, she asked about her servants' wages, she asked for money, she asked to see leading nobles, she asked how her kingdoms fared. Almost ten years' incarceration were beginning to take their toll – she was afraid that Prince Ferdinand might be given 'something to kill him', for example – but she was not the constantly unbalanced creature that carefully phrased propaganda promulgated.

Secrecy was to be the order of the day. In one of his first letters to Denia, Charles stressed just that. The marquis was not 'to speak or write anything concerning her Highness to any other person except to me', Charles emphasised, and such letters should be sent only 'by trusty messengers'. Moreover, whenever Denia spoke to Juana, he should ensure that no one heard what was going on. 'The affairs of her Highness being of such kind as you know, you must not consent that any of the women or any other person be present when she speaks to you about them,' Charles instructed. Quickly Denia affirmed that Charles could

'rest assured' that 'precaution is and will be observed ... by not per-
mitting anyone to be present when her Highness speaks to me, as well
as by keeping the secret, as it stands to reason'. In fact, he said that 'for
writing certain things', he would 'like to have a cipher'. Denia is silent
on whether the 'secret' was that Juana was so unbalanced that she was
an embarrassment to herself and others, or that she was in fact quite
sane. It is left to us to make up our minds.

Denia understood completely that what went on at Tordesillas was
to be kept confidential, even from Juana's other children. When Prince
Ferdinand left the country, Denia thought he should send a note of
farewell, a 'message of courtesy', the essence of which he was quick to
convey to Charles:

> I wrote to him that the Queen our lady was better treated than she
> had been before, thinking it advantageous to your Highness that
> the better treatment of her highness should be known in these
> kingdoms, and everywhere else, and that it was due to your High-
> ness. Besides this I wrote to the senor Infante on the occasion of
> his departure what a good vassal and servant of your Highness
> ought to write, but if he had remained a hundred years in these
> kingdoms I should not have written or told him a word of what is
> going on here.

Denia became obsessed with the need for stealth, especially because
Juana 'speaks words to move stones'. Those words should be for his
implacable ears alone. Therefore he was quick to stop her meeting the
nobles whom she often said she wished to consult, always pretending
that pestilence or distance had stopped them coming. Juana's women,
too, were a perennial problem to him because they went out into the
town and gossiped 'of things which ought not to be known, because in
all that passes here, secrecy indeed is necessary'. He was particularly
worried because one of them was married to an official of the Council
of State who could then hear things that 'ought to be a secret from all,
and much more so from the Members of the Council'. Even if the
women did not indulge in tittle-tattle, and he thought most of them
did, they brought news back from the town to Juana, thus depriving

her 'of her rest and tranquility'. The danger that such news might include the fact of Ferdinand's death did not bear thinking of. Charles's quick response was to dismiss those women thought untrustworthy.

But even with the women dismissed, there were other anxieties for Denia to contend with. A major concern was always illness. As outsiders, doctors could be dangerous. When Juana complained of toothache, Denia's response was that everyone was unwell because the weather was so bad; when Juana felt so awful after suffering 'strong fevers and shiverings' for ten days that she begged for a doctor, Denia refused. The fever subsided, he said. And when Catalina became so ill that he had no option but to seek medical help, Denia sent for Dr Soto, an elderly physician who had accompanied Juana from Burgundy. Denia thought Dr Soto would stay silent in the hope that a small pension he had once received would be reinstated. It was not.

Even if Juana and Catalina seemed healthy, Denia was forever troubled by the spread of plague and disease in the countryside around them. Fearing contagion, he told Charles that he had 'taken measures of great precaution, walling up all the gates of the town, with the exception of two' at which he posted guards. This served only to so upset the townsfolk who were unable to go about their normal business that Denia entreated Charles to send them a personal note of thanks for their cooperation. What really kept Denia awake at night was what he should do if the outside sickness became so bad that Juana had to be moved. How he would keep her away from prying eyes occupied much of his thought, so much so that he was constantly writing to Charles about it.

While Charles pondered over other possible destinations, Juana's existence continued its monotonous pace. She 'lives in her room, goes to bed and gets up, and dines every second day', wrote Denia. Food rarely tempted her, although her gaoler happily reported when she 'improved in eating'. Her religious observances, or apparent lack of them, were a persistent thorn in Denia's flesh. Charles wanted her to hear Mass often. She demurred, unless it was said in a corridor rather than in the room of Denia's choice. Such issues, petty in themselves, were crucial to Juana's self-esteem; religion was the one area which she understood really mattered to those in charge of her, the one area in which she could still defy them. She contrived to get her way: a small chapel was 'constructed out of drapery' in the corridor just where she wanted it. With the hangings in place, she finally consented to hear Mass with Catalina. Receiving the sacrament she 'chanted Paternosters and Ave Marias so loud that they could be heard', wrote an exultant Denia. Charles could rest easy that his mother's soul was being safe-guarded even if her overall welfare was not. Such was his sense of priorities.

Catalina's welfare did trouble Charles, though. Lovingly brought up with most of his siblings by his aunt Margaret, he believed that he cared deeply about family, and about his sisters in particular. The records bulge with affectionate letters he wrote to them. Catalina's plight, growing up in the same bleak castle in which their mother declared herself to be 'locked up and a prisoner', pained him. He immediately set about providing her with all she might need as a royal princess, requesting Denia's wife to send him a list of 'what appears to be necessary'. Once he received it, he said, he would 'provide for it at once'. Yet in a note he sent to Catalina, in which he called her his 'very dear and beloved sister' and signed himself 'your good brother', he also told her to 'follow the council and advice of the Marquis of Denia and of the Marchioness his wife' because 'persons who are so prudent and so much desire to serve' him could not 'err in any respect'.

Perhaps to give Catalina more experiences, and to prepare her for a royal marriage, Charles ordered that she should be removed from Tordesillas six months or so after he first saw her. But Catalina was all that Juana had – even some of the queen's possessions were being spirited away to provide items for Eleanor's trousseau – and her reaction was so pitiful that Catalina was quickly restored to her mother's side. From then on, Juana tried not to let her daughter out of her sight, constantly 'calling for her' if she disappeared even for a minute. She was afraid, she told Denia, that 'the King my lord will take her from me as he has taken the Infante [Prince Ferdinand]'. Should that happen, she said that she would throw herself out of the window or kill herself 'with a knife'. The fact that it was her son not her father who had removed Catalina never occurred to her. Fortunately, Charles heeded her warnings and allowed his sister to stay with their mother for a while yet.

Some years later, when Catalina did leave her in order to marry her Portuguese cousin and become a queen herself, Juana would become almost broken by her grief at the girl's loss. She stayed for twenty-four hours in the corridor from where she had had her last glimpse of her daughter, before shutting herself away and taking to her bed for two days prostrate with despair.

From the moment of his accession, Charles had been in a dilemma over what to do with Juana. She was an enigma, her behaviour so often puzzling and contradictory. Whenever she wanted to get her own way at Tordesillas, she would try anything. She would orchestrate scene after scene; she had temper tantrums; she would not eat regularly; she attacked two of her female attendants with a broom. Yet she would then spend hours in coherent and sensible conversation with Denia and his wife, and Catalina never begged Charles to save her from an irrational mother.

However, if he accepted that Juana was not insane but, with rest and a change of scene, might be able to play some part in ruling her kingdoms, no matter how limited, his own position would be undermined. His father had ruled in partnership with Isabella, but that was not Charles's style. He had a deep inner conviction of his own destiny and monarchy was, in his opinion, a male preserve. 'Think what troubles might not ensue if your sisters and their husbands came to inherit what was yours,' he was later to write to his own son, counselling the young man to take very good care of himself in order to keep such 'troubles' away.

It is true that Charles relied upon his aunt Margaret to act as regent for him in the Netherlands again and would use his son and other female members of his family similarly, but his regents had no inherent right to their position; they worked under his direction and could be removed at the stroke of a pen should he so wish. His mother's case was entirely different because she was a sovereign in her own right. If he released her, there was no saying what she might do; genies do not willingly jump back into bottles. She could even attempt to take over the sole government of her realms herself and, because Charles was highly unpopular with many Castilian grandees, they might support her.

We cannot know whether Charles really did think Juana was totally unbalanced, whether he chose to convince himself that she was, or whether he knew that she was quite sane. All of those are possible, but there is no denying that his mother's supposedly deranged mental state was remarkably convenient for him. So, when he was in a position to change her life, he did not do so. He did not deliberately have her badly handled, indeed he was assiduous in requiring Denia to treat her well, but he did continue her imprisonment.

Maximilian's death in January 1519 made Juana's confinement still more essential because Charles was clearly the prime candidate to take over from his grandfather as Holy Roman Emperor. Success would mean Charles leaving Spain, at least for a while; he did not want existing tensions increasing in his absence. Although the office of emperor was not hereditary, for its holder had to be elected by seven electors, Charles's Habsburg blood, his ownership of land within the conglomerate of states that comprised the Empire, and the astronomical sums he was prepared to advance in bribes, gave him a key advantage over other potential contestants. He knew it; so did Francis I and Henry. And if Charles gained the Empire in addition to his existing territories, France was encircled and England outshone. In such circumstances, the only course open to Francis and Henry was to put themselves forward for election too. But, although Francis lobbied hard and efficiently, 'straining every nerve, by art or cunning' as Wolsey so aptly put it, and promising to double Charles's bribes to those electors who would support him, while Henry also offered promises of cash to anyone who would switch to his side, it was Charles who triumphed. Already the possessor of Spain, the Low Countries, parts of the New World and Italy, and now the Holy Roman Empire, Juana's son was the man of the moment.

Juana was told of his election, but she was not told of Maximilian's death. Instead, she was fed the usual pack of lies. The emperor had abdicated, she was informed, so that Charles could take over. Denia even suggested that she write to Maximilian to thank him for 'the favour' he had shown her son. Such a letter, written to a decaying corpse, really would have illustrated her insanity, but Juana perspicaciously ignored his advice. She suggested that Denia should write it instead, since 'she had never written to him [Maximilan] since the death of the King her lord [Philip]'.

In England, Wolsey celebrated a high Mass at St Paul's in Charles's honour as Henry, who had thought he stood a chance of winning as a compromise candidate, made the best he could of his disappointment. Pointedly, the French ambassador did not attend the service, an action which 'offended many', or so the Venetian representative, Giustinian, assures us. Katherine, naturally, was delighted by her family's increased power and Charles's new position in European politics. Giustinian reported that 'as a Spaniard', Katherine was 'gratified at the success of her nephew'. And that was the rub: Katherine would always be thought of as Spanish. When her father's perfidy had given her little option, she had chosen her husband over her Spanish heritage, but that had not meant that she had relinquished it for ever: if presented with a choice between France and Spain as English allies, she would not have hesitated for an instant. The choice, though, was not hers to make.

And, for a brief while, it looked as though there was no choice to make in any case. Before Charles's coup in securing his new title, Cardinal Wolsey, shamelessly hijacking the pope's plans for a major European truce so that Christians could fight the Muslims rather than each other, had encouraged Henry to abandon thoughts of conflict (always expensive and usually risky) and consider himself a warrior for peace instead of war. The result had been the Treaty of London of 1518, which provided a form of collective security for those who signed: should any be attacked by anyone else, the others would rush to their aid. Because of Wolsey's skilful negotiations, the signatories included the key Italian city states, the pope and Francis, soon to be joined by Charles himself. Henry basked in admiration, his ego satisfied. As 'the chief author of the proceedings', Wolsey fared just as well. 'Nothing pleases him [Wolsey] more', announced Giustinian shrewdly, 'than to be styled the arbitrator of Christendom.'

This rush of universal brotherhood and warmth, moreover, had directly affected Katherine: Princess Mary, although only two, was betrothed to the dauphin. At Greenwich on 5 October 1518, Henry had stood before his throne with Katherine beside him. Princess Mary, wearing 'cloth of gold, with a cap of black velvet on her head, adorned with many jewels' stood in front of her mother. Wolsey, naturally, was there, and so was the pope's representative, Cardinal Campeggio. All listened while the French ambassadors formally asked for Mary's hand in marriage for the dauphin. Henry and Katherine having given their consent, Wolsey gave the little girl a ring containing a huge diamond which, it was said, he had purchased for her himself. Once one of the ambassadors symbolically 'passed it over the second joint' of the child's wedding finger, the betrothal was complete, the ring's shape, a circle without a break, supposed to represent the eternal nature of love.

To cement this new-found amity between the old enemies, Henry and Francis pledged to meet each other near Calais. It was while Wolsey settled down to the complex and convoluted preparations required for this summit that an additional scheme was hatched: on his way to his new empire, Charles should stop off in England and meet Henry. It was in both their interests. Since Charles and Francis were so evenly matched, Henry's backing might tip the balance between them should the current mood of universal brotherhood disintegrate into war. Henry would then be in the envious position of being wooed by both sides and could attempt to exact a high price for his support.

Katherine, never likely to be overjoyed at a French match for her only daughter but thrilled at the idea of bringing together her nephew and her husband, played her part in trying to engineer the encounter. After all, friendship with France was one thing, friendship with Spain quite another; it would be a rekindling of everything she had come to England to foster. And, for the first time since those few precious hours she had spent with Juana all those years ago, Katherine would be able to see a member of her own family. No wonder that when Henry announced to her that they would meet Charles on their way to the rendezvous with Francis, she was ecstatic. 'Raising her eyes to heaven, with clasped hands', she praised God 'for the grace she hoped he would do her that she might see Charles, which was her greatest desire in the world'. And, knowing her husband as she did, she thanked him profusely, making a low curtsy to him as she did so.

The timing of the meeting was tight, largely because Francis could not delay too long because of his wife's pregnancy. The king wanted Queen Claude to be present when he greeted Henry in France, but also wanted to allow time for her to rest before her delivery. Thus, if Charles did not arrive in England by 26 May, there would be no time for talks before Henry would have to start for Calais. Katherine was on tenterhooks as Charles did his utmost to meet the deadline, but was hindered by bad winds and treacherous weather. Finally, his ship scraped into Dover harbour on the twenty-sixth itself.

Katherine was about to have her wish and meet her sister's son for the very first time. What she did not realise as she waited anxiously for him was that, like her sister, her own fate was eventually to rest in his hands.

Fool's Gold

Early on the morning of Whit Sunday, 27 May 1520, Katherine's ladies helped her into a gown of cloth of gold lined with ermine, carefully lowering strings of pearls over her small, neat head. For her, this was a very happy day: she was about to meet Charles, Juana's eldest son, one of the most important men in Europe, for the very first time.

Now thirty-four, worn out by frequent pregnancies, Katherine looked very different to the young girl who had so enchanted everyone when she had arrived from Spain nineteen years before. Her face was plumper, the set of her jaw more decided, her skin less taut, her waistline thicker. But her demeanour was as regal as ever, her manner as gracious, and she had determined to look her best for her sister's son.

She and Henry had left Greenwich on Monday, 21 May to travel to Canterbury where they would wait for Charles to arrive. For Katherine in particular it had been nerve-wracking as no one really knew whether Charles would make the rendezvous before the English party had to set off for Calais, so news of his arrival off Dover on the late afternoon of Saturday the twenty-sixth gladdened her heart. Cardinal Wolsey, Archbishop of York, immediately rushed to welcome him.

Wolsey, the butcher's son, was now rich beyond belief, his hubris increasing as his wealth multiplied. When he travelled, he did so with as much pomp as though he was a king or pope himself, accompanied by a bodyguard of 200 archers and as many as 200 gentlemen dressed in crimson velvet, heavy gold chains gleaming upon their breasts. Even his cardinal's mule was covered in crimson velvet and boasted trappings made of gold. He was, wrote an anonymous French gentleman who watched one of his progresses, 'the proudest prelate that ever breathed'. His position as papal legate made him supreme within the English Church, his overall authority surpassing that of Archbishop Warham of

Canterbury, and his role as Henry's minister and fixer was universally recognised. England's government, the Venetian ambassador once reported, was 'exclusively in the hands of the Cardinal of York'. It was Wolsey who ruled 'the entire kingdom' and 'may be considered King in so far as its administration is concerned', the ambassador affirmed. The cardinal was 'alter Rex', the other king, a man whom it was never wise to antagonise.

The days when Henry might have asked Buckingham to greet Charles were long since gone; now Wolsey had that honour. So, the moment he heard that Charles's ships were off the coast, Wolsey and fifty of his gentlemen set off smartly from Canterbury to Dover to receive him in the king's name. With Wolsey's Latin address ringing in his ears, Charles was escorted to Dover Castle where apartments had been prepared for him. Henry followed his minister as quickly as he could, although Charles was already in bed by the time the English king rode into the courtyard. Nonetheless, Charles, swiftly rising, 'exchanged embraces and other loving compliments' with his aunt's husband.

On the following morning, Katherine, resplendent in her cloth of gold and pearls, waited in Warham's palace while Henry and Charles, who had ridden over to Canterbury from Dover together, went into the great church for prayers, accompanied by the ubiquitous Wolsey, the Dukes of Suffolk and Buckingham, and members of Charles's entourage. Before the altar, Warham sprinkled holy water upon the two kings, gave them 'the wood of the holy cross to kiss' and began the hymn *Veni Creator Spiritus* which the Venetian ambassador, possibly tongue in cheek, informs us 'was suited ... to the conference between the two Sovereigns, united by spiritual love and goodwill for the benefit of Christendom'.

As the last notes faded away, Henry and Charles progressed along a purple velvet carpet out of the church and to Warham's official residence. After being met at the entrance by twenty-five of the 'handsomest and best apparelled' court ladies, and passing along the corridor lined with twenty of Katherine's pages sporting 'gold brocade and crimson satin in checquers', Charles and Henry went up the fifteen steps of the main marble staircase to where Katherine was waiting. Aunt and nephew embraced tenderly, she being unable to hold back the tears as she clasped the tall, thin young man in her arms.

After breakfast came Mass. Henry and Charles, each sparkling in cloth of gold and silver and arrayed in precious jewels, walked in procession to their special pew to the right of the altar, a pew decorated with gold-and-silver brocade embroidered with roses and carpeted in crimson velvet. Once the two kings were settled, it was Katherine's turn to make a grand entrance. Now changed into a gown of cloth of gold lined with violet velvet, her underskirt of silver clearly visible, her hair covered by a black-and-gold headdress dotted with jewels, and wearing a magnificent necklace of 'very large pearls' from which hung a diamond cross, the queen entered a second pew sited to the left of the altar. With her was her sister-in-law Mary, 'the French Queen', in silver cloth, gold and pearls. Wolsey, in crimson and ermine, sat on a gilt chair close to the altar as Warham celebrated the Mass.

There was another Mass on the following day, Whit Monday, and again Katherine's ladies dressed their mistress sumptuously, this time in a dress of cloth of gold and violet velvet, intricately embroidered with flowers of gold thread and pearls. Around her neck they arranged a pearl necklace with a diamond pendant of St George killing the dragon. Wonderful though she appeared, as did Charles in his silver-and-gold brocade, nobody quite matched Henry himself. In cloth of gold and grey velvet, a jewelled belt around his thickening waist, buttons made from rubies, sapphires and diamonds and with a breathtaking jewelled collar around his neck, Henry stole the show.

After dinner, Henry joined in the dancing while Charles quietly watched. In the evening came a banquet at which guests included Henry's leading nobles, key figures from Charles's retinue and the ambassadors from France, Spain and Venice. Henry, Charles, Katherine, Mary 'the French Queen', and Wolsey sat at the top table. There was so much food that the banquet lasted for four hours, there were special dances, there were entertainments. The festivities went on throughout the night, no one getting to bed before daybreak.

As Katherine rested on the following day, Charles and Henry, no doubt with the attentive and indispensable Wolsey on hand, 'sat in council until late in the evening'. For Katherine, it was enough to see

Charles and perhaps start the process of renewing Anglo-Spanish amity. Charles wanted to renew that amity, too, but he also wanted something more concrete. In theory, he was incredibly mighty, certainly infinitely mightier than Henry and, on paper, mightier even than Francis. But Charles knew that the discontent he had left behind in Spain could erupt at any minute, that his treasury was depleted, that the office of emperor gave him a title but limited power, that the Turks were forever pushing towards the empire's eastern frontiers, and that Francis would never rest until he had extended his control in Italy, largely at Charles's expense. To cap it all, an obscure German monk, Martin Luther, had caused a sensation with his outspoken criticisms of Holy Mother Church.

The problems facing Charles were immense. He suspected that the universal peace and brotherhood, to which he was ostensibly committed, would quickly evaporate. When trouble came, he wanted Henry with him not against him. So if he could disengage Henry from Francis, preferably scuppering his meeting with the French king and breaking up the proposed marriage of Princess Mary and the dauphin, he would be in a much healthier position. He argued in vain. With the prospect of sailing to Calais imminent, Henry made it plain to Charles that he was adhering to the Treaty of London, to Francis, and to Mary's marriage to the dauphin. However, he did agree to meet Charles again once his French summit had ended.

So Charles did not come away from Dover entirely empty-handed. And he had made contact with his aunt: she could be a willing channel to Henry. Ever a pragmatist, Charles was ready to flatter and court Wolsey, as did everyone else (the Venetians were busily selecting sixty 'beautiful and choice carpets' for his delectation), but the ties of flesh and blood were likely to prove more reliable than putting his faith in the wily Wolsey. Katherine, Charles appreciated, was at heart still Spanish. Since her parents had sent her to England she had acted as Spain's ambassador, and she was as willing as ever to foster excellent relations between the two countries and do what she could to advance the interests of her native land. This did not mean she would encourage war against France necessarily, nor that she would dare openly to support Spain over England, for Katherine knew that, should her nephew's relationship with Henry founder, she could bear the brunt of English rage.

After fond goodbyes, Charles set off for the port of Sandwich to board his ship for the Netherlands while Katherine and Henry travelled to Dover to sail the twenty or so miles to Calais. The meeting with Francis could not be delayed. Any Channel crossing was unpredictable. With mill-pond seas and a favourable wind, it could be done in three hours; equally, if the weather turned, it could take a day or two, possibly even longer. Fortunately, this time, the weather was perfect and the royal fleet spied Calais's defensive walls within a few hours of setting off from Dover.

Henry and his queen were not alone. Buckingham and Suffolk were in attendance, along with Wolsey, Sir William Compton of the privy chamber, Sir Nicholas Carew, one of Henry's favourite jousting companions, Sir Edward Boleyn and his brother, Sir Thomas, the latter a man often close to Henry these days. Ten earls, twenty-one barons, three Knights of the Garter, several bishops and countless knights from the shires, all sailed with their king in this wonderful adventure. Erasmus's friend Thomas More, Henry's secretary who was fast becoming a man to be reckoned with, was present too. The lists of names go on and on and on. Nor is that the end of it, for each knight or nobleman was entitled to bring a prescribed number of family members and a fixed number of servants. Buckingham was permitted five chaplains, ten gentlemen, sixty other servants and thirty horses. Not surprisingly, Wolsey allocated himself an entourage that was larger than those of Buckingham, Suffolk and Archbishop Warham combined.

Katherine, too, was entitled to her own establishment, just as she had her own household for her normal day-to-day existence. Some were male: we hear of Lord Morley, whose wife was a distant relation of Margaret Beaufort; Lord Mountjoy, Katherine's chamberlain; Lord Willoughby, Maria de Salinas's husband. Then there was the Earl of Derby and John Fisher, Bishop of Rochester, as well as knights like Sir John Shelton and Sir Robert Poyntz. Katherine's almoner, Robert Bekynsall, came with her; so did her doctor, her apothecary, Master John, and her chaplains Dr Peter and Dr Christopher. And just like her husband,

Katherine was served by an army of domestics, there to ensure that her every need was catered for.

Most of all, she needed her women. Maria de Salinas was there, and so was Lady Morley. Lady Mountjoy (alas, not Agnes de Vanegas, who had sadly died, but Mountjoy's next wife, Lady Alice), Lady Elizabeth Boleyn, Sir Thomas's wife, Lady Anne Boleyn, Sir Edward's wife, and many, many more are named as being part of Katherine's party. Included among the gentlewomen was Sir Thomas Boleyn's pretty young daughter Mary, who had recently married William Carey. Boleyn's other daughter, Anne, was currently one of Queen Claude's ladies, so perhaps the Boleyns were able to snatch an albeit brief family reunion.

One sadness for Katherine was that she had to leave her daughter behind; such a junket was hardly suitable for a four-year-old child. Entrusted to the safe and loving hands of Margaret Pole, Mary stayed at Richmond where she was visited by those members of Henry's council left to run the country while the king was away. The little girl was 'right merry and in prosperous health', her parents were informed and was 'daily exercising her self in vertuous pastymes and occupacions', much as Katherine would have expected.

Another absentee was Henry's mistress, Elizabeth Blount, now Lady Tailboys, who was rarely seen at court these days. That, at least, did not displease Katherine. Elizabeth had readily made the transition from dance floor to bedroom, presenting the king with a bouncing baby whom he acknowledged as his. To add to Katherine's distress, the baby was a boy, christened Henry after his father and always known as Henry Fitzroy; her rival had given him the son that she could not.

Fitzroy's birth had been humiliating to Katherine, but if she shed tears, she did so privately. Kings had had affairs since time immemorial, Henry's fling was no worse than those of her own father. And she was confident in her own status; Elizabeth was Henry's mistress, she was his wife. In any case, Katherine still hoped that her prayers would be answered and she would have a son, a son who survived as Prince Henry had not. Then again, if there was to be no son, her daughter Mary would rule England as Isabella had Spain. Either way, Katherine's position was sacrosanct. So, casting aside her hurt about Fitzroy, she performed her duties in Calais with the serene dignity that was her trademark.

Wolsey had invested a good deal of time in arranging the meeting with Francis, negotiating dates, the number of retainers that each king would bring, organising supplies, arranging for ships and horses; the sheer scale of the task stretched even his considerable logistical talents. But he managed it, as he managed everything else. The plan was for Henry to stay in Calais, the only English part of France remaining after the military victories of the Hundred Years War. After a few days he would move on to the small town of Guisnes, about five miles south of Calais, where a temporary palace had been erected for the royal party. It was at this amazing construction that Katherine and Henry arrived on 5 June 1520.

Though temporary, the palace was a masterpiece of engineering. The chronicler, Edward Hall, has left us one of the many descriptions of what he called 'the most noble and royal lodgynge before sene'. Stone foundations supported walls of brick and wood, into which tall diamond-shaped windows set with particularly clear glass were installed. There were towers and arches, there were monumental statues of ancient princes and heroes, there were battlements, there was a gilded fountain, topped by an image of Bacchus, from which red and white wine flowed freely. The high ceilings of the palace were hung with silk or embellished with gilt and gold; floors were carpeted in silks; tapestries adorned the walls, their silver and gold threads iridescent in the shafts of light streaming through the windows or from the tiny flames of hundreds of flickering candles. There was even a chapel, its walls lined with cloth of gold, where worshippers could see the glint of gold everywhere they looked. There were golden ornaments and basins; five pairs of huge golden candlesticks stood on the gold- and pearl-draped altar; jewel-encrusted vestments, brought specially from St Peter's at Westminster, lay ready for use. And when Henry or Katherine wanted to pray, they did so in individual enclosures which were draped with cloth of gold and had altars furnished with glittering religious images and crucifixes laden with precious stones. 'I suppose never suche like were seen,' boasted the patriotic Hall.

The palace contained four separate sets of apartments: one each for Henry, Katherine and the king's sister, Mary 'the French Queen', and the last reserved for Wolsey. The king and queen had chambers embellished and decorated with the finest materials that money could buy and with silver and gold plate bursting from open-fronted cupboards. However, as Katherine retired to her own chambers, walking past the vibrant and costly tapestries, described by an awestruck onlooker as 'marvellous' and with figures who 'really seemed alive', she would have done well to ponder some of their subject matter. One sumptuous set of hangings which Henry had brought with him depicted King David, an Old Testament king for whom he had a perennial fascination. But David had a darker side: his lust for the married Bathsheba led him to incur the wrath of God and earned him divine punishment when the couple's only son died soon after birth.

The palace was but a backdrop to the seemingly endless round of jousts and banquets and mummeries and masques all so beloved by Henry and all so magnificent that the whole extravaganza came to be thought of as the Field of Cloth of Gold, an eighth wonder of the world. It was in these jollities that Katherine had to play her part. The talks, squeezed in between the serious business of tilting, feasting and dancing, were for Francis, Henry and Wolsey, not for any of the women. She was there to smile, to be gracious, to entertain. Together with Queen Claude she presided over several of the jousts, sitting almost enthroned within her private enclosure, presenting diamonds and rubies as a reward to the valiant Francis while Queen Claude charmingly did the same for a delighted Henry. When Claude entertained Henry to a banquet, Katherine followed suit for Francis. Good manners, chivalrous behaviour and courtesy were the order of the day, even if nobles on both sides found it hard to hide their mutual distrust and the English felt smug pleasure in hearing that the French king's enormous, and very expensive, pavilion had blown down in the wind.

Finally, about two weeks after Henry and Francis first rode out of their respective camps to talk to each other, almost inevitably in a golden tent, the two kings and their wives bade each other farewell. All were laden with gifts, Henry and Francis having vied not to be outdone by their counterpart. In the jewellery stakes, they were about equal, Henry's gift of a jewelled collar with a ruby pendant similar in value to Francis's offering of a jewelled bracelet. In horseflesh, though, Francis seems to have triumphed, for it was said that a proud mare Francis gave to Henry was worth more than the entire string of beasts that Henry bestowed upon him. Katherine gave Claude horses too, each 'well trapped', receiving in return a cloth of gold litter which came complete with mules.

For everyone there was much to think about as Francis, Claude and their army of nobles, attendants and servants departed for French territory on 24 June. Wolsey had done his best to cement the French agreement which Charles would have loved to destroy, but there was another meeting to attend before Henry and Katherine could return home, one to which she was eagerly and anxiously looking forward: Charles was due again, and this time he was bringing Katherine's childhood friend, Margaret, the woman who had married Katherine's only brother, Juan, and who was back in charge of the Netherlands now that Charles had other, more onerous, commitments. Again Wolsey undertook the complex preliminary negotiations, during which time Katherine and Henry rested at Calais.

Finally, on Tuesday 10 July, Henry, together with Wolsey, Buckingham and Suffolk, and about three hundred courtiers and council members, set off towards the small town of Gravelines, some twenty miles west of Calais, which Charles controlled. It had been agreed that he would escort the English party to Gravelines itself, having met them all about halfway along the route. Henry, naturally, donned cloth of gold and silver, as did Charles, and they rode together into the town where Margaret was already waiting. The two had met before, when a slightly younger Henry, flushed with his victories against the French, had joined her at Lille in 1513.

Two days later, it was Henry's turn to reciprocate Charles's lavish hospitality. The key buildings in Calais, like the Staple Hall and the Exchequer, had been exquisitely furnished for the royal group, lodgings arranged within the town for everyone else, hay provided in abundance for the horses, cooks preparing the food with which the tables would soon be laden. Masques, entertainments and banquets were to be laid on, many intended to be held in an enormous, specially erected pavilion whose decoration was primarily the responsibility of Thomas More's brother-in-law, John Rastell. Everything was to be splendid, if on a lesser scale than at the Field of Cloth of Gold. For Katherine at least, the next few days were a sheer delight.

When the two kings and Margaret reached Calais, Katherine was awaiting them impatiently. Good though it was to see her nephew again, it was also wonderful to see her former sister-in-law. It had been twenty years since the two women had last met. Then, both had been young, both had believed their futures established and secure. Now fast approaching middle age, they had learned the hard way that life can hold tragic surprises. But, as they kissed and embraced on that Thursday evening at Calais, their lives seemed to have settled down. Margaret had been widowed again after Juan's death and, with no babies of her own, her family had become Charles and his sisters, Juana's children. As regent of the Netherlands, a post she filled with vigour and ability, she had also tasted power, just as Katherine had so briefly when given charge of England while Henry was gallivanting in the French wars.

As for Katherine, she too had faced her demons and had conquered them. Her marriage to Henry was steady rather than passionate, her political influence reduced, and she had only a daughter, a fact which she knew distressed her husband, but she was a royal consort in the realm chosen for her by her parents and which, as things stood, the Catholic Monarchs' granddaughter would inherit. Katherine had not let down her family. And, for a couple of days, she could talk to Margaret of times past, of people whom they had both known, of experiences they had shared, leaving Henry and Charles to discuss and debate state affairs.

On Saturday 16 July, Margaret and Charles departed for Bruges. Not all had gone according to plan. The pavilion's roof blew off in a storm, much to its architect's chagrin, but the banquets still took place and Henry dressed up and danced to his heart's content. As for the talks, Charles did not get what he wanted. Henry made it clear that he was still unwilling to ditch the French marriage plan or the Treaty of London's ethos of collective security. On the other hand, no one had quarrelled and the new emperor had made himself very popular among the English, possibly because of the scale of his welcome in Gravelines, possibly because of his courteous demeanour, most likely because he was not French.

Katherine, for whom family ties had been re-established, would never see Margaret again. It would be two years before she and Charles met one final time. By then, Juana's existence in Spain had been seriously threatened and the diplomatic carousel had revolved yet again.

Family First and Last

On 23 August 1520, as Henry settled down to a refreshing summer of hunting after his exertions in Guisnes and Gravelines, a group of officials insisted on seeing Juana at Tordesillas. Receiving visitors was a very unusual occurrence. Normally Denia would have prevented anyone coming near her, apart from those whom he had personally vetted. This time he had no choice, for the officials were insistent. Their business was so crucial, they declared, that it was imperative they saw the queen.

The news they delivered would have shaken Juana to the core. They began by telling her that Ferdinand had died in 1516, totally exposing the lies fed to her by Denia and, indirectly, by her son. Although shocked to realise that she had been deceived for four years, Juana had no time to grieve, for the officials went on to tell her that Castile was in a state of turmoil which only she could remedy.

Castile was indeed in uproar. Charles had barely bade farewell to Katherine and Henry at Gravelines before the discontent, quietly simmering away since the emperor had left to take up his imperial crown, erupted into riots and disturbances. The reasons were many and complex, some involving grievances that stretched back over decades. Some people were angered by the Inquisition's cavalier abuse of power; some felt that the authority of the various Cortes was being whittled away; some hated foreigners, especially the Burgundians who had accompanied Charles and who seemed so adept at gaining offices and benefices that many thought should be reserved for native Castilians; some resented her son's massive taxation demands; some thought he would simply be too busy with his other dominions to bother about Spain; some saw Spain's traditional culture under threat; some just wanted to pursue local quarrels and vendettas. These rebels, or Comuneros, had now come together to form a Junta that would determine a joint strategy and unite their various groups and communities.

Charles's supporters, headed by his regent Cardinal Adrian of Utrecht, desperately tried to uphold their master's rights and possessions. But Adrian had little money, resources or concrete support. When the cardinal told Charles bluntly that 'the affairs of these kingdoms are on the way to utter ruin', he was not exaggerating. And Adrian knew that the key to preventing that 'ruin' was Juana. How she behaved would be crucial.

Shut away in Tordesillas for eleven years, deliberately kept out of touch with politics, Juana had had no idea that the country was anything other than tranquil. And she had just heard of her father's death. If Spain was in turmoil, so was she. She wanted independent counsel. So, faced by these earnest men, who wanted her help in organising opposition to the rebels, she asked them to send for four specified advisers, one of whom was the Bishop of Malaga, taking the precaution of issuing her instructions by word of mouth, rather than giving the officials signed authorisation.

Before her designated councillors could arrive, however, Tordesillas fell under rebel control. The townsfolk, having barred the gates to Charles's men, were happy to open them for his enemies. The main rebel leader, Juan de Padilla, whose father had served Juana's mother, was no ill-educated firebrand but a man who considered himself a true patriot. It would be de Padilla and his associates with whom Juana would have to deal.

She was now caught in the middle, needed by both the rebels and her son's chief representative, Cardinal Adrian. Terrified by what she might do, the cardinal warned Charles that, if she made a mistake when negotiating with the rebels, 'without any doubt, the whole kingdom' would be 'lost' and would 'throw off the royal obedience to your Majesty'. He need have had no fears. Juana's conduct from the time the officials first saw her until the revolt was beginning to subside, throws into question the assertions of those who label her as 'mad', a woman living only in 'hopeless darkness', and from whom it was impossible 'to get any sense'. In fact, she behaved with a degree of caution that would have done justice to her much revered parents, and she showed an ability to dissemble that rivalled the not inconsiderable skills of her sister

Katherine. And we know just what happened because letters and accounts from both sides of the conflict are still extant.

What Juana appreciated right from the start of the 'tumults' was that the rebels wanted her signature on their various documents to give them legitimacy. They could then say that everything they did was done by her authority. But Juana was not one to sign anything lightly; indeed, she was not one to sign anything at all if she was unsure or under pressure. She had not even signed for her own officials. Once the rebels were inside the castle, though, she had little choice but to hear them out. After being sidelined for so long, she may even have welcomed a chance to hear their version of what was going on in her kingdoms; listening committed her to nothing.

Denia was horrified by the turn of events. He managed to write to the cardinal to let him know that he was 'almost a prisoner, and had been ordered not to leave the fortress'. When it dawned on them, however, that his presence was a hindrance to their cause, the Comuneros summarily turfed him and his wife out of the town. Purporting to view it as a 'great and daring affront' to his mother, Charles declared himself so angry at the Denias' dismissal that he was unable 'to express in words how much' he had been 'grieved' to hear of it. That Juana herself did not lift a finger to retain the Denias' service says it all. When Denia begged her to intercede for him, 'she told him to leave her alone and not to speak of it with her'.

Over the next hundred days Juana had meeting after meeting with their representatives, once asking for a cushion so that she would be more comfortable as they discoursed before her. She listened for hour upon hour as they told of her the unrest gripping so many of her cities. They promised her that they were loyal subjects, wanting only to serve their country and her; they 'entreated' her 'to have confidence in herself and govern her kingdoms'; they said the country was in the grip of 'bad government', that 'foreigners' accompanying Charles had milked the land, committed 'great evils', and 'ruthlessly plundered and tyrannized' her realms and her people. And they wanted her to help them restore order, justice, and their traditional way of life. If she would only sign proclamations and orders when they asked her, they all said, then all would be well again and she would be able to take up the reins of government. If she would but 'rule, and govern and command', there was 'no one in the world to forbid or impede' her. Everyone in her kingdoms was 'ready to obey and serve her Highness, and place her, their queen and born sovereign, at their head, and die for her'. Castile would once again become a land flowing with milk and honey.

For a woman shut away for so long, it was intoxicating. It was also tempting. Having been ignored, not even allowed to go out without permission, she was suddenly the focus of attention. On the face of it, the Comuneros were offering her freedom, the chance to be a queen like her mother. If they failed, and their rebellion was suppressed, Denia could return, her life resume its tedious monotony, and she might never again have the chance to escape. And the well-educated, polite men standing respectfully before her asking her to help them to bring order back to Castile and return it to what it had been under what they portrayed as the Golden Age of her parents, the time before the land was, as they said, ransacked by Burgundian foreigners, seemed so reasonable. They did not appear to be dangerous revolutionaries. Yet she held back.

While agreeing that she would be 'glad to concert with them [the Junta] what is serviceable' for her kingdoms, professing that she loved all her people 'very much' and was 'very sorry for any injury or damage they may have received', she found excuse after excuse not to sign anything they put in front of her. Sometimes she blamed her grief, saying sadly that she could not concentrate on state business at that precise moment as she wanted 'time to comfort' her heart and 'console' herself for Ferdinand's death. Sometimes she said that she would meet with just a few of them rather than a whole group, probably aware that it would take them a while to decide who should comprise the smaller number. Sometimes she announced herself 'unwell and tired', after which she swiftly 'retired to her cabinet'. Often she declared that she could do nothing without the advice of her councillors, established ones who she remembered had advised her father. Once they arrived, she said, she would be in a position to 'decide what is suitable'. On one occasion, putting aside the documents they thrust at her, she said that 'such decrees must be signed first by her councillors on the back of the paper, else she could not ratify them by her signature'; when the Junta members professed themselves ready to sign instead of the councillors, she took refuge in illness. Using stratagem after stratagem, Juana managed to avoid signing anything.

Fears that one day she would give in tormented Adrian. As he saw it, and as he despairingly wrote to Charles with urgent frequency, the emperor's rule in Spain was on a knife-edge. Just one signature from the queen was all it would take, he believed, to turn the situation from dangerous to catastrophic. 'Your Majesty may believe me', he said, 'if they could obtain only one signature from her Highness the revolt and confusion of these kingdoms would become much greater than they are, if that is possible.' In another letter, he spelt out the danger even more dramatically: Charles was in peril 'of losing this kingdom ... if her Highness should sign'. Unless Juana behaved with circumspection and Charles acted with guile, promising pardons to those rebels having second thoughts, there could be 'total and everlasting downfall'. The cardinal could not have been plainer. And he wanted Charles to come in person to Spain to sort things out.

But Juana stood her ground with the Junta. She had chosen her side, and it was not theirs. She resisted them. She argued her case with passion and apparent ease whenever necessary. She began to wage her own crusade, setting herself to maintain the welfare and honour of her family against the insurgents. When the Junta accused her father's councillors of betraying him, she refused to believe them. If her father had chosen them they 'could not be wicked, at least not all of them'. While forced to concede that Ferdinand had kept her at Tordesillas, she suggested that perhaps it had been due to Queen Germaine's malign influence. In any case, her father must have had 'considerations which were known to his Highness alone': she would not condemn him simply on the rebels' word. She even stood up for the cardinal, her son's regent, saying that she was informed that 'although a foreigner' he 'was a good man, harbouring the best intentions and [leading an irreproachable] life'. And when the rebels dared to try to drive a wedge between herself and her son by alleging that he 'styled' himself king 'in prejudice of her Highness', she was having none of it. Rebuking them firmly, she asserted that 'such was the custom of the kingdom', and that 'no one shall set her at variance with her son', for 'all that belonged to her was his, and he would take good care of it'.

Her trust in Charles may have been misplaced, but she certainly felt that she could not trust the rebels. This was particularly true as the weeks passed and the tide very slowly, and very slightly, began to turn in Charles's favour as the more headstrong rebel elements altered course, diverting what had begun as a fight to maintain traditions into a more revolutionary movement demanding social change. There was no way that Juana, brought up to believe that the monarchy and the status quo were sacrosanct, would ever countenance that. But with the Junta's cause beginning to flounder, possession of the queen's person became a trump card. And she knew it.

So, when rumours started to circulate that a royal army was approaching Tordesillas, she would not order the gates to be barred and she would not flee the city. However enticing their promises, however much the Communeros threatened that the royal army would 'do her much harm', and however much she may have yearned to leave Tordesillas, she could appreciate when she was being duped. Thus, when they suggested she should live in Valladolid, a city which she had praised to Denia as one in which she had always felt well, she declined to move. She kept the rebels waiting overnight for her decision before telling them that, while 'much pleased with their offer', she had 'not yet decided on leaving Tordesillas' but should she 'come to such a decision' she would 'let them know'. She understood only too well that she could become just as much a hostage in Valladolid as she already was.

And when, in the first week of December, a royal army drew nearer to Tordesillas, Juana ordered the gates to be left open. Despite her instructions, the Communeros kept them firmly closed as Charles's troops attacked; they were not about to surrender meekly. Juana, along with Catalina who had rushed to her mother's side, were marooned in the palace as fierce fighting broke out all around them. Fierce fighting it was as the defenders blocked gates and manned the walls, battling with an intensity born of desperation. Finally, one of Charles's soldiers managed to dig a hole through the walls with a pickaxe so that his comrades could get in. Even then it took two and a half hours of bloody hand-to-hand combat before the town fell and all was quiet.

During that two and a half hours, Juana and Catalina escaped from the palace to the nearby church. If they ended up being forced to flee, the queen knew exactly what she intended to take with her: a chest of jewellery, and Philip's coffin, which she remained adamant would be buried only in Granada. Her determination on that score had never changed. But the battle raged so ferociously that she and Catalina made their way back to the comparative safety of the palace. It was there that mother and daughter were found when the town was taken. Gently they were led back into their former apartments. Tordesillas was back under Charles's control, and so was his mother. It took another five months or so, and a pitched battle, before the rebels were finally defeated and their leaders executed but, for Juana, all was over as soon as she walked back into the familiar surroundings of her own rooms.

Thus, when it came to choosing between the Communeros and soldiers sent by her son, Juana had not hesitated. Had she truly gone along with the Junta from the beginning, trusting in their vows of allegiance and protestations of loyalty to the old Spain, the Spain of Ferdinand and Isabella, the Spain of her childhood, she might perhaps have broken free. Perhaps the Communeros really would have allowed her to head a new government and rule as the queen she rightfully was. Perhaps, more cynically, they would have used her as a puppet ruler, and she would have been just as much their prisoner as she was that of her son. We can never be sure. The nineteenth-century historian, Bergenroth, a great apologist for Juana, thinks that the Communeros represented her one chance of liberation and that, by refusing to sign their various declarations or commit herself publicly to their cause, she 'finally and irrevocably rejected her only true friends'. But Juana did not see it that way.

What mattered to her was her family. Just as she could never accept that Ferdinand meant her anything other than good, neither could she believe that her son would deliberately, and for his own 'criminal purpose ... rob his mother of her crown'. Juana had a stark choice: to throw in her lot with the rebels or rely on Charles's honour to treat her decently. Despite all the pressures and indignities she had suffered since her father had sent her to Tordesillas, despite all the efforts of Denia and his wife to break her spirit and quell her defiance, she knew she must not yield. Her own position might, or might not, improve if she opted for the Communeros, but Charles's succession would be threatened. Anything could happen: the rebels might be trustworthy but, equally they might drag out la Beltraneja from her Portuguese convent and install her on the throne instead. With Juana, her children came first. She would not risk their inheritance.

During the three months Juana had been in Communero hands, the issue of her mental state had been crucial: it was in Communero interests that she was sane, it was in Charles's interests that she was not. Only by declaring her to be of sound mind could the rebels maintain that they were acting for her and that Charles had usurped his mother's throne; only by regretfully declaring her unbalanced could Adrian legitimise Charles's rule. Right from the beginning of their occupation of Tordesillas, therefore, the Junta had emphasised how intelligently she responded in their discussions. She received them 'graciously and gladly', they said; she answered them with 'wisdom and prudence'; she gave 'a long and comprehensive answer' to their remarks; they even recorded her more tart defences of her family and her reasons for not signing anything as indicating her ability to think and to reason, even if they had wished she had replied differently. A fearful Adrian reported back to his master that the Junta had spread a rumour throughout the kingdom that Juana was 'perfectly sane, and as able to command as the Queen Doña Isabel, her mother of glorious memory'.

To Adrian's further discomfiture, when questioned, Juana's servants had tended to confirm not only that she was as 'sane and prudent as she was when first she was married' but that she had been 'tyrannically detained'. And it was patently obvious that the man detaining her, currently at least, was Charles. It was 'as though your Highness had usurped the royal name and imprisoned the Queen, pretending that she was insane, whilst she is in her right mind', wrote Adrian. Forced by the facts to accept that he had heard of times when she had spoken with 'prudence', the cardinal was careful to point out that he had also heard that she had added 'some things, from which it is easy to understand that her Highness is not perfectly in her right mind'. A frequent refrain in Adrian's letters is that the Communeros were referring to Juana as though she was sane, his innuendo to Charles being that she was not. Yet he himself had been swift to warn her confessor to advise her to sign nothing; clearly he did not think her beyond rational understanding.

He was accordingly overjoyed and relieved when the rebels had suddenly called in physicians and priests to restore her 'health' and had prayers said for her recovery in the various churches under their jurisdiction, actions which might suggest that they too doubted her sanity. Maybe they did, or maybe, as Bergenroth plausibly suggests, they brought in doctors and holy men because of her constant complaints of ill health; interestingly, they did not mention her 'ill health' until they realised that she was unlikely to sign the documents they put before her.

No clear-cut evidence exists to prove conclusively whether Juana was sane or not but, whatever the truth, Charles had what he wanted. The defeat of the rebels meant Spain was back in his hands thanks, in no little part, to his mother's loyalty. She had chosen family over possible freedom. And soon Denia was back at Tordesillas. Having learnt nothing from his summary dismissal, which he considered only as undeserved and a great affront, he immediately started to throw his weight around in his usual tactless, hubristic and overbearing fashion. Charles's commander in chief, the Count of Haro, who was not one of Denia's sycophants, could not have been blunter when he told his master that Denia came 'with more passion than was necessary' and aroused nothing but 'ill will'.

Juana settled back into her old routine. Isolated once more, her wishes and requests ignored, she resorted to her customary tactics of refusing to eat or dress, providing further ammunition for those who stressed her incapacity. Denia blamed her recalcitrance on the attention she had received during the revolt. She had become so 'spoilt' and 'haughty', he grumbled, 'that there is no man who has not had great difficulty with her'. Should she continue in her defiance, he advised Charles that there was but one suitable remedy: 'In truth, if your Majesty would apply the torture it would in many respects be a service and a good thing rendered to God and to her Highness. Persons in her frame of mind require it.' Fortunately, Charles does not appear to have sanctioned such stringent measures, but the prospect of whipping, or even the use of rack, were never explicitly ruled out.

Worried by Denia's zeal in coping with Juana's behaviour, Haro begged Charles to 'command him to be more moderate'. Haro was also stung by the marchioness's demeanour, requesting the emperor to order her to behave 'better than she was in the habit of doing'. Certainly Catalina was becoming increasingly annoyed by Denia's wife and was obviously showing her displeasure all too plainly. Seven months after Tordesillas was re-taken, the marchioness penned an angry letter to Charles, complaining that while Catalina was 'the best-intentioned person in the whole world', she was growing up and her 'age gives opportunity to those who are near her Highness to prejudice in some degree the service and education of her Highness'. She herself was kept out of the princess's bedroom, she complained, because only those encouraging the young girl in her defiance were allowed to enter.

A month later, Catalina told her brother the truth. Always, she said, she had written only what the Denias 'desired' because they would not give her 'permission to do anything else'. They watched her 'so closely' that she could not 'write anything but what they like'. This time, though, she would let him know just how bad things really were. Her life and that of her mother, she said, were 'spent without any profit to your Majesty'. She was 'ill-treated'. And she went on to list her resentments, chapter and verse.

In the aftermath of the Communero troubles, various nobles had stayed at the castle, among them the Countess of Modica, with whom Catalina had struck up a friendship. Naturally, she wanted to write to the countess afterwards and receive letters from her in return. This was anathema to the marchioness who, wrote Catalina graphically, 'wants to tear out my eyes, searches me, and makes enquiries by whom I send and who brings me letters from the countess and her sisters'. The Denias 'set guards' over her to prevent her 'speaking or writing'.

The fourteen-year-old princess, becoming conscious of her status, also complained of the familiarity with which the Denias treated her. 'I beseech your Majesty', she begged, 'to write and order them to treat me in a different manner, and that some difference be made in public between me and their daughters.' Clearly she wanted them to give her the respect that she believed was her due. And she did not want her possessions mauled over by the marchioness's servants. 'They take everything, use it, and spoil it, so that I have nothing of my own, and nothing lasts me,' she wrote despondently.

Her most telling comments came when she described what was

happening to Juana. The queen's property, too, was being filched, the Denias obviously pretending that anything they took was for Catalina. The princess could see exactly what they were doing:

> Of the linen, headdresses, dresses, gold, jewels, and other things belonging to the Queen, my lady, nothing ought to be taken for my use, although I should write that I want it, unless I ask your majesty in a letter written with my own hand. For all that has hitherto been taken in virtue of the orders of your Majesty has not been given to me, nor did I ask it. They have taken it from me, and it will be lost.

Not content with robbing Juana, the Denias also literally imprisoned her in her room. Again, Catalina could not have expressed herself more forcefully:

> Your majesty ought for the love of God to provide that, if the Queen my lady wishes to walk for her recreation in the corridor on the river ... or if she wishes to go to the large room to refresh herself, she be not prevented from doing so ... They [the Denias] direct the women not to let her go to the large room or to the corridors, but lock her up in her chamber where no other light enters except by candlelight, and there is no room whither she could retire from that chamber.

The princess's pleas fell largely on deaf ears. Charles seems to have believed he genuinely cared for all his sisters, but his trust in the Denias remained unshaken.

Craftily, the marchioness contrived to enlist the support of the cardinal in the way she was handling her young charge. Blaming the women around Catalina, the marchioness whined to Adrian (who she knew would pass on her comments to his master), that the princess did 'not pay the respect to the admonitions of the marchioness which she ought'. The cardinal backed the marchioness to the hilt, giving it as his considered opinion that, until she grew up, Catalina should 'obey the marchioness'. Obviously catching a glimpse of Catalina's list of grumbles, he did concede that 'consideration' should be shown to the princess's 'person and authority'. On Juana's living conditions, the good cardinal, shortly to be elevated to the papacy, was silent. So was Charles.

Thus, at Tordesillas, once the excitement of the rebellion had died down, little changed. The Denias stayed and Catalina's miserable existence dragged on, as did her mother's. That was not the case for other members of the imperial family: by the time he returned to Spain in July 1522, the European situation had undergone a major shift and, in the process, Charles found himself betrothed. His intended bride was Catalina's cousin, Katherine's only daughter, Princess Mary.

The Landscape Changes

Little, other than the birth of a son, could have pleased Katherine as much as a Spanish match for her daughter. But the young princess was already betrothed to the dauphin, her marriage designed to cement the spirit of peace, brotherhood and neutrality which Henry and Francis had had such a wonderful time professing at the Field of Cloth of Gold. Indeed, Henry and Wolsey were still basking in the glory of their achievements as Katherine and Charles had bade each other farewell at Gravelines. Only if the international scene changed would there be any chance of renewing the Anglo-Spanish family compact which had originated in Henry VII's tentative approaches to Ferdinand and Isabella all those years before. To Katherine's great joy, the international situation did indeed change.

For that she had to thank Francis. Never one to accept second place, he had looked at Charles with envy. And then he realised that Charles's acquisition of the conglomerate that was the Holy Roman Empire brought huge problems in its wake. The individual princes within it often quarrelled; the Turks, superb warriors, were a constant threat to its eastern borders; religious differences resulting from Luther's challenge to the Church were becoming increasingly volatile and bitter, dividing one state from another. Once the Communero revolt broke out in Spain, Charles was suddenly vulnerable. Francis could not have hoped for more. His response to his rival's difficulties was to re-open the Italian wars. The days of amity were over. After Charles came to an agreement with the pope, war between himself and Francis was imminent. And Charles wanted Henry on his side. In that, Katherine would concur.

Henry, wanted by everyone, felt important. Not only was he the great peacemaker, he also had a new title: because he had written a book denouncing Luther, he was given the title of 'Defender of the Faith' by the pope in 1521. Previously, Henry had been all too conscious that while Francis was the 'Most Christian King', he had no official soubriquet, despite his constant support for the papacy. Now he felt a true equal on the European stage.

Katherine, no doubt delighted by her husband's stance against the heretical Luther, was not to be outdone. Her Spanish confessor, Alfonso de Villasancta, began his own rebuttal of Luther's ideas. His book, *Problema indulgentiarum adversus Lutherum*, which was published in 1523, and owed much to the work of Bishop John Fisher, was dedicated to Katherine. She was, declared Villasancta, the 'Defendress of the Faith'. For the woman whose religion was the mainstay of her life and whose parents had defeated the Moors and established the Inquisition, such a dedication was exhilarating. Luther's ideas were spreading, his followers multiplying. As far as Katherine was concerned, crusades were not just fought against Muslims, they must be fought against any and every enemy of the Catholic Church. She would be her faith's defendress until her dying day.

Meanwhile the 'Defender of the Faith' turned his attention to the growing threat from France. He sent Wolsey to Bruges to negotiate with Charles, ostensibly to see whether some accommodation might be arranged between Charles and Francis. It could not. But what could be arranged was that Henry and Charles would wage war on France. In 1523 Henry, eager to turn his assumed designation of King of France into reality, joined forces with Charles to attack the French. Wonderful. Equally wonderful for Wolsey was Charles's promise to support him in the next papal election. Already a cardinal and a legatus a latere, the highest form of papal representative aside from the Holy Father himself, Wolsey would attain the ultimate of religious offices, an amazing triumph for a butcher's son; or he would if Charles, grandson of the duplicitous Ferdinand, kept his promise.

That her husband and her nephew were allies was excellent news for the queen. Even better was that the new alliance would be marked by a marriage between her daughter Mary and Charles. Since Charles was twenty and Mary only six, the nuptials would have to wait for some years, but the principle of a renewal of the Anglo-Spanish family compact was established.

Mary was soon informed of her good fortune. When Charles's envoys came to England, they were introduced to the princess who was wearing, so they told Charles, 'a golden brooch ornamented with jewels forming your Majesty's name, which name she had taken on St Valentine's Day for her valentine'. When the ambassadors were leaving, Katherine made sure that they took with them a very favourable impression of Mary's accomplishments. Having expressed her desire to see Charles and to receive him 'with the greatest honour and best cheer possible', the queen insisted that Mary should dance. Since she obviously enjoyed dancing, she 'did not have to be asked twice'. She performed two dances, in one of which we hear that she 'twirled so prettily that no woman in the world could do better'. Then, showing that Henry was not the only Tudor to have musical talent, she played 'two or three songs on the spinet' showing, apparently, 'unbelievable grace and skill and such self-command as a woman of twenty might envy'. Clearly, she would one day make Charles a fine consort, and he would help her rule England if Providence left her as England's heir. And the newly affianced pair were soon to meet. Before Charles returned to Spain in the aftermath of the Communero revolt, he would visit England.

The preparations for this state visit were intense and meticulous. Henry wanted to put on a show. The guilds of London were ordered to produce a series of pageants at their own expense; the prospect of safe and perhaps increased trade with the Netherlands, England's main trading outlet, smoothing over many a grumble about the cost. Eleven wine merchants and twenty-eight major taverns were required to procure ample supplies of wine to keep conversations flowing. We even have a list of the billets that were organised for the emperor's followers, each entry mentioning how many rooms every householder was expected to offer and how many feather beds could be provided. Nothing was left to chance.

Thus, the king's officials in Calais, where Charles was due to spend a night on his way to England, were warned well in advance to give him a truly memorable welcome. They fulfilled their brief to the letter. On Sunday 26 May 1522, the Marquis of Dorset headed the delegation which met Charles at Gravelines and escorted him into Calais itself. All the ships moored in the harbour fired their guns in tribute; the clergy, wearing their best copes and carrying jewel-studded crosses, lined the streets; the emperor's lodging, the Exchequer, was made as sumptuous and inviting as possible; Charles was wined and dined by the chief men of the town, as were his retinue. It was a very promising start.

On the following day, Charles set off for Dover, arriving at about four in the afternoon to begin his month's stay. Wolsey, naturally, was there to greet him, the two men embracing before Charles honoured the cardinal by taking his arm. A week later Charles and Henry rode into Gravesend, where more than thirty barges were moored, the oarsmen in place to row the two kings and their entourages along the Thames to Greenwich. It was at Greenwich that Katherine and an excited Princess Mary were waiting.

The river voyage, which took almost five hours, was like a pageant in itself, with ships along the banks 'well garnished with stremers and banners, gunnes and ordynaunce', firing a salute as Henry and Charles passed by. Finally, at about six in the evening, the royal barge, cushioned for comfort, decked with sweet herbs to mask any nauseous odours, pulled into the private landing stage. Katherine could at last introduce her nephew to her daughter. Katherine greeted Charles with genuine affection. The chronicler Edward Hall has left an account of what happened. Charles, he said, 'asked the Quene blessing (for that is the fashyon of Spain, betwene the Aunte and the Nephew), the Emperor had great joye to se the Quene hys Aunte, and in especyall his young cosyn ... the lady Mary'. And Mary could see her valentine in person.

The next few days were filled with festivities and sports. Charles was treated royally, Katherine loving every minute that he was there. She was with him as he watched Henry, ever true to form, having a wonderful day capering manfully in the jousts designed for the emperor's pleasure. She banqueted with Charles, she looked on while her ladies danced for him, she enjoyed the masque which formed the climax of the evening's revelry. Henry relished participating in all that was going on. He still took a childish pleasure in dressing up and playing a part, donning a long gown complete with a hood of cloth of gold as his disguise, as his courtiers and those of the emperor intermingled amicably. In another of the jousts, Charles himself joined the lists, mounted on a 'richly trapped' charger, and glittering in cloth of tissue. Katherine could watch happily as the two most important men in her life behaved like comrades and allies.

Charles stayed at Greenwich from Monday 2 June until Friday 6 June 1522 when he and Henry were scheduled to make a ceremonial entry into London, just as Katherine herself had done on her marriage to Arthur and for her coronation. As the two kings reached the city, they were met by the lord mayor, John Milborn, and key figures in the various guilds, all in their finest scarlet robes and wearing their gold chains. Thomas More was there too, his task to give a Latin oration on the topic of peace and amity. For the city officials, Charles's entry was the climax of over three months' anxious work on the series of pageants for which they were responsible. Every one of the nine tableaux, stationed at central positions along the processional route, involved stunning costumes, elaborate sets and the compilation of verses. Visually, all were amazing. There were castles, turrets, giants, beautiful maidens. There were some elements clearly aimed at flattering the emperor, such as Charlemagne restoring the pope (for Charles and Henry were posing as guardians of the Church) and a tableau about Jason and the Golden Fleece, the chivalric order to which Charles was so attached.

Possibly the most inspired pageant was that devised by More's brother-in-law, John Rastell, fresh from his work at Calais two years before. The centrepiece of Rastell's effort was an island representing England set in a silver sea surrounded by waves and rocks. On the island were woods and mountains, flowers, birds, animals, fish; there were actors who resembled Charles and Henry but who were carrying swords; there were planets and stars and the Holy Trinity and angels. Suddenly at the approach of the real Charles and Henry, the whole contraption burst into life. The mechanical birds sang, the toy fish leapt from their pools, the animals moved and the actors symbolically cast aside their swords to embrace each other instead of fighting. It was a masterpiece of invention and imagination.

Although each of them was an entity in itself, the major overall pageant theme, echoing More's oration, could not have been closer to Katherine's heart: friendship between Charles and Henry, between the Spanish dynasty and the Tudors. And some of the individual pageants were very reminiscent of those offered to honour her as a young bride.

King Alfonso was there again, so was King Arthur and his Round Table, there was a tree with John of Gaunt at its head to symbolise the family links between England and Spain. On a more sinister note, the message was a blatant warning to Francis of the combined might shortly to be ranged against him.

At Windsor, to which the two monarchs travelled in easy stages and where Katherine and Mary joined them, that message was rammed home even more clumsily in an evening entertainment held in the great hall. A fierce horse, unresponsive to all efforts to be ridden or bridled, was miraculously tamed courtesy of the friendship between Henry and Charles; no one could fail to realise that the horse was meant to be the French king.

Katherine bade her nephew farewell at Windsor, but Charles did not leave empty-handed. Both monarchs had agreed to the treaty of Windsor, promising unity and mutual aid in the ensuing conflict against France; Charles reaffirmed his match with Mary; and Henry lent him money, much of which the king had to squeeze out of the reluctant Londoners as a loan, a demand that 'sore chafed the citizens', Hall states, and which forced many of the guildsmen to sell their plate. Still, overall the visit was an overwhelming success. Providing both sides kept to the bargain, and really did work together, the future augured well.

Within three years, however, Katherine's world was disintegrating. Had she but realised it, the rot had started even before Charles's arrival. At the centre of the cataclysm that eventually would engulf her was her failure to bear a male heir. All her prayers, her pilgrimages and her hopes for a miracle such as that granted to St Elizabeth when she gave birth to John the Baptist, came to nothing. Mary's prettiness, her musical talent, her dancing and her attention to her studies could not compensate for her gender. To Henry, a female heir was terrifying. The embers of the Wars of the Roses still smouldered; a woman on the throne could rekindle them. Way back in 1514, the Venetians had reported whispers that Henry was about to repudiate Katherine because he thought she could not give him a son; although then the rumours were false, the lack of an heir was obviously already arousing comment.

As the years passed, Henry's patience dwindled; Katherine had not even conceived since 1518. Virtually certain that God was not going to grant him legitimate sons, Henry's developing anxiety over a succession crisis is the most plausible explanation for one of the most extraordinary missives that he ever penned. Probably in 1521, about a year before Charles came back to England, Henry had written a letter in his own hand to the man he trusted above all others: Cardinal Wolsey. Quite what prompted his suspicions in this undated note we do not know because, frustratingly, he says that 'the most part of this business' he had 'committed to our trusty counsellor this bearer'. What he did put on paper, however, is dynamite: he ordered the cardinal 'to make good watch on the duke of Suffolk, on the duke of Buckingham, on my lord of Northumberland, on my lord of Wiltshire and on others which you suspect'.

Buckingham, who could trace his descent straight back to Edward III, was one of the leading aristocrats in the realm, his lineage and pedigree unimpeachable. His lands were vast, his wealth phenomenal, his tapestries and possessions monumental. One estimate saw him netting over £6000 for one year alone. His spending matched his income, making him highly popular with the London merchants. He could afford to give a £5 tip to one of Katherine's servants for bringing him her New Year's Gift; he thought nothing of ordering a pomander and chain of gold to give to Katherine. He was a man whom the queen knew well, a man with whom Henry had jousted, a man to whom one of Henry's many presents had been 'a goodly course [a horse], a rich gown, a like jacket doublet and hosen', a man who had taken a prominent role in almost all major celebrations and events of Henry's reign. Yet none of this would save him. In fact, it helped cause his downfall. He was just too powerful, his claim to the throne all too real to a king worried about leaving England to a woman ruler. In 1513 Henry had experienced no qualms in executing the Yorkist Earl of Suffolk, breaking the undertaking that Henry VII had given to Juana's husband when Suffolk had been handed over; he suffered none in ordering Buckingham's arrest either.

The essence of the crown's case, presented when Buckingham faced a panel of his peers at Westminster Hall in May 1521, was that he had listened intently when a Carthusian monk, Nicholas Hopkins, who was alleged to have the gift of prophecy, foresaw that the duke would rule

England when Henry died. Then, said one of the witnesses against him, Buckingham vowed to stab the king should he ever be arrested. If true, this was treason, and the arrogant duke faced the prospect of a traitor's ignominious and excruciatingly painful death. Depositions were meticulously collected and presented to the court, some from a handful of Buckingham's disgruntled ex-employees. What the peers were not told was the extent of Henry's interference in the proceedings.

The monarch who believed himself a true son of the Church was not above coaching witnesses privately and frightening the duke's chaplain into breaking the seal of the confessional. Needless to say, the duke was declared guilty. He was decapitated by a blundering executioner who took three blows from a 'woodman's axe' to sever his head, the king having decided to exercise his prerogative of mercy by commuting the sentence to beheading rather than hanging, drawing and quartering. Buckingham was fully conscious until that third blow, bravely attempting to pray while in excruciating pain. His brutal demise sent shock waves through London, and through Henry's court. While it was wiser not to speculate on whether the evidence was rigged and merely accept the verdict at face value, no one could feel entirely safe from this point onwards. Except Henry. With Buckingham a decaying corpse, Henry had removed one potential danger to the continuation of his dynasty. He had also emerged much richer because, as the law allowed, Buckingham's property was forfeit to the crown. Henry retained a few choice estates such as Kimbolton Castle in Huntingdonshire, but distributed some of the remainder to lucky recipients. Thomas More accepted the manor of South (now Southborough) in Kent, despite his inner scruples about the nature of the duke's fall.

Katherine knew to keep her own counsel on Buckingham's death. She certainly would never have broached the subject with Charles when she saw him thirteen months later. Nor would she have mentioned her misgivings on another subject: Henry's infidelity with one of Thomas Boleyn's daughters.

As a family, the Boleyns were formidable. Clever, astute and ambitious, Thomas's son George was married to Lord Morley's daughter, Jane Parker, and was clearly destined for a successful career at court. Thomas's daughters had both served at the French court; Mary, pretty and enticing, was married to William Carey, while Anne, stylish, possessed of an indefinable chic and vivacity, was unmarried but already beginning to arouse interest from the young bloods at court. But it was upon Mary, who had gained a reputation in France as a 'very great bawd', that Henry's eyes first alighted.

Quite when their relationship became sexual is impossible to say, but there is no doubt that the king was only too happy to share his bed with the delectable Mistress Carey. There were even those who whispered that her son, coincidentally named Henry, was more than the king's namesake. Henry and Mary's affair may have started shortly after the Field of Cloth of Gold, but it was almost certainly under way when Charles arrived in 1522. Mary had even performed in a masque for Charles's ambassadors a couple of months before the emperor kissed his aunt so lovingly at Greenwich. Ironically, she played 'Kindness' in the entertainment; her sister Anne, yet more tellingly, was 'Perseverance'. Just as Mary was kind to him, so the king was kind to her husband. The acquiescent Carey grew rich upon the profits of offices and perquisites allocated to him by his grateful sovereign. Indeed, Carey's tax demand was nearly half that of Thomas Boleyn and more than that required from Lord Morley, a peer of the realm.

Katherine, who had learnt to tolerate her husband's extra-marital adventures, maintained her customary dignified silence as Henry frolicked with Mary. As with Elizabeth Blount, Henry was bound to tire of his new amour. While a blow to her pride, she did not envisage the liaison affecting Princess Mary's inheritance as Henry's legitimate heir, especially now that the princess was affianced to the most powerful monarch in Europe. The queen did not lose much sleep on her daughter's behalf. Yet.

But by 1525, three years after Charles's departure, that was no longer true. While Mary Boleyn was no real threat to either Katherine or to her daughter, little Henry Fitzroy, Henry's child by Elizabeth Blount, most definitely was. Henry loved him 'like his own soul'. He proved it to the world.

In the middle of June 1525, a select band of lords and courtiers assembled at Bridewell in London. Preceded by the Earl of Northumberland carrying the special sword and girdle which would be used for the investiture, six-year-old Fitzroy walked in procession along the long gallery, the Earl of Arundel on his right and the Earl of Oxford on his left. They reached the king's chamber, where Henry stood under his cloth of estate surrounded by other lords and the ever-present Wolsey. Standing to one side was Thomas More who read out the official patent which created the child Earl of Nottingham. Henry gently draped the girdle and sword over his kneeling son's neck. The first part of the deed was done. But there was more. The new Earl of Nottingham briefly left the room, to return for the second part of the proceedings. This time, Henry bestowed the dukedoms of Richmond and Somerset upon the kneeling boy.

The significance of the event escaped no one: Henry Fitzroy now bore the same titles as those held by Henry VII before he seized the crown at Bosworth. Just as significant was that a former Duke of Somerset, born a royal bastard, had been legitimised. The unspoken question was whether this was a prelude to legitimising Fitzroy and showering him with still more titles and offices. Many speculated that the child would become King of Ireland; others, more ominously, began to wonder if what Henry really had in mind for the boy was England itself. Perhaps. Certainly the boy's tutor always referred to him as 'the Prince'.

For Katherine, the entire episode was a nightmare. This time she did not adhere to her usual prudent stance. As she saw it, Mary's future could be in jeopardy. History could be about to repeat itself: Katherine did not want Mary to face a damaging civil war against Richmond for England, as Isabella had done against la Beltraneja for Castile. Lightning quick to nose out scandal, the Venetians reported her reaction. 'The Queen', they said, 'resents the earldom and dukedom conferred on the King's natural son.' She did indeed. She also resented that Henry blamed three of her Spanish ladies for inciting her anger and dismissed them from her service. She could do nothing to stop him. Instead, the Venetians say, she 'was obliged to submit and to have patience'. There was one thing she could do, however: it was in this year that she commissioned a treatise on marriage from Erasmus. It is tempting to wonder whether she was aware just how far the sands were shifting beneath her own marriage.

And Fitzroy's triumph was only one of the troubles besetting her. The alliance with Charles that had begun so well had collapsed. Henry, relishing the prospect of attacking France again, had sent armies across the Channel in 1523 in the so-called 'Great Enterprise'. Charles was committed to assist, and there were high hopes that a rebellious French noble, the Duke of Bourbon, would bring so many troops to the conflict on Henry's side that Francis would not stand a chance. Events had not gone as expected. Bourbon's forces, such as they were, were useless, Charles was more interested in Italy than fighting in France, and Henry had run out of money. With insufficient resources to pay and equip his own men, he could not cope with Charles's incessant pleas for more loans.

To cap it all, Henry suspected that Charles had no intention of waiting for Mary to grow old enough for marriage and instead intended to wed his cousin, Princess Isabella of Portugal, the daughter of Katherine's sister Maria. Equally, Charles thought Henry was angling for Mary to marry the young King of Scotland, James V, his nephew, who had acceded to the Scottish throne after the Battle of Flodden. It was a mess.

As the atmosphere of mutual mistrust increased, Wolsey toyed with peace with France. Katherine was once more caught in the middle. Charles was forever trying to seek her support, but getting messages to him was so awkward that she occasionally resorted to using her confessor as an intermediary, warning her nephew of Henry's 'discontent'. Then, in February 1525, came news which stunned Europe: Francis was not only comprehensively defeated by Charles at the Battle of Pavia in northern Italy, he was taken prisoner. Suddenly, everything had changed. With its king in Spanish hands, France lay defenceless. This was Henry's moment. Now, he could do what no king of England had done since the heady days of Henry V. He could conquer France. All he needed was Charles's support. He did not get it. Charles, his treasury depleted, facing religious discord in Germany and a victorious Turkish army on the empire's eastern borders, was not about to bankrupt himself further to increase Henry's power and feed the English king's vanity. Instead, Charles made peace with Francis at Madrid the following January.

Katherine's dreams were shattered: her husband felt betrayed by her nephew. It was an awful repetition of his earlier fury against Ferdinand.

And then, as now, she had no option but to back her husband. But this time it was almost past bearing, her catalogue of woes seemed endless. Now beyond the age of childbirth, she had to accept that she would never give Henry a son; Fitzroy was Duke of Richmond; Henry's infidelity with Mary Carey was an open secret. Worst of all, Charles had jilted Princess Mary and was strolling through the shaded gardens of the Alhambra with his new bride, Katherine's niece Isabella. Never had Katherine's influence over Henry, or over the events of her life, been so slight.

And yet, appalling though all of this was, it was trivial compared with what was still to come. Katherine would one day have to fight the battle of her life: and what would then be at stake was her own marriage.

PART VI

Adversity

'A Blind, Detestable
and Wretched Passion'

For almost two years after Richmond's elevation, Katherine's life continued much as usual despite her grief over the utter collapse of the family compact with Charles. She dined in state with Henry on days of estate, as the special feast days when the king wore his crown and purple robes were known; they celebrated Christmas together; they exchanged gifts at New Year; sometimes she dined with him in her privy chamber; she travelled with him from palace to palace, even if she tended to prefer a pilgrimage to hunting these days; she watched the court revels and entertainments just as she always had; she read and she sewed as her mother had taught her.

One hopeful sign that Henry was not ready to exclude Mary from the succession was that he arranged for her to travel to Wales to preside over the Council there just as Arthur had once done. Like the young Katherine, Mary even resided at Ludlow. Parting with her daughter was a wrench for the queen, but she was reassured that Mary was in good hands for Margaret Pole, the queen's own friend over so many years, went with the young princess. And, while Henry had not bestowed the title of Princess of Wales upon Mary officially, he had not given Wales to Richmond either. Nor was Mary's future neglected. Although cast aside by Charles in favour of Isabella of Portugal, she retained considerable value on the marriage market; Wolsey was already busy negotiating to achieve a French wedding for her, perhaps even with the recently widowed Francis himself. Such a union was not one that Katherine relished – indeed she went so far as to ask the French ambassadors if the 'alliance would make the King [Henry] suspected by the Emperor' – but at least it proved that her child was not to be disowned and could still have a glittering match.

Life at court continued its customary pattern too, outwardly anyway. Wolsey remained the most powerful man in England next to the king, with no one daring to say or do anything to antagonise him. The Dukes of Suffolk and Norfolk were constantly at her husband's side. If she noticed the prominence and aggrandisement of Norfolk's brother-in-law, Sir Thomas Boleyn, who had been created Earl of Rochford on the same day that Fitzroy became Earl of Richmond, Katherine said nothing. She would not have thought it important. Escaping her too was Boleyn's gradual accumulation of perquisites, such as lands and offices around Tonbridge in Kent, which had once belonged to the Duke of Buckingham.

Then there were the Boleyn children, quite permanent fixtures in court circles by now. By late 1525, Mary Carey's affair with Henry was probably over but her husband William, a member of the king's privy chamber, had profited well from his wife's readiness to serve her king in the way she knew best. Thomas's only son, George, was starting to accumulate property and connections on his own account. His marriage to Lord Morley's daughter, Jane Parker, not only linked George to the established peerage, but was very lucrative. Jane's dowry of 1000 marks (about £666), half of which was paid by a generous Henry, was huge. And although the Eltham Ordinances, a series of reforms to Henry's privy chamber initiated by Wolsey, meant that George lost his coveted place there, he did not lose out entirely. Anyone examining the original draft of the Eltham Ordinances under ultraviolet light can see that the cardinal wrote in his own highly distinctive hand that 'Young Boleyn' was 'to have twenty pounds yearly above the eighty pounds he hath gotten to him and his wife to live thereupon'. In addition, George shared Buckingham's Kent lands with his father and the king gave him the manor of Grimstone in Norfolk for himself. George was certainly a man to watch.

So, too, although again Katherine did not realise it at first, was Thomas's other daughter, Anne. Elegant, exotic, vivacious and witty, she was already turning heads even if her dark complexion did not fit the conventional idea of feminine beauty, which favoured delicately pale skin and blonde hair. The poet, Thomas Wyatt, it was rumoured, found her captivating, as did Harry Percy, the Earl of Northumberland's son and heir. Clearly, the Boleyns' fortunes were rising. That Anne had moved on to higher things from Harry Percy (hastily married off by his father, who wanted a better match for his son than a Boleyn) and was leading Katherine's husband into what the Spanish ambassador was to describe as a 'blind, wretched and detestable passion', was something the queen could never have imagined.

But by 1527 that was exactly what was happening, in fact had happened. We will never know for sure when Henry's love for Anne started. According to George Cavendish, Wolsey's contemporary biographer and gentleman-usher, Anne's burgeoning romance with Percy was stifled by Wolsey, acting upon Henry's instructions because the king confessed to his loyal cardinal that he had a 'secret affection' for the lady himself. Possibly so.

What we do know, however, is that it was indeed a deep love on his part, a love for which he even did something he admitted to finding 'tedious and painful': he settled down at his writing desk to compose love letters to her, writing them in his own hand. The letters, many of them filled with sentiments that are touchingly genuine and heartfelt, almost boyish, still survive, preserved within the archives of the Vatican; frustratingly, Anne's replies have disappeared. In these letters Henry declared himself 'wounded by the dart of love', Anne's absence causing him 'more pain' than he 'should ever have thought could be felt'. She was the woman he most esteemed in the whole world, his 'darling', his 'own sweetheart'. Prolonged absence would be 'intolerable'. 'I and my heart put ourselves in your hands,' wrote the besotted Henry.

Had Katherine any idea that Henry was penning such missives, she would have assumed that another mistress was about to appear on the scene. And that she should become his new paramour is probably all that Henry envisaged when he first gazed into Anne's 'black and beautiful eyes'. If she would only surrender herself to him 'body and heart', he told her, then he would do her the honour of making her his 'sole mistress, remove all others from my affection, and serve you only'. To Henry's mind, no woman could refuse such a magnanimous offer. But this one did. Having seen Elizabeth Blount and her own sister discarded once the king's interest faded, Anne wanted more. She wanted to become

Henry's wife and his queen, not his mistress. Unfortunately, Katherine was in her way.

But this is where fortune's wheel favoured Anne not the queen. For Henry now had scruples about the legality of his marriage, and it is far more likely that these scruples developed before he was bewitched by Anne rather than afterwards. She merely crystallised them, focused them and gave him an additional reason to exploit them.

Central to Henry's thinking was the succession. He wanted a son. And he could not understand why Katherine could not provide one. There must be a reason, and that reason, Henry decided, was because, somehow, he had sinned against God. Such a sin could not possibly have come from his own conduct as king, for he was a dutiful son of the Church, had written against Luther and acted against heretics within his own realms. So there must be a much more basic cause of God's anger with a man whom the pope had declared to be 'Defender of the Faith'.

That cause, Henry decided, was that his very marriage was at fault: marrying his brother's widow had been contrary to God's law and he was being punished because of it. The origins of his case, he thought, lay in a verse (20:21) in the Old Testament book of Leviticus which stated that a man who married his brother's widow would remain childless. Henry had a healthy daughter, Mary, but taking advice from a Hebrew expert, he came to think that the meaning of the original verse of the Scripture was that he would lack sons. This fitted his own situation perfectly: Katherine was Arthur's widow, and the death of little Prince Henry, in addition to the queen's failure to produce another male heir, was evidence of God's anger.

He could even see his sin depicted in the tapestries on his own walls. We cannot know whether Katherine drew parallels between her husband with the Old Testament king, David, but Henry did; he had always felt drawn to David, believing that they shared a sincere and special relationship with God, and like David he coveted military victories for the glory of God. But David had displeased his maker. Loving Bathsheba, the wife of Uriah the Hittite, David had deliberately sent Uriah off to fight knowing that he was almost certain to be killed; he was. The death of David's son by Bathsheba was the terrible manifestation of

God's vengeance. For Henry, the story was further proof that his own marriage was damned. He had not killed Arthur but he had taken to wife a woman whom he should not have touched. And their only son had died.

Clearly, then, Henry should not have been allowed to marry Katherine in the first place and the pope should never have issued a dispensation. The only remedy now was for the king to appease God, and the only way to do that was to repudiate Katherine so that he would no longer be living in sin and his conscience would be clear. Once free, of course, he could marry again and thus ensure the succession. What could be simpler?

All the king needed was the Church's agreement that his marriage was wrong in the sight of God and was therefore invalid. While there was no divorce in the modern sense, the Church could, and sometimes did, pronounce what amounted to a sentence of nullity on unions that had somehow contravened church law. That was what Henry wanted, and he had various precedents to encourage him: the Duke of Suffolk, his brother-in-law, had managed this with regard to his first marriage; Louis XII of France had divorced his wife to marry Anne of Brittany; and his own sister, Margaret, the widow of James IV, who had been killed at Flodden, had managed to have her second marriage, to the Earl of Angus, annulled. Henry saw no reason why the pope would not be just as obliging for him.

In reality, the whole question of who could marry whom was far more complex than Henry's argument suggests. Church law forbade marriage between those who were related in some degree or had become related through the marriage of a relative. But, over the centuries, there had been considerable discussion and debate over the exact nature of these relationships, how they were created, and whether the pope could grant dispensations to take people out of the prohibited degrees of affinity (as the relationships were called). Dispensations had indeed been issued in very similar cases to Henry and Katherine's; as Ferdinand had once pointed out, Manuel of Portugal had been allowed to marry Katherine and Juana's sister, Maria, when their eldest sister, Isabella, had died. Maria and Manuel had subsequently produced numerous offspring, one of whom had just married Charles. Manuel had even gone one stage further: when Maria died, he took Juana's eldest daughter, Eleanor, as his third wife. And no one had suggested that any of these instances of close family inter-marriage had been invalid.

Then again, the Bible itself appeared to be contradictory: a verse in the book of Deuteronomy (25:5) pronounced it a brother's duty to marry his brother's widow, if they had no children, so that the brother's line could nonetheless continue. And Arthur and Katherine had no children, so that verse could apply too.

However, should there be any disputes over precisely what church law asserted, the pope was there to sort it out. It was his role to reconcile what seemed to be contradictory, to define and differentiate between what was the law of God, and therefore immutable, and what was the law of man, and thus could be open to alternative interpretations. Once he had done that, all should be well. Certainly, when Wolsey sounded him out, the learned Bishop John Fisher could see no 'sound reason to show that it is prohibited by divine law for a brother to marry the wife of a brother who has died without children'. Moreover, said Fisher, 'considering the fulness of authority given by our Lord to the Pope', it belonged to the pope 'to clear ambiguous passages of Scripture, after hearing the opinions of the best divines'. Since the pope had dispensed in similar cases, 'this alone should determine the question'. Henry's marriage, therefore, was solid. And Fisher would not be the only person who would say exactly that. It was a minefield, one that Henry wanted Wolsey to enter on his behalf.

Katherine had no idea that any of these thoughts were running through her husband's mind. The last thing he wanted was to discuss his fears with her, probably because he appreciated only too well what her answer would be, and how effective an opponent she could become. Anne Boleyn, who was in no doubt as to the steely nature of her adversary, was later to say that if Henry tried to dispute with Katherine 'she was sure to have the upper hand'. Anne's assessment could not have been more accurate. As far as Katherine was concerned, she and Henry were man and wife and would stay man and wife until parted by death. There was no equivocation. She had 'truth and right' on her side, she was to say, and Henry was her 'lawful lord and husband'. He had been so since 1509 and that was that.

And that most likely was Wolsey's viewpoint as well when he first heard what Henry intended. Henry wanted the cardinal to use his legatine powers to convene a secret 'court' to investigate the legalities of the royal marriage and come up with the correct answer: that the marriage was against God's law, a palpable fact against which no dispensation was possible. Reluctantly, the king would then put away the woman he had innocently thought his wife. The pope, Henry thought, would not interfere but would rubber-stamp Wolsey's judgment. Problem solved.

Except that, far from being solved, the problem was only just beginning. When he had time to digest the idea, Wolsey appreciated that, if the marriage could be ended, the king would be available for a new one, one that was diplomatically advantageous. Blissfully ignorant that Henry had already determined that his new bride would be Anne Boleyn, the cardinal looked to France: a French wife would cement the growing relationship with Francis and act as a strong counter-weight to Charles. Most satisfactory. Nonetheless, Wolsey was under no illusion that everything would be plain sailing. Labyrinthine scheming would be required; and, at that, he was a practised expert.

So the cardinal set about fulfilling his master's bidding. On 17 May 1527, a select group of clerics and scholars, including William Warham, Archbishop of Canterbury, Stephen Gardiner and Dr Richard Wolman, scuttled to Wolsey's London residence, York Place. Their task was to investigate the King's 'secret matter' by analysing every word of the pope's dispensation and examining all relevant canon law. Speed would be essential, secrecy maintained. But the end result was pre-determined: Henry would be reprimanded and the marriage annulled. Assuming that the pope was amenable, the matter would be settled before Katherine had time to do anything about it.

That is where the plan began to go wrong. Despite all the cloak-and-dagger skulduggery, the queen heard that something was afoot. We do not know who her informant was; neither did a fuming Henry, although he left no stone unturned in his efforts to find out. But, whoever told her, Katherine acted immediately. With no one to advise her, she turned to the one place where she was certain she would get help: Spain.

Katherine instinctively knew that Charles would not desert her, even though the cooler political climate between her adopted country and her native land had ruined her own rapport with him. Affectionate correspondence had stopped. In a very telling letter to her nephew, which is dated 26 November 1526, Katherine had made no attempt to conceal her distress at their estrangement: 'I cannot imagine what may be the cause of your Highness having been so angry, and having so forgotten me, that for upwards of two years I have had no letters from Spain,' she had written. Characteristically though, she had not been able to resist driving home the point that she did not 'deserve this treatment' because her 'affection and readiness' for Charles's cause surely meant that she 'deserved a better reward'. She had returned to the same theme in a subsequent note. After thanking him for 'favours conferred' upon her, and promising to serve him in whatever way her 'scanty' abilities and 'small' powers permitted, she had bluntly reminded him of the paucity of his attention: 'I hold it to be that Your Highness has chosen to show sorrow for my death, perceiving that neither my existence nor my services are such as to deserve being recalled to your memory.' It could hardly have been otherwise, especially with Henry's rapprochement with France and Charles's Portuguese marriage. Ironically, it was within the bright, intricately carved rooms of Boabdil's former palace that the new empress conceived her first child, a boy whom a delighted Charles named Philip after his own father, Philip of Burgundy.

But, in times of crisis, all ill-feeling would be forgotten. So, when whispers of Henry's underhand divorce attempts first filtered through to her, Katherine's immediate thought was her nephew. In a dispatch to Charles dated 18 May 1527, the Spanish ambassador, Iñigo de Mendoza, conveyed the devastating tidings. He had heard 'on reliable authority' that Wolsey, 'as the finishing stroke to all his iniquities has been scheming to bring about the Queen's divorce'. Still worse, the king was 'so bent on this divorce' that he had 'secretly assembled certain bishops and lawyers that they may sign a declaration to the effect that his marriage with the Queen is null and void on account of her having been his brother's wife', Mendoza elaborated. His information was remarkably accurate.

It is safe to speculate that the 'reliable authority' was Katherine herself, because the ambassador not only knew of the secret court's existence and purpose, he also knew of the queen's trepidation and fears. And this though he claimed she was 'so full of apprehension' that she had not 'ventured to speak' with him. Clearly, the queen had her own methods of communication. Dissembling was an art she had already mastered; ingenious subterfuge was to be next on her list of useful accomplishments.

However, there was always a chance that events might go no further. The king had had whims before. 'She [Katherine] always fancied that the King, after pursuing his course for some time, would turn away, and yielding to his conscience, would change his purposes as he had done at other times and return to reason,' the Spanish ambassador would tell his master. Fancy it was, but it was a straw she was to clutch until her dying day.

Yet any early hopes of Henry abandoning the matter were dashed on 22 June 1527 when he tentatively broached the subject with her himself. He began quite forcefully, boldly stating that they had been living in 'mortal sin' since the day of their wedding; he knew this because it was 'the opinion of many canonists and theologians' he had consulted. So, he went on, probably a little more hesitantly, he had 'come to the resolution, as his conscience was much troubled thereby, to separate himself from her'. He then had the temerity to ask her 'to choose the place to which she would retire'.

Katherine's response was to burst into tears. Perhaps this was simply because her worst fears were now realised; equally, after eighteen years of wedlock, she knew that her sobs were the best way to discomfort Henry and she was not a woman to discard a useful weapon. She once said that he was 'more accessible to persuasion than to threat'; few means of persuasion could rival the witnessing of female tears. And certainly her tears did move the king. Clumsily, he tried to assure her that 'all should be done for the best' as he swiftly made his exit. But his sympathy only went so far: before leaving her to the ministrations of her ladies, he begged her to keep secret all he had said. Since the account we have of the incident comes from Mendoza who passed it on to Charles, Katherine took no notice of that particular request. Secrecy benefited Henry; she wanted publicity and she wanted outside help. That could only come from the pope himself and from Charles. She would assiduously court and badger both.

For her, there came to be three main issues. The most immediate was that her marriage was sacrosanct and so must be defended. Her parents had arranged it and the pope allowed it. There was nothing questionable about it. And she would forever maintain that it had to be valid for the most intimate of reasons: she had never been Arthur's wife in the fullest sense of that term. If she had not known Arthur 'carnally', then 'truth and right' were hers. To deny her marital status, to put asunder those whom God had joined together, was to imperil her soul because she would be denying truth. And if Henry persisted in his wanton folly, he would imperil his soul too. Thus, she was trying to preserve more than her own marriage, she was trying to rescue her husband. The fires of the Inquisition were but a taster of what the damned would face if they did not repent. She must redeem Henry from himself.

But there was Mary too. If she gave way, her daughter could be illegitimised, becoming no better than Richmond and with no more right to the throne than the king's bastard. Dismayed at Richmond's possible prospects before the divorce was mooted, she was even more horrified now. A wild rumour reached Charles that the projected French marriage for Mary was designed so that she could be sent to France and leave the coast clear for Richmond. Then, 'in course of time the said illegitimate son might be appointed to the succession of the Crown'. With her daughter's royal status and future at stake, Katherine would battle to the bitter end, just as Juana had fought for Charles during the Communero revolt. Eustace Chapuys, the Spanish ambassador who succeeded Mendoza upon the latter's return to Spain in 1529, once remarked that Anne Boleyn was 'fiercer than a lioness'; the same could be said of Katherine. The two women were well matched.

Yet, as time went on, a wider point gradually emerged: the supremacy of Holy Mother Church. If the pope's dispensation was cast aside, papal power itself would be discredited. Katherine expressed this very clearly in a letter to Charles and his empress in October 1528: 'Were this present Pope to undo what his predecessors have done, it must inevitably weigh on his honour and conscience, and lead ultimately to the discredit of the Apostolic See, which should stand firmly on one foundation.'

Her conviction that her personal struggle was bound up with the survival of the Church, even its very soul, was to become a constant theme for her. To protect her God, no price was too high to pay for the 'Defendress of the Faith'. In 1531, worried that the English Parliament would act against both herself and Mary, she would write to Chapuys that their deaths would be 'martyrdom', a fate they would willingly accept as they would be suffering 'for the sake of truth'. Hyperbole had run through her letters to Ferdinand when complaining of her neglect by Henry VII after Arthur's death; so it does again – but, arguably, with more cause.

And once she realised that her replacement was to be Anne Boleyn, the situation assumed yet another dimension, for Anne represented a threat to all that Katherine stood for. Over the years, she had managed to accept the presence of mistresses in her husband's life with a reasonable degree of sangfroid. A quick glance in her mirror would have shown her that constant child-bearing had taken its toll upon her physical appearance. While the king was still in his prime, albeit starting to put on a little weight, the passing years had not treated her so kindly; the soft prettiness that once had attracted Henry had long since disappeared. Her face was fuller, her figure stouter. 'If not handsome, she is not ugly,' wrote one Venetian as tactfully as he could; another remarked on her 'modest countenance'. Both men stressed her gentle character. She was 'prudent and good', she was 'replete with goodness and religion'. Even Katherine understood that the plain face and goodness of a son-less wife was no competition to the youthful promise of Anne. What truly appalled Katherine, though, was not so much that Henry was tempted by Anne's blatant allure but the prospect of Anne becoming queen. No mistress should be able to oust a wife.

Even worse, Anne leaned towards the new religious ideas that, to traditionalists like Katherine, were surfacing frighteningly fast. And where Anne went, Henry was sure to follow. To Chapuys, and presumably to Katherine, Anne and her father were 'more Lutheran than Luther' himself. Chapuys's assessment was not entirely wrong. Religion was as central to Anne's being as it was to her father, her brother and had been to her grandfather. Yet Anne was not one mindlessly to accept the concepts taught by the Church for generations. Like a modern woman, she wanted to question and probe, she revelled in the buzzing debates that were beginning to take place in intellectual circles, finding such discussions genuinely thrilling and exhilarating. Once the divorce got into its stride, her views became more pronounced, more extreme. A fluent French speaker, she soon shared with Henry a translation of the New Testament by Lefèvre d'Étaples, a copy whose cover was engraved in gold with her initials and those of the king. That Henry and Anne should own such a work was truly shocking for Katherine, herself safely brought up on the Latin Vulgate and agreeing that vernacular versions of the sacred text were heretical. Anne's brother George was no better, forever dabbling in the exciting new ways of looking at the world and religion's place within it. Neither Anne nor George was anything but devout, but they wanted to bring the gospels to the people, they wanted preachers to preach and enlighten not just repeat age-old homilies, they wanted all to share a much more relevant religious experience. They represented the new ways, while Katherine stood firmly behind the old.

For Katherine, then, it was as though the Crusades were on her own doorstep. The 'secret matter' started off for the queen as a straightforward struggle to make Henry overcome his unfounded scruples of conscience and return to her as his God-given wife, but escalated over the years into a battle not just for herself and her daughter but for the preservation of nothing less than her 'Holy Catholic Faith' itself. As a girl, she had witnessed the fall of Granada, a fitting climax to Isabella's crusade for her God. Now, thirty years or so later, it was her own turn to carry on the fight.

Like her formidable mother, Katherine would not flinch from her duty. It is romantic nonsense to imagine her a patient Griselda, a saintly being quietly waiting for her husband to come to his senses while she stoically endured mental torment and anguish. It is also grossly to underestimate her. Katherine was brave, feisty, a ferocious and tenacious warrior for what she believed to be right. If Henry would not cease from risking his own soul and the souls of the people entrusted by God to his care, and if he continued to threaten the very existence of God's Church, then she must and would oppose him every inch of the way. A lioness indeed.

Crusader Queen

The instant Katherine heard of Wolsey's shabby, secret court, she sprang into action and the first salvoes were fired in a war which would end only when she took her final breath. At first glance the odds against her seem overwhelming. Surely, she did not stand a chance. Or did she?

After virtually twenty years on the throne, Henry was awe-inspiring, commanding, egotistical, confident that no one could prevent him from getting his own way. Those who had opposed or threatened him in the past had been swept aside. Empson and Dudley had been executed to bring cheap popularity; the rotting bodies of those unfortunate apprentices chosen to pay the price after Evil May Day had filled the gibbets; the Yorkist Earl of Suffolk had been beheaded; even Buckingham had proved just as mortal as everyone else when he had knelt before that bungling headsman on Tower Hill. With such grim memories so fresh, who among the clergy or laity would dare take Katherine's side against Henry, a man whose forceful personality dominated every sphere of their lives and who could buy their loyalty with perquisites, offices and grants of land?

And behind Henry was the great cardinal. Courted by kings, trusted by Henry, feared by English courtiers, rich beyond measure, a true prince of the church, his workload was incredible. So was his success rate. When Katherine viewed him as the originator of the terrible trouble that had befallen her, she was wrong. But she was right to be wary of his incisive mind, his intellect and his sheer logistical ability. He was an opponent to be dreaded.

So was Anne. With her quick, agile brain, and a dogged determination that equalled Katherine's, she was a force in herself, especially with the enticing prospect of the king's ring upon her finger and a glittering crown upon her dark hair. She would take just as active a part in the proceedings as did Katherine. After all, Katherine's loss would be her gain.

It would be her relatives' gain as well, for Anne came equipped with formidable family back-up only too happy to share in whatever loot was on offer. Neither Anne's brother-in-law, the acquiescent William Carey, nor her father had ever refused the flood of gifts accruing from Mary Carey's affair with the king. The prospect of Anne replacing her sister in the royal bed, and becoming queen in the process, aroused nothing but gleeful anticipation among her nearest and dearest. Indeed, Anne's father, Thomas, is the only one who could have afforded to pay for a jewelled ship in which a 'solitary damsel is tossed about' that Anne presented to Henry to mark her surrender to his masculine charms. With a little sleuthing, we can find a reference in Thomas's accounts 'to Corneyls [Cornelius Hayes], the king's goldsmith, £4' which might well have gone some way to settling that particular bill.

Then there was Anne's brother, George; a fluent French speaker and ever his sister's confidant, Anne counted on him to champion her cause with Francis. Her maternal uncle just happened to be the Duke of Norfolk, a man constantly at Henry's side and in his confidence. And her father's brother, James Boleyn, was another useful member of the family firm, partly because his former tutor was Robert Wakefield, England's most respected Hebrew expert. It was none other than Wakefield who had countered those who had pointed to the existence of the Princess Mary as the obvious flaw in Henry's use of the verse in Leviticus promising childlessness to those who married their brother's widow. For it was Wakefield who had proved to Henry's satisfaction that the original Hebrew text had been incorrectly translated and gendered.

Katherine was undaunted by the forces ranged against her. Although often presenting herself as a weak, friendless woman, alone in a foreign land, with no one daring to stand up for her, she knew she was nothing of the kind. With her mother's courage and strong spirit, she was not one meekly to surrender to what she saw as an injustice. Even Wolsey, while deriding her stubbornness, paid reluctant homage to her 'stiff heart'. Her innate political acumen, honed during her widowhood, when she had learnt the priceless skills of manipulation, dissembling and scheming, had matured in those early halcyon days of her marriage to Henry. As a young wife, she had felt the thrill of advising her doting husband, having her support respectfully sought by the various ambassadors, ruling the country as its regent in her husband's stead, even emerging victorious in the most thorough routing of Scotland's armies that England had ever inflicted. She was no novice on the world stage.

Nor, as she was quite aware, was she friendless. She had supporters even within Henry's innermost circles. To the obsequious Suffolk's obvious dismay, his wife, Mary 'the French Queen', Henry's sister, remained her staunch ally throughout, even recklessly uttering 'opprobrious language against Madam Anne' at the height of the latter's ascendancy. Mountjoy's daughter, the Marchioness of Exeter, was solidly in Katherine's camp. Margaret Pole, Countess of Salisbury, Katherine's friend since Ludlow, was considered too suspect to be left in charge of Princess Mary, her replacement eventually being Lady Anne Shelton, Thomas Boleyn's sister. While having no real influence, Lady Willoughby, Katherine's dearest Maria de Salinas, would never forsake her much-loved mistress. Women, in particular, flocked to Katherine's cause as, to Henry's fury, did many of the ordinary citizens. So, more significantly, did Bishop John Fisher. Initially bamboozled by Henry's mendacious protestations about merely wanting his doubts about the legality of his marriage allayed so that he could live with the queen in peace and harmony until death did them part, Fisher soon appreciated the extent of Henry's duplicity. From then onwards, Katherine could not have had a better friend or better advocate. Her own servants did not desert her either. Her physician, Dr Fernando Vittorio, and her 'sewer' (a sort of waiter and general factotum), Francisco Felipez, proved her valiant defenders, selflessly putting themselves in personal danger for her sake. And there were so many whose names we do not know but who gave her information, warnings, comfort. In the early years of the divorce at least, Katherine was far from alone or friendless.

But concrete support could only come from Spain. The ambassadors, Iñigo de Mendoza and later his successor, Eustace Chapuys, were stalwart in her defence, doing whatever their remit would allow. Most of all, she pinned her hopes on Juana's son, Charles. He alone had the sheer clout to act on her behalf against her husband and his advisers, against Francis (whom Henry was forever trying to bring firmly on his side) and, crucially, to negotiate with the pope, Clement VII.

Filling Charles in on what was going on was a constant headache. Clearly a born conspirator, Katherine devised ingenious methods to get her letters and messages through to the ambassadors, to foreign rulers, and to Charles himself. One of her first attempts was quite crude but, incredibly, it worked. Francisco Felipez, her 'sewer', asked Henry for permission to return to Spain to visit his dying mother. In normal circumstances, the king would have granted it without a thought. Now, though, he was bound to be suspicious and this is where Katherine launched her scheme to outwit him. Pretending to think Felipez a liar, she advised Henry to withhold his consent, hoping that he would grant it just to be perverse. Seeing straight through her scheme, but eager to know the contents of her agent's letter pouch, Henry attempted a double bluff: he said that Felipez could leave, but Wolsey sent messages that he should be arrested in France and his baggage searched. Unfortunately for the king, Felipez contrived to reach Spain without arrest and rushed straight to Charles with the news that Katherine's marriage really was in jeopardy.

Charles listened. Katherine was his 'dear aunt', his 'most beloved aunt', a woman for whom he felt 'love and affection ... of the same kind as that of a son towards his parent'. He would not let her down. 'Her cause is ours', he instructed Mendoza to warn Henry. At first, however, believing that Henry merely needed reassurance, Charles tried a direct man-to-man approach, writing to his fellow monarch expressing his own confidence that the marriage was definitely valid. The English king should have no anxieties about it. But Charles took the added precaution of alerting Pope Clement, suggesting that he should send a letter or brief couched 'in the mildest terms' to persuade Henry to drop the whole business. Should he persist in his folly, then Clement should judge the suit in Rome.

Having a hearing at Rome was precisely what Katherine wanted, fearing that she would not get fair treatment in England where she was surrounded by Henry's cronies. Revocation of the case to Rome was what she would go on demanding over the next seven or so years. And this is where the international situation tipped her way. After the battle of Pavia, Charles and Francis had eventually agreed a peace deal of sorts, but the conflicts between them had not really ended. Although weakened, Francis carried on plotting and Charles still had armies in Italy. On 6 May 1527 mutinous soldiers under the command of one of Charles's allies attacked and sacked the holy city of Rome.

Lurid stories of the soldiers' misdeeds reverberated throughout Europe: 'They violated nuns.' They 'burnt the most magnificent buildings'. They 'turned churches into stables'. They 'trod underfoot the relics of the saints to spoil [steal] their ornaments'. They used 'crucifixes and other images' for target practice. Caught in the midst of such outrages, Clement fled to the safety of the Castel Sant'Angelo. He was completely in Charles's power. A pragmatic man of the world, as much a temporal as a religious leader, Clement might have liked to ease Henry's path but that was not an option. Charles would never allow it.

In England, news of the pope's plight ruined Wolsey's court. The cardinal had already realised that the intricacies of the case were monumental. He knew that Katherine would refuse to acknowledge his jurisdiction and appeal directly to the pope – and he feared that her messengers would elude his own spies and agents. With Clement now subject to Charles, the cardinal had no alternative but to end his secret court and try something else. Katherine, while suitably distressed to learn of the Sack of Rome, had breathing space. It was not to last.

Over the next year the talking never stopped. Charles, genuinely perplexed about Henry's alleged 'scruple' of conscience, hoped that all could be settled amicably. While concerned for Katherine, and ready to challenge slights upon his family, he did not want yet more war. Wolsey, desperate to fulfil his master's wishes and to please the ever-present and ever-pressing Anne, negotiated frenetically to free the pope or to persuade his fellow cardinals to allow him to act in the Holy Father's place. Henry resorted to a little back-handed diplomacy of his own. Without telling Wolsey, he sent a trusted envoy, William Knight, to Rome. His mission was to pave the way for Henry to marry Anne. Henry was all too aware that, having slept with Anne's sister, Mary Carey, he had created an affinity between himself and his 'own darling' almost identical to the one which he insisted was the obstacle between himself and Katherine – an irony that cannot have been lost on the

incredulous Clement. A further complication was that Anne's relationship with Harry Percy, juvenile though it probably was, might well
be construed as a betrothal, and perhaps was. Even an unofficial
betrothal introduced another impediment to a future marriage. If
Henry's existing union was a mess, his next one could be too. Better to
clear it up in advance. Eventually, Knight did secure a dispensation on
the lines that Henry wanted, but crucially it was only to operate if the
king's original marriage was first declared invalid, and there was no
imminent prospect of this.

Meanwhile, Katherine continued to bide her time. In public, she
remained the perfect wife, ever polite and gracious. Mindful of her
mother's teaching on housewifely skills, she went on sewing Henry's
shirts for him as though no discord existed. Behind the closed doors of
her privy chamber, however, she wrote to Charles whenever she could,
she sent messages to Mendoza via her servants, she plotted the lines of
her defence and, since the king's supporters preferred to tell her as little
as possible, she agonised over how Henry intended to proceed.

She was soon to find out. After weeks of constant pressure, Clement
gave way to Henry's demands and allowed a commission of inquiry to
be set up, headed by Wolsey and his fellow legate, Cardinal Campeggio.
The latter arrived in England at the very end of September 1528, tired,
in agony from the gout that afflicted him sorely, to discover just how
many hopes were pinned upon him.

Katherine prayed that Campeggio had been sent to make sure that
the case was transferred to Rome. 'The Queen's friends', wrote Mendoza,
'think he only comes to institute a judicial inquiry, and then, with the
result of the same, return to Rome.' Her nightmare, that Campeggio
intended to hear and judge the case in London, was Henry and Anne's
dream. They were happily contemplating a court case held in London
and a judgment in their favour. 'Then I trust within a while to enjoy
that which I have so longed for to God's pleasure and our both comfort,'
Henry wrote to his beloved.

Wolsey was praying for the king's comfort too. His fear was that
Katherine would protest against the jurisdiction of the court and appeal
directly to Clement; then the king's cause might be lost and Henry
would blame Wolsey. So the cardinal had worked to cajole Clement

into allowing him to try the case on the basis of a 'decretal' commission, rather than a more general one. A 'decretal' commission meant that instead of merely allowing the outline of the suit to be aired, as Katherine's friends anticipated, the legates were empowered to decide upon the various canon law issues involved in what all recognised was tantamount to a final trial of the matters central to the case. If Wolsey and Campeggio were entitled to pronounce on these issues, Katherine could not appeal to Rome against their decisions on points of law. Effectively, the ground would have been cut from beneath her feet. Tragically for Wolsey, the pope gave Campeggio possession of such a document but with strict instructions that, while he could show it to the king and his fellow cardinal, he could not use it.

Clement was on a tightrope. With Luther's ideas spreading, he was desperate to keep Henry within the Church, but trying to achieve this without antagonising Charles was a very tricky business. One solution was for Campeggio to use his 'utmost skill and address in diverting the King from his present desire, and restoring him to his former love towards the Queen'. If this proved 'impossible' he was ordered 'not to pronounce in any manner without a new and express commission from hence [Rome]'. In other words, he was to drag the proceedings out as long as he could but give no judgment. Had Katherine only known that, she could have slept a little more easily. She would not have slept at all had she known that at one point Clement had pondered appeasing Henry by allowing Princess Mary to marry her half-brother, Richmond, thus settling the succession. Even Henry might have baulked at that.

As it was, Campeggio's attempts to bring the king to reason failed miserably. Henry, Campeggio told Clement's secretary despondently, was so sure that his marriage was invalid, that 'an angel descending from heaven would be unable to persuade him otherwise'. Therefore the resourceful Campeggio tried another tack. Perhaps Katherine would succumb to gentle arguments and be persuaded to repair to the nearest nunnery and spend the rest of her life in contemplation and prayer. Once she was safely immured, the case could proceed without her interference and Clement would no doubt be in a better position to grant an annulment of her marriage to Henry. The king thought it a wonderfully neat idea.

So, on 24 October 1528, Katherine received visitors: Campeggio and Wolsey. It was her first chance to gauge what Campeggio's mission might mean for her, and for him to assess her position. Wolsey, naturally, tried to take charge. When Katherine asked whether it would be better to hold the meeting in her public chambers or in private, he was quick to propose that a more intimate setting was preferable. From his standpoint, the fewer witnesses the better; Katherine lost that round. But she won the next. She listened wryly as Campeggio suggested that the solution to what was such an awful situation for everyone lay in her own hands. Campeggio, writing to the pope's secretary, flattered himself that he had managed this delicate matter remarkably well. While refraining from actually mentioning a convent, he said, he had left the queen to come to see the attractions of the cloister as the best way of giving 'general satisfaction'. As a good, religious woman she would not want to see 'many and incalculable evils' arising if the case came to trial.

No novice in dissembling, Katherine saw straight through Campeggio's clumsy efforts, remarking placidly that she had already heard that the legates would try to make her enter a convent. Then, Campeggio had to concede, he 'did not deny it'. In fact, the peace and tranquillity of a nunnery was not an unattractive proposition in itself for the daughter of the Catholic Monarchs, but that was not the role in life that her parents and God had chosen for her. She was a married woman, she was Henry's wife, and she would die his wife. It was as simple as that. Campeggio was wasting his time, not that she told him so immediately. Better to leave him wondering for while.

Katherine was too adept a politician not to use Campeggio as he had tried to use her. With Henry and Wolsey intent on curtailing her channels of communication with her potential supporters, she had been forced to resort to using her doctor, her 'sewer', anyone she could, to get messages to Mendoza and to smuggle out letters to Charles and to those who, like her old friend Margaret, Regent of the Netherlands, might help her. To seize upon the opportunity to contact Clement through Campeggio was a stroke of genius. When she begged Henry to allow her to see the cardinal and make her confession to him, the king, unsuspecting, agreed.

So, on 26 October, cardinal and queen met again. He was lodged at

Bath Place, the London residence of John Clerk, the Bishop of Bath and Wells – much to Clerk's chagrin for the bishop furiously complained that there were plenty of other places far more suitable and that Campeggio's presence left him with nowhere to stay himself. Since Campeggio was in severe pain with his gout, Katherine came to visit him. She arrived at Bath Place at nine in the morning, perfectly sure of what she was going to say and why she was saying it.

Katherine had no need to confess to Campeggio, she had her own chaplains. That she chose to do so suggests she had an ulterior motive, especially because we should not know what was said between confessor and penitent. In this instance, though, we do. And we know because Katherine gave Campeggio permission to break the seal of the confessional. For a priest, the words spoken in confession are sacrosanct; he should never reveal them even when threatened with death. True, Henry had once bullied Buckingham's confessor into doing so, but Katherine applied no such pressure to Campeggio. She simply asked him, and he complied.

For most priests, speaking about what they had been told would be a terrible sin, but Campeggio appears to have had no such qualms. Just as the 'Defendress of the Faith' clearly had no qualms about using, some might say abusing, the confessional for her own ends.

In such circumstances, it is hardly surprising that Mendoza soon knew about everything too. Besides Mendoza's report, which he quickly sent to Charles, and a confirmation provided by the Venetian ambassador (albeit five years afterwards), we have Campeggio's own account of this remarkable interview. Katherine asked that his secretaries should take an oath of silence, but that did not apply to the cardinal: 'Although she told me all under the seal of confession, yet she gave me liberty, indeed she besought me, to write to our Lord (the Pope) certain resolutions.' And he tells us just what those resolutions were:

She affirmed, on her conscience, that from 14 November, when she was espoused to the late [prince] Arthur, to 2 April following, when he died, she did not sleep with him more than seven nights *et che da liu restò intacta et incorrupta, come venne dal ventre di sua madre.*

These last words, stating that she had remained as intact and uncorrupted as when she had left her mother's womb, were startlingly similar to those used by Isabella when she had read Doña's Elvira's letter about Katherine's virgin status on Arthur's death.

The other things that Katherine said, such as begging Campeggio to bring Henry to reason and that she could never become a nun, pale into insignificance compared with her statement of virginity. Mendoza knew all about it and passed on his information to Charles:

> I have reasons to believe, though the Queen herself has not said so to me, that she told the Legate that she was a virgin when she married this her second husband, and that the first (Prince Arthur) had never consummated the marriage.

Katherine could not have better served her cause. The pope would hear what she wanted him to hear, and would know that she had made her declaration under the sacred seal of the confessional.

Her virginity was the essence of her case: if she was a virgin, then her marriage to Arthur was no true marriage so her union with Henry was legal in God's eyes. But the strategy was not without risk. 'Virginity', remarked Mendoza shrewdly, 'is a thing not easily proved, except by oath of the party herself.'

By her assertion in the confessional, Katherine might be assumed to have placed herself above suspicion. Yet Katherine was not above dissembling. She could deceive and she could lie. Indeed that is, in effect, what she had done when she misdated one of her earlier miscarriages to her father. And, while lying was intrinsically wrong, motivation was key; even Thomas More and Bishop John Fisher, canonised saints that they became, advised their servants that lies told for a godly purpose were likely to earn God's forgiveness. But they both agreed that to lie upon oath was another matter entirely. It imperilled the soul.

Lying in the confessional involved a similar hazard. For Katherine to jeopardise her soul is surely unthinkable – unless, just maybe, she convinced herself that she would confess her lie in another confession another day. As long as she was not *in extremis*, there would be time to seek God's mercy and entreat forgiveness and understanding for her sin.

Yet in the Spanish archives we can find references to an oath in which she placed her hands between those of Cardinal Campeggio, and stated her virginity. We do not know precisely when this oath was taken; it could have been on the occasion of her confession. If she both confessed, and took a separate oath, it would be to gamble with her soul not once but twice. We can only speculate as to whether Katherine, seeing her marriage, her child and her Church at stake, would dare to risk such a sacrifice.

Certainly Henry's investigators thought that she would. It was an issue to which they would return again and again. Hidden among a long list of questions, now in the National Archives, that were later put to John Fisher, and which are rarely noticed, are several about the queen. Three are of considerable significance. Did he write any letters to Katherine, Fisher was asked, 'as if she despaired of the mercy of God'? The follow-up question was 'whether the cause of this despair was that she committed perjury, and, as some say, received the Host, that she was never carnally known by prince Arthur'. Pursuing the point, the interrogators asked 'why he should exhort her not to despair of the mercy of God unless he knew she despaired thereof'.

Fisher answered each question with precision, clearly choosing his words with care. 'Not for one time only', he said, did Katherine consult him about 'certain scruples which offended her conscience', but such consultations were known to Henry and had happened 'long before this affair began'. He did not say what those scruples were. Yet his response to the second question was exact. 'I never heard from her that she despaired of mercy, or had committed perjury,' he declared. And, if he ever wrote to her about the mercy of God, it was only 'that she might put away all scruples of conscience' and 'establish her mind in the hope and trust of the promises of Christ'. He does not say why he mentioned the mercy of God in the first place.

The matter of Katherine's maidenhood, then, is a minefield. In the last resort, we have to decide whether or not we believe what she said. Perhaps our best clue is that we know that nothing mattered to her more than her faith. She would never betray that lightly nor for personal gain.

But she did have another card to play. Knowing that Wolsey hoped to seize upon an easy way out by finding so many faults in the pope's original bull of dispensation that it could be dismissed on technical grounds, she suddenly announced that she possessed both a copy of the bull and a copy of a brief on the same subject. The brief, found in Dr de Puebla's papers after the ambassador's death, had been sent by the pope to comfort Katherine's mother Isabella in her final illness. Over the years the brief had been forgotten. Its sudden appearance now threw the legatine proceedings into disarray. Clement's commission, decretal or not, had empowered the court to look only into the bull; it said nothing about the mysterious brief. Katherine's copy of the bull was identical to that of her husband, so all hinged on the wording of the brief. Should it differ from the bull, the court's mandate was inadequate. And Katherine knew very well that there were indeed discrepancies between the two documents.

And one of the divergences overturned a central plank of Wolsey's case. He had been arguing that one reason why the bull of dispensation was useless was because it had stated that the marriage between Henry and Katherine would ensure peace between England and Spain. Wolsey's thesis, tenuous as it might seem to us, was that since England and Spain were at peace then anyway, there was no need for the marriage to ensure its continuance. So, the pope's motive for allowing something so controversial in canon law as a union with a brother's widow was thus invalidated. Unfortunately, the brief said that there had been other (unspecified) reasons why the pope had agreed to the match.

Wolsey and the king were furious with Katherine. She was inter-rogated by Warham and Bishop Tunstall over how she had got hold of her copy of the brief in the first place. She remained firm, even when they virtually accused her of plotting against Henry's life. Such a ludicrous allegation was beyond contempt, but the question concerning the brief had to be answered. Katherine, by now a mistress of evasion, replied that Mendoza had given it to her six months earlier. We do not know for sure how she had obtained the brief, but Mendoza was obviously puzzled over the part she had allocated to him in its discovery. Clearly, Katherine knew that he would be, so she forewarned him. His dispatch to Charles on how he would respond if questioned is illuminating for those who believe that Katherine could never equivocate. 'I shall so shape my answer', said the loyal Mendoza, 'that it may not disagree with the Queen's declaration, nor make it appear as if she had stated an untruth.'

In fact, while explosive at the time, the brief did not change the outcome of the 'secret matter' but, because of it, Katherine took yet another oath on the subject of her virginity. Although the wording of the brief seriously undermined Henry's case, it also affected her own: it referred to her marriage to Arthur having been consummated, as Julius had assumed that it was. As a result of Spanish protests, the final bull of dispensation had contained the words 'perhaps consummated' rather than just 'consummated'. The damning words of the brief and the 'perhaps' of the bull left doubts that Katherine needed to remove.

She was up to the challenge. On 7 November 1528, and 'in the presence' of leading churchmen including Warham and Fisher, she made a 'protest and declaration ... that she does not admit those words inserted in the brief' (i.e. carnally known by Prince Arthur). Such words, she said 'holding the Holy Gospel in her hand', were 'lacking any decree or knowledge'. 'No presumptions' were therefore to be drawn from them. Her casuistry is intriguing; she does not actually say that the words are untrue, simply that she does not admit them.

She never would admit them. And she was about to be given the chance to say so in public. On 31 May 1529 Wolsey and Campeggio opened their inquiry into the royal divorce. Katherine steeled herself to appear in person. Arguably, it was her finest hour.

Taking a Stand

A stone's throw from the River Thames and from Henry's palace of Bridewell lies the monastic complex known as Blackfriars. Here, black-garbed Dominicans chanted their prayers, studied in the cloisters, ate in the lofty refectory, and meditated in the gardens and orchards. It was Blackfriars that the king chose as the venue for Campeggio and Wolsey to thrash out the intimate details of his marriage. Within its walls, he hoped, they would reach what for him was the correct decision, and he could at last marry his Anne. That is, unless Katherine managed to prevent him.

By now she was as prepared as she could be. Her position had not changed: she would not surrender and she would maintain that her marriage to Henry was true because she had never consummated her union with Arthur. 'No marriages will be secure if this is dissolved,' she told Pope Clement. She had no choice but to take a stand if truth was to be upheld.

But no court in England, she maintained, could bring her justice because its personnel were bound to be under Henry's sway, as were any counsel assigned to her. Agreeing, Katherine's friend Margaret appointed lawyers from the Netherlands to assist her former sister-in-law. As it turned out, they were unable to stay in England for very long as they felt intimidated, probably with reason. One whose advice she sought was the scholar Vives, who had written treatises on education with Princess Mary in mind. After listening politely to all the queen said concerning her marriage, doing his best to console her and generally singing her praises, he agreed to pass on a message to Mendoza. Other than that, he was reluctant to 'willingly meddle in the affairs of princes'.

Luckily for Katherine, there was one man who would 'meddle in the affairs of princes', a man of integrity and fierce courage: Bishop John

Fisher. One of the legal team appointed by Henry to work for Katherine's defence, Fisher was to become her most resolute and valiant champion. Pointing out to a furious Henry that, in a dispute with Herod, John the Baptist had declared that it was 'impossible ... to die more gloriously than in the cause of marriage', Fisher vowed that he himself would 'dare any great or extreme peril whatever' for a similar principle. Equating Henry with Herod was tantamount to putting his own life on the line, but the bishop did not flinch.

When the court at Blackfriars opened at the end of May 1529, Katherine certainly had need of him. But she also relied upon her own instincts. The proceedings presented her with a dilemma. If she appeared in person, some might see it as a tacit acceptance of the trial's legality; if she refused to appear, she would miss a rare opportunity to air her case in public. Such a chance might not come again. The choice was simple.

Katherine knew how to create an impression and how to play the many roles thrust upon royal women. Every inch a queen, she had fulfilled her myriad of public duties with regal aplomb, while never losing sight of her essential feminine status. She was, after all, a woman who was not too proud to make her husband's shirts. Indeed, Wolsey's biographer, Cavendish, describes how she once appeared to the legates with a skein of white thread around her neck, apologising that they had arrived while she was 'at work' among her ladies. Perhaps she was indeed working, or perhaps she knew the importance of cultivating a good image to the worldly Campeggio, a man who had only taken holy orders following the death of his wife.

Nothing she had ever done, though, could match her superb display in that chamber at Blackfriars. The tapestry-decorated hall was set up as a court room, with benches for the various lawyers, chairs draped with cloth of gold for Wolsey and Campeggio, cushioned chairs set under gold brocade cloths of estate for Henry and Katherine, and plenty of room for spectators. Far from the surroundings daunting Katherine, they provided her with the best of all possible stage sets. Truly magnificent, she gave the performance of her life.

Her petition to transfer the trial to Rome rejected by the legates, she listened sceptically while Henry declared himself tormented by living in mortal sin for twenty years, vowing earnestly that he could never be 'at ease' while the legality of his marriage was unclear. After Wolsey and Campeggio promised to judge the dispute fairly and justly, Katherine took control.

Rising from her seat, she crossed the floor and knelt at Henry's feet. Cavendish has left us a very full version of what she said. She addressed herself only to her husband, it was as if she and he were the only two people in that packed room. Begging him for 'justice and right ... pity and compassion', she reiterated her feelings of being 'a poor woman', 'a stranger' born out of Henry's lands. She had she said, 'no assured friend', no neutral counsel.

Then, with everyone's eyes upon her, their ears straining to catch her every word, she cut to the quick, asking what she had done to offend her husband. 'I take God and the world to witness', she said, 'that I have been to you a true humble and obedient wife, ever conformable to your will and pleasure.' No one could have said otherwise. And when she touched on the question of children, few would have been unmoved:

> This twenty years I have been your true wife or more, and by me
> ye have had divers children, although it hath pleased God to call
> them out of this world, which hath been no default in me.

It was then that she broadcast to the world that she had been a virgin upon her marriage to Henry: 'And when ye had me at the first, I take God to be my judge, I was a true maid without touch of man.' No one listening could mistake what was in fact her key point. Devastatingly, she went on to remind Henry that he knew she was telling the truth. 'Whether it be true or no, I put it to your conscience,' she challenged, knowing perfectly well how much Henry's conscience mattered to him.

Henry VII and Ferdinand, she continued, both 'excellent kings in wisdom and princely behaviour', as well as the 'wise counsellors' around them, had thought the marriage 'good and lawful', so she could not understand why Henry could entertain such doubts himself, and cause her so much pain.

Returning to her point about having no proper advisers, she implored the king to spare her the 'extremity' of the court until she received counsel from Spain. If he would not, she said, delivering yet another body blow, she could only commit her cause to God.

In the stunned silence that greeted her totally unexpected speech, she curtsied deeply to Henry and swept from the room leaning upon the arm of one of her household officials, accompanied by her supportive ladies. Requests that she return to her seat were treated disdainfully. 'It is no indifferent [neutral] court for me,' she pronounced, 'therefore I will not tarry.' She had thrown everything into disarray, just as she must have planned. She would never go back.

With her empty chair a constant accusation for Henry, he had little choice but to press on. The trial continued in her absence, the queen being pronounced 'contumacious', her cause maintained by her legal advisers who remained after her dramatic departure. Katherine had often proved herself a poor judge of character: she had eulogised over the calculating and grasping Friar Diego, she had criticised the efforts of the hard-working Dr de Puebla. Her belief that Wolsey was anything but an impartial judge was correct, but when she dismissed her advocates as Henry's stooges, she did Fisher in particular a gross disservice. He never gave an inch. He fought her corner with erudition, skill and consummate bravery.

He needed to, for Henry's counsellors pursued the king's case as if their lives depended on it. Katherine's claim of virginity, so difficult for her to prove, was bound to be the crux. The obvious approach was to try to reinvestigate what had happened in the bedroom on Arthur's wedding night and at Ludlow. After Isabella and Ferdinand's first night spent as man and wife, their blood-flecked sheets had been proudly displayed; that had not happened with those used by Arthur and Katherine. Wolsey's clumsy attempt to suggest to Katherine's almoner that they had been smuggled to Ferdinand to prove consummation was a blatant lie. Had Ferdinand received bloodied sheets, neither he nor Isabella would have had any reason to order their ambassador to try to find out whether or not their daughter was still a maiden, which is precisely what they did when news had reached them of Arthur's sudden death. And Wolsey did not seek to produce anyone able to testify to seeing soiled sheets removed from the royal couple's bed, either on that first morning or on any other occasion when Katherine and Arthur had been supposedly living as man and wife. Perhaps the reason was simply that there really had been no bloodstained sheets in the first place?

Wolsey therefore tried a different avenue. He amassed a huge dossier, but almost everything in it is hearsay. This is the run of often voyeuristic documents in which those who had escorted Arthur to his bedchamber or had met him outside his bedroom door on the following morning now told their stories. Henry's cronies certainly did their best for their master and, incidentally, for themselves. The king's favourite and former jousting partner Charles Brandon, now elevated to the dukedom of Suffolk and married to Henry's sister, 'the French Queen', described Arthur's boasts of being 'in the midst of Spain', and repeated insinuations that it had been too much sex that had caused Arthur 'to decay', thus bringing about his premature death. Anne's father, Thomas Boleyn, was quick to reiterate the 'in Spain' stories, even though he had not heard the words himself; in any case, he said, he 'believed' the marriage consummated 'from their [Katherine's and Arthur's] age'. In other words, he knew precisely nothing. And that was the sum of it: mostly, these so-called witnesses affirmed that they 'believed' or 'assumed' consummation because they had not heard otherwise or because they had overheard someone else talking about it.

Wolsey would have been aware of this, but had an ace up his sleeve, or so he thought. He had tracked down William Thomas, the man who had helped Arthur into his nightgown and taken him to Katherine's chamber, leaving him there all night long. His is perhaps the most crucial piece of evidence in Henry's favour as he confirms that Arthur and Katherine did indeed sleep in the same room on more than one occasion. However, since Katherine herself admitted to Campeggio that she had slept with Arthur, although not 'more than seven nights', his testimony loses much of its value. By the time of the Blackfriars trial, Thomas was a prosperous Welsh country gentleman. Sheriff of Carmarthenshire, with a coat of arms of five golden moons and three boar's heads, he was rich enough to leave plenty of silver plate including a silver salt and silver goblets to his family in his will. Although he had transferred to Henry's service shortly after Arthur's death, he stayed at the English court for only a year or so after Henry's marriage to Katherine before returning to his native Wales, making himself respected enough for a Welsh poet, Dafydd ap Hywel, to compose an ode in his honour. The poet describes him as 'Marchog Wiliam' (William the Knight), a man similar in prowess to Galath, one of the legendary knights of King Arthur, as a giant comparable to the warriors of Troy, as one of Henry VIII's hawks ('gwalch Hari') whose privilege was to guard and serve his king. Serving his king, however, did not mean lying for his king; he could not say what he did not see.

A couple of statements in the dossier stand out, since they reveal that not everyone was on Henry's side. Bishop Fox, once one of Henry VII's ministers, had been interviewed in 1527 in the very early stages of Wolsey's investigations. By then seventy-nine years old, he professed not to remember many things but there was one point on which he was very definite: after Arthur's demise, there had been 'frequent deliberations' in Henry's council 'in reference to the impediment'. He knew about the deliberations because he had been present. Nicholas West, Bishop of Ely, was another dissenting voice. While he could 'say nothing of the consummation' other than that Katherine and Arthur had been old enough, West expressed 'doubts of it' because the queen had denied it to him 'on the testimony of her conscience'.

Overall, however, Wolsey's dossier remains thoroughly uncon- vincing. And this did not escape Katherine's shrewd mind. Lying buried in the Spanish archives where it was first discovered by the leading Spanish historian and antiquarian Pascual de Gayangos in 1879, is a 'list of persons likely to give evidence on the first and second marriage of the queen of England' who had returned to Spain over the years, together with the questions they were to be asked. Among those named is Catalina the Moor, 'once the Queen's slave, who used to make her bed and attend to other services of the chamber'. Then there is Catalina Fortes, a former lady-in-waiting to Katherine, 'and much in her confidence'. Another 'waiting maid to the Queen', now married to one of her former male attendants, Juan Cuero, is also mentioned, as is Maria de Rojas, who (says the compiler of the list) 'used to sleep in the same bed' with Katherine 'after the death of Prince Arthur, her first husband'.

The questions put to these former servants leave us in no doubt as to the line that was being pursued:

[1] How long did the said Queen live with Arthur, prince of Wales, and whether the councillors of the king of England [Henry VII] were of opinion that the said Queen and Arthur, her first husband, did not consummate matrimony, owing to his extreme debility, and to the act being exceedingly injurious to his health?

[2] Whether it be true that the said Arthur was very young and thin, delicate and of a weak complexion, and unfit for a woman, and whether he looked as if he were impotent for marriage?

Here was a completely fresh approach to the problem. Had Arthur, after all, been a sickly boy and 'unfit for a woman' even before he had first entered the bedroom on his wedding night to make love to his bride? Had he all along been impotent: unable to do more than manage a teenage fumble?

It would take a considerable time for Charles's agents to track down the people on the list, notably Catalina the Moor, who had married a crossbow maker and was said to be living near Granada. As to Catalina Fortes, she had become a nun at the convent of Madre de Dios at Toledo, while Maria de Rojas had made her home close to either Najera or Vitoria. Their testimony, whatever it finally was, was for some reason never produced at the Blackfriars trial and did not affect its outcome. Nevertheless, the Spanish initiative on Katherine's behalf shows that she had been more than happy for her former servants to give their evidence, clearly believing that she had nothing to fear from what they might have to say. On the other hand, the likelihood that they would have contradicted the official Spanish line so clearly dictated by Charles was about the same as Henry's nobles and Arthur's former servants contradicting the English one. And in the last resort, the evidence on both sides could only have been hearsay, because no one, not even Katherine's Spanish bedchamber servants, had actually been in the room or watched her and Arthur enjoy, or attempt, sexual intercourse together, or not.

And so the case dragged on. Despite all Wolsey's – and Katherine's – best efforts, nothing could be proved on either side, and since there was also no consensus on how the canon law surrounding the case should be interpreted, with Campeggio adhering to his secret instructions from Clement not to decide any substantive points of law, no decision could be reached. Campeggio, who went so far as to say that he hated the entire business as a 'heavy burden' and a 'travail', could see no way out. It thus fell to him to deliver the coup de grâce. On 1 September he transferred the entire case to Rome.

No one had won. Katherine still did not have her husband back, Henry had not received a papal judgment that would allow him to marry Anne with impunity, Clement had antagonised Henry. And, as Katherine had foreseen when she told Mendoza that she thought Wolsey 'would be the victim' of Henry's 'rage', the court's failure presaged the great cardinal's fall. Try as he might, Wolsey could do nothing to placate Henry. In September 1529, Mendoza's replacement, Eustace Chapuys, summed up Wolsey's predicament: 'The affairs of the old Cardinal are beginning to take a very bad turn. Formerly no one dared to say a word against him, but now the tables are turned.'

Turned they were. In October, Wolsey was forced to surrender the king's great seal so he was no longer chancellor; five days after that he pleaded guilty to praemunire (the catch-all crime of accepting foreign jurisdiction contrary to the royal prerogative). Katherine had come to loathe Wolsey, believing him an enemy of Charles and imagining him to be the main instigator of the divorce, but his spectacular fall, and its consequences, shocked even her. His property confiscated by the king, the humiliated and scared cardinal had to write out in his own hand an inventory of every single item he possessed to make sure that nothing was missed. His silver and gold plate, his embroidered hangings and tapestries, his sumptuously furnished houses were all now Henry's. Gloating over the gleaming treasure trove and the glories of Wolsey's London residence, Henry could not resist showing everything off to Anne and her mother.

Meanwhile the disgraced Wolsey was packed off to the city of York to take up his somewhat neglected duties as archbishop, a move that would not satisfy his enemies, who were soon baying for his blood as well as his property. 'Those who have raised this storm against the Cardinal will not rest until they have entirely done for him, knowing full well that were he to recover his lost ascendancy and power their own lives would be in jeopardy,' wrote a perspicacious Chapuys. They did not have long to wait: Wolsey died of a flux the following year while on his way to London to face trial for treason.

Although never in danger of her life, Katherine's own position was worse after the trial than before, as Henry plotted and schemed how to be rid of her. In outward appearance, little seemed to have changed. She carried out her duties as punctiliously as before; ever solicitous, she wrote to Charles asking him for a benefice for one of Campeggio's servants who had lost all his property in the sack of Rome. She continued to sew Henry's shirts – until Anne Boleyn found out, stormed into Henry's presence and demanded that the custom be stopped. It was. In public, Henry continued to treat her with respect. They were together at Whitsun in 1530, they dined in state on major church festivals, they hunted together 'as usual' in the summer of that year. But in private, things were very different. Katherine was bypassed and more personal conversations and meetings with her husband were less and less frequent. Henry was beginning to ostracise her.

Katherine's demeanour remained serene and dignified. Just once she upbraided Henry and took him to task. She exhorted him 'to be again to her a good prince and husband', to 'quit the evil life he was leading and the bad example he was setting', reminding him that she was, as he 'well knew', his 'true and lawful wife'. Henry, who hated scenes, retorted that there were many of his persuasion and that, anyway, the pope was in the emperor's power. With that, he left the room 'abruptly without saying another word'. Not only was such a visible display of defiance uncharacteristic of Katherine, she knew it would achieve nothing. She herself had once said that it was better to cajole Henry than to berate him.

What made matters as intolerable as they were painful for her was Anne's prominence. No longer bothering to disguise his intentions, Henry flaunted his 'own sweetheart' as if she was already his wife. With unconcealed distaste, Chapuys reported to Charles that Anne had sat at the king's side at a banquet 'occupying the very place allotted to a crowned queen'. Still more scandalous in Chapuys's eyes, Henry rode through the countryside with Anne mounted upon his own horse in a pillion, an action so unusual and provocative that it 'greatly called forth people's attention'. And, as the months passed, no one could be unaware of the gifts lavished upon her by Katherine's besotted husband. A raft of new saddles was ordered for her. Among them was one 'of the French fashion', which came with a down pillow 'covered with black velvet, fringed with silk and gold'. Another, again 'of the French fashion', was accompanied by 'a pillow of fine down covered with black velvet, lined with buckram, fringed with silk and gold'. There was a harness 'of black velvet, fringed with silk and gold, with buttons pear fashion, and tassels of silk and gold'. The list is endless, more and more saddles and riding accessories were provided for Anne to accompany her king outdoors in considerable style.

The multitude of riding items pale into insignificance when compared with the jewels Anne accumulated. There was a huge emerald ring, golden buttons, a girdle of gold, a diamond brooch featuring a figure of the Virgin, rubies, gold rings, gold borders 'set with 10 diamonds and 8 pearls' for her sleeves, diamonds for her hair. And, because Anne, like Katherine, was well read, there was material 'for furnishing a book with silver and gilt' and bindings of velvet for other volumes. The king even settled the bill for 'mending a little book which was garnished in France'. Then, to provide a suitable backdrop to show off so many sparkling items, the king paid for yards and yards of the best fabric for her ever-growing wardrobe, some satins costing almost as much by the yard as Henry's servants earned in a month.

And where Anne went, so did her grasping family. They were all forever in the king's company, riding with him, playing cards with him, racing greyhounds with him, hunting with him, playing bowls with him. As they did so, they gathered titles and lands. Her father became Earl of Wiltshire, leaving the title of Viscount Rochford conveniently available for Anne's sharp, astute brother, George. Her uncle, James, so closely associated with the Hebrew scholar, Robert Wakefield, entered Parliament. And Durham House, the stunning riverside home where Katherine had recuperated after Arthur's death, was given to the new Earl of Wiltshire.

Katherine could only watch aghast as her rival was fêted, paraded and flattered while she was being systematically sidelined. What Henry really wanted, or perhaps what Anne demanded, was that she was no longer at court at all. Because Katherine dug in her heels, that took time to arrange, despite a crafty Henry offering the inducement of a precious reunion with their daughter. Seeing straight through his stratagem, Katherine's immediate response was that nothing would make her separate from her husband; a wife's duty was to be constantly at hand. And, when he left her to spend time with Anne without even a farewell, she carried on treating him as she always had by attempting to continue their joint custom of sending messages to each other every three days.

However, with this she miscalculated. What she thought a harmless action, provoked an appallingly vicious response. She sent a message asking after his health and saying how sorry she had been at not seeing him before his departure. Since she had been told that she could not have 'the pleasure and happiness' of going with him, she had imagined that she might have 'the consolation of bidding him adieu'. By meekly stating that nonetheless it was 'for him to order and for her to obey his commands', Katherine probably infuriated him, but his answer left her reeling. He 'cared not for her adieux', he railed, nor did he 'wish to afford her the consolation' of which she had spoken. In fact he had no desire to afford her any consolation at all and was 'indifferent' about her cares for his health. Katherine's attempts at placating him met with another stinging reply, this time in a letter, telling her that she was 'very pertinacious' in her oath that she had 'never been carnally known by prince Arthur, as likewise making public such an assertion'. He would prove her wrong, he threatened. Her time would be more profitably spent in trying to find witnesses 'to prove her pretended virginity' than in sending messages or writing to him. We know of all this from Chapuys's detailed report to Charles on the matter; we also know that it took the ambassador a while to 'soothe' Katherine's 'sorrow' and 'calm her fears'. His efforts were doubtless needed again shortly afterwards, when Henry returned Katherine's carefully chosen New Year's Gift, a 'gold cup of great value and singular workmanship', after hardly glancing at it, while gratefully accepting Anne's present of ornamented darts.

The very foundations of Katherine's life were being undermined. Her husband wanted nothing to do with her; despite his promises and encouragement, Charles seemed to be achieving little for her; and her case dragged on endlessly in Rome. Everyday matters were becoming increasingly troublesome, subject to petty restrictions. With spies planted in her privy chamber, getting messages and letters to her supporters was a major challenge, although her physician Fernando Vittorio acted as her go-between whenever he could. Ever resourceful, the supportive Duchess of Norfolk once sent her a message concealed in an orange stuffed inside a gift of poultry. Even when given permission to visit her, Chapuys told Charles of how the duchess's husband tried to fob him off by saying Katherine had gone out to 'hear a sermon', when she was sitting quietly in her apartments all the time.

Yet somehow she kept up her stream of letters and messages to those she thought might come to her aid. While it never occurred to her to write to her sister Juana, shut up incommunicado at Tordesillas as she was, she communicated with the pope, with Margaret, with Juana's daughter Maria Queen of Hungary, with Charles, with his wife, Isabella, whom he often left as regent in Spain while he attended to the rest of his vast dominions. She told them her news, she begged for their help, and she made it very clear that she would never, ever, give up even though, as she complained to her nephew, her treatment was 'enough to shorten ten lives, much more mine'. She would persevere, for pain and suffering were part of the human condition, designed to be endured and overcome through faith and struggle. This was particularly so when religion itself was threatened. And, since the fiasco of the Blackfriars trial, Katherine had watched helplessly as her fears for her Church gradually materialised.

In a quandary about what road to follow as Campeggio left English shores, Henry tried anything and everything. Constant embassies were sent to Francis to elicit his support. Weakened after Pavia and a second defeat in the battle of Landriano, the French king was prepared to listen, but did very little. He had no desire to defer to Charles but wanted peace rather than war. Thomas Boleyn had the idea of trying to reason directly with Charles himself; unsurprisingly, his arguments fell on deaf ears. Then, possibly acting on the suggestion of a Boleyn protégé, the young Cambridge don, Thomas Cranmer, Henry sought opinions on his case from various European universities. The results were predictable, the institutions declaring their verdicts according to their political allegiances or the value of the king's bribes. Katherine could breathe easily on that score. For Henry, nothing seemed to be working.

And then she suffered another, very cruel blow: enforced separation from her daughter. After a very brief, almost happy, interlude with Princess Mary who had been allowed to visit her in Windsor, Katherine was ordered to move to Wolsey's former Hertfordshire residence, The Moor. Mary was not to go with her, but was to travel to Richmond. While the queen stayed put for another couple of months, Mary dutifully obeyed her father and left for Richmond.

Mother and daughter were never to meet again.

Dangerous Times

Three months after being forced to leave court and travel into exile, Katherine settled down to write yet another letter to her nephew. 'I shall never cease praying God to enlighten his [Henry's] mind, sure as I am that my prayers so just and pious shall in the end be heard,' she wrote, ending poignantly, if a little self-righteously, 'separated from my husband without having ever offended him'. Separated she was. Her household reduced, bundled from residence to residence, brutally parted from her cherished only child, Katherine was also kept out of sight as much as possible, for the ordinary people had no doubts about where their sympathies lay. Nor did they have qualms about expressing them. When Anne travelled with Henry the following summer, people lined the route 'hooting and hissing at her passage'. For most, as for Chapuys who could never bring himself to write of Anne as anything other than 'the Lady' or 'the Concubine', there was only one queen in England and it was not Anne. She was nothing but a strumpet, a 'whore', a 'harlot'.

Anne's name was reviled as far afield as the Welsh hinterland, areas staying loyal to Katherine and to Princess Mary who, like her mother, had lived for a while at Ludlow. In 2004, a forgotten sixteenth-century Welsh poem by Lewys Morgannwg entitled 'To Henry VIII because he married Anne Boleyn', was reliably edited. In this fascinating piece, the poet echoes popular opinion by choosing to castigate Anne as the reincarnation of Alice and Rowena, two legendary women synonymous in Welsh literature with betrayal, poison and murder. 'Do not suppress those of gentle birth and favour those of lowly state,' the poet warns Henry in a clear reference to the differences between Anne and Katherine. Nor should Henry elevate 'one of low blood to be a prince' – a possible allusion to Richmond, or to the son Anne promised to give him. While it is unlikely that the poet would have dared to publish his work while Anne's star was so high, its very existence, and the feelings it expressed, would have comforted the exiled Katherine.

As the months turned into years, she needed such comfort. Try as she might through her prayers and through her frequent messages to her supporters, Katherine could do nothing to halt Anne's meteoric rise. 'The Lady commands absolutely and her will is done in all things,' wrote Chapuys sadly; 'the king cannot be one hour away from her.' Being forever in Henry's company was not enough for Anne: she wanted Katherine's crown as well as her husband.

Snatching her jewels would be a good start. And Anne had a perfect excuse. In May 1532, in a ceremony as glittering as it was controversial, her indulgent suitor elevated her to the peerage in her own right with the male title of Marquess of Pembroke, a title which could be inherited by her sons, whether legitimate or not, and which came complete with lands worth a staggering £1000 per year. Henry, planning a state visit to Calais to meet Francis, intended to take Anne as though she was already queen, her new designation but a taste of what was in store for her. If she was wearing Katherine's jewels it would look even better.

When she was asked for them, Katherine's distress gave way swiftly to anger. She told Chapuys exactly what she thought:

> I would consider it a sin and a load upon my conscience if I were persuaded to give up my jewels for such a wicked purpose as that of ornamenting a person who is the scandal of Christendom and is bringing vituperation upon the king.

Brave words but useless; when the Lady wanted something, the Lady got it. Katherine was forced to accede to the king's direct command and hand over the jewels.

To see Anne go to Calais in her place was anathema to Katherine, though she was gratified to note that the most important ladies in France declined to accompany Francis to see the English monarch's notorious paramour. Among the absentees was Juana's daughter, Eleanor, the widowed Queen of Portugal, now Francis's new wife. Keen to show her support for her aunt and conscious of what was seemly, she would not demean herself by meeting Katherine's foe. However, as she confided to Chapuys, Katherine had an additional worry: that Henry would marry Anne while in France. For, as Anne and Henry boarded the king's ship, the *Swallow*, on a cold October day in 1532, Katherine's world was changing so fast that anything was possible.

Certainly her fears for her beloved Church were coming all too true. She said as much to Charles, comparing events in England with the Turkish onslaught on the Holy Roman Empire. 'Almost equal offence is being offered to God,' she wrote, by what 'these people are attempting here' as 'what the enemy of our Holy Catholic Faith is aiming at there where you are'. She looked to recent events as proof.

A portent of things to come had been a series of anticlerical reforms allowed to pass through the Parliament which Henry called immediately after Blackfriars. Then, in 1531, Henry, convinced that the pope had usurped powers that were rightly his, had attacked the Church more directly by forcing Convocation, as the bench of bishops was known, to agree that he was Supreme Head of the English Church, albeit as far as the law of Christ allowed. The writing was on the wall: Henry was coming round to the idea that the divorce could be granted within England by his own Church rather than by the pope in Rome.

Katherine, 'Defendress of the Faith', watched in genuine anguish as her husband, who had once written against Luther and had been happy to allow the burning of heretical books and even the burning of the occasional heretic, turned from the Church's valiant knight into its vicious scourge. When, at Anne's instigation, he had given safe-conduct to two notorious Protestants, Robert Barnes and Simon Grynaeus, so that they could visit England and discuss the divorce, Katherine had been as shocked as Thomas More, chancellor after Wolsey, who set spies to track their every move. The enemy was not just at the gate, it was everywhere. No wonder, then, that she saw the struggle to preserve the faith in England as comparable to the crusades waged by her parents.

In 1532, there was another calamity, the so-called Submission of the Clergy, when a cowed Convocation accepted Henry's rights to vet and revise their canon law. Thomas More, realising that the game was lost, resigned his office and left court. Anne was delighted by the Submission. She 'made such demonstrations of joy as if she had gained paradise', a horrified Katherine wrote to Chapuys. Just as Katherine had predicted, the dispute over her marriage was leading towards the destruction of her Church and the damnation of the people of England. That she might prevent further damage by stepping aside, as Campeggio had once urged, was not an option to her; she was fighting for a holy cause.

In this, Charles supported her. So did his wife, Empress Isabella, Maria of Portugal's daughter, who told him that the 'case closely concerns the Christian religion itself'. Unfortunately, for Katherine, her affairs were but one on the huge list of Charles's concerns.

For the exiled Katherine, though, her 'case' was all that mattered. With her royal duties suddenly curtailed, she had the time to devote her every waking moment to thinking about it, to writing about it, to talking about it to anyone who would listen. She was beginning to experience the loneliness and powerlessness so familiar to her sister Juana as the years of her own seclusion had lengthened.

We cannot be sure quite what, if anything, Juana knew of her sister's plight, but she kept a portrait of Katherine at Tordesillas and she was not entirely cut off from news of her family. Denia, writing to Empress Isabella in 1530, remarked that Juana had enquired after her health. She had also asked about Charles's health and, suggesting that she was not quite as ignorant of political affairs as Charles might have wished, requested details on how his 'affairs in Italy' were progressing. So, while unable to assist, she may well have had some idea of Katherine's plight.

Anne returned from Calais in triumph. There she had 'lived like a queen', dined from plates of gold, danced with Francis at a masque and graciously accepted his gift of a breathtaking diamond. And, although Anne and Henry had not chosen to marry while away, he moved swiftly into action once they were back. He had to, for Anne had finally surrendered to his entreaties, most likely on the return journey from Dover to London. At long last she gave him her 'body' as well as her 'heart', and he married her secretly and bigamously early in 1533. Within weeks, she was pregnant. Katherine's misery was now abject.

Of course, Katherine's marriage had still not been officially annulled. With Henry ready to brush the pope aside and have his own clergy act for him, that was just a matter of time. In March 1533, Thomas Cranmer was consecrated as the new Archbishop of Canterbury, the elderly Warham having gone to meet his maker seven months earlier. With such an avid Boleyn champion in such a key position, Katherine's days as a married woman were numbered. And, under the aegis of Thomas Cromwell, the king's Machiavellian new minister who was by now directing and controlling divorce policies, all avenues were being covered. Anticipating that she would appeal once more to the pope over any decision that Cranmer might make in her case, Cromwell ensured that such appeals to outside authority were made illegal by act of Parliament.

Then in the second week of April 1533, Katherine's attendants told her that she had visitors. Four members of the royal council, including the Dukes of Suffolk and Norfolk, had arrived to see her. As she listened to what her husband had sent them to say – for Henry never undertook unpleasant business in person – she learnt the full implications of all that was happening. Henry's blunt message was that she should 'not trouble herself about returning to him, for he had already taken another wife'. Almost as an afterthought, the councillors informed her that she 'must abstain from calling herself or being addressed as queen'. She had now lost her husband and was within weeks of losing her throne.

The point was rammed home to Katherine and to everyone else just a few days later. On Easter Saturday, Anne processed to Mass along the corridors of Greenwich Palace. She did so in regal style, sparkling in cloth of golden tissue, 'loaded with diamonds and other precious stones', her train carried by Norfolk's daughter. Chapuys, who reported the incident, tells us that Anne was 'conducted to and from the church with the same or perhaps greater ceremonies and solemnities than those used with former queens on such occasions'.

Cranmer then stepped into the picture, intensifying Katherine's misery. At a hearing in Dunstable, the archbishop declared her marriage null and void. Anne was therefore Henry's lawful wife, Katherine merely the widow of Prince Arthur. Again Katherine could do nothing but hope that somehow her prayers would be answered, and that the pope would rescue her by ordering Henry under pain of excommunication to put Anne aside and return to his true queen. Instead the pope prevaricated, and when, eventually, he did declare the marriage to Anne invalid, Henry simply ignored him.

As it was, Henry provided Anne with the most spectacular and lavish of coronation festivities. After waiting so long, she savoured every moment of her triumph. Just as Katherine had once done, she progressed through London along streets hung with velvet and cloth of gold. Sir Stephen Peacock, the lord mayor, took his place in the procession, desperately hoping that nothing could go wrong with the preparations over which he had spent many an anxious hour. Members of the city guilds lined the route, Londoners pushed forwards behind barriers or leant dangerously out of windows to catch a glimpse of the woman who had bewitched their king.

Anne followed the protocol of the Royal Book, for royal she now was. Dressed in pure white cloth of gold, a jewelled circlet on her rich dark hair, she rode in her silver cloth-of-gold-draped litter, an embroidered canopy held above her. With Anne were her ladies, resplendent in new gowns of crimson velvet trimmed with cloth of gold, her servants, her attendants, the blue-clad Knights of the Bath, the scarlet-robed judges and the leading nobles of the land, all vying for the attention and approval of the woman who represented their future whether they liked it or not. Suffolk, made Constable of England just for the day so that he could help oversee the proceedings, rode towards the head of the long cavalcade, proud in his crimson velvet and pearl-encrusted doublet. His wife, Mary 'the French Queen', Katherine's friend, was not present; she lay sick and dying more than one hundred miles away at Westhorpe in Suffolk.

Mourning the loss of his wife's French pension as much as he did her person, the financially canny Suffolk was to wed his fourteen-year-old ward, Katherine Willoughby, less than three months after his dead wife was entombed within the abbey-church of Bury St Edmunds; Katherine Willoughby's mother was the widowed Maria de Salinas. That rather shabby marriage, though, was yet to come.

The day after her magnificent reception in the city, in the abbey-church of St Peter's and close to the tomb of Katherine's deceased son, little Prince Henry, Anne was crowned England's queen. But she was not crowned with Queen Edith's crown, as Katherine had been. For Anne, it was St Edward's crown itself. This was the crown intended for kings not for consorts. It had been used for generations of monarchs. It was used for Edward IV, Henry's grandfather; it was used for Henry

VII. And it was used for Henry VIII himself in the coronation he had shared with Katherine, then his much-loved wife, all those years ago. Such days were over. Now, nothing was too good for Anne. The very chair upon which she sat while Cranmer placed the crown upon her head was special: it was St Edward's Chair, the chair used for sovereigns. Anne, pregnant with the child that Henry was convinced would be a son, had achieved everything she had set out to gain.

If Anne was the future, Katherine was now the past, a position bluntly spelt out to her a few weeks later when members of Henry's council visited her at Ampthill, a royal residence in Bedfordshire, where she had been staying. Coughing, ill, suffering acute pain in her foot caused when she accidentally trod on a pin, Katherine received them lying on a low pallet bed. She listened as they informed her that, because she was queen no more, she must never use the title which now belonged to the king's genuine wife, Queen Anne. Henceforth, as Arthur's widow, Katherine was to be known as the Princess Dowager.

If the councillors thought Katherine too weak to respond, they underestimated her. Gathering her strength, she demanded to read the king's instructions. After quickly perusing them, she defiantly scored out every reference to 'Princess Dowager'. She was not Princess Dowager, she snapped, she was Henry's wife just as much now as she had been on the day of her wedding. She would be Henry's wife until she drew her last breath. And woe betide any luckless servant who dared to address her with anything other than queenly respect. Henry's demands held no terrors for the daughter of the Catholic Monarchs.

Yet she was certainly anxious about the damage that Anne might now do, not just to her but to Princess Mary as well, a nagging worry that Chapuys expressed very clearly in a dispatch to Charles: 'It is to be feared that the moment this accursed Anne sets her foot firmly in the stirrup she will try to do the Queen all the harm she possibly can, and the Princess also.' Katherine was right to feel some trepidation. Anne was indeed an enemy to Henry's former wife and to the girl she saw as a danger to her own children. And, over the next three years, her foot very firmly in the stirrup, Anne did her utmost to destroy both of them.

But first, she had to give birth. As Anne's pregnancy advanced, Katherine had a further spat with her. This time the two quarrelled over a special christening cloth that Katherine had brought with her from Spain, and had used for Princess Mary: Anne demanded that it be sent to her in readiness for her own baby. Just as she had over the question of her jewels, an incredulous Katherine resolutely refused to surrender something so precious. Her rebuke to Anne was stinging: 'God forbid that I should ever be so badly advised as to give help, assistance, or favour directly or indirectly in a case so horrible and abominable as this.' Perhaps embarrassed by Anne's sheer effrontery, Henry did not insist that Katherine satisfy the brazen demand. Katherine kept her cloth, a small but very welcome victory for her against the woman who she believed had ruined her life. And, when Anne's longed-for baby turned out to be another girl, Katherine could be excused for feeling a measure of quiet satisfaction. Anne was discovering that the duties of a queen were not always so easy to fulfil. Although the child, named Elizabeth after Anne's own mother as well as Henry's, was given a sumptuous christening, no one could pretend that she was anything other than another princess rather than a prince. And she was not draped in Katherine's cloth.

Yet, although Anne had faced her first failure, the birth of a daughter being 'to the great disappointment and sorrow of the King' and to 'the Lady herself', as Chapuys informed Charles gleefully, it did nothing to alleviate Katherine's overall treatment or that of Princess Mary.

Three months after Elizabeth was born, Mary was told that there was but one princess in England, and it was not her. From now onwards, she would be the Lady Mary. Her household was curtailed, her allowance reduced. To make matters worse, she was to be part of Elizabeth's establishment, expected to serve her half-sister.

If Henry thought to intimidate Katherine by browbeating her daughter, he should have known better. Her entire life based on what she saw as moral truth and religious devotion, Katherine treated threats with contemptuous disdain. And she knew her daughter: although only seventeen years old, and frequently ill, especially when menstruating, Mary possessed an inner strength almost as deep as Katherine's. Thus she moved residence only with vehement, and highly audible, protests; when Norfolk carelessly referred to Elizabeth as 'Princess of Wales', Mary silenced the hapless duke by retorting, 'That is a title which belongs to me by right, and to no one else'; she had the temerity to write directly to her father stating that while she would always obey his commands she 'could not renounce the titles, rights and privileges given her by God, Nature and her parents'. A princess she had been born, a princess she would forever be — this despite Anne's shrewish order that Mary should be handled as 'the accursed bastard that she was'. Mary was even capable of roundly answering back Henry's 'own darling'. When Anne proffered an olive branch to her step-daughter, saying that 'the Queen' would be prepared to intercede with the king on her behalf, Mary's reply could not have been more audacious. While she knew of no other queen but her mother, she said, she would be 'most grateful' if 'the King's mistress' would plead for her with Henry.

No, Katherine had little need to fear that her daughter would submit. Yet she missed her terribly. Now in a similar position herself, Katherine could finally appreciate the unhappiness Juana had suffered in 1525 when Charles had taken her daughter, Catalina, away so that his sister could prepare for her marriage with the new king of Portugal, John III.

With Katherine marginalised, Cromwell went into action, rooting out and punishing opposition to Henry and his new queen with the relentlessness that was fast becoming his trademark. He began with Elizabeth Barton, known as the Holy Maid of Kent. A sick young servant girl, she became a nun at St Sepulchre in Canterbury after being miraculously cured by lying in front of a statue of the Virgin Mary. Had the girl then slipped quietly out of sight behind convent walls, no harm would have been done. But she became revered for her gift of prophecy, and widely listened to, even by members of the court entranced by her account of her mystical visions. Unfortunately, while her visions were sometimes of Wolsey, or angels, or popes, or Mary Magdalen, they also included Henry and the dire consequences of his new wedding: she said she had seen the place reserved for him in hell.

Cromwell moved in, literally, for the kill. Barton, compelled to confess that her visions were bogus, was publicly hanged along with her key supporters. They were small fry. Katherine, who had always had the sense to ignore the nun despite the girl's entreaties to 'speak with her and console her in great affliction', was uninvolved. Chapuys, writing to Charles, said that it seemed 'as if God inspires the Queen on all occasions to conduct herself well, and avoid all inconveniences and suspicions'. But the Maid's downfall provided Cromwell with a pretext for attacking Katherine's adherents. The Marchioness of Exeter, once described by Chapuys as Katherine and Mary's 'only true comforter and friend', and already humiliated by being required to act as godmother to Anne's daughter, was humbled again. This time she was forced to write a self-deprecating letter of apology to Henry for her involvement with Barton. Offending her king, even if only through 'simplicity and lack of knowledge', the scared marchioness wrote, made her 'the most sorrowful and heavy creature alive'. All she could do was to beg his 'gracious pardon'.

With Henry looking for trouble, any expressions of sympathy for the disgraced marchioness from Katherine would have been futile and foolhardy. Wisely, she said nothing. Silence was her only refuge when Cromwell moved on to bigger targets: Fisher and More, both figures of international repute and known integrity. More, who was included in a parliamentary bill against the Maid's alleged supporters, protested his innocence so forcefully that his name was removed from the list. Fisher was not so lucky. Ascetic and brave, terrier-like in his determination to fight for Katherine and for the Church which was the essence of his being, he was swiftly imprisoned, his goods forfeited, his papers seized, because, as Bishop of Rochester in Kent, he had heard the Holy Maid but had failed to condemn her quickly enough.

He was not alone in arousing Henry's wrath. Even ordinary people who chanced to speak against the royal marriage were being rounded up, threatened and terrified into submission. After Henry bullied Parliament into declaring him to be the Supreme Head of the Church in England and approving an oath of loyalty to the king and his new queen that everyone who really mattered must take, the net was widened. Now all of his subjects must abide by the king's desire to settle the succession on the children he was sure he would have with Anne, and accept his title of Supreme Head (this time without the face-saving words 'as far as the law of Christ allows'). Since assent was gauged by taking the oath of loyalty, any who did not take the oath faced death. The Kafka-like nightmare really had come terrifyingly true.

Among the first to suffer were Carthusian monks, and those of some

Juana's son, the Emperor Charles V, also King of Aragon and Castile.

Prince Ferdinand, Juana's second son, who eventually succeeded his brother Charles V as Holy Roman Emperor.

FRANCOIS I.
Roy LVII.

FRANCISCVS·I·DEI·GRATIA·FRANCOR·REX·CHRISTIANISS·

FRANÇOIS le Favory des Lettres & des armes,
Pour qui la belle gloire estaloit tous ses charmes,
Honora les Sçavants à l'égal des Guerriers;
Doctes Filles du Ciel qu'il traittoit de Princesses,
Puisqu'à vous appartient de donner des Lauriers,
Couronnez ses vertus, celebrez ses largesses!

King Francis I of France, the rival of Charles V and Henry VIII.

The entrance to the Royal Convent of St Clare at Tordesillas, founded in 1363.

Anne Boleyn, Henry VIII's second wife.

Sir Thomas More, Henry VIII's councillor and chancellor, later beheaded for refusing to accept Henry as Supreme Head of the Church in England.

John Fisher, Bishop of Rochester, Margaret Beaufort's favourite cleric and Katherine's staunch champion at the Blackfriars Court in 1529, who was executed in 1535. Engraving after Hans Holbein the Younger.

An eighteenth-century depiction of Cardinal Wolsey surrendering the Great Seal after the failure of the Blackfriars Court.

Thomas Cromwell, Henry VIII's second chief minister, who masterminded the divorce proceedings after Wolsey's fall.

The tiny chapel in the Franciscan monastery at the Alhambra where the bodies of Ferdinand and Isabella lay until their removal to the specially built Royal Chapel in the town of Granada.

Exterior view of the
Royal Chapel,
Granada.

(left) Juana and
Philip's mausoleum in
the Royal Chapel,
Granada.

Katherine's tomb,
Peterborough
Cathedral. She rests
under the unmarked
stone slab in the
foreground. The gold
letters spelling out her
name date from the
nineteenth century.

The tomb of Henry VIII's illegitimate son, Henry Fitzroy, Duke of Richmond, in the Church of St Michael, Framlingham, Suffolk.

Framlingham Castle, Suffolk, from where Katherine's daughter, Mary, launched her successful bid for the crown against the forces of Lady Jane Grey in 1553.

Philip II of Spain, Juana's grandson, and his wife, Mary I of England, Katherine's daughter.

other orders, who could not comply – any more than Katherine could – with Henry's new status as head of the Church. Henry and Cromwell brought some to trial, leaving others to rot in chains in prison until they starved or until disease and 'stink' did the king's work for him. Found guilty, the first group, Richard Reynolds, John Houghton, Augustus Webster and Robert Lawrence, were sentenced to the full horrors reserved for traitors: hanging, drawing and quartering. Taken from the Tower, they were tied to hurdles, dragged along the bumpy cobbled streets and sharp stony ground, their bodies bruised and gashed, until they reached Tyburn over three miles away. There the grisly butchery could begin. With Anne's brother, her father, the Duke of Richmond and other members of Henry's council settled comfortably among the spectators in the gentle May sunshine, the victims were hanged to within an inch of their lives. But they were not killed. Coughing and choking, they were laid flat as the executioners cut hearts, bowels and testicles from their writhing bodies. The mutilated corpses could then be cut into quarters for public display. To stop those who tried to sing psalms with their dying breath as the abominations were inflicted, the executioner stuffed their testicles into their mouths.

Then it was the turn of Fisher and More. Fisher, in his mid-sixties, frail and weakened by the penetrating damp and cold of the Tower, remained courageous to the last. Questioned on all he had done over the last few years, including his alleged dealings with Katherine, he held firm. Even in peril of his life, he would not give way. He would not take the oath. He would not deny papal supremacy even if he had to die for it. Die he did, a month or so after the first batch of the Carthusians, his sentence mercifully commuted to beheading. A last-ditch attempt by the new pope, Paul III, to save him by raising him to the cardinalate failed abysmally, Henry raging that if the pope did send him a red cardinal's hat, 'I will provide that whensoever it commeth, he shall wear it on his shoulders; for head shall he have none to set it on.'

More was next. With Thomas and George Boleyn sitting ostentatiously beside the judges deputed to try him, More faced his accusers in Westminster Hall in July 1535, just over a week after Fisher's execution. Born in Milk Street in London, just around the corner from the birthplace of Thomas Becket, and an honorary member of the Mercers'

Company, whose hall stood on the site of what once had been Becket's London residence, More had always revered Becket as his favourite saint. And Becket had been murdered in Canterbury Cathedral for his spirited defiance against what he saw as the tyranny of Henry II. Almost four hundred years after Becket's brains had spilled out on to the floor at Canterbury, his namesake prepared to fight his own battle against what he believed was the tyranny of another Henry.

Taking no chances – for More was not only a lawyer by profession but possessed one of the most incisive legal brains of the century – Cromwell, never a scrupulous upholder of the spirit of the law, packed the jury of so-called ordinary citizens with a handful of the former chancellor's bitterest enemies. More's defence was indeed formidable but the guilty verdict was already assured. Unlike Fisher, he was not an outright papalist, but he did not believe that the king had the right to contradict the received wisdom of the Catholic Church without the deliberations and the permission of a Church Council: for upholding that principle, he would die. As he did.

Katherine, like so many both within England and beyond, watched Henry's assault on the Church and upon men of honour with alarm and despondency. 'It is impossible to describe the distress of the Queen and Princess on account of these two persons,' wrote Chapuys to Charles shortly after Fisher and More had paid the price Henry demanded from those disagreeing with him. But, above all, Chapuys continued, mother and daughter greatly feared that heresy was spreading like a plague, heretics swarming like ants (as Thomas More had once said) and that the one and only true faith was being systematically dismantled.

They were also fearful for themselves. If lives of respected men like the Carthusians, Fisher and More could be so wantonly extinguished, then, under the influence of 'the Lady', would even Katherine and Mary be safe? Chapuys, who thought not, began to hatch a series of ingenious rescue plans to spirit them out of the country. Rumours abounded that Katherine and her daughter would be sentenced to death because 'the Lady' wished it. 'It is she [Anne] who now rules over, and governs the nation,' wrote Chapuys to his master.

Dangerous times indeed.

'Mine Eyes Desire You'

As Bishop Fisher, thin, frail, indomitable, lowered his neck to receive the headsman's blow, and Thomas More prayed in his cell in the Tower for the strength to face his own oncoming ordeal, Katherine sat helplessly in exile at Kimbolton. One of the king's provincial residences, Kimbolton was about twenty miles or so from Cambridge, the university of which, in happier times, Fisher had been chancellor.

While Kimbolton was reasonably well appointed, Katherine's day-to-day existence was far from comfortable. Like Juana, incarcerated at Tordesillas, Katherine still had some of her precious possessions around her. There is a list in the archives of precisely what plate and other items she was allowed to retain, the rest being parcelled up for storage in the king's jewel-house. Among the plate designated for her private chapel and for her table, we read of a small gilt crucifix and a crucifix 'of Spanish work standing on a foot', both of which are marked as 'of her own', maybe brought with her from Spain when she had arrived as a young princess.

Like her property, her expenditure was also regulated. Her intimate household was small: she had her physician, her apothecary, her confessor and a couple of maids, the rest of her staff being organised by the men Henry had appointed as her gaolers, with whom she had as little contact as possible. The honourable Mountjoy, perhaps having divided loyalties, had asked to be excused from her service. Even with such a tiny establishment she was considered a drain on Henry's purse. Cromwell often inserted a note to himself in his 'remembrances' that he must not forget to take the accounts of the 'Princess Dowager' to the king for royal approval. Maybe as a result, she was not always allowed the wine she preferred. And, in a bizarre repeat of what had so often happened to her as a young widow, she found herself frequently in arrears for tradesmen's everyday bills. Unlike former times, though, she did not send begging letter after begging letter. Her life had moved on: while often complaining in general terms about poor treatment, she had more important things to worry about than money.

Crucial to everything was how best to win her husband back. Her early hopes that Henry would return had been dashed. When, in 1534, Clement had pronounced that her marriage was legal, Henry had simply taken no notice. He had continued to take no notice ever since.

And the general situation was getting worse. All around her, Katherine saw her beloved Church attacked, honourable men suffering hideous deaths, monasteries closed, heresy gaining ground. Perhaps war was the answer, but this Katherine refused to contemplate, even if Charles, beset with problems in his own dominions, could have found time to pursue it. Just as Juana had backed away from supporting the Communero rebels against her son, so Katherine confessed to Chapuys that she 'would consider herself irretrievably doomed to everlasting perdition' if she encouraged Charles to make war on her husband.

To assume that she was always of this opinion, though, is wrong. As the years passed, there are hints that her attitude began to harden. In a telling dispatch to Charles written shortly after the papal sentence was issued, Chapuys expressed her view very clearly:

> She [Katherine] hitherto imagined that the Papal sentence once delivered and intimated to the parties, this King would return to the right path; but she now perceives that it is absolutely necessary to apply stronger remedies to this evil. What these are to be, she durst not point out . . .

When nothing had happened after Fisher's death, her tones became more strident. Swift action should be taken. If there was 'the least hesitation or delay', it would 'be tantamount to letting the Devil . . . entirely loose and at liberty to do mischief'.

Perhaps fortunately for Katherine's conscience, Fisher's death, and the advent of Paul III, a new and more belligerent pope than the recently deceased Clement, took things out of her hands. Furious with Henry's intransigence and his wanton execution of a cardinal, Paul began making overtures among European princes to remove Henry from the throne.

While the princes pondered, Katherine feared for her own life and for Mary's. Refusal to take the oath to the succession and denying Henry's supremacy carried the death penalty. Katherine's talk of martyrdom was not entirely far-fetched. Whether Henry really would have executed them is probably unlikely, but Charles was sufficiently worried that he advised Chapuys to tell the two women that taking the oath would be preferable to losing their lives. Fortunately, despite bluster and threats, the choice never became that stark. Yet the danger was ever present. Neither woman could enjoy untroubled sleep.

And each desperately missed the other. To Mary, Katherine was not just her beloved mother, but her 'chief refuge in her troubles'. For Katherine, being kept apart from Mary was heartbreaking. It was still worse when Mary was ill. Once, after hearing that her daughter was sick again, Katherine penned a plaintive letter to Chapuys, her 'especial friend'. Desperate to nurse her daughter, but not daring to write personally to Henry, she begged Chapuys to ask him to send Mary to Kimbolton. There she would care for her lovingly, letting her sleep in her own bed and watching over her 'when needful'. Henry refused, fearing that if the two were together, he would never be able to make them conform to his will.

Towards Christmas 1535, Katherine herself became ill. Chapuys heard only obliquely when Cromwell let slip that he was about to inform Henry that Katherine was 'very poorly'. Anxiously, Chapuys begged for permission to visit her but, before it was granted, the ambassador heard better news from Katherine's physician: she was apparently much improved but he would let Chapuys know should her condition worsen.

Worsen it did, and quite suddenly on Christmas Day morning. Unhappy, missing her daughter, and troubled in her conscience about whether, by acting differently, she could have prevented the turmoil she saw shattering the world she had once known, Katherine's strength began to ebb away. Racked with stomach pains, unable either to eat or drink, she tossed and turned as she tried to sleep. Even that brief release eluded her. She slept for no more than one and a half hours over a two-day period. She was too weak to stand, or even to sit up in bed.

By Wednesday 29 December Chapuys had received letters from her physician and her apothecary warning him that she had relapsed. Though the apothecary's note advised him to come at once, Chapuys was not unduly disturbed as the physician's missive was more optimistic. Nonetheless, Katherine's 'especial friend' rushed to get the necessary permit to visit her. Even though Suffolk told him she was '*in extremis*', Chapuys did not believe 'the danger' to be 'too great' as he relied on the physician's hopeful message. Still, with the permissions agreed, he 'took horse at once' and rode the ninety or so miles to Kimbolton.

He was not the only one to do so. Knowing that Henry would not visit her, and Mary could not, Chapuys was the person Katherine most wanted to see – except perhaps for one other. The moment Maria de Salinas, now the Dowager Lady Willoughby, was told that her mistress was 'very sore sick again', she implored Cromwell 'to labour with the King' to get her 'licence to go to her [Katherine] before God send for her'. When nothing came, the resourceful Maria decided to go anyway.

She arrived at Kimbolton in pouring rain at about six in the evening of 1 January 1536, the night before Chapuys. Forbidden entry by Katherine's keepers, Maria brazened it out, telling them that they had to admit her since she had just fallen from her horse and that, anyway, her permit would arrive on the following day. Before anyone realised what had happened, she had slipped into the house and into Katherine's apart-ments. She managed to disappear, no one could find her. But Katherine would have seen her. The two women, who had shared so much together, were reunited at the last.

Chapuys turned up the next day, accompanied by Cromwell's man, Thomas Vaughan, clearly sent to 'spy and note all that was said and done' (as the ambassador shrewdly put it). Chapuys has left us his own account of the four days he spent with the dying woman. The queen suggested that 'the principal persons of the house' as well as Vaughan should be present at her first meeting with the ambassador; even immi-nent death did not rob Katherine of her well-honed political judgment.

Relieved and delighted to see him, Katherine greeted Chapuys as the loyal friend he undoubtedly was. Thanking him for taking the trouble to make the journey, not easy in mid-winter, and for his 'numerous services' over the years, she expressed her joy at having him with her so

that 'if it pleased God to take her', he would be there. She might even
die in his arms. With an eye towards Vaughan and those of her household
installed by Henry, Chapuys craftily dissembled about his talks with
Henry about Katherine's illness. The king, he told Katherine, and
everyone else in the room, was 'very sorry for her illness' and intended
to provide better treatment and accommodation for her. In fact the king
had expressed no sorrow whatsoever, but by insinuating that it was
Henry's belief that only Katherine alive could preserve the 'union and
peace of Christendom', Chapuys hoped to persuade his listeners to 'have
the greater care of her life'; the ambassador always thought that one day
someone would poison the queen (and that someone was his bête noire,
Anne). Since Chapuys mentions that this line of conversation had
already been agreed with Katherine via an intermediary, we have yet
another indication that she remained politically astute even in such dire
circumstances.

Over the next few days, Katherine was well enough to spend some
time talking with Chapuys. To do so gave her 'great pleasure and
consolation' he tells us, for she prolonged their discussions for up to
two hours at a time, often asking him to stay despite his anxiety that he
was tiring her. Comforted though she felt in chatting to him, Katherine
knew that he was her channel to the outside world. So, while they talked
of Charles and Mary, Katherine also talked of the heresies spreading
within England and of the perils endured by 'honest and worthy people'.
Unless something was done quickly, she insisted, more and more damage
would occur. Chapuys, dedicated to his master's interests as well as to
hers, reassured her that Charles, busy though he was, was an assiduous
champion of her cause. And, as it had turned out, he continued, delay
had proved beneficial because Pope Paul was now vehement in her
defence. In any case, he concluded, Henry could hardly blame her for
action which she had not herself incited. Chapuys must have presented
his arguments well, for he felt that Katherine 'seemed satisfied' with his
'reasoning, and entirely approved of the delay'.

She also took comfort from his soothing response to her 'scruple of
conscience' that heresy in England 'had arisen from her affair'. As one
of her recent biographers has pointed out, her fear was substantially
correct. Quite what changes would have been introduced even had she

taken the veil and removed herself from the political arena remains speculative, but because she would not surrender, Henry had broken with the pope, met notorious heretics, and allowed new doctrines and concepts to creep into the country. At Kimbolton, though, as she felt her death approaching, Katherine needed her mind setting at rest. Chapuys managed to do just that by confirming that heresy was not yet so entrenched that it could not be 'uprooted'. 'This speech of mine made the Queen happy and contented,' Chapuys afterwards told Charles.

The few happy days she spent with the ambassador cheered Katherine up immeasurably. She began to sleep, she could eat and drink, and she began to feel so much stronger that she advised Chapuys to return to London. She did not want him to risk Henry's displeasure by staying with her longer than was absolutely necessary. So, when her physician thought her 'out of danger', Chapuys set off for the capital, having elicited the doctor's promise to send for him should she relapse again. Leaving on Wednesday 5 January 1536, the kindly ambassador 'rode as leisurely as possible' just in case there was a message before he was too far on the road. No message came.

For Katherine did indeed feel better. She sat up again, she even brushed and arranged her own hair. This proved a temporary reprieve. By midnight on Thursday evening, she had weakened considerably. And she knew it. In her last hours, she wanted the peace and solace that only her faith could give her. With death approaching, she was desperate to hear Mass and receive the Sacrament, but she was determined to wait until dawn. Despite her confessor's offer to say Mass whenever she needed it, she could not bring herself to break the habits of a lifetime. To her, the holding of such a service before dawn was wrong – biblical authorities said so (as she soundly proved to the confessor, Jorge de Ateca, Bishop of Llandaff).

At last dawn came. The bishop recited the familiar words and she 'heard mass and took the Holy Sacrament with the greatest fervour and devotion that could be imagined'. There were more prayers, she entreated God's pardon and forgiveness for her husband, she dictated her last requests, summoning the strength to sign what amounted to her will. Under English law no woman was allowed to make a formal will while her husband was still alive, so the document Katherine signed was more like a list of requests. She wanted Mary to have her furs and a special necklace with a cross which she had brought from Spain; mindful of her duty, there were bequests for her servants; there was a plea for five hundred Masses to be said for her soul; she wanted an unnamed 'personage' to undertake a pilgrimage to Walsingham on her behalf; she wanted her gowns cut up and used for church vestments; she asked to be buried in a convent of the Observant Friars, always a favoured order for herself and for her mother.

Katherine died at 2 p.m. on Friday 7 January 1536, her crusade ended. It would be up to Mary to fight on in her place. Whether Katherine died in the loving arms of Maria de Salinas, as has been suggested, is not documented. One hopes that she did.

Interestingly, she did not make a death bed affirmation that she had never consummated her marriage with Arthur, as Chapuys had wanted. Since few people would risk their soul by lying when there was no time to retract and beg God's forgiveness, Chapuys knew that had Katherine made such an affirmation, it would have carried considerable weight. Perhaps her physician (the man primed by Chapuys to secure the statement) simply forgot to ask her as he strove to make her last moments as pain-free as he could; more probably, Katherine was too weak to think of anything else but God. No one knows.

We cannot be completely sure about something else either: her last letter to Henry, allegedly dictated in her final moments. The letter, addressed to her 'dear Lord, King and Husband', has been quoted for centuries as a wonderful example of Katherine's saintly nature. In some ways it is highly characteristic: she tells him of the 'love' she bears him; she reminds him to take care of his soul, which he 'ought to prefer before all considerations of the world or flesh whatsoever'; she forgives him for the 'many calamities' he has inflicted upon her; she asks him to be a 'good father' to their daughter; and, as in most wills of the period, she asks for his generous help to her servants to ensure that they are not 'unprovided for'. The simple beauty of the epistle's ending has almost become legendary: 'Lastly, I make this vow that mine eyes have desired you above all things.'

It is truly wonderful. With its note of forgiveness, its concern for her daughter and her servants, but with the warning that Henry should have a care to his 'soul's health', it is just the sort of letter we would expect Katherine to write. But is it genuine?

The original has not survived. The text is printed in Polydore Vergil's *Anglica Historia*, a contemporary history of England from pre-Conquest times until the reign of Henry VIII, written, naturally, in Latin, and dedicated to Henry VIII. Intriguingly, Vergil quotes Katherine's letter two paragraphs before briefly mentioning the birth of Prince Edward, Henry's son by his third wife, Jane Seymour. At that point the book abruptly stops. It is as if Vergil sees Katherine's death and the future Edward VI's birth as marking the end of an era, the end of Catholic England, even the end of England itself as he had known it.

Vergil, an Italian, had spent most of his life in England after arriving in 1502, when he accompanied one of the pope's tax collectors. He did well for himself, accumulating various church benefices and becoming a well-known figure before falling foul of Cardinal Wolsey. After that he spent much of his time writing. His sympathy for Katherine is overt. She is the 'worthy queen', her letter causing Henry 'to weep' because, alleges Vergil, the king was moved by being 'the object of such pure and earnest benevolence'.

A slightly abridged version of the letter is included by Lord Herbert of Cherbury in his own history, printed in 1649, and by Peter Heylin in 1660. Herbert gives his source as Vergil, Heylin gives no source but his translation from the Latin follows Herbert's word for word. Other chroniclers of the time, such as John Stow and Edward Hall, do not mention the letter at all. The plot thickens because one account of Katherine's death refers to 'a writing . . . made in her name addressed to the King', and to a letter to Charles. Yet Chapuys alleges that 'among the last words she said', she sent apologies to Charles for not being able to write. And, according to the account of Katherine's last hours given to Chapuys from the servant he sent to find out what had happened, while Katherine certainly dictated her final requests (which she wanted sent to Chapuys), her only other messages were verbal. Also, Chapuys's account of Henry's reaction to Katherine's death is markedly different from the affecting scene described by Vergil.

A man of the Renaissance, Vergil was aware of the classical tradition by which speeches, of the sort expected of them, were inserted into the mouths of heroes and heroines. He could have followed that exemplar in the case of Katherine's letter. Yet, except when referring to Wolsey, whom he loathed, Vergil is largely reliable and he has not inserted other fake letters into the Tudor sections of his *Anglica Historia*. On balance, therefore, Katherine's letter may be genuine: somehow it, or a copy of it, fell into Vergil's hands through a contact at court, and then the missive subsequently disappeared or was destroyed. But until the handwritten original is suddenly discovered slumbering in an archive or some other reliable information comes to light, the letter must remain a tease.

Chapuys did not hear of Katherine's death until Sunday. Learning that her heart, removed as part of the very swift embalming process, was said to be black, he was convinced that she had been poisoned, with Anne Boleyn as his chief suspect. However, even though Anne was becoming increasingly worried by Henry's growing attraction for Jane Seymour, to take such a risk could have been suicidal. To rejoice at Katherine's death was one thing, murdering her quite another.

As for Henry, if he shed regretful tears for the remarkable woman he had once loved, he did so privately. Chapuys, admittedly not a neutral observer, instead reports the king declaring 'God be praised that we are free from all suspicion of war', sporting bright yellow, and showing off Elizabeth, his 'Little Bastard' as the ambassador called her, to all and sundry. Far from rushing into deep mourning, Henry continued his tilting and appeared like 'one transported with joy'. He did manage to tear himself away from his usual round of pleasure long enough to order Katherine's funeral ceremonies, however.

And on the question of Katherine's funeral, Henry was adamant. Much to Chapuys's chagrin, she was buried as Dowager Princess of Wales, not as a queen. There was to be no elaborate tomb. Thus, she was afforded a solid, respectful interment in the abbey-church at Peterborough (now cathedral), the convents of the Observant Friars having been suppressed. There were candles, banners with the various royal arms of England and Spain and her pomegranate device. There were Masses and official mourners. The chief mourner was the eldest daughter of the Duke of Suffolk by his dead wife Mary 'the French Queen', but, among the rest were Maria de Salinas and her daughter, by then the new Duchess of Suffolk. Chapuys chose not to attend.

Visitors to Peterborough Cathedral today are drawn to the site of Katherine's grave by two flags, flying horizontally, fastened to the stone Norman arches. One is of the royal arms of England, the other features the symbols of her homeland, including her own pomegranate emblem. There is no elaborate mausoleum to see. Instead, she lies to the left of the altar, in the North Presbytery Aisle, beneath an unmarked stone slab on the floor. On the railings behind her tomb, the words 'Katharine the Queen' are picked out in large gold letters; both the railings and the letters were positioned there in simple tribute in the nineteenth century. Although Chapuys was not present at the original obsequies in 1536, the current Spanish ambassador to the United Kingdom is one of those who travel to Peterborough for the special service which is now held every January in her memory.

Katherine's death was devastating for Mary, but she retained her fierce pride and courage. She spurned Anne's offer to become like a second mother, she resisted attempts to make her take the dreaded oath, and she relied very much on Katherine's 'especial friend' to help her through the coming years. He did not let her down.

The news took a while to reach Charles, who was in Italy. He had heard rumours by 23 January but was inclined to caution because he had not yet received Chapuys's reports. It was not 'certain', he thought. By 1 February, though, he was writing to his wife, Isabella, who was acting as his regent in Spain, saying that he had heard of Katherine's death 'five or six days' previously. He told her that he and his court had donned mourning and that suitable obsequies had been performed. 'May God receive her [Katherine] in Paradise which she certainly deserved on account of her extreme goodness and virtue, and the excellent life she led,' he wrote. When Charles told his mother Juana of Katherine's death is unknown, as is her reaction. Perhaps the two sisters had been apart for too long for it to have much impact.

It certainly had an impact on Charles's brother, Ferdinand, who took the news badly. Wearing 'deep mourning', he told the Venetian ambassador that his aunt had been 'a sage, virtuous and sainted' wife, cast aside for 'a harlot'. She had borne her adversity 'with patience and wisdom' and had 'died like a saint'. He could not 'refrain from shedding tears' for the woman he had never even met but whose cause had reverberated around Europe.

Katherine could not have been a better wife to Henry. Chaste, virtuous, regal, dignified, she was a gracious and dedicated queen; if at heart she remained Spanish, she knew when to champion the interests of England. But she had failed in the most fundamental of all areas: she had not given Henry the son he needed to assure his succession. And because of that, she had watched in horror as her religion was attacked, her daughter disinherited, the friendship she had been sent to foster between England and Spain replaced by suspicion and distrust, and the heretic Anne and her circle crowing and triumphant.

Katherine died safely cocooned within the Church that meant everything to her, but she died knowing that her efforts to ensure the survival of her world had been fruitless. Only if a miracle occurred and Mary somehow succeeded would all come right again. Then, Mary would restore true religion, rekindle the alliance with Spain and bring peace and harmony back to a fractured nation. Perhaps.

The Final Release

In 1543, seven years after Katherine's death had left Juana as the sole surviving child of the Catholic Monarchs, her sixteen-year-old grandson, Philip, was ushered into her room at Tordesillas. He had come to ask her blessing before leaving to meet his Portuguese bride and escort her across the border and into her new homeland. Wearing a long garment with wide sleeves, the queen, now almost sixty-four, asked him about his betrothed and was delighted when he promised faithfully to bring the girl to meet her. Philip's bride, Maria Manuel, was very special to Juana, for she was yet another grandchild, the daughter of her beloved Catalina. And Philip did indeed keep his word. When he returned to his grandmother, Maria Manuel was with him. Unfortunately, the marriage proved short but in 1554, after being prematurely widowed, Philip would come again, this time to bid her farewell before leaving Spain for a second marriage.

Seeing her close relatives brought Juana great joy. Although abused by her husband and her father and neglected by her eldest son, her family and her dynasty were the cornerstones of her entire life. She had endured much over the long years at Tordesillas because she had convinced herself that it had been Ferdinand's wish; she had robustly defended her father and her son as she had squared up to the Comuneros; no word of criticism of Charles had ever passed her lips. She never complained that his visits to her were so rare. For her, it was always so good when he was there at all.

So, whenever Juana saw Charles's son, Philip, and the other members of her family, it was a rare delight. She and Philip had first met some years previously when he had been only four and Empress Isabella, Juana's niece, had brought him with his two-year-old sister, Maria, to visit her. As a letter from her custodian, the Marquis of Denia, to the empress proves, she had loved every moment of the meeting. She had kept on and on talking about it. She had declared herself 'much satisfied' with her son's wife, and wanted to discover all she could about her. In particular, she had asked Denia to find out how she 'comported' herself on horseback; image was always so crucial in a sovereign. As for the children, she had often asked how they 'proceeded'. Denia had left the empress in no doubt that the visit had been a great success. 'As often as her Highness has spoken to me since', he had written, 'she has inquired for your Majesty, the señor Prince and the señora Infanta.' Isabella, too, had valued the contact. When her next daughter had been born, she and Charles had named the baby 'Juana' in the queen's honour. Juana had been thrilled by that; she had not been forgotten by those who mattered to her.

And whenever her family visited her, she behaved impeccably. There was never a hint of the deranged woman of legend. Had there been anything worrying, the empress would never have risked bringing her children; nor would Philip, or his sisters, or his cousins, have wanted to make the journey to Tordesillas. For that is what several of them did over the years. While there is little or no information about what transpired on each occasion, sixteen visits are recorded from 1535 until 1555.

We do know a little about a visit in 1550, however, when two more of the queen's grandchildren came to see her, showing her pictures of their own children. She looked at each portrait carefully, asking questions about each child, but what really pleased her was that they also brought her word from her second son, Ferdinand. With his message of love and respect came a gift: a golden cross which was said to date from 1451. 'In good truth, my son gives me great pleasure by remembering me and sending me such a devout and distinguished piece,' she said after examining it thoroughly and asking about its history. She was to treasure that cross until the day she died. Then it was given to Denia's son; that she would have hated.

But while her family treated Juana with consideration and deference when in her presence, Charles, Isabella and Philip were forever quick to help themselves to any of her possessions they fancied. 'The chamberlain Ryvera takes to your Majesty the things which you saw here,' Denia had written to the empress after one of her visits. And none of her relatives ever suggested that she might like to return to court. It was perhaps too late for such a change anyway; she had probably grown beyond it, too accustomed to seclusion to venture into society even had that been mooted. She had first come to Tordesillas in 1509; she was entering her twenty-seventh year of captivity even as Katherine's cortège wound its way towards Peterborough, and, after that, she still had almost another twenty years before death would release her. It was inevitable that the world was moving on without her.

It was not moving on without Charles. The days that passed so slowly for his mother were often too short for him to make much inroad into the demands of ruling his vast swathes of territory. Early rapprochement with Henry following Katherine's death largely survived over the years – with Henry once seriously considering marrying the rather fetching Christina of Denmark, yet another of Juana's granddaughters, although nothing came of it – yet Charles never really felt he could trust the English king. In that, he was probably right. Agreements with France came and went. The French were uneasy, slippery allies at best, dogged foes at worst. Within the Empire, Charles found himself powerless to prevent the spread of Lutheranism as the various independent princes chose one side or another of the religious divide and fierce fighting broke out among them: the emperor's attempts to broker peace and reconciliation at the Diet of Regensburg in 1541 largely failed. He did no better against the Moslems: Turkish attacks on the eastern side of the Empire were frequent; his own assault on the Moslem stronghold of Algiers ended in ignominious failure in 1542.

Little seemed to go right for him. Yet always he battled on, despite his own failing health, taking his duties as a sacred trust, travelling from one region to another, trying desperately to hold his disparate lands together against all odds. With so many troubles, his mother could never be his main concern. His burden was grinding him down just as relentlessly as the years of imprisonment were taking their toll on her.

Juana's bleak existence at Tordesillas continued from day to day much as it always had. Other than scanty information on her family's occasional visits, we have little real idea of just how she passed her time. She still had her books and her religious texts, so could read or contemplate. Or she could wage war on the women set to guard her, women she was certain were enemies and spies, even witches, and whom she was constantly trying to have dismissed and sent away. And always there were the Denias, whom she had loathed virtually since Charles had appointed them way back in 1518. Her 'dissatisfaction' with them was said by observers to be 'discernible'. Sometimes Juana could bear neither them nor the sound of their voices. Merely catching snippets of their conversation could make her 'suffer' even more than she had when her youngest daughter, Catalina, had left for Portugal. Charles knew just how much she hated them, for outsiders told him so, but he chose to do nothing. He relied upon them too much. Knowing just how valuable he found them made them bold, allowing their avaricious natures full rein.

While still with her mother, Catalina had noticed that items went missing, but when she had told her brother in the letter she smuggled out to him, he had brushed it aside as usual. Juana herself was forever trying to keep track of her personal belongings, sometimes demanding that chests be opened so that she could check their contents. She was constantly terrified that things she really prized, such as Ferdinand's cross, would suddenly disappear.

Over the years the Denias had grabbed every chance they had to enrich their family as well as themselves. Juana was forever fascinated by the progress of her dynasty; the marquis was busily founding his own. He was never slow to ask the emperor for offices within both Church and state for his brother, for his nephews, for his sons, even for his daughters. Requesting a post for his brother, Denia had pointed out forcefully, if respectfully, that his brother deserved it, for he had 'served very well with his person, and spent all the property he had with which he could have bought estates worth as much as what he now begs to have given him for life'; the position, then, was but a just reward. Another nephew, Denia maintained, was an ideal candidate to become Charles's chaplain. Once, he had managed to inveigle the emperor into contributing towards one of his daughters' dowries because he stated that he had been compelled to spend 'her marriage portion in the service of your Majesty'.

To Juana's distress, the Denias had also managed to tighten their grip on what went on within the castle by gradually filling the posts around the queen with their nominees. No position, however menial, was beyond their notice. When her laundress died, Denia had promptly sent his own messenger to Charles begging him 'to appoint the person he will name' for then she would be 'well served'. Even when Denia himself had died, just a few months after Katherine, Juana did not escape from his family's clutches: Charles appointed the marquis's son in his father's place. Gaolers though they were, the Denias were as tied to Tordesillas as she was.

Religion remained the one issue that continually caused her relatives far more anxiety than any other. In total contrast to Katherine's clear-cut adherence to traditional Catholicism, every so often Juana decided that she would not hear Mass and she would not confess. This had been her practice even when her father had been alive. But, after 1523, when her confessor, Friar Juan de Avila, had been summarily dismissed, she became far more truculent, refusing to make a full confession at all. No one had been able to persuade her.

Charles had agonised over this many a time, so had his empress and, once they were grown up, so did Philip and his second sister, the queen's namesake, Princess Juana. All had sent confessors to try to tempt her back to the correct path; all had failed. Thus, she was putting her soul at risk, or so it seemed to them. The spectre of heresy, never far from anyone's thoughts in a society in which the Inquisition was so dominant, reared its head. Ironically, Juana's piety, if that is indeed what was at the heart of her religious rebellion, made her particularly vulnerable.

With heresy so dominant within the Empire, the Inquisition stamped down firmly and ferociously whenever its officials sniffed anything that smacked of the slightest deviation from accepted norms; at least they could halt the spread of Lutheranism on home turf. Accepted norms meant outward compliance to Catholicism's established rituals, but by the early 1520s, a growing number of people had begun to be attracted by a form of religious experience popularised by, among others, a Franciscan nun, Isabel de la Cruz. Her theories, which followed Burgundian ideas about mental prayer based on inner piety and intense contemplation, had not placed so much emphasis on attending Mass or confession on a rigidly routine basis as was customary. Convinced that individualism was highly dangerous, the Inquisition had stepped in, arresting Isabel and many of her adherents for heresy. By her own refusal to attend Mass or confession, Juana may well have been viewed by her relatives as linking herself to the same type of heresy.

Like so much about her, Juana's true religious beliefs are a tantalising puzzle. Perhaps she really did come to see contemplation and inner prayers as valid additions or even substitutes, to Mass and confession in the sight of God, just as her conventionally devout relatives feared. She had certainly been exposed to such concepts while in Burgundy as a young archduchess. If she did indeed choose such a path, she may even have come to consider her seclusion as a blessing, a chance to become closer to God without worldly responsibilities. Yet, it is equally possible that she simply used religious defiance as one of her weapons to get her own way. For she never stopped feuding with her ladies, or being as difficult as ever with her gaolers. It is impossible to be sure.

By 1555, and after forty-six years of incarceration, seventy-five-year-old Juana had grown very frail. Sometimes she spent weeks at a time just lying in bed, too weak to move even for her attendants to change her soiled bed linen. Anxious that she might die outside the protection of the Church, her family made further strenuous attempts to cajole her into confession. Again it was to no avail but, just before the end finally came on 12 April 1555, it would seem that she accepted Extreme Unction from the Jesuit Francisco de Borja who had been sent by her worried relatives for that very purpose; even then, it would seem that she did not make a full confession in the Spanish manner.

Obsequies were dutifully said for her throughout Charles's lands but signs of true grief within her family appear conspicuous by their absence. Alive, she could be seen as an inconvenience; dead, she could be suitably, even magnificently, interred.

Dwarfed by the fame of her father and especially by her son, she is so often remembered simply as 'Juana La Loca' (Juana the Mad), a woman whose key role in Spanish history can be so easily ignored. Yet, like Katherine, she has attracted defenders and apologists among historians and writers over the centuries, drawn by the speculation and mystery which inevitably surround her. Thus to Tamayo y Baus, whose play about her was published in 1855, she is a woman willing to sacrifice everything, even her own freedom and eventual sanity, for love; in Benito Perez Galdós's work, published after the carnage of the First World War, she is a queen whose main concern was for the poor and the oppressed; in 1976, Martín Recuerda, whose play's central character is a sixteenth-century Spanish saint who founds a hospital in Granada, links her to social justice, to helping the victims of war, to upholding pure ideals, her own mental frailty enabling her to recognise the values of truth and goodness.

While Juana's life can be so variously and effectively portrayed in drama or fiction, what is clear for historians is that to consider her only in terms of her mental state – about which the evidence is deeply ambiguous – is to do her just as much of an injustice as viewing Katherine solely in terms of her role as a discarded wife. And much of Juana's character and what she stood for can be securely documented. Like Katherine, she had set out from Spain with the very best of intentions. Both sisters were strong-willed, both could be impulsive, both could be passionate in their allegiances and in their dislikes, both had raw determination and courage, both loved their children with a fierce intensity and commitment. But, especially as she matured, Katherine could be detached, thoughtful, able to dissemble and scheme. She enjoyed wielding what power she could. Compared to Juana, she was by far more politically astute. Although it is true that Juana sometimes weighed up situations before acting, she could also take too long to move decisively and, of the two sisters, she was far more volatile, far more subject to her emotions. It is ironic that while Katherine was a consort, she was a sovereign.

Although their mother Isabella had inherited Castile, she had been obliged to fight a civil war to gain control of it. Of all her family, she was the one who could conjure the will to keep her independence as a sovereign ruler and had the skill to ensure that her husband remained a support rather than a threat. She had battled against the Moors with the same degree of single-minded intensity that had earned her the Castilian crown. With neither her mother's ruthlessness not her innate ability, Juana was more easily manipulated, more easily controlled, more easily subdued. So she became an easy prey to her ambitious husband, father and son. And this is where she faced odds that her mother had happily been spared: Isabella had to contend with external conflicts but with the defeat of la Beltraneja, she never had to wage war within her immediate family circle.

Yet there was one area in which Juana excelled, surpassing even the great Isabella. In contrast to Katherine, who suffered miscarriage after miscarriage, she bore six healthy children: two sons and four daughters. She may have died almost forgotten at Tordesillas, but her descendants dominated Europe for at least two centuries after her death. As a woman to whom protecting and promoting her family represented her own crusade, that would have pleased her.

Her eldest son, Charles, became the most powerful monarch in Europe. Ferdinand, her second son, made his life within the Habsburg lands of the Empire and was elected Holy Roman Emperor when his brother died in 1558. His own son succeeded him.

Of Juana's female children, Maria became Queen of Hungary, although she was left a childless widow when her young husband died. She then helped Charles by acting as his regent in the Netherlands. Isabella eked out a miserable existence with the bullying and inept King Christian II of Denmark, eventually sharing his exile when his foolish political manoeuvrings cost him his throne.

Two of Juana's daughters became Queens of Portugal. Eleanor married Manuel I when her aunt, Maria, died. Having married two daughters of the Catholic Monarchs, Manuel was very happy to wed his niece. When he died, Eleanor's sister, Catalina, left Tordesillas to marry his successor, John III, while the widowed Eleanor became the wife of Francis I of France.

And, gradually, a complex family web developed and grew as cousin married cousin and Juana's descendants branched forever outward. But there was not yet even a toe-hold in England. That soon would change.

The Sisters' Legacy

In death, if not in life, Juana had her due. While Katherine had been buried as a princess, Juana was entombed as a queen. In front of the altar in the Royal Chapel at Granada stand two magnificent marble mausoleums. Effigies of Ferdinand and Isabella, resplendent in royal robes, dominate one; the other has effigies of Juana and her husband, Philip, looking equally as regal and serene. Philip carries a sword, Juana a sceptre.

Their bodies rest below the mausoleums. Just beneath the impressive tombs, approached by a narrow stairway and dominated by a plain wooden crucifix, is a small crypt. Here lie five simple lead coffins. Two are those of Ferdinand and Isabella. Juana is at her mother's side. Next to Juana's casket is a much smaller coffin containing the remains of her eldest sister's son, Prince Miguel, the child upon whom had been pinned so many hopes. Close by, next to Ferdinand, is Philip. He and Juana are together in death, exactly where she always wanted them to be. They had reached Granada at last. But neither Juana's story, nor Katherine's, was over quite yet.

In 1553, seventeen years after Katherine had been interred at Peterborough and two years before Juana died, momentous events had taken place in England. The miracle that Katherine had prayed for had taken place: Mary had become queen.

The miracle had started on the very day that Katherine had been buried. A jubilant Chapuys had conveyed the stunning news to Charles that 'the Concubine had an abortion [a miscarriage] which seemed to be a male child'. With the fickle Henry already tiring of her and giving 'great presents' to the demure, well-coached Jane Seymour, Anne's days had been numbered. Within five months of Katherine's death, Anne had faced the executioner's sword on Tower Green, having been found guilty of adultery with five courtiers, one of whom had been her own brother. Her fall, according to Chapuys, had been 'the judgment of God'.

Anne's dramatic exit had not immediately resulted in Mary's reconciliation with her father. Before that could happen, there had been the matter of the dreaded oath to be sorted out. Grieving for Katherine, bullied and threatened, Mary had at last given way and had accepted everything that the oath implied: the invalidity of her mother's marriage, her own bastardy, Henry as Supreme Head of the Church in England rather than the pope. Making such a complete denial of all that she really believed had almost broken her.

But it had worked. Graciously forgiven at last, Mary had returned to court and, with the sudden death of Henry's son, the Duke of Richmond, she had taken a step nearer the throne. Her chances of inheriting had plunged when Jane Seymour, whom Henry had married with indecent haste almost before Anne's body was cold, had given birth to the longed-for prince in October 1537. Named Edward, the child had seemed healthy and likely to live. But Jane's premature death, followed by three more marriages for Henry, all of which were childless, had kept Mary very much in the line of succession. And Henry had recognised her claims in his will. Naturally, he had left everything to Edward and to his heirs, but Mary was to be next, with Anne Boleyn's daughter, Elizabeth, after her should she have no heirs.

Mary's good fortune had continued when Edward, who had become king on Henry's death in 1547, sickened and died in July 1553. He had not quite reached his sixteenth birthday. But Mary's accession had proved far from straightforward. Edward had hated Catholicism and everything associated with it so much that he could not bear to think of England, which he had pushed into Protestantism, being governed by his Catholic half-sister; all of his work would then have been swept away. So, determined to protect the religion that had dominated his life, the dying boy had left a will, a 'device', disinheriting both Mary and Elizabeth and bequeathing the crown to the equally fanatically Protestant Lady Jane Grey, the granddaughter of Katherine's former friend, Mary the French Queen. The girl had been proclaimed queen and had taken up residence in the Tower.

But this had been to reckon without Mary. With the blood of Isabella the Catholic flowing through her veins, she knew a crusade when she saw one. And, unlike her aunt Juana, who had tended to cogitate too long before taking action, Mary had grasped that hesitation could spell defeat. Ignoring the Spanish ambassador, who urged caution, she had fled to the security of Framlingham Castle in Norfolk – coincidentally a stone's throw from the church where the Duke of Richmond is buried – and declared herself queen. It had been a huge gamble, but it had succeeded. Jane's forces had simply melted away, bowing to the justice of Mary's cause. 'Our Lord guided events,' Charles was to write to his son, Philip. Mary had expressed similar sentiments. 'By God's goodness and design, we have come to the enjoyment of our rights,' she affirmed.

She had returned to London in triumph, the people wearing themselves out in cheering her to the rafters, fears of the consequences of female rule dissipating in the general euphoria as bonfires were lit in the streets to celebrate Katherine's daughter at last coming into her rightful inheritance. But the pretty young princess who had danced, sung and played to the ambassadors had long since gone. She was thirty-seven, her features had hardened, her short-sightedness had become so pronounced that many commented on her piercing stare. 'Of low stature', like her mother, she was very thin and still prone to the various minor ailments that had plagued her all her life. She was also unmarried and knew nothing of administration or how to govern. No matter, God was with her, or so she thought.

Therefore, as quickly as she could, Mary had followed in her mother's footsteps as 'Defendress of the Faith'. She had set herself to do everything in her power to lead her people back to Rome. Cranmer, the man whose Dunstable Judgment had given the coup de grâce to Katherine's marriage, had been arrested and imprisoned, his archbishopric taken by Margaret Pole's son, Reginald Pole. In a ceremony in which Mary knelt with tears of happiness running down her face, England was reconciled to the papacy. The Mass was restored, the churches refurbished, priests reinstated, heresy attacked. Those who would not abjure Protestantism would eventually burn at the stake, crowds watching their agonised writhings as the flames licked around their bodies.

Katherine, who had looked on helplessly as her beloved faith had been attacked from all sides, would have been overjoyed by her daughter's godly endeavours. She had taught her well. She would have been still more ecstatic when Mary decided to marry, for her choice was Charles's son, Philip, who had been widowed when his first wife, Maria Manuel, had died so suddenly. Nothing could have pleased Katherine more than to have the Anglo-Spanish union reawakened through the marriage of her daughter with her sister's grandson. So much that the Catholic Monarchs had worked to engineer through their lengthy negotiations with Henry VII half a century before could now be fulfilled.

All that was needed now was the birth of a son. Then the past would reach down to touch the present and shape the future. Juana, the successful advancement of her own dynasty forever in her mind, would have prayed for that. And she knew about the wedding because when Philip had come to see her for the last time about a year before her death, it had been to bid her farewell before embarking for England to marry his cousin, Mary.

The marriage, naturally, was one of convenience for both sides. Charles had realised the potential of a union with England almost as soon as he had heard that Mary was safely, if remarkably, on the throne. Too old and ill to marry her himself even if she was hardly in the first flush of youth, sending his son instead was the ideal solution. Though Philip was eleven years younger than his intended bride, and was part-way through negotiations for another Portuguese match, Mary's hand was a prize worth winning: controlling English ports would give Spain a massive advantage against France should the French attack the Netherlands. A Spanish gentleman, Rue Gomez de Silva, summed up the situation with admirable clarity. The queen, he said, was 'old and flabby'; that would not matter because Philip fully realised 'that the marriage was concluded for no fleshly consideration, but in order to remedy the disorders of this kingdom and preserve the Low Countries'.

Mary had thought about marriage very carefully. As a sovereign queen, she knew she risked male influence, even domination, if she married. But to stay a spinster was irresponsible. As things stood, Anne Boleyn's daughter, Elizabeth, was next in line. To allow 'the Lady's' child to wear St Edward's crown was unthinkable: her religion was suspect, her mother the cause of Katherine's misery. Only by marrying and having an heir of her own could Mary save England from heresy and prevent her half-sister from taking over and leading the country back towards damnation. And marriage could bring other benefits. Mary could gain the support of a loving husband, an ally in any possible wars against France. And in marrying Philip she would bring her mother's country and her father's together again. Philip, the son of the man to whom Mary had once been betrothed, was bound to be an ideal husband. Thus, the decision had been straightforward.

For a while, at least, Mary found that she liked having a husband. Writing to Charles, she confided that the marriage 'renders me happier than I can say, as I daily discover in the King my husband and your son, so many virtues and perfections that I constantly pray God to grant me grace to please him and behave in all things as befits one who is so deeply embounden to him'. Clearly her feelings for Philip were similar to those experienced by her aunt, Juana, for Philip's grandfather all those years before. That did not bode well.

Philip has not left us his true thoughts on his 'old and flabby' wife. In public he was punctiliously polite and considerate. He never left her side; he helped her 'to mount and dismount'; he dined with her; he danced with her. And he was happy to accept her gifts. Among the items she gave him was a 'richly wrought' dagger studded with gems. On another occasion, she presented him with two robes, one of which was 'as rich and beautiful as could be imagined'. Then there was a velvet cap decorated with jewels and pearls. And for her, diamonds from Philip, 'dresses and coifs' from Philip's sister which were so lovely that she spent ages in 'looking at them and rejoicing over them', and a wonderful pearl known as 'La Pelegrina' from Charles V (which would one day be bought by the actor Richard Burton for his wife, Elizabeth Taylor).

If the royal couple seemed happy, many of the English were not. Even from the start, the marriage was unpopular. 'The English hate us Spaniards worse than they hate the Devil, and treat us accordingly,' a Spanish gentleman was to write to his friend. English fears of a Spanish take-over meant that the marriage treaty was intended to be water-tight in preserving English independence and Philip was hemmed in by restrictions on his powers. Mary was to make the major decisions; posts were to be filled only by Englishmen; Philip could not take her out of the country without her consent; should she die childless, he was to have no further claim to England.

In 1555, ten months after his glorious nuptials in Winchester Cathedral, Philip received the news of Juana's death at Tordesillas. Initially he tried to prevent Mary from hearing of it because, by then, she was said to be carrying the child that they both longed for. Already she had taken to her chamber at Hampton Court to prepare herself for the ordeal of childbirth. Somehow the news filtered through to her, however, and she was quick to order that suitable obsequies should be said in St Paul's for the woman who had been Philip's grandmother and her aunt as well as a sovereign queen. Family, especially her Spanish family, mattered to her just as much as it always had done to Juana. Indeed, Giacomo Soranzo, the Venetian ambassador, once remarked that 'being born of a Spanish mother' she 'was always inclined towards that nation, scorning to be English, and boasting of her descent from Spain'.

At a cost of over £1000, the obsequies, held on 17 June 1555 in the very building where Katherine and Arthur's wedding had taken place fifty years before and where Henry VIII had ordered a *Te Deum* sung to mark Charles's election as Holy Roman Emperor, were more than merely suitable. London craftsmen toiled for almost a month on the preparations. Merchants, such as Sir Thomas White, Francis Pope and William Cock, ordered copious supplies of black cloth which was needed both to drape the dazzling interior of the church and for dozens of tailors to use to make mourning garments. Thus, Mary Wilkinson measured out 21 pounds of black silk fringe and 12 pounds of 'fringes of Venice gold' to edge the canopy which would be placed over the hearse provided for a symbolically empty coffin. John Greenhill, a wax chandler, amassed huge quantities of wax to make hundreds of candles. Nicholas Lizard, Serjeant Painter, who once had worked for Henry VIII, gilded and painted banners, skilfully turned brightly coloured bolts of cloth of red, blue and white into a visual delight, glowing with images of saints and representations of family arms. The Dean of St Paul's, John Feckenham, settled down quietly in his 'fair old house' at the side of the churchyard to compose his sermon. One hundred and twenty poor men, who would chant the obligatory prayers to help

Juana's soul on its journey to God, tried on the black cloth mourning robes with which they were issued. The official mourners, some English such as the Marquis of Winchester and the Earls of Shrewsbury and Pembroke, some Spanish, like the Count of Feria, the Count of Fuensalida and the Marquis of Valea, all gathered in London ready to play their part in the proceedings.

And when those proceedings took place, everything went according to plan. In death, Juana attracted more attention in England than she had done in life. Indeed, her only time on English soil had been when she and Philip had been shipwrecked on their way to Spain to claim Isabella's thrones. Mary, who was waiting in her darkened apartments at Hampton Court, eager to feel the first pangs of labour, could have done no more for her mother's sister.

Unfortunately, the pains did not come. Mary waited and waited as the weeks passed but nothing happened. Eventually, Philip, her ladies, her doctors and finally Mary herself faced the sad truth that she was not about to give birth. We cannot know precisely what had happened: perhaps her swollen stomach was due to a phantom pregnancy, perhaps it was the result of a tumour. But, just as Katherine had once done when the 'twin' her doctors had confidently asserted that she was carrying had proved illusory, Mary had no choice but to emerge from her rooms and brazen it out.

It was the first of many disappointments she would endure. Katherine's life had been blighted by her failure to bear a son, Juana's by the ruthless ambition of the men around her. Mary had the great misfortune to be beset by both of these calamities. For she quickly found that Philip was hardly the stuff of dreams.

Like his grandfather, Juana's husband, Philip was not one to sit back quietly and accept a subservient role. He was a king in his own right, because Charles had granted him the titles of King of Naples and Milan so that he could marry Mary on an equal footing; he was an experienced ruler, for Charles used him as regent and relied upon him; and, above all, he was male. Thus he readily acquiesced when his father advised him to 'busy' himself in the 'affairs of government'. In a letter to his sister, Juana, who was then acting as their father's regent in Spain, Philip confirmed that busying himself in government was precisely how he was spending his time. And there was plenty of state business for him to attend to, for Mary's Council organised the translation of all state papers into Latin or Spanish so that Philip, or 'the King', as he was increasingly known, could access them. And they did so only two days after the marriage ceremonies and subsequent consummation had occurred.

Remarkably quickly, Philip was becoming enmeshed in political matters. The reign of Queen Mary soon became that of King Philip and Queen Mary. In official documents, which it was agreed that both would sign, his name came before hers. His face, as well as hers, was on the coins. And, with the establishment of the so-called Select Council, a sort of overseeing Council of State very much on the lines of that which was used in Spain, Philip became involved in a myriad of decisions ranging from appointments to the economy, from defence to foreign policy. Philip, as Mary found, was no mere figurehead.

He also soon became an absentee husband. After the fiasco of her false pregnancy, having spent just over thirteen months in England, he left for the Netherlands. He returned for three months or so in 1557, solely to persuade Mary to give him the troops he wanted for his French war. She did, but since the result was the loss of Calais, England's last bastion on the French mainland, the outcry in England was phenomenal. Expensive and difficult to maintain though it might be, Calais was a symbol of English might; to lose it was as devastating to Mary as to her xenophobic people.

Still Philip stayed away. Realising that his middle-aged wife would never have a child, no matter how many hours she spent on her knees praying for one, Philip read the Select Council's reports to keep abreast of events in his English realms but devoted his time to his many other responsibilities, responsibilities which increased when an exhausted Charles abdicated in 1557 to spend the final year of his life in a palace complex he had built next to the monastery of San Jeronimo de Yuste in Castile (ironically, one of the possessions he took with him was his mother's set of 'golden hangings' tapestries). Philip sent Mary his best wishes for her good health, he sent apologies for his absence but, once he had the forces he required for his French wars, he never saw her again.

And there is a story reported in the State Papers which illustrates just how far her initial happiness had evaporated. Receiving news from Philip that displeased her, she vented her frustration on his portrait. Unable to berate the man, she berated his picture, which she then 'kicked out of the chamber'.

Thus, like her mother before her, Mary faced death with the knowledge that she had failed. There was no child, her marriage had turned into little more than a sham. She had lost Calais. Her people were dying from hunger after poor harvests, and from the 'great maladies' of a terrible outbreak of influenza. The Catholic faith might be officially restored, but she had not been able to bring back more than a tiny handful of monasteries for no one wanted to relinquish the monastic land they had acquired and, despite the horrible burnings, Protestantism was alive and well.

And, perhaps, the hardest thing of all to bear, she had no option but to endorse Elizabeth's accession. The Concubine's daughter would wear a crown after all. While Juana triumphed in Europe as her descendants ruled and multiplied, the victor in England was not Katherine but Anne Boleyn. In 1558, it was Henry's 'own sweetheart' who triumphed from her unmarked grave within the Tower's high walls: at Hatfield House in Hertfordshire, Elizabeth heard the news of Mary's death and held the ring that had so recently been on her finger. She rode from Hatfield to London and into English legend. Ever Anne's daughter, Elizabeth would find her own solution to the dilemma of female monarchy.

The hopes nurtured by Ferdinand and Isabella in 1501 when they had sent their youngest child to marry into the English royal family and usher in an era of friendship and alliance finally crumbled. Philip began his own crusade against the land he had once ruled as king. In 1588, he ordered a fleet of ships to set sail from Spanish ports once more: this time priests and soldiers, instructed to conquer England and restore the true faith, were on board rather than a young princess.

The Spanish Armada was on its way.

References and Abbreviations

The Harvard system is used in citing references to sources. Abbreviated citations of primary and secondary material identify the works listed in the Bibliography, where full references are given. For example, Starkey (2004) refers to D. R. Starkey, *Six Wives, The Queens of Henry VIII* (London, 2004); Starkey (2008) refers to D. R. Starkey, *Henry, Virtuous Prince* (London, 2008). Manuscripts are cited by the reference numbers used to request the documents in the archives and libraries. In citations the following abbreviations are used:

BL	British Library, London
CSPMilan	*Calendar of State Papers and Manuscripts, Existing in the Archives and Collections of Milan*, ed. A. B. Hinds (London, 1912)
CSPSp	*Calendar of Letters, Despatches and State Papers Relating to the Negotiations between England and Spain, Preserved in the Archives at Vienna, Brussels, Simancas and Elsewhere*, 13 vols in 19 parts (London, 1862–1954)
CSPSp, Supp	*Calendar of Letters, Despatches, and State Papers Relating to the Negotiations Between England and Spain, Supplement to Volume I and Volume II* (London, 1868)
CSPSp, Further Supp	*Further Supplement to the Negotiations Between England and Spain*, ed. G. Mattingly (London, 1940)
CSPVen	*Calendar of State Papers and Manuscripts Relating to English Affairs, Existing in the Archives and Collections of Venice and in Other Libraries of Northern Italy*, 38 vols (London, 1864–1947)
CWE	*Collected Works of Erasmus*, 76 vols (Toronto, 1974–)
HLRO	House of Lords, Record Office
LA	Lincolnshire Archives Office

LP	*Letters and Papers, Foreign and Domestic, of the Reign of Henry VIII*, ed. J. S. Brewer, J. Gairdner, R. H. Brodie, 21 vols in 32 parts and *Addenda*, with revised edition of vol. I in 3 parts (London, 1862–1932)
LP Ric III and Hen VII	*Letters and Papers illustrative of the Reigns of Richard III and Henry VII*, ed. J. Gairdner, 2 vols (London, 1861–63)
MS	Manuscript
NA	The National Archives, Kew
NLW	The National Library of Wales
ODNB	*The New Oxford Dictionary of National Biography*, ed. Colin Matthew and Brian Harrison, 60 vols (Oxford, 2004)
STC	*A Short-Title Catalogue of Books Printed in England, Scotland and Ireland, and of English Books Printed Abroad*, ed. W. A. Jackson, F. S. Ferguson and K. F. Pantzer, 2nd edition, 3 vols (London, 1976–91)
WRO	Worcester Record Office

Notes

CHAPTER 1   *A Triumph of Faith*

An excellent and very readable account of Isabella's early life and her marriage to Ferdinand can be found in Liss (1992), pp. 11–81. Fernández-Armesto (1975), pp. 1–45, is also indispensable. For general information on the fall of Granada, see Kamen (1983), pp. 32–37; Elliott (1963), pp. 32–41. Prescott (1854), pp. 241–251, is a rich source. In particular, however, see Liss (1992), pp. 194–237, which gives a full account of the wars against the Moors, including a description of the fall of Granada; Fernández-Armesto (1975), pp. 89–106. Readers wanting more detail and information will find these works very helpful.

The quotation which describes Ferdinand and Isabella as more than mortal is from Prescott (1854), p. 247. Ferdinand's letter to Elizabeth of York is from *CSPSp*, I, no. 40. Ferdinand's letter to Pope Innocent is quoted in Kamen (1983), p. 35. The reference to the bed-sheet is by Liss (1992), p. 79. *Ibid.*, p. 47, Liss mentions the failure to show the bed-sheet after Henry's marriage. The biographer who says that Isabella had a 'youthful freshness' is Fernández-Armesto (1975), p. 5. Ferdinand's letter to Katherine about marriage is *CSPSp*, II, no. 22. Ferdinand's cast is mentioned *ibid.*, no. 437. Isabella's comments on la Beltraneja are from *ibid.*, no. 379. The Catholic Monarchs' assertion that their lands were united is quoted in Boruchoff et al. (2003), p. 27. Isabella's early promise to protect the Jews is mentioned by Liss (1992), p. 267. Talavera's comment on the Moors is from Elliott (1963), p. 40. Isabella's joy at Boabdil's departure is mentioned by Liss (1992), p. 314.

CHAPTER 2   *Royal Siblings*

Katherine's choice of badge is fully discussed by Starkey (2004), pp. 14–15. Charles V's comment on the beauty of the Alhambra is taken from Irwin (2004), p. 63. For details and comments on Isabella's art collection, see Fernández-Armesto (1975), pp. 113–114; Ruiz (2004), pp. 52–53; Boruchoff et al. (2003), pp. 103–119. The references to the queen's tapestry collection are from Campbell (2002), pp. 20, 26. The children's presents and fondness for sweet food items are mentioned by Fernández-Armesto (1975), pp. 60, 65; Liss (1992),

p. 251. Isabella's letter to her confessor is quoted in Hume (1906), p. 102. My comments on the girls' (and the queen's) clothing are based on Aram (2005), pp. 24–26; Kamen (1983), p. 49; Gairdner (1858), pp. 344, 345, 350. For Machado's reference to Princess Isabella dancing with one of her ladies, see *ibid.*, pp. 345–346. For details on Isabella's own education and her library, see Liss (1992), pp. 17–22, 254–258; Fernández-Armesto (1975), pp. 109–114. Readers interested in further analysis of the part played in Isabella's image by her patronage of learning will find Boruchoff et al. (2003), pp. 91–102, fascinating. Juan's birth and the festivities it engendered are described by Liss (1992), pp. 152–154. Hume (1906), p. 96, records Isabella calling Juan her 'angel'. Harris (2002), pp. 99–107, is very useful for details concerning childbirth. The remark that Juana was 'handsome' is taken from *CSPVen*, I, no. 854. Fernández-Armesto (1975), p. 123–124, states that Maria was one of twins. Information on Katherine's birth comes from Mattingly (1942), p. 15. Prince Arthur's praise for Katherine's 'sweet face' is taken from *CSPSp*, I, no. 312. For the education of the royal children, see Fernández-Armesto (1975), pp. 58–61; Liss (1992), pp. 251–253; Aram (2005), pp. 24–27; Mattingly (1942), pp. 17–18; Prawdin (1939), p. 15; Starkey (2004), pp. 15–18. It is Starkey who points out the girls were inadequately trained in foreign languages and that this was hardly conducive to bedroom chit-chat, *ibid.*, p. 18. See also Vives (2000), p. 24, for the reference to Alessandro's book on female education.

CHAPTER 3   *Of Weddings and Funerals*

Useful accounts of the background to Isabella's marriage to Afonso and the celebrations connected with it can be found in Liss (1992), pp. 113, 225–226; Fernández-Armesto (1975), pp. 118–120. See also Mattingly (1942), p. 20. Details on the Portuguese celebrations for the marriage and the reactions to Afonso's death are taken from Marques (1971), pp. 33–35, 264–265, 278. The princess's determination never to marry again is mentioned in *CSPSp*, I, no. 150. Machado's descriptions of the unmarried girl dancing are taken from Gairdner (1858), pp. 345 and 349. The Catholic Monarchs' reluctance to send Juan overseas is taken from *CSPSp*, I, no. 41. Maximilian's letter in which he describes his wife, Mary, Duchess of Burgundy and her love of hunting is quoted in Hare (1913), p. 46. The Venetian ambassador's description of Philip is from *CSPVen*, I, no. 842. The suggestion that the widowed Maximilian should marry one of Ferdinand and Isabella's daughters is taken from *CSPSp*, I, no. 21 (p. 11). Good general details on the marriages of Juana and Juan can be found in Liss (1992), pp. 322–323; Fernández-Armesto (1975), pp. 120–121. Isabella's requests to Henry VII that he should help if Juana or Margaret became stranded in an English port are from *CSPSp*, I, nos. 151, 152. Juana's voyage and arrival in the Low Countries is described by Aram (2005), p. 34;

Margaret's voyage and arrival is described by Liss (1992), pp. 323–324. Henry VII's letters to Margaret offering her every assistance are from *CSPSp*, I, nos. 173, 174. For Isabella's stoic comment on Juan's death and the country's reaction, see Prescott (1854), p. 342. The need to accept God's will in such matters is from *LP*, XII, ii, no. 1030. For details on Isabella of Portugal's succession, the birth of her son Miguel, and both her own and the child's death, see Liss (1991), pp. 325 and 332; Fernández-Armesto (1975), p. 123; Prescott (1854), pp. 343–346. Isabella's letter to de Puebla is *CSPSp*, I, no. 296.

CHAPTER 4 *'Our Illustrious Children'*

Isabella's request that Katherine's reception should not cause too much expense is mentioned in *CSPSp*, I, no. 293. Details on Katherine's journey, arrival and reception are taken from Starkey (2004), pp. 40–44; *The Receyt of the Ladie Kateryne* (1990), pp. 4–6; *CSPSp*, I, nos. 298, 299, 300, 302, 304, 305; Leland, III (1770), pp. 352–353 The reference to Katherine's dowry is taken from *CSPSp*, I, no. 29. Henry's letter to Katherine is in *LP Ric III and Hen VII*, I, no. 16. For Katherine's household, see *CSPSp*, I, nos. 249, 280, 288. Margaret Beaufort's life is taken from the entry in *ODNB* written by Michael K. Jones and Malcolm G. Underwood. Margaret's letters to Henry VII are printed by Wood (1846), I, pp. 118–120; Ellis (1824–46), 1st Series, I, pp. 46–48. Henry's letter to his mother is *ibid.*, pp. 43–46. Of the many references to Margaret's influence over Henry and over Elizabeth of York, I have chosen *CSPSp*, I, no. 210. I have used Rosemary Horrox's *ODNB* entry on Elizabeth of York for basic details of the queen's life. See also *CSPVen*, I, no. 833 and *CSPSp*, I, no. 210. Elizabeth's letter to Isabella suggesting they exchange news about their children is printed by Wood (1846), I, pp. 114–116. See also *CSPSp*, I, nos. 185, 202, 203, 221. The possibility that Margaret of Burgundy should teach Katherine French is mentioned in *ibid.*, no. 203. Arthur's letter to Katherine is from Wood (1846), I, pp. 121–122. Of the many references to Katherine bringing a special cloth to be used in the christening of her children, I have used *CSPSp*, IV, ii, no. 1107.

CHAPTER 5 *Face to Face*

For accounts of Juana's first few weeks in the Netherlands see Aram (2005), pp. 34–41; Prawdin (1939), pp. 16–23; Hare (1913), pp. 91–92; Miller (1963), pp. 181–186. Details on Katherine's reception and the Dogmersfield meeting are based on Leland, III (1770), pp. 353–356; *The Receyt of the Ladie Kateryne* (1990), p. 1; Starkey (2004), pp. 44–47; Mattingly (1942), pp. 31–37. It is Mattingly who suggests that Henry might have determined to see Katherine for himself in case Ferdinand had somehow tricked him. Warbeck's letter asking Isabella to help him is *CSPSp*, I, no. 86. The suggestion that Juana's presence in the Netherlands might be a useful disincentive to fostering further Yorkist plots there comes from *ibid.*, no. 113. An excellent starting point for the main details of Arthur's life can be found in Rosemary Horrox's entry for *ODNB*. Arthur's letter to Katherine is printed by Wood (1846), I, pp. 121–122. Of the many accounts of Arthur's birth, early infancy and Arthurian legends, see Starkey (2008), pp. 41–58; Anglo (1969), pp. 44–47, 55–56, 62–64; *The Receyt of the Ladie Kateryne* (1990), pp. xvii–xix. Arthur's education is discussed by Starkey (2008), pp. 122–123, but see also the articles by Carlson (1991) and Hepburn (1997), both of which are particularly useful on this topic despite their areas of disagreement. The quotation from André comes from Constance Pike's unpublished translation of his *Life*. Juan's court is described by Fernández-Armesto (1975), pp. 58–61. Arthur's letter to Ferdinand and Isabella is *CSPSp*, I, no. 312.

CHAPTER 6 *Wedding Pageantry*

My account of the pageants is pieced together from *The Receyt of the Ladie Kateryne* (1990), pp. 12–38; *Chronicles of London* (1905), pp. 234–248; *The Great Chronicle of London* (1893), pp. 296–309. Quotations concerning the pageants are taken from these three sources, but are mainly from *Chronicles of London*. The themes of the pageants and their meaning are superbly explored by Anglo (1969), pp. 56–97, and by Gordon Kipling in his notes to *The Receyt of the Ladie Kateryne* (1990), pp. 119–142. See also Starkey (2004), pp. 48–57, for an excellent summary and description of Katherine's reception and the pageants. That Henry VII had intended that Katherine should enter London in a carriage is mentioned in *LP Ric III and Hen VII*, I, p. 410. Anglo (1969), p. 77, suggests that in the fourth pageant Arthur is seated in a chair while Kipling in the notes to *The Receyt of the Ladie Kateryne* believes that Arthur is seated in a chariot; since Arthur is in armour, I feel that the latter is more credible and consequently I have portrayed the prince in a chariot in my account. For those interested in the City of London, and Cheapside in particular, see Stow (1956), pp. 231–247. The remarks of Sir Thomas More and his quotation on Katherine are taken from Rogers (1961), pp. 2–3. The assessment of Henry VII's avarice is from Bacon (1881), p. 213. Mention of 500 marks being levied for gifts for Katherine can be found in Guildhall Library, London, MS Repertory of the Court of Aldermen, 1, fo. 87.

CHAPTER 7 *The Estate of Matrimony*

My account of the wedding of Katherine and Arthur is pieced together from *The Receyt of the Ladie Kateryne* (1990), pp. 39–51; *Chronicles of London* (1905), pp. 248–250; *The Great Chronicle of London* (1893), pp. 309–312. For a full description of St Paul's, see Stow (1956), pp. 290–302. For a detailed account of sixteenth-century wedding services, see Sarum Missal (1913), II, pp. 143–161. The feasting, jousts and entertainments which followed the wedding are described in *The Receyt of the Ladie Kateryne* (1990), pp. 47–76; *Chronicles of London* (1905), pp. 250–253; *The Great Chronicle of London* (1893), pp. 312–316. See also Anglo (1969), pp. 100–103. *The Receyt of the Ladie Kateryne* (1990), p. 47, refers to the consummation of the marriage; the other two chronicles I have relied upon do not mention it at all. The printed versions of the depositions concerning Katherine and Arthur's wedding night can be found in *LP,* IV iii, nos. 5774, 5778; Herbert (1649), pp. 242–245. The originals are BL, Cotton MS, Appendix XXVII, fos. 58–82v. See also BL, Cotton MS, Vitellius B. XII, fos. 109–124, for William Thomas's statement. The curious thoughtfulness displayed by Henry VII in showing Katherine his library and giving her a jewel when she exhibited signs of strain is described in *The Receyt of the Ladie Kateryne* (1990), pp. 77–78. Don Pedro de Ayala's dispatch to Ferdinand and Isabella in which he describes the discussions concerning Katherine travelling to Wales with Arthur is *CSPSp, Supp*, no. 1. For Arthur's part in the proceedings, see Starkey (2004), pp. 69, 72; Mattingly (1942), p. 40. Charles V's remarks on the dangers of too much sexual intercourse for young men come from Brandi (1939), p. 488. For an excellent analysis of the consummation issue, see Starkey (2004), in particular pp. 83–84. Starkey puts forward the interesting theory that, perhaps, Katherine blocked out what really happened concerning the physical side of her marriage to Arthur.

CHAPTER 8 *Marital Harmony*

For a full account of the early years of Juana's marriage, her sojourn in Spain and the events following her return to Burgundy, see Aram (2005), pp. 41–75. Aram also includes an analysis of Juana's feelings for Philip, *ibid.*, pp. 68–69. The extracts I have chosen from the reports sent to Ferdinand and Isabella from Friar Tomás de Matienzo, the Sub-Prior of Santa Cruz, are from *CSPSp, Supp*, nos. 1, 2, 4.

CHAPTER 9 *Death of a Prince*

Much of this chapter is based on the information given in *The Receyt of the Ladie Kateryne* (1990), pp. 80–93, together with Kipling's admirable notes, *ibid.*, pp. 164–168. See also Starkey (2004), pp. 73–78; Mattingley (1942), pp. 42–45. For William Thomas's deposition, see BL, Cotton MS, Vitellius B. XII, fos. 109–124. For details on Sir Richard and Margaret Pole, see Pierce (2003), pp. 14–27. Starkey's assertion (2004), p. 75, that Katherine knew that the execution of the Earl of Warwick was probably linked to her own arrival is supported by Margaret's son, Reginald Pole, *CSPVen*, V, pp. 257–258, but

Pole does not say that it was his mother who told her, nor that the princess heard about it at Ludlow. The quotation concerning Arthur's rule in Wales is from *The Receyt of the Ladie Kateryne* (1990), pp. 78–79. For details of Arthur's work as Prince of Wales, see Robinson (2002). It is Starkey (2004), pp. 76–77, who posits the suggestion that Arthur may have died from testicular cancer; Mattingley (1942), p. 44, mentions the suggestion that the young prince died from tuberculosis, although he inclines more towards the view that the sweating sickness may have been the cause. The fact that the author of *The Receyt of the Ladie Kateryne* (1990), p. 91, mentions illness in Worcester, and that Katherine herself became ill, seems to support the latter view. I am greatly indebted to Dr Dafydd Wyn Wiliam for transcribing Rhys Nanmor's ode and for providing me with an English translation of the entire poem from the original Welsh. The poem is a masterpiece of Welsh artistry and, like other works of the period, deserves to be much better known and used. It can be found in 'Barddoniaeth Llawdden a Rhys Nanmor', M.A. dissertation by Mary Headley, 1938 (poem no. 71), in NLW. Isabella's order to Dr de Puebla that Katherine should be removed from Ludlow is in *CSPSp*, I, no. 319.

CHAPTER 10   *To Be a Wife*

The description of Katherine's litter is from Nicolas (1830), p. 103. The letter from Ferdinand and Isabella concerning Arthur's death is in *CSPSp*, I, no. 319. The danger of French attack is mentioned *ibid.*, no. 333. Early marriage negotiations are *ibid.*, nos. 318, 360. For a description of Durham House, see Fox (2007), p. 82. Starkey (2004), p. 79, discusses the timing of Henry's creation as Prince of Wales. I am grateful to Dr Starkey for reminding me of the time lag between Arthur's death and Henry's assumption of his dead brother's title. References to the issue of consummation are from *CSPSp*, I, nos. 325, 327. See also references to the papal dispensation, *ibid.*, nos. 354, 370, 389, 396. Chrimes (1972), pp. 285–286, discusses the issue of consummation thoroughly. Intriguingly, Scarisbrick (1968), p. 188, states that Katherine had written to her father immediately after Arthur's death declaring that she remained a virgin. Unfortunately Scarisbrick does not give a reference for this assertion and I can find no trace of the vital letter; it would also contradict Ferdinand's own puzzlement over the issue which is fully documented in *CSPSp*, I, no. 325, so I can only treat it with caution. In any case, if the letter does, or did, exist, it merely supports the line that Katherine was to take throughout her life. For the suggestion that bloodstained bed-sheets were smuggled to Spain, see Cavendish (1825), pp. 289–290. The caustic comment that Henry guarded every coin he possessed is *CSPSp*, I, no. 239. The references to Katherine's grief over Arthur and that of the Queen of Portugal when her first husband died are *ibid.*, nos. 321, 343. Isabella's conviction that serving

God did not preclude serving the state at the same time is *ibid.*, no. 142. Her lie to the King of Scotland is mentioned *ibid.*, no. 132. Her order that Katherine should return to Spain comes from *ibid.*, no. 343. My account of the death of Queen Elizabeth of York and her funeral is based on *The Great Chronicle of London* (1893), pp. 321–322; Nicolas (1830), pp. xciii, xcv, xcvii–ci. There is a discrepancy between the number of horses used to draw Elizabeth's bier: Nicolas states that there were six, while *The Great Chronicle of London* says that there were eight. Starkey (2008), pp. 169–170, gives Henry VIII's reaction to his mother's death. Isabella's condolences on the death of Elizabeth, her refusal to countenance her daughter's marriage with Henry VII and her comment that Arthur had actually been more suitable for Katherine than his brother are all taken from *CSPSp*, I, no. 360. Chrimes (1972), p. 287, effectively dismisses the suggestion that Henry VII really did want to marry Katherine. The ratification of the marriage treaty and the betrothal are mentioned *CSPSp*, I, nos. 375, 376. For the full terms of the treaty, see *ibid.*, no. 364. My references to Katherine's jaunts to court, her illnesses, and her letters to Henry are taken from *ibid.*, nos. 398, 400.

CHAPTER 11 *'The Greatest Affliction'*

Isabella's will can be found in the *CSPSp, Supp*, nos. 5, 6 (pp. 63–69). Liss (1992), pp. 342–343, has a very full and moving account of Isabella's last days. Ferdinand's letter to Henry VII announcing Isabella's death is *CSPSp*, I, no. 409. See also Gairdner (1858), p. 416. Katherine's letters to her parents are from *CSPSp*, I, nos. 412, 413. For very full and readable accounts of Juana's conduct and treatment upon her return to Burgundy, see Liss (1992), p. 342; Aram (2005), pp. 76–81. It is Aram who points out, to my mind convincingly, that Isabella may well have inserted the caveat clause in her will because she was only too conscious of Philip's Svengali-like hold over Juana. Isabella's letter to Philip requesting that he treat Juana more kindly is mentioned by Liss (1992), p. 342. According to Liss, this letter states that Juana is 'of unsound mind'. Bergenroth's suggestion of religious anxiety as a possible explanation for the clause can be read in the Introduction to the *CSPSp, Supp*, pp. xxi–xxiii. See also Aram's analysis in Gómez et al. (2008), p. 38. Ferdinand's proclaiming of Juana is from *CSPSp*, I, no. 472. For a very full, and completely convincing, discussion of the episode concerning Juana's alleged relinquishing of her powers to her husband, see Aram (1998). Examples of Henry VII writing to Juana are *CSPSp*, I, nos. 175, 177. The Venetian ambassador's reports concerning Juana's demeanour, the joust, and her jealousy, are from *CSPVen*, I, nos. 854, 875, 880. The proceedings of the Council of Toro can be found in *CSPSp, Supp*, no. 7 (pp. 70–71).

CHAPTER 12   *'A Happiness Rare'*

The remark concerning 'a happiness rare' is taken from Herbert (1649), p. 67. Problems for English merchants in Spain are mentioned in *CSPSp*, I, no. 438. Mattingly (1942), pp. 56–64, and Starkey (2004), pp. 88–91, give very full and highly readable accounts of Katherine's involvement in the machinations of Doña Elvira and her brother. For Doña Elvira's general influence over Katherine see *CSPSp*, I, nos. 401, 420, 439. Ferdinand's distrust of Doña Elvira is mentioned *ibid.*, no. 432. The entire story of the letters is given in de Puebla's dispatches, *ibid.*, nos. 440, 441, 443. Wood (1845), I, p. 132, says that Doña Elvira went to Burgundy to see an eye specialist. My account of Philip and Juana's unexpected visit to England is pieced together from Gairdner (1858), pp. 282–303; *CSPVen*, I, nos. 863, 864, 865, 867, 868, 869, 870; Mattingly (1942), pp. 65–70; Starkey (2004), pp. 91–93; Starkey (2008), pp. 206–220. The very plausible explanation of Philip's strange words about being a mariner is from Starkey (2004), p. 92. Mattingly's suggestion, (1942), p. 68, that the words were uttered by Katherine is contradicted by Gairdner (1858), p. 288. It is Starkey (2008), p. 213, who suggests that Philip wanted to keep Katherine and Juana apart. My extract from Katherine's letter to her sister is printed in *CSPSp, Supp*, no. 23 (p. 132).

CHAPTER 13   *A Sea of Troubles*

For further reading on Katherine's early life as a widow and the 1503 marriage treaty, see Mattingly (1942), pp. 53–58; Starkey (2004), pp. 80–82, 87–88, 93–97. The terms of the 1503 marriage treaty are printed in *CSPSp*, I, no. 364. Interestingly, Mattingly (1942), p. 54, states that the marriage treaty said that Henry, Prince of Wales, would be free to marry Katherine when he had completed his fifteenth year; Scarisbrick (1968), p. 8, confirms that the treaty said that the prince had to have completed his fourteenth year. Prince Henry's repudiation of the marriage treaty is from *CSPSp*, I, no. 435. Katherine's early money problems are described *ibid.*, nos. 321, 323. Ferdinand's instruction to her to preserve her 'treasures' is *ibid.*, no. 431. The Venetian ambassador's remarks about Philip's councillors' fears about Juana are taken from *CSPVen*, I, no. 873. Those readers wanting a brief but highly readable and informative summary of the general background to the situation in Spain, and the relationship between Philip and Ferdinand, will find Elliott (1963), pp. 127–130, very helpful. The best overall account of Juana's return to Spain and the aftermath of Philip's death is Aram (2002), pp. 83–93. See also Aram (1998), a masterly essay which is essential reading for those who wish to approach the question of Juana's alleged insanity from a fresh, unbiased point of view. I have taken Juan Lopez's defence of Juana's sanity from *ibid.*, p. 342. *Ibid.*, p. 333, refers to the suggestion made by Juana's nineteenth-century biographer,

Antonio Rodriguez Villa, that the queen was 'crazy from love'. See also Prawdin (1939), pp. 111–155, for an enthralling account of this period of Juana's life. Loades (1989), pp. 5f, and Chrimes (1972), p. 292, n. 5 and also p. 296, n. 1, are sceptical of Juana's alleged insanity. The Spanish ambassador's account of his meeting with Juana is taken from *CSPVen*, I, no. 872. Juana's growing confidence is mentioned *ibid.*, no. 875. The suggestion that Philip's councillors were feeding her lies is from *ibid.*, no. 873. Her seclusion and continued sexual relationship with Philip are referred to *ibid.*, no. 881. The various negotiations and agreements between Philip and Ferdinand are pieced together from *CSPSp, Supp*, nos. 10, 11, 12 (pp. 78–84). Ferdinand's letter justifying his actions is *CSPSp*, I, no. 471, and his suggestion that Philip should treat Juana kindly is *ibid.*, no. 470. Ferdinand's letter to Katherine is *CSPSp, Supp*, no. 13 (pp. 85–90).

CHAPTER 14 *The Art of Politics*

The most balanced assessment of Dr de Puebla can be found in Mattingly (1940). Examples of de Puebla's pleas for money can be seen in *CSPSp*, I, nos. 221, 511, 552 and *ibid.*, no. 204, mentions the amusement he caused to Margaret Beaufort and Henry VII. From Katherine's frequent letters of complaint about de Puebla, I have chosen examples from *ibid.*, nos. 443, 448, 449, 551. Examples of when she asked for a better ambassador can be found *ibid.*, nos. 449, 551. Ferdinand's love for Katherine, which was often expressed, comes from *ibid.*, no. 502; *CSPSp*, II, no. 13. The reference to him treating her communications as gospel truth is from *CSPSp*, I, no. 575. His conciliatory letter to Fuensalida is *CSPSp*, II, no. 13. The suggestion that Katherine should regard her marriage as beyond doubt is from *CSPSp*, I, no. 502. Readers interested in Margaret Tudor should see her biography written by Richard Glen Eaves in *ODNB*. Katherine's letter to Juana is calendared in *CSPSp*, I, no. 492; the full text is printed by Wood (1845), I, p. 141. Wood believes this letter to be written to Germaine de Foix because it is so politely and submissively couched but, as Bergenroth rightly points out, Germaine was never Queen of Castile and, in fact, the language in which Katherine addresses her sister is similar to that which she uses elsewhere (compare *CSPSp*, I, no. 553). Details of Ferdinand's letter to Katherine explaining his return to Spain can be found in *CSPSp, Supp*, no. 13 (pp. 85–90). Her response is *ibid.*, no. 16 (pp. 99–105). The reference to Juana having suffered an 'unspeakable affliction' is taken from *CSPSp*, I, no. 501. Ferdinand's dispatch to de Puebla describing Juana's refusal to have Philip buried is *CSPSp, Supp*, no. 24 (pp. 137–139). Manuel's support for Ferdinand is mentioned in *CSPSp*, I, no. 437. Katherine writing in cipher is from *ibid.*, no. 541. Her statement that she could no longer endure her treatment is from *CSPSp, Supp*, no. 3 (pp. 16–22), and her assertion that she has suffered more than any other woman is from *CSPSp*, I, no. 432.

CHAPTER 15 *A Knife's Edge*

An excellent summary of Henry VII's foreign policy can be found in Chrimes (1972), pp. 272–297. Ferdinand's letter to Katherine about his rapturous welcome home is printed in *CSPSp*, I, no. 554. The unknown chronicler is cited by Aram (2005), p. 94. For an example of a letter ostensibly in Juana's name but actually signed by Ferdinand, see *CSPSp*, II, no. 6. My reference to Henry VII telling Katherine that she could live wherever she wanted is taken from *CSPSp*, I, no. 496. It is Mattingly (1942), p. 73, who states that her apartments were inferior. Katherine's letter to Ferdinand asking for help to fund her ladies' dowries is from *CSPSp*, I, no. 446; printed in full by Wood (1845), I, pp. 129–130. The reference to Francesca de Caceres comes from *CSPSp, Supp*, no. 3 (pp. 19–20). Mattingly (1942), pp. 89–90, suggests that de Caceres was involved in a clique in Katherine's household which aimed to secure their return to Spain and that this was why Katherine came to dislike her. Henry VII's reluctance to settle disputes within Katherine's household is mentioned in *CSPSp*, I, no. 400. My account of Friar Diego is pieced together from *CSPSp, Supp*, nos. 2, 3, 4 and 5 (pp. 13–32). Katherine's assertion that she has been a 'martyr' for Spain is mentioned *ibid.*, no. 16 (p. 105). For further details and analysis of Henry's marriage portrait see Glück (1933). Henry's request for a portrait of Queen Joanna is mentioned in *CSPSp*, I, no. 401, and his envoys' reports on the physical attributes of the queen is *ibid.*, no. 436. Katherine's lament that she always had the 'worst part' is taken from *CSPSp, Supp*, no. 21 (p. 122). Ferdinand's letter accrediting Katherine as his ambassador is *CSPSp*, I, no. 526. The references to Henry's marriage to Juana come from *CSPSp, Supp*, nos. 13 and 14 (pp. 85–97); *CSPSp*, I, no. 586, which also contains references to Henry's envoy meeting Juana (pp. 458–459) and to the marriage between Charles and Mary (p. 459). Katherine's letter to Juana is *CSPSp, Supp*, no. 23 (pp. 132–135) and her letter to Cisneros is *ibid.*, no. 22 (pp. 125–126). Ferdinand's letter concerning Katherine's dowry and marriage settlement is *CSPSp*, I, no. 598. For the possibility of Henry switching sides, see *ibid.*, I, no. 600. Katherine's letter of despair is *CSPSp, Supp*, no. 3 (pp. 16–22, especially p. 22).

CHAPTER 16 *The Triumph of Hope*

The wedding oath taken by Henry and Katherine is printed in *CSPSp*, II, no. 17. Of the many descriptions of Henry, the ones I have chosen come from *CSPVen*, II, nos. 918, 1287; Hall (1904), I, p. 5; *LP*, I, i, no. 51. References to Maria's marriage to Manuel of Portugal are from *CSPSp*, II, no. 8. For fuller consideration of why Henry chose to marry Katherine, see Mattingly (1942), pp. 95–96; Starkey (2004), pp. 111–113; Starkey (2008), pp. 277–291. Ferdinand's Spanish festivities are mentioned by Halliwell (1848), I, p. 197. For contemporary references to the legality of the match, see *CSPSp*, II, no. 8; Hall (1904), I, p. 4. My account of the procession and the coronation come from *ibid.*, pp. 5–10; Guy (2008), pp. 27–29; Starkey (2004), pp. 109–111; Starkey (2008), pp. 286–296; *LP*, I, i, nos. 82, 112. For the traditional protocol, see also Royal Book (1790), pp. 123–124. Henry's letter praising Katherine is summarised in *LP*, I, i, no. 119; printed in full in Halliwell (1848), I, pp. 196–199. It was David Starkey who referred to Margaret Beaufort as the 'mother-in-law from hell' in Starkey (2004), p. 28. For the tournament following the coronation, see Anglo (1969), p. 11; Starkey (2008), p. 295; Hall (1904), I, pp. 11–14. Henry's letter speaking of passing time in innocent pleasures is *CSPSp*, II, no. 19. Katherine's letter to her father is summarised in *LP*, I, i, no. 127; printed in full in Wood (1845), I, pp. 157–161. Juana's message of congratulation is from *CSPSp*, II, no. 21. John Stile's report to Henry VII is from *LP*, I, i, no. 6.

CHAPTER 17 *To Be a Queen*

Stile's dispatch to Henry VIII is printed in *LP*, I, i, no. 162. Juana's tapestries are discussed by Campbell (2002), pp. 94, 131–133, 146–148. Katherine's dower settlement is printed in *LP*, I, i, no. 94 (35); its value is mentioned in *LP*, II, i, no. 1363. For Baynard's Castle, see Thurley (1993), p. 36; Colvin (1982), pp. 50–52. For Havering see *ibid.*, pp. 150–153; Thurley (1993), p. 78. Those members of Katherine's household who attended Henry VII's funeral are listed in *LP*, I, i, no. 20, and her household at the time of the coronation is detailed in *ibid.*, no. 82. Margaret Beaufort's will is discussed in Nichols (1780), pp. 356–403; see also *LP*, II, ii, no. 4183. The scope of the financial demands made upon queens and Elizabeth of York's loans from Henry VII are mentioned in Nicolas (1830), pp. cii–ciii. Hayward (2007), pp. 84–86, discusses Margaret Beaufort's clothes. For details on the people Katherine employed in connection with her dress, jewels etc., see *ibid.*, pp. 323–325, 327, 328–329, 333, 335–336, 340; for Katherine's clothes, see *ibid.*, pp. 177–180; for Katherine's household expenses see *ibid.*, p. 180. Readers interested in costume, fabrics, jewellery and material culture will find in Hayward a thrilling treasure trove. I have taken my references to individual officials of Katherine's household from *LP*, I, i, no. 82. Readers interested in Lord Mountjoy should read James P. Carley's account in *ODNB*; those interested in Jane Seymour will find Barrett L. Beer's article in *ODNB* useful. Staverton's case is described by Guy (2008), p. 144, and it is Guy who calls Staverton the 'black sheep of the family'. Katherine's council is discussed by Mattingly (1942), p. 133. For information concerning how royal palaces were organised and what rooms were used for, see Thurley (1993), pp. 113–161. Those readers interested in pursuing this topic further, will find Starkey et al. (1987), particularly valuable. Katherine's recycling of New Year's Gifts is mentioned in *LP,* Add. I, i, no. 367. Erasmus's boast that the queen wanted him as her teacher is from *LP,* I, ii, no. 3063 and her chess sets and cloth of estate are included in the inventory of her possessions taken at Baynard's Castle printed in *LP,* VIII, no. 209. Katherine's reaction to the widowed Francesca Grimaldo's attempts to find another post is mentioned by Starkey (2004), p. 149; Mattingly (1942), p. 111. See also *LP,* I, ii, no. 2120. I have based my account of Alessandro Geraldini on *LP,* II, ii, nos. 3164, 3774, 3775, 4195, 4196; see also Mattingly (1942), p. 49; Dowling (1986), pp. 144–145; Starkey (2004), pp. 70, 73, 82; *CSPSp,* I, no. 322. Other historians who have noticed that Katherine's nature was not a forgiving one are Dowling (1986), pp. 144–145; Mattingly, (1942), p. 111; Starkey, (2004), p. 149. Henry's letter to Ferdinand announcing Katherine's pregnancy is *CSPSp,* II, no. 23, and Ferdinand's response to Katherine is *ibid.,* no. 28. The items ordered for the royal nursery are listed in *LP,* I, i, no. 381 (95).

CHAPTER 18 *Motherhood*

Bergenroth's account of how he managed to access those documents originally withheld from him can be found in his Introduction to *CSPSp, Supp.* It makes fascinating reading. Starkey (2004), pp. 115–123, gives a superb description and analysis of Katherine's miscarriage and false pregnancy, and of the episode concerning Buckingham's sisters. Mattingly (1942), pp. 11–12, discusses the trouble over Buckingham's sisters, but ignores the issue of the false pregnancy. I have based my account on *CSPSp, Supp,* nos. 8 (pp. 34–36) and 9 (pp. 36–44). It is Starkey (2004), p. 119, who points out, quite rightly, that Katherine lied to her father. Ferdinand's letter demanding information is *LP,* I, i, no. 482, *CSPSp,* II, no. 49. Henry's letter to Ferdinand is *LP,* I, ii, no. 472, *CSPSp,* II, no. 42. Katherine's letter to Ferdinand is *LP,* I, i, no. 473, *CSPSp,* II, no. 43. Ferdinand's letter wondering about the progress of her pregnancy is *LP,* I, i, no. 482, *CSPSp,* II, no. 49. Caroz' comment that Henry was not interested in state business is from *CSPSp,* II, no. 44. Ferdinand's instruction that Katherine could be influenced by Friar Diego if necessary is contained in *LP,* I, i, no. 483; *CSPSp,* II, no. 50. My description of Richmond Palace is from Thurley (1993), pp. 27–32, 104. The mummery is described by Hall (1904), I, p. 21. Details on childbirth rituals are from Cressy (1997), pp. 80–86; Harris (2002), pp. 99–107. Prince Henry's christening is pieced together from *LP,* I, i, nos. 670, 674, 675. The jousts are described by Anglo (1964), pp. 111–112; Hall (1904), I, pp. 23–27.

CHAPTER 19 *A Taste of Power*

For the death and burial of Prince Henry, see *LP,* I, i, no. 707; Hall (1904), I, p. 27; Fox (2007), pp. 1–3. I also used the original handwritten primary account of the burial, NA, LC 2/1, fos. 159–174v, which contains information that is not available in the printed sources. Archbishop Warham's letter of condolence to his niece is printed by Ellis (1824–46), 3rd Series, II, pp. 46–47. Katherine's letter to Cardinal Bainbridge is from *CSPVen,* II, no. 203. Her questions on the cost of galleys and her desire for war are mentioned in *ibid.,* no. 211; *LP,* II, ii, no. 1407. Lists of names of those involved in the French war can be found in *LP,* I, ii, no. 2052. Katherine's letter to Margaret is *ibid.,* no. 2138. Her letters to Wolsey about her anxieties concerning Henry's safety are *ibid.,* nos. 2120, 2162; printed in Ellis (1824–46), 1st Series, I, pp. 78–82, 84–85. Katherine's powers as regent are taken from *LP,* I, ii, nos. 1985, 2005 (g. 46, 47). Her letter to Wolsey about sewing banners is *ibid.,* no. 2162; printed in Ellis (1824–46), 1st Series, I, pp. 82–84. I have pieced together my account of Katherine's actions and preparations for the Scottish war from *LP,* I, ii, nos. 2143, 2162, 2204, 2278, 2299, 2330 (3); *CSPVen,* II, no. 297. The fall of Norham is mentioned in *CSPMilan,* I, no. 655; *LP,* I, ii, no. 2279. From the many excellent references to Flodden, I mainly used *ibid.,* nos. 2246, 2260, 2283. Henry's reception in Lille is mentioned *ibid.,* no. 2391. Katherine's letter to Wolsey about Henry's victory is from *ibid.,* no. 2200; printed in Ellis (1824–46), 1st Series, I, pp. 84–85. For details concerning the housing of the Duke of Longueville, see *LP,* I, ii, no. 2226; printed in Ellis (1824–46), 3rd Series, I, pp. 152–154. The ambassadors' letters are from *CSPMilan,* I, no. 654; *LP,* I, ii, no. 2261; *CSPVen,* II, no. 329. Katherine's letter telling Henry about Flodden is *LP,* I, ii, no. 2268; printed in Ellis (1824–46), 1st Series, I, pp. 88–89. The reference to 'ungracious dogholes' can be found in *LP,* III, ii, no. 2958 (p. 1248). *CSPVen,* II, no. 331, mentions (I think erroneously) that Katherine had given birth to a child. Additionally, Mattingly (1942), pp. 118–122, covers the period of the French war and Katherine's regency succinctly and intelligibly, but I would also recommend that those interested in these events should read Starkey's highly perceptive analysis in Starkey (2004), pp. 135–149.

CHAPTER 20 *Happy Families*

Henry's instructions to his ambassadors are from *LP,* I, ii, no. 2656. Details of Mary's marriage to Louis are from *ibid.,* no. 3146; *CSPVen,* II, no. 505. Ferdinand's excuse for his truce with the French is *LP,* I, ii, no. 2744, and Henry's response is *ibid.,* no. 2707. The Spanish ambassador's acknowledgement that Katherine chose her husband over her father is *ibid.,* no. 3524; *CSPSp,* II, nos. 201–202. Details of Katherine's miscarriage are taken from *LP,* I, ii, nos. 3332, 3333, 3364, 3440, 3500, 3581; *CSPVen,* II, no. 555. For readers interested in Elizabeth Blount, Beverly Murphy's *ODNB* entry provides a good starting point. The revels are mentioned in *LP,* II, ii, p. 1501. Katherine's letter to her father mentioning the Candlemas miscarriage is *CSPSp,* II, no. 238. For details on protocol surrounding royal childbirth, see the Royal Book (1790), pp. 125–126; *CSPVen,* II, no. 691; *LP,* II, i, no. 1573 (interestingly, this document is still using the system of beginning the new year in March rather than January so states that Mary was born on Monday 18 February 1515 and christened on Wednesday 20 February 1515, whereas we would date these events to Tuesday 18 February 1516 and Thursday 20 February 1516). The letters sent by Katherine and Henry to Ferdinand concerning the reconciliation and the treaty are *CSPSp,* II, nos. 229, 230, 231, 238. See also *CSPVen,* II, no. 635. *ODNB* has a life of Mary, the French Queen by David Loades; see also *LP,* II, i, nos. 222, 223, 227, for details on Mary's life and her marriage to Suffolk. For Ferdinand's death and the accession of Charles see *ibid.,* nos. 1563, 1610; *CSPSp,* II, no. 246. The story of Charles plucking the hawk is from *CSPVen,* II, no. 505. The reference to Juana's madness is from *ibid.,* no. 564. For a full description of Charles's behaviour at Ferdinand's requiem Mass see Brandi (1939), p. 60.

CHAPTER 21 *The Twisting Path*

My account of Juana in these years is based on Aram (2005), pp. 104–110, 145; Bergenroth's Introduction to *CSPSp, Supp,* pp. xli–xliii; *ibid.,* nos. 25, 26 and 27 (pp. 141–153). The Venetian ambassador's comment on Wolsey's power is from *CSPVen,* II, nos. 635, 894. Katherine's involvement in Maria de Salinas's jointure is documented in LA, 2ANC3/A/35, 2ANC3/A/36. Readers interested in the expulsion of Friar Diego should read his letter to Henry VIII upon his departure for Spain. It is printed (in Latin) in *CSPSp, Supp,* no. 8 (pp. 44–46). My account of Evil May Day is pieced together from *CSPVen,* II, no. 887; *LP,* II, ii, nos. 3218, 3230, 3259; Hall (1904), I, pp. 153–164. Katherine's pregnancy is taken from *CSPVen,* II, nos. 903, 1103; *LP,* II, ii, nos. 4074, 4213, 4288, 4308, 4326, 4529, 4568; Halliwell (1848), I, pp. 234–235. Henry's letter is undated but most authorities believe that it concerns this particular pregnancy e.g. Starkey (2004), p. 159. Henry's writing desk was exhibited at the 2009 exhibition at the British Library, London, which marked the 500th anniversary of Henry's accession. For a picture and description of the desk, see Doran, ed. and Starkey (2009), p. 116. My reference to moving Mary and her household because of the sweat is from *LP,* II, ii, no. 4326. The payment for moving the font to and from Canterbury is mentioned *ibid.,* pp. 1479, 1480. My references to the contents of Katherine's chamber are taken from Camden Miscellany (1855), pp. 24, 30, 34, 37, 38; *LP,* VIII, no. 209. Those interested in Mary's upbringing will find much fuller and more detailed accounts than the one I have given in

Starkey (2004), pp. 164–179; Loades (1989), pp. 28–35; Mattingly (1942), pp. 140–143. See also *LP,* II, ii, pp. 1473, 1476, 1538, 1539, 1542; Ellis (1824–46), Ist Series, II, pp. 19–20. Erasmus's comments on Henry's courts are mentioned in *LP,* II, ii, nos. 4115, 4340. Carlson (1991), discusses the controversial issue of whether or not Thomas Linacre was one of Arthur's tutors, as is often suggested, and proves, conclusively to my mind, that he was not selected despite his hopes.

CHAPTER 22   *The Man of the Moment*

Aram (2005), pp. 112–125, gives an excellent account of Juana's life in the early years of Charles's rule and is a key source. Additionally, my information on Juana's captivity in this period is largely pieced together from *CSPSp, Supp,* nos. 28–50. See particularly p. 154 (*ibid.,* no. 29); pp. 157–158 (*ibid.,* no. 30); p. 160 (*ibid.,* no. 31); p. 162 (*ibid.,* no. 32); pp. 164–165 (*ibid.,* no. 33); pp. 166–167 (*ibid.,* no. 34); p. 171 (*ibid.,* no. 36); p. 184 (*ibid.,* no. 42); p. 187 (*ibid.,* no. 43); p. 190 (*ibid.,* no. 45); p. 196 (*ibid.,* no. 47); pp. 197–199 (*ibid.,* no. 48); p. 200 (*ibid.,* no. 49). See Brandi (1939), p. 81, for Charles's early life. See *CSPVen,* II, no. 1187 for the reference to Juana's distress when Catalina was first removed from her. The quotation concerning Charles's view of women rulers is taken from Brandi (1939), p. 488. For the final removal of Catalina, see *CSPSp, Supp,* no. 97 (p. 418). Charles's use of bribery in the imperial election is mentioned *LP,* III, i, no. 50. Wolsey's comment on Francis's attempts to secure the election for himself is *ibid.,* nos. 137, 318. The absence of the French ambassadors is noted in *ibid.,* no. 383. Katherine's joyful reaction to the news of Charles's election is *ibid.,* no. 402. My description of Mary's betrothal is from *CSPVen,* II, no. 1085. Katherine's pleasure at the projected meeting with Charles is *LP,* III, i, no. 637. Francis's need for haste in his own meeting with Henry is *ibid.,* no. 728. Charles's letter of thanks to Katherine for helping to bring about his meeting with Henry is *ibid.,* ii, no. 778.

CHAPTER 23   *Fool's Gold*

I have taken my comments on Wolsey from *CSPVen,* III, nos. 3, 18, 56, 232. Hall (1904), I, pp. 188–189, gives a brief account of Charles's first visit to England, but for more details see *CSPVen,* III, nos. 3, 50, 53, 54, 55. The Venetian gift of carpets to Wolsey is mentioned *ibid.,* no. 30. From the many sources of the Field of Cloth of Gold, I have based my account on the *Calais Chronicle* (1846), pp. 19–27; the *Rutland Papers* (1842), pp. 28–42; *CSPVen,* III, nos. 50, 60, 67, 68, 69, 74, 94; *LP,* III, i, nos. 632, 702, 704, 852, 869, 870; Hall (1904), I, pp. 188–218. Anglo (1969), pp. 124–158, gives an excellent analysis and overview of the entire event. Campbell (2007), p. 145, identifies the King David hanging as one of Henry's tapestries hanging in the palace at Guisnes. Ives (2004), p. 32, suggests that Anne Boleyn may have accompanied Queen Claude to the Field of Cloth of Gold. It is Anglo (1969), who points out that Wolsey's retinue was bigger than those of Buckingham, Suffolk and the Archbishop of Canterbury combined. For Mountjoy's marriages see James P. Carley's masterly *ODNB* entry. The Council's letter mentioning Mary at Richmond is printed in Ellis (1824–46), 1st Series, I, pp. 174–176; *Calais Chronicle* (1846), p. 92. My account of the discussions at Gravelines is pieced together from *Calais Chronicle* (1846), pp. 28–30; the *Rutland Papers* (1842), pp. 49–59; Hall (1904), I, pp. 219–221; *LP*, III, i, nos. 907, 908, 914; *CSPVen*, III, no. 106. Anglo (1969), pp. 158–168, gives a superb analysis of the spectacle and background of this meeting which is particularly useful for those readers wanting to discover more on the temporary pavilion and the masques.

CHAPTER 24 *Family First and Last*

The best account of Juana's situation during the revolt of the Communeros is Aram (2005), pp. 125–128. Neither Aram's succinct account of what happened nor her critical analysis of the effects on Juana and her behaviour can be bettered. For basic details of the major events, see Elliott (1963), pp. 141–150; Kamen (1983), pp. 73–81; Brandi (1939), pp. 142–149. The adverse comments on Juana's state of mind come from Elliott (1963), p. 145; Kamen (1983), p. 77; Brandi (1939), p. 144. Bergenroth's Introduction to *CSPSp, Supp*, pp. lxi–lxxiv, provides instructive commentary from one of Juana's apologists. My account of the rising and its aftermath is largely based on *ibid.*, nos. 49 (p. 201); 51 (pp. 204–205); 52 (p. 207); 53 (pp. 209–210); 54 (p. 214); 55 (p. 218); 57 (pp. 225, 227); 58 (p. 232); 61 (pp. 247–252); 62 (pp. 254–255); 63 (p. 258); 64 (p. 261); 65 (p. 270); 67 (pp. 289–291, 293); 69 (p. 304); 71 (p. 325); 75 (pp. 340–341); 76 (p. 344); 79 (p. 354); 92 (p. 394); 93 (p. 395); 94 (pp. 397–401); 95 (pp. 401–402); 96 (pp. 404–405).

CHAPTER 25 *The Landscape Changes*

For Katherine's confessor's book against Luther, see Carley (2004), pp. 115–116. The most recent account of the foreign policy leading up to the agreement with Charles can be found in Sharkey (2008). I am much indebted to Dr Sharkey, my former student, for permission to refer to her work. A description of Wolsey's visit to Bruges can be found in Hall (1904), I, pp. 228–229. Charles's promise to assist Wolsey's papal candidature is from *LP*, III, ii, no. 1887. References to Mary claiming Charles as her valentine and her performances for his ambassadors are taken from *CSPSp, Further Supp*, pp. 71, 73–74. My account of Charles's visit in 1522 is pieced together from *LP*, III, ii, nos. 2288, 2289, 2305, 2306, 2333, 2360; Hall (1904), I, pp. 244–258; *CSPVen*, II, nos.

466, 467; the *Rutland Papers* (1842), pp. 59–100, which give a very full account of the entire visit; Starkey (2004), pp. 186–189. Anglo (1969), pp. 170–206, provides a masterly analysis of the London pageants which cannot be bettered. For a description of Greenwich Palace and the royal barge, see Thurley (1993), pp. 75–78. Venetian reports that Henry was considering divorcing Katherine in 1514 are mentioned in *CSPVen*, II, no. 479. Readers interested in the life of the Duke of Buckingham should see C. S. L. Davies's entry in *ODNB*. Henry's gift to Buckingham is from *LP*, II, ii, no. 4075. My account of his arrest, trial and execution is based on *LP*, III, i, nos. 1070, 1284, 1285, 1286, 1288; *CSPVen*, III, no. 213; Guy (2008), pp. 70–73. Thomas More's acquisition of the manor of South in Kent is from *LP*, III, i, no. 2239. A good starting point for Mary Boleyn is Jonathan Hughes's *ODNB* entry, but the details I have included on her and on William Carey come from *LP*, III, i, no. 317; *LP*, III, ii, nos. 2074 (5), 2297 (12); *LP*, IV, ii, no. 2972, (p. 1331). Rumours about the parentage of Mary's son, Henry Carey, can be found in *LP*, VIII, no. 567. For Fitzroy's investitures, see *CSPVen*, III, nos. 1037, 1053; *LP*, IV, ii, no. 1431. A letter from Fitzroy's tutor referring to the boy as 'the prince' is printed in *ibid.*, no. 3135. My reference to Katherine using her chaplain to send a warning to Charles concerning Henry's growing discontent comes from *CSPSp, Further Supp*, p. 325. Charles's fear of a possible Scottish match for Mary is from *CSPSp*, III, no. 16.

CHAPTER 26 *'A Blind, Detestable and Wretched Passion'*

For a much fuller account of the divorce proceedings, see Starkey (2004), and Scarisbrick (1968). Kelly (1976), provides an excellent and fascinating analysis of the various court proceedings and the theories behind them; his book is essential reading for anyone wishing to study the divorce in more depth than I am able to provide. See also Parmiter (1967), for a very informative general account.

Katherine's comment to the French ambassadors about antagonising Charles is from *LP*, IV, ii, no. 3105 (p. 1402). The Boleyns' acquisition of Tonbridge is mentioned in *LP*, III, ii, no. 2214 (29) while Grimstone is listed in *LP*, IV, i, no. 546 (2). The king's contribution to Jane Parker's jointure is mentioned in *LP*, X, no. 1010; Ellis (1824–46), 1st Series, p. 67. Readers interested in pursuing the fascinating details of Jane's jointure further should refer to unprinted sources: WRO, microfilm 705:349/12946/498729 is illuminating but should be read together with HLRO, MS PO1/1539 (Original Acts, 31 Henry VIII, c.20). The printed version of the Eltham Ordinances is *LP*, IV, i, no. 1939 (4). To read those parts which were undecipherable to the Victorian transcribers, see NA, SP 1/37, fo. 102. Chapuys's description of Henry's feelings for Anne Boleyn as a 'blind, wretched and detestable passion' is from *CSPSp*, IV, ii, no. 584. For Cavendish's comment on Henry's passion for Anne beginning as she was courted by Percy, see Cavendish (1825), I, p. 58. The chronology of Henry's affair with Anne is discussed by Ives (2004), pp. 81–92; Starkey (2004), pp. 271–285. Starkey's discoveries on the date of Percy's marriage are particularly interesting. Henry's comment about hating writing is from *LP*, III, i, no. 1. The extracts from Henry's love letters which I have chosen to include are from Halliwell (1848), I, pp. 302–303 (*LP*, IV, ii, no. 3221); Halliwell (1848), I, pp. 303–304 (*LP*, IV, ii, no. 3326); Halliwell (1848), I, pp. 305–306 (*LP*, IV, ii, no. 3218); Halliwell (1848), I, p. 317 (*LP*, IV, ii, no. 3990). Anne's beautiful eyes are mentioned in *CSPVen*, IV, no. 872. The David tapestries and their significance are discussed by MacCulloch (1995), p. 180; Herman (1994), pp. 193–218; Campbell (2007), pp. 177–187. Readers interested in the Duke of Suffolk's convoluted marital history should read *LP*, IV, iii, no. 5859 which covers the ground with admirable, if salacious, clarity. Fisher's comments on the marriage question are from *LP*, IV, ii, no. 3148. Katherine's assertions on the validity of her marriage are from *CSPSp*, IV, ii, nos. 681, 1077. Anne Boleyn's remark that Henry would never beat Katherine in argument is from *CSPSp*, IV, i, no. 224. A Latin account of Wolsey's May 1527 court is printed in *LP*, IV, ii, no. 3140, but parts are missing. It was Wolsey who tells us that Henry was anxious to discover the name of Katherine's informant in *ibid.*, no. 3231. Katherine's letters to Charles when she felt he was paying her insufficient attention are from *CSPSp*, III, i, no. 621; *CSPSp*, III, ii, no. 67. The dispatch in which Mendoza told Charles of Wolsey's court is *ibid.*, no. 69. Katherine's hopes that the affair was only a passing fancy on Henry's part is *CSPSp*, IV, i, no. 241. The account of the meeting at which the king told Katherine of his scruples is *CSPSp*, III, ii, no. 113 (p. 276). Katherine's belief that Henry responded to persuasion is from *CSPSp*, IV, i, no. 160. The suggestion that Mary might be sent to France to clear the way for Richmond is *ibid.*, no. 252 (p. 482). Anne Boleyn's resemblance to a lioness comes from *CSPSp*, IV, ii, no. 584. Katherine's letter to Charles and Isabella is printed in *CSPSp*, III, ii. no. 571. The queen's assertion that she and Mary might face martyrdom is *CSPSp*, IV, ii, no. 833. The Venetians' unflattering descriptions of Katherine are from *CSPVen*, IV, nos. 682, 694. Chapuys describes Anne and Thomas Boleyn as Lutherans in *CSPSp*, IV, ii, no. 664. For Anne's possession of a French bible, see Fox (2007), p. 346. Readers interested in religious texts possessed by the Boleyns should refer to James Carley's unequalled work on the subject: see, for example, Carley (2004), especially pp. 125–131. Additionally, Ives (2004), pp. 239–240 and 269–273, also gives an excellent analysis and Starkey (2004), pp. 368–375, gives a particularly incisive and informative examination of Anne's religious values.

CHAPTER 27 *Crusader Queen*

Again, I would refer those seeking more detailed analysis of the divorce to Parmiter (1967); Scarisbrick (1968); Kelly (1976); Starkey (2004). Because my main focus is upon how the divorce affected Katherine and upon how she reacted towards it, I have not attempted to give anything other than relatively basic consideration to the wider issues involved or to the broader international repercussions and diplomacy. Nor have I examined the view explored in Scarisbrick (1968), pp. 163–197, that Wolsey suggested that the bull was insufficient because it did not cover the impediment of public honesty.

Of the many references to Katherine's belief that Wolsey was the main instigator of the divorce, *LP*, V, no. 702 provides one example. The reference to Thomas Boleyn paying £4 to Hayes is *LP*, IV, Appendix 99, p. 3116. For an analysis of the significance of the ship jewel, see Ives (1994), pp. 86–87; Starkey (2004), pp. 282–283; Arnold (1988), p. 76; Fox (2007), p. 60. Susan Wabuda's entry on James Boleyn in *ODNB* mentions his interest in religion, and for his links with Wakefield and Wakefield's significance see Fox (2007), p. 68. Wolsey's reference to Katherine's 'stiff heart' is *LP*, IV, iii, no. 5923. The Duchess of Suffolk's outburst against Anne Boleyn is from *CSPVen*, IV, no. 761. For the Felipez mission see *LP*, IV, ii, nos. 3265, 3278, 3283. References to Charles's affection for Katherine and his early actions on her behalf can be found in *CSPSp*, III, ii, nos. 131, 166, 674; *LP*, IV, ii, no. 3312. Of the many accounts of the Sack of Rome, my quotations come from *ibid.*, no. 3200. For an analysis of the Knight Mission, see Starkey (2004), pp. 302–310. See also Sharkey (2008). My reference to Katherine continuing to make Henry's shirts, which caused friction with Anne Boleyn, comes from *CSPSp*, IV, i, no. 354. Mendoza's comment that Katherine hoped Campeggio would refer the case to Rome is in *CSPSp*, III, ii, no. 570, while her fears that he would not are *ibid.*, no. 562. Henry's letter to Anne is *LP*, IV, ii, no. 4742. Campeggio's instructions are printed *ibid.*, no. 4737. But see also *ibid.*, no. 5073 for the suggestion that Mary might marry Richmond. Campeggio's belief that even an angel could not change Henry's mind is *ibid.*, no. 4858. For Chapuys's visit to Katherine and the nunnery suggestion, see *ibid.*, no. 4856; *CSPSp*, III, ii, no. 586 (pp. 840–841). For Clerk's complaints about the requisitioning of his house, see *ibid.*, nos. 4753, 4754. Of the many examples which show how difficult Katherine found it to send messages to the pope, see *ibid.*, no. 4881. For her confession to Campeggio, see *ibid.*, no. 4875; *CSPVen*, IV, no. 860; *CSPSp*, III, ii, no. 586 (pp. 842–843). For Doña Elvira's comments on Katherine's virginity, see *CSPSp*, I, no. 327 (p. 272). Mendoza's comment on the difficulties involved in proving virginity is *CSPSp*, III, ii, no. 570. That it was permissible to lie except when on oath is taken from Guy (2008), pp. 236–237. Starkey (2004), p. 119, rightly points out that Katherine lied to Ferdinand. Katherine's oath to Campeggio is from *CSPSp*, III, ii, no. 600 (p. 861). Details on Fisher's interrogation can be found in *LP*, VIII, no. 859 (p. 335, questions 29, 30 and 31 and p. 337, answers 29, 30 and 31). For the brief see *CSPSp*, III, ii, no. 644 (p. 973); *LP*, IV, iii, nos. 5154, 5177, 5301, 5376, 5468, 5469. See also Parmiter (1967), pp. 72–95; Kelly (1976), pp. 62–67; Starkey (2004), especially pp. 226–232. For Katherine's interrogation, see *CSPSp*, III, ii, no. 586 (pp. 844–845). For her oath concerning the wording of the brief see *LP*, IV, iii, Appendix 211; Pocock (1870), II, p. 431. Interestingly, Chrimes (1972), p. 286 n. 1, points out that Katherine did not protest against consummation during the negotiations for the treaty for her to marry Henry.

CHAPTER 28 *Taking a Stand*

Once again I would refer readers interested in more detailed explanations and analysis of the issues touched on in this chapter to Parmiter (1967); Scarisbrick (1968); Kelly (1976); Starkey (2004). An example of the many references to Katherine's belief that she would never secure justice in England is *LP*, IV, ii, no. 4535; her assertion that no marriage would be secure if hers is dissolved is from the same source. References to Margaret sending lawyers include *ibid.*, nos. 4943, 4944, 4945, 4946, 5681; *LP*, IV, iii, no. 5687 (p. 2516); *CSPSp*, III, ii, no. 586. Vives's comment is *LP*, IV, ii, no. 4900. Fisher's allusion to John the Baptist is *LP*, IV, iii, no. 5732. The comment about Katherine appearing with thread draped around her neck comes from Cavendish (1825), I, pp. 162–163. For her speech see *ibid.*, pp. 149–152; *CSPVen*, IV, no. 482; *LP*, IV, iii, no. 5702. Hall (1904), II, pp. 150–153 provides an overall description of the Blackfriars trial. Of the many references to Katherine being declared contumacious, see *LP*, IV, iii, no. 5732. For the question of the bed-sheets see Cavendish (1825), pp. 289–290; *LP*, IV, ii, no. 4685; *CSPSp*, I, no. 325. Liss (1992), p. 79, mentions that the sheets used by Ferdinand and Isabella were displayed after their wedding night. The list of those who had returned to Spain but who should be contacted to give evidence on Katherine's behalf is *CSPSp*, IV, i, nos. 573, 574, 575. The list of the questions that were to be asked is from *ibid.*, IV, i, no. 572. For the trial depositions *LP*, IV, iii, nos. 5774, 5778 and 5791 form a useful beginning, but also see the original documents BL, Cotton MS, Appendix XXVII, fos. 58–82v and Cotton Vitellius B. XII fos. 109–124. Starkey (2008), pp. 108, 164, 199, 281, 317–318, 339, has examined Thomas's evidence and explored his relationship with Henry VIII with consummate skill. Starkey intriguingly questions whether Thomas perhaps left Henry's service so shortly after the king's marriage to Katherine because Thomas's knowledge of her marriage with Arthur made her feel uncomfortable. While this is, of course, a possibility, I would suggest that it is doubtful since she did not deny spending up to seven nights or so with Arthur (and Thomas certainly did not witness consummation). It is entirely possible that Thomas simply wanted to return to his native Wales where he made a very good career for himself. The details I have included from his will can be found in NA, PROB 11/29, fo. 121v. I am deeply indebted to the kindness of Dr Dafydd Wyn Wiliam for alerting me to the Welsh ode on Thomas and for transcribing and translating the poem for me. The ode itself can be found in NLW, Brogyntyn 2, p. 431b. Campeggio's complaints of the burden the trial was to him are *LP*, IV, iii, nos. 5713, 4881. My references to Wolsey's fall and its aftermath are from *CSPSp*, IV, i, nos. 83, 135, 182; *LP*, IV, iii, nos. 5803, 6026 (p. 2683). Katherine's plea to Charles for Campeggio's associate is *ibid.*, no. 177; *LP*, IV, iii, no. 5980. Anne Boleyn's anger that Katherine made Henry's shirts and Katherine's open chastising of Henry is *CSPSp*, IV, i, no. 354. Examples of the queen's continued contacts with Henry can be found *ibid.*, nos. 345, 373; *CSPSp*, IV, ii, 720 (p. 153). Anne's presence at a banquet is referred to in *CSPSp*, IV, i, no. 222. That she rode pillion with Henry is stated *ibid.*, no. 302. Examples of gifts for Anne can be found in *LP* IV, iii, Appendix 256; *LP* V, no. 276. For Durham House see Starkey (2004), pp. 356–358; Colvin (1982), p. 76. My examples of the ways in which Henry and the Boleyns passed their time are from *LP*, V, Privy Purse Expenses, pp. 755, 757, 758, 760. The cost of a yard of satin is mentioned *ibid.*, p. 752. Katherine's refusal to leave court even to spend time with Mary is *CSPSp*, IV, ii, no. 720 and the letters/message episode between the queen and Henry is *ibid.*, no. 775. Henry's refusal of Katherine's New Year's Gift is *ibid.*, no. 860. References to Katherine leaving the court can be found *ibid.*, nos. 778, 786. Examples of the problems she faced in trying to receive or send letters and messages to her supporters can be found *ibid.*, nos. 160, 422, 509. Her complaint to Charles about her treatment is *LP*, V, no. 513 (p. 239).

CHAPTER 29 *Dangerous Times*

Katherine's letter to Charles is *CSPSp*, IV, ii, no. 860. An example of Chapuys's derogatory names for Anne can be found *ibid.*, no. 838. Anne's hostile reception is mentioned *ibid.*, no. 980 (p. 964). *LP* VI, nos. 923, 964 include references to Anne as a harlot and a whore. I am once more indebted to Dr Dafydd Wyn Wiliam for bringing the long-lost Welsh poem about Anne to my attention. Fascinating to read, it provides incredible insight into Welsh feelings towards Anne and their loyalty towards Katherine. It can be found in Cynfael Lake (2004), II, pp. 478–479. Anne's power and the king's unwillingness to leave her side is from *CSPSp*, IV, ii, nos. 838, 995 (p. 512). Katherine's response to Anne's request for her jewels is *ibid.*, no. 1003 (pp. 524–525). *LP* V, no. 1274, is an account of Anne's investiture as Marquess of Pembroke. Readers interested in the wider implications of this event should see Friedmann (1884), I, pp.

162–163. Katherine's letter to Charles comparing events in England with Turkish attacks on the Holy Roman Empire is *CSPSp*, IV, ii, no. 994. For the visit of Barnes and Grynaeus, see Guy (2008), p. 195. Anne's jubilant response to the Submission of the Clergy is *CSPSp*, IV, ii, no. 635. Isabella's letter to Charles is *CSPSp*, VIII, Addenda no. 401. Aram (2005), p. 138, mentions Juana's possession of Katherine's portrait. Denia's letter outlining Juana's interest in her family and in political affairs is *CSPSp*, IV, i, no. 247. The Calais visit is briefly covered in Anglo (1969), pp. 245–246. See also Hall (1904), II, pp. 218–221; *CSPVen*, IV, no. 824; *LP*, V, nos. 1484, 1485, 1492; *STC*, nos. 4350, 4351; *Calais Chronicle* (1846), pp. 116–122. See also *CSPSp*, IV, ii, no. 1003 (p. 527) for the fear that Henry might marry Anne at Calais. The words 'body' and 'heart' come from one of Henry's love letters to Anne, printed in *LP*, IV, ii, no. 3128; Halliwell (1848), I, p. 305. For the secret marriage of Henry and Anne see Friedmann (1884), I, pp. 182–184; Ives (2004), p. 161; Starkey (2004), pp. 461, 463, 474–477; MacCulloch (1996), pp. 637–638. My account of when Katherine was officially told of the marriage comes from *CSPSp*, IV, ii, no. 1058 (p. 629). Anne's procession to Mass as queen is *ibid.*, no. 1061 (p. 643). For the Dunstable Judgment see *LP*, VI, no. 528. I based my very brief account of Anne's coronation on Fox (2007), pp. 109–114; Hall (1904), II, pp. 237–239; Ives (2004), pp. 178–179; Starkey (2004), pp. 500–501; Anon. (1533); *LP*, VI, nos. 584, 601, 661. For the major point that Anne was not only crowned with St Edward's Crown but was crowned on St Edward's Chair, see Fox (2007), pp. 111, 343. My reference to Mary, 'the French Queen's' death and burial comes from David Loades's *ODNB* entry. Mary herself refers to her sickness in a letter to Henry, *LP*, VI, no. 693. Suffolk's hasty remarriage is mentioned in *CSPSp*, IV, ii, no. 1123 (p. 786). The meeting at which Katherine is ordered not to use the title of queen again is referred to in *LP*, VI, nos. 759, 760, 765. Chapuys's fears that Anne might harm Katherine and Mary is *CSPSp*, IV, ii, no. 1058 (p. 630). The spat over the christening cloth is *ibid.*, no. 1107. Disappointment over Elizabeth's gender comes from *ibid.*, no. 1124 (p. 789). My details concerning Princess Mary are compiled from *ibid.*, nos. 1123 (p. 819), 1137 (p. 830), 1144 (p. 839), 1161 (pp. 881–882); *CSPSp*, V, i, nos. 10, 23. For the removal of Catalina see *CSPSp, Supp*, no. 97 (p. 418); *CSPVen*, III, no. 910. Bernard (2005), pp. 87–101, 101–125, 125–151, 160–167, gives excellent accounts of the opposition of Elizabeth Barton, Fisher, More and the Carthusians respectively. See also *LP*, VI, nos. 522, 1419, 1464, 1465, 1466, 1519, 1546; *LP*, VII, nos. 498, 499, 500, 1114, 1116, 1563; *LP*, VIII, nos. 661, 666, 815, 876, 895, 988, 996; *CSPSp*, V, no. 156; Guy (2008), p. 3. The remark that the Marchioness of Exeter was Katherine and Mary's only true friend is from *CSPSp*, IV, ii, no. 1127 (p. 800). For More's trial and the packing of the jury see Guy (2008), pp. 185–205. I must thank my husband, John Guy, for the information that Thomas More adopted Thomas Becket as his favourite saint. The reference to Anne's power is *CSPSp*, V, i, no. 229 (p. 571).

CHAPTER 30 *'Mine Eyes Desire You'*

Excellent accounts of Katherine's final years, her illness and her death will be found in Mattingly (1942), pp. 279–311; Starkey (2004), pp. 541–549. For her plate and possessions, see *LP*, VI, nos. 340, 1194. Her household is mentioned in *CSPSp*, IV, ii, no. 1165. The refusal to provide her favourite wine is *CSPSp*, V, i, no. 26. References to her arrears are from *LP*, IX, nos. 178, 964. Katherine's remark to Chapuys that she did not want war is *CSPSp*, IV, ii, no. 1107 (p. 775). Of the many references to her change of heart in this matter, I have taken *CSPSp*, V, i, nos. 57 (p. 153), 237. Charles's recommendation that it was better for Katherine and Mary to take the oath than to die is *LP*, IX, no. 1035. Mary's comment about her mother is mentioned by Chapuys in *LP*, X, no. 141 (p. 52). For Katherine's request to nurse Mary, see *LP*, VIII, no. 200; *CSPSp*, V, i, no. 134. Henry's determination to keep Mary and Katherine apart is mentioned in *CSPSp*, V, i, no. 142 (p. 430). I have based my account of Katherine's illness and death on *LP*, IX, nos. 964 (p. 323), 1036 (pp. 356, 358), 1037, 1040; *LP*, X, nos. 28, 59, 60, 141 (pp. 49–51); *CSPSp*, V, i, no. 238 (pp. 585–586); *CSPSp*, V, ii, nos. 3, 4, 9 (pp. 15–16). The historian who agrees that Katherine's actions, albeit beyond her control, helped usher in consequences which horrified her is Starkey (2004), p. 547. Katherine's 'will' is *LP*, X, no. 40; *CSPSp*, V, ii, no. 9 (p. 16); see also BL, Cotton MS, Otho C. X, fo. 216. The lack of an affirmation concerning the consummation of her marriage to Arthur is *LP*, X, no. 142. For Katherine's last letter, see *LP*, X, nos. 141 (p. 50), 142, 284. I have used Herbert's translation from Vergil's Latin, printed in Herbert (1649), pp. 403–404. See also Heylin (1660), p. 9; Vergil (1950), pp. 334–337. For a very full analysis of Vergil's place in Tudor historiography, see *ibid.*, pp. xxiii–xl. Interestingly, Mattingly (1942), p. 308, prints the letter in full and has no doubt that it is genuine. However *ibid.*, p. 329 n. 16 (wrongly numbered as n. 15) states that Chapuys gives the gist of this letter and that Katherine also wrote to Charles. In fact, while the ambassador confirms the existence of Katherine's will (which is extant) the terms in which he refers to Katherine's last messages suggests that they were verbal rather than written – see *CSPSp*, V, ii, no. 9 (p. 15) and he also passes on her apologies to Charles for not having written personally – see *LP* X, no. 142. In contrast to Mattingly, Starkey (2004), p. 550, appears more sceptical of the genuineness of the letter to Henry. Henry's reaction to Katherine's death is *LP*, X, 141 (p. 51); *CSPSp*, V, ii, no. 9 (p. 19). For her funeral, see *LP*, X, nos. 75, 76, 141 (pp. 50, 51, 53), 282 (p. 102), 284. For Mary's rejection of Anne's offer to be a second mother and her fears concerning the oath, see *ibid.*, no. 141 (p. 48). My details on Charles's reaction come from *ibid.*, nos. 167, 237; *CSPSp*, V, ii, no. 16. Ferdinand's reaction is *CSPVen*, V, no. 90.

CHAPTER 31 *The Final Release*

The best account and most thoughtful analysis of Juana's last years can be found in Aram (2005), pp. 132–161. For the various visits Juana's family made to her, see *ibid.*, pp. 137–138, 143–146. It is Aram who mentions Juana's delight when her granddaughter is named after her, *ibid.*, p. 134. Juana's words when she received Ferdinand's cross are printed *ibid.*, p. 145. Catalina's letter to Charles mentioning missing possessions is from *CSPSp, Supp*, no. 94 (pp. 400–401). For Denia's letter to the empress, see *ibid.*, no. 99 (p. 422) and for various perquisites, see *ibid.*, nos. 96 (pp. 410–411, 416); 103 (p. 428). Details concerning the beliefs of Isabel de la Cruz and of the concept of inner piety can be found in Elliott (1963), pp. 204–209. See also Aram (2005), pp. 146–156, 168–171. For further analysis of Juana's life and of her religious views in particular, see Aram's article in Gómez et al. (2008). Readers interested in how Juana has been portrayed in drama will find Halsey (1978–1979) fascinating. For Juana's last years, I have also used *CSPSp, Supp*, nos. 99 (pp. 422–423), 100 (pp. 423–424), 104 (pp. 429–430).

CHAPTER 32 *The Sisters' Legacy*

For Anne's miscarriage and the presents to Jane Seymour, see *CSPSp*, V, ii, no. 21 (p. 39). My references to Anne's fall are taken from *ibid.*, no. 48; *LP,* X, no. 782. Readers who want a full and detailed analysis of the events surrounding this controversial event should see Ives (2004); Starkey (2004); Warnicke (1989); and, for an intriguing new take on the issue, Bernard (2010). The background to Mary's submission to her father is well described in *CSPSp*, V, ii, no. 70. For a good and comprehensive account of Edward's life and reign, see Dale Hoak's *ODNB* entry. Hoak also analyses the possible causes of Edward's death. For Mary's accession, I have chosen to use *CSPSp*, XI, pp. 106–109, 112–113, 126, 155. Mary is described as being of 'low stature' in *CSPVen*, V, no. 934. De Silva's unflattering comment on Mary's appearance and the reason why Philip married her can be found in *CSPSp*, XIII, no. 7. Mary's letter to Charles praising Philip is *ibid.*, no. 33. Of the many references to presents, I have chosen to use *ibid.*, nos. 1, 7, 503. Duffy (2009) refers to La Pelegrina, Plate 1, opposite p. 114. Philip's attempts to be pleasant to Mary are from *CSPSp*, XIII, no. 37 (p. 31). Mary's comment on her Spanish heritage is from *CSPVen*, V, no. 934. There are many references to the St Paul's obsequies for Juana in *CSPVen*, VI, nos. 89, 138. See also Machyn (1848), p. 90; Strype (1822), Part I, pp. 349–350. The Privy Council meeting at which orders were given for the ceremony to take place is in Acts of the Privy Council of England

(1892), Vol. V, pp. 134–135. Feckenham's sermon was printed in 1555 and can be found in *STC* 10744, *A Notable sermon made within S. Paules church in London ... at the celebration of the exequies of the right excellent and famous princess, lady Jane, Quene of Spayne.* The best, most thorough and most detailed information on the copious preparations for the ceremony, which includes much of what I have said, is not printed and can only be obtained by using the original document source, E 101/427/14. For a full analysis of Mary's phantom pregnancy, see Loades (1989), pp. 248–251. Charles's advice to Philip to become involved in English political affairs is *ibid.*, no. 12, advice which Philip confirms he has accepted *ibid.*, no. 59. See also Guy (2000a), pp. 56–58, for a useful summary of Philip's involvement. The source for my reference to Mary attacking Philip's picture is from NA, SP 11/7, no. 66.

Bibliography

Acts of the Privy Council of England. (1890–1964). New Series. Ed. J. R. Dasent et al., 46 vols. London.

Anglo, S. (1969). *Spectacle, Pageantry, and Early Tudor Policy*. Oxford.

Anon. (1533). *The noble tryumphaunt coronacyon of quene Anne wyfe unto the moost noble kynge Henry the viij*. London.

Aram, B. (1998). 'Juana "the Mad's" Signature: The Problem of Invoking Royal Authority, 1505–1507', *Sixteenth Century Journal*, 29, no. 2 (Summer, 1998), pp. 331–358.

—— (2005). *Juana the Mad: Sovereignty and Dynasty in Renaissance Europe*. Baltimore and London.

Bacon, F. (1881). *Bacon's history of the reign of King Henry VII*, with notes by J. Rawson Lumby. Cambridge.

Baker, J. (2003). *The Oxford History of the Laws of England, Volume VI, 1483–1558*. (Oxford)

Bernard, G. W. (1996). 'The Fall of Wolsey Reconsidered', *Journal of British Studies*, 35, pp. 227–310.

—— (2005). *The King's Reformation: Henry VIII and the Remaking of the English Church*. New Haven and London.

—— (2010). *Anne Boleyn: Fatal Attractions*. New Haven and London.

Boruchoff, D. et al. (2003). *Isabel La Catolica, Queen of Castile: Critical Essays*. New York and Hampshire, England.

Brandi, K. (1939). *The Emperor Charles V, the Growth and Destiny of a Man and of a World–Empire*. Trans. by C. V. Wedgwood. London.

Brigden, S. (1989). *London and the Reformation*. Oxford.

Burnet, Gilbert. (1679–1714). *History of the Reformation of the Church of England*. 3 vols. London.

—— (1820). *History of the Reformation of the Church of England*. New ed., 6 vols. London.

Calais Chronicle. (1846). *The Chronicle of Calais in the Reigns of Henry VII and Henry VIII to the Year 1540*, ed. J. G. Nicholls (Camden Society, 1st Series, 35), London.

Calendar of Letters, Despatches, and State Papers Relating to the Negotiations

Between England and Spain, Preserved in the Archives at Vienna, Brussels, Simancas and Elsewhere. (1863–1954). 13 vols. London.

Calendar of Letters, Despatches, and State Papers Relating to the Negotiations Between England and Spain, Supplement to Volume I and Volume II. (1868). London.

Calendar of Letters, Despatches, and State Papers Relating to the Negotiations Between England and Spain, Further Supplement to the Negotiations between England and Spain, ed. G. Mattingly (1940). London.

Calendar of Patent Rolls, 1485–1509. (1914–16). 2 vols. London.

Calendar of State Papers and Manuscripts, Existing in the Archives and Collections of Milan. (1912). Vol. I. London.

Calendar of State Papers and Manuscripts Relating to English Affairs, Existing in the Archives and Collections of Venice and in Other Libraries of Northern Italy. (1846–1947). 38 vols. London.

Camden Miscellany. (1855). *The Camden Miscellany,* Volume the Third. Printed for the Camden Society. London.

Campbell, T. P. (2002). *Tapestry in the Renaissance, Art and Magnificence.* New York.

—— (2007) *The Art of Majesty: Henry VIII's Tapestry Collection.* New Haven and London.

Carley, J. P. (1998). '"Her moost lovying and fryndely brother sendeth gretying": Anne Boleyn's Manuscripts and Their Sources'. In Michelle P. Brown and Scot McKendrick, eds., *Illuminating the Book: Makers and Interpreters.* London and Toronto, pp. 261–280.

—— (2000). *The Libraries of King Henry VIII.* London.

—— (2004). *The Books of King Henry VIII and His Wives.* London.

Carlson, D. (1991). 'Royal Tutors in the Reign of Henry VII', *Sixteenth Century Journal,* 22. no. 2 (Summer, 1991), pp. 253–279.

Cavendish, George. (1825). *The Life of Cardinal Wolsey and Metrical Visions.* Ed. Samuel Weller Singer, 2 vols. London.

Chrimes, S. B. (1972). *Henry VII.* London.

The Chronicle of Calais in the Reigns of Henry VII and Henry VIII to the Year 1540. (1846). Ed. J. G. Nicholls (Camden Society, 1st Series, vol. 35). London.

Chronicles of London. (1905). Ed. with Introduction and Notes by Charles Lethbridge Kingsford, M. A. Oxford.

Colvin, H. M. (1982). *The History of the King's Works, IV, 1485–1625* (Part 2). London.

The Complete Peerage of England, Scotland, Ireland, Great Britain and the United Kingdom by G. E. C[ockayne]. (1987). 6 vols. Gloucester.

Crawford, A. (2001). 'The Queen's Council in the Middle Ages', *The English Historical Review,* 116 (Nov. 2001), pp. 1193–1211.

Cressy, D. (1997). *Birth, Marriage and Death: Ritual, Religion and the Life-Cycle in Tudor and Stuart England*. Oxford and New York.

Cynfael Lake, A. (2004). *Gwaith Lewys Morgannwg*. Aberystwyth.

Dewhurst, J. (1984). 'The Alleged Miscarriages of Catherine of Aragon and Anne Boleyn', *Medical History*, 28, pp. 49–56.

Doran, S. ed. and Starkey, D. R. (2009). *Henry VIII: Man and Monarch*. The British Library, London.

Dowling, M. (1984). 'Anne Boleyn and Reform', *Journal of Ecclesiastical History*, 35, pp. 30–46.

—— (1986). *Humanism in the Age of Henry VIII*. Beckenham and Dover, N. H.

—— (1990). 'William Latymer's Chronickille of Anne Bulleyne'. In *Camden Miscellany*, 30 (Camden Society, 4th Series, vol. 39), pp. 23–65, 501–3.

Doyle, D. R. (2000). 'The Sinews of Habsburg Governance in the Sixteenth Century: Mary of Hungary and Political Patronage', *Sixteenth Century Journal*, 31, no. 2 (Summer, 2000), pp. 349–360.

Duffy, E. (1992). *The Stripping of the Altars: Traditional Religion in England, 1400–1580*. New Haven and London.

—— (2009). *Fires of Faith, Catholic England under Mary Tudor*. New Haven and London.

Duncan, J. and Derrett, M. (1963). 'Henry Fitzroy and Henry VIII's Scruple of Conscience', *Renaissance News*, 16. no. 1 (Spring, 1963), pp. 1–9.

Dyer, A. (1997). 'The English Sweating Sickness of 1551: An Epidemic Anatomized', *Medical History*, 41, pp. 362–384.

Elliott, J. H. (1963). *Imperial Spain 1469–1716*. London.

Ellis, H. (1824–46). *Original Letters, Illustrative of British History*, 3 series, 11 vols. London.

Elton, G. R. (1972). *Policy and Police: The Enforcement of the Reformation in the Age of Thomas Cromwell*. Cambridge.

Fernández–Armesto, F. (1975). *Ferdinand and Isabella*. London.

Fiddes, R. (1724). *The Life of Cardinal Wolsey*. London.

Flood, J. L. (2003). '"Safer on the Battlefield than in the City": England, the "Sweating Sickness" and the Continent', *Renaissance Studies*, 17, pp. 146–176.

Fox, A., and Guy, J. A. (1986). *Reassessing the Henrician Age: Humanism, Politics, and Reform*. Oxford and New York.

Fox, J. (2007). *Jane Boleyn, The Infamous Lady Rochford*. (London).

Foxe, John. (1563). *Actes and monuments of these latter and perillous dayes touching matters of the Church, wherein are comprehended and described the great persecutions [and] horrible troubles, that have bene wrought and practiced by the Romishe prelates, speciallye in this realme of England and Scotlande . . .* London.

—— (1576). *The first volume of the ecclesiasticall history contayning the actes [and] momumentes of thinges passed in euery kinges time, in this realme, especialli in the Churche of England principally to be noted . . . Newly recognised and inlarged by the author.* 2 vols. London.

—— (1583). *Actes and monuments of matters most speciall and memorable, happenying in the Church with an vniuersall history of the same, wherein is set forth at large the whole race and course of the Church, from the primitiue age to these latter tymes of ours . . . Newly reuised and re cognzed, partly also augmented, and now the fourth time agayne published.* 2 vols. London.

—— (1843–49). *The Acts and Monuments of John Foxe.* Ed. G. Townsend. 8 vols. London.

Friedmann, P. (1884). *Anne Boleyn: A Chapter of English History, 1527–1536.* 2 vols. London.

Glück. G. (1933). 'The Henry VII in the National Portrait Gallery', *The Burlington Magazine for Connoisseurs*, 63, no. 366 (Spring, 1933), pp. 100, 104–108.

Gómez, M. et al. (2008). *Juana of Castile: history and myth of the mad queen.* Lewisburg, Pa: Bucknell University Press.

The Great Chronicle of London. (1983). Ed. by A. H. Thomas and I. D. Thornley. Gloucester, England.

Green, V. H. H. (1952). *Renaissance and Reformation: A Survey of European History between 1450 and 1660.* London.

Gunn, S. J. (1988). *Charles Brandon, Duke of Suffolk, 1484–1545.* Oxford and New York.

Guy, John. (1988). *Tudor England.* Oxford.

—— (2000a). *The Tudors: A Very Short Introduction.* Oxford.

—— (2000b). *Thomas More.* London and New York.

—— (2004). *'My Heart is My Own': The Life of Mary Queen of Scots.* London.

—— (2008). *A Daughter's Love: Thomas and Margaret More.* London and New York.

Haigh, C. A. (1993). *English Reformations: Religion, Politics and Society under the Tudors.* Oxford and New York.

Hall, Edward. (1904). *Henry VIII* [an edition of Hall's Chronicle]. Ed. C. Whibley, 2 vols. London.

Halliwell, J. O. (1884). *Letters of the Kings of England.* 2 vols. London.

Halsey, M. 'Juana La Loca in Three Dramas of Tamayo y Baus, Galdós, and Martín Recuerda', *Modern Language Studies*, Vol. 9, No. 1 (Winter, 1978–1979), pp. 47–59.

Hare, C. (1913). *Maximilian the Dreamer: Holy Roman Emperor, 1459–1519.* London.

Harpsfield, N. (1932). *The life and death of Sir Thomas Moore, knight, sometymes Lord high Chancellor of England, written in the tyme of Queene Marie.* Ed. E. V. Hitchcock (Early English Text Society, Original Series, no. 186). London.

Harris, B. (1986). *Edward Stafford, Third Duke of Buckingham, 1478–1521.* Stanford, Calif.

—— (2002). *English Aristocratic Women 1450–1550: Marriage and family, Property and Careers.* Oxford and New York.

Hayward, M. (2004). *The 1542 Inventory of Whitehall: The Palace and its Keeper.* 2 vols. Society of Antiquaries. London.

—— *Dress at the court of King Henry VIII: the Wardrobe Book of the Wardrobe of the Robes prepared by James Worsley in December 1516, edited from Harley MS 2284, and his inventory prepared on 17 January 1521, edited from Harley MS 4217, both in the British Library,* edited and with a commentary by Maria Hayward. Leeds.

Hepburn, F. (1997). 'Arthur, Prince of Wales and his Training for Kingship', *The Historian,* no. 55 (1997).

Herbert of Cherbury, Edward. (1649). *The Life and Raigne of King Henry the Eighth.* London.

Herman, P. C. (1994). *Rethinking the Henrician Era: Essays on Early Tudor Texts and Contexts.* Urbana and Chicago, Il.

Heylin, P. (1660). *Affairs of Church and State in England during the Life and Reign of Queen Mary.* London.

Hume, M. (1906). *Queens of Old Spain.* New York.

Irwin, R. (2004). *The Alhambra.* London.

Ives, E.W. (1972). 'Faction at the Court of Henry VIII: The Fall of Anne Boleyn', *History,* 57, pp. 169–188.

—— (1994). 'Anne Boleyn and the Early Reformation in England: the Contemporary Evidence', *Historical Journal,* 37, pp. 389–400.

—— (2004). *The Life and Death of Anne Boleyn.* 2nd ed. Oxford and Malden, Mass.

Kamen, H. (1983). *Spain 1469–1714: A Society of Conflict.* New York.

Keay, A. (2001). *The Elizabethan Tower of London: The Haiward and Gascoyne Plan of 1597.* London.

Kelly, H. A. (1976). *The Matrimonial Trials of Henry VIII.* Stanford, Calif.

Kingsford, C. L. *Chronicles of London.* Oxford.

Knecht, R. J. (1994). *Renaissance Warrior and Patron: The Reign of Francis I.* Cambridge.

Lehmberg, S. E. (1970). *The Reformation Parliament, 1529–1536.* Cambridge.

Leland, J. (1770). *Antiquarii de Rebus Britannicus Collectanea, Volume III.* London.

Letters and Papers, Foreign and Domestic, of the Reign of Henry VIII (1862–1932). Ed. J. S. Brewer, J. Gairdner, and R. H. Brodie. 21 vols. in 32 parts, and Addenda, with rev. ed. of vol. 1 in 3 parts. London.

Letters and Papers illustrative of the Reigns of Richard III and Henry VII (1861–63). Ed. J. Gairdner. 2 vols. London.

The Lisle Letters. (1981). Ed. M. St Clare Byrne. 6 vols. Chicago and London.

Liss, P. K. (1992). *Isabel the Queen: Life and Times*. New York and Oxford.

Livermore, H. V. (1966). *A New History of Portugal*. London.

Lloyd Jones, G. (1983). *The Discovery of Hebrew in Tudor England: A Third Language*. Manchester and Dover, N.H.

—— (1989). *Robert Wakefield: On the Three Languages (1524)*. Ed. and trans. with introduction and notes. New York.

Loach, J. (1994). 'The Function of Ceremonial in the Reign of Henry VIII', *Past and Present*, no. 143, pp. 43–68.

Loades, D. M. (1986). *The Tudor Court*. London.

—— (1989). *Mary Tudor: a Life*. Oxford and Cambridge, Mass.

—— (1991). *The Reign of Mary Tudor: Politics, Government and Religion in England, 1553–1558*. 2nd ed. London and New York.

MacCulloch, D. (1995). 'Henry VIII and the Reform of the Church'. In D. MacCulloch, ed., *The Reign of Henry VIII: Politics, Policy and Piety*. London and New York, pp. 159–80.

—— (1996). *Thomas Cranmer. A Life*. New Haven and London.

Machyn, H. (1848), *The Diary of Henry Machyn, Citizen and Merchant-Taylor of London, from A.D. 1550 to A.D. 1563*. Edited by John Gough Nichols. London.

Manuale et Processionale ad Usum Insignis Ecclesiae Eboracensis [with appendix 1: *Manuale ad Usum Insignis Ecclesiae Sarum*]. (1875). Surtees Society, York.

Marques, A. H. de Oliveira. (1971). *Daily Life in Portugal in the Late Middle Ages*. Trans. by S. S. Wyatt. Madison, Wis. and London.

Mattingly, G. (1940). 'The Reputation of Dr De Puebla', *The English Historical Review*, 55 (Jan. 1940), pp. 27–46.

—— (1942). *Catherine of Aragon*. London.

McIntosh, M. K. (1991). *A Community Transformed: The Manor and Liberty of Havering, 1500–1620*. Cambridge.

Mendelson, S. and Crawford, P. (1998). *Women in Early Modern England, 1550–1720*. Oxford and New York.

Merriman, R. B. (1902). *Life and Letters of Thomas Cromwell*. 2 vols. Oxford.

Miller, Townsend. (1963). *The Castles and the Crown. Spain: 1451–1555*. London.

Monumenta Westmonasteriensa. Or an Historical Account of the Original, Increase, and Present State of St Peter's, or the Abbey Church of Westminster, with all the Epitaphs, Inscriptions, Coats of Arms and Achievements of Honor Belonging to the Tombs and Gravestones. (1683). London.

Murphy, B. A. (2003). *Bastard Prince: Henry VIII's Lost Son.* Stroud.

Murphy, V. M. (1984). 'The Debate over Henry VIII's First Divorce: An Analysis of the Contemporary Treatises'. Unpublished Ph.D. dissertation, Cambridge.

Murphy, V. M. (1995). 'The Literature and Propaganda of Henry VIII's First Divorce'. In D. MacCulloch, ed., *The Reign of Henry VIII: Politics, Policy and Piety.* pp. 135–158.

Nichols, J. (1780). *A Collection of all the Wills now known to be extant of the Kings and Queens of England, Princes and Princesses of Wales, and every branch of the Blood Royal, from the reign of William the Conqueror, to that of Henry the Seventh exclusive, with explanatory notes and a glossary.* London.

Nicholson, G. D. (1988). 'The Acts of Appeals and the English Reformation'. In Claire Cross, et al., eds., *Law and Government under the Tudors.* Cambridge and New York, pp. 19–30.

Nicolas, N. H. (1830). *Privy Purse expense of Elizabeth of York: Wardrobe Accounts of Edward the Fourth, with a Memoir of Elizabeth of York*, and notes by Nicholas Harris Nicolas. London.

—— (1834–37). *Proceedings and Ordinances of the Privy Council of England.* 7 vols. London.

Norris, Herbert. (1997). *Tudor Fashion and Costume.* New York.

Parmiter, Geoffrey de C. (1967). *The King's Great Matter: A Study of Anglo-Papal Relations 1527–1534.* London.

Pierce, Hazel. (2003). *Margaret Pole, Countess of Salisbury, 1473–1541.* Cardiff.

Pocock, N. ed. (1870). *Records of the Reformation: the Divorce, 1527–1533.* 2 vols. Oxford.

Pollard, A. E. (1902). *Henry VIII.* London and New York.

Prawdin, M. (1939). *The Mad Queen of Spain.* New York.

Prescott, W. H. (1854). *History of the Reign of Ferdinand and Isabella, the Catholic, of Spain.* London.

Prockter, A. and Taylor, R. (1979). *The A to Z of Elizabethan London.* London.

Rex, Richard. (1993). *Henry VIII and the English Reformation.* London.

Robinson, W. R. B. (2002). 'Prince Arthur in the Marches of Wales, 1493–1502' in *Studia Celtica*, 36, pp. 89–97.

Rogers, E. F. (1961). *St Thomas More: Selected Letters.* New Haven and London.

Royal Book. (1790). *A Collection of Ordinances and Regulations for the Government of the Royal Household.* Society of Antiquaries, London, pp. 109–133.

Ruiz, M. R. (2004). *The Royal Chapel of Granada, The Exchange ('Lonja'), the Church, the Museum, Visitor's Guide.* Granada.

Rutland Papers. (1842). *Original Documents illustrative of the Courts and Times of Henry VII and Henry VIII ... from the Private Archives of His Grace the Duke of Rutland.* Ed. W. Jerdan (Camden Society, 1st Series, vol. 21). London.

The Sarum Missal in English. (1913). Ed. and trans. F. E. Warren, 2 vols. Alcuin Club, Oxford.

Scarisbrick, J. J. (1968). *Henry VIII.* London and Berkeley.

Searle, W. G. (1867). *The History of the Queens' College of St Margaret and St Bernard in the University of Cambridge.* Cambridge.

Sharkey, J. (2008). '*The Politics of Wolsey's Cardinalate, 1515–1530*'. Unpublished Ph.D. dissertation, Cambridge.

A Short-Title Catalogue of Books Printed in England, Scotland and Ireland, and of English Books Printed Abroad. (1976–91). Ed. W. A. Jackson et al., 2nd ed., 3 vols. London.

Spruyt, B. J. (1994). '"En bruit d'estre bonne luteriene": Mary of Hungary (1505–58) and Religious Reform', *The English Historical Review*, 109 (Apr., 1994), pp. 275–307.

Starkey, D. R. (1987a). 'Court History in Perspective', In D. R. Starkey et al., eds., *The English Court from the Wars of the Roses to the Civil War.* London and New York, pp. 1–24.

—— (1987b). 'Intimacy and Innovation: The Rise of the Privy Chamber'. In D. R. Starkey et al., eds., *The English Court from the Wars of the Roses to the Civil War.* London and New York, pp. 71–118.

—— (1991a). *Henry VIII: A European Court in England.* London.

—— (1991b). *The Reign of Henry VIII: Personalities and Politics.* London.

—— (2004). *Six Wives: The Queens of Henry VIII.* London and New York.

—— (2008). *Henry, Virtuous Prince.* London.

Starkey, D. R. and Ward, P., Hawkyard, A. (1998). *The Inventory of King Henry VIII. Volume. 1. The Transcript.* Society of Antiquaries, London.

State Papers During the Reign of Henry VIII. (1830–52). 11 vols. Record Commission, London.

Statutes of the Realm. (1810–28). Ed. A. Luders, et al., 11 vols. London.

Stow, John. (1592). The *Annales of England faithfully collected out of the most autenticall authors, records, and other monuments of antiquitie, from the first inhabitation vntill this present yeere, 1592.* London.

—— (1956). *Stow's Survey of London.* Ed. H. B. Wheatley. London.

Strype, J. (1822). *Ecclesiastical memorials Relating chiefly to Religion and the Reformation ... under King Henry VIII, King Edward VI, and Queen Mary I.* 3 vols. Oxford.

The Receyt of the Ladie Kateryne. (1990). Ed. G. Kipling (Early English Text Society). Oxford.

Thompson, G. G. (1984). 'Mary of Hungary and Music Patronage', *Sixteenth Century Journal,* 15 (Winter, 1984), pp. 401–418.

Thurley, S. (1993). *The Royal Palaces of Tudor England. Architecture and Court Life, 1460–1547.* New Haven and London.

—— (1999). *Whitehall Palace. An Architectural History of the Royal Apartments, 1240–1698.* New Haven and London.

Thwaites, G., Taviner, M., and Gant. V. (1997). 'The English Sweating Sickness, 1485–1551', *New England Journal of Medicine,* 336, pp. 580–582.

—— 'The English Sweating Sickness, 1485–1551: A Viral Pulmonary Disease?' *Medical History,* 42, pp. 96–98.

Vergil, P. (1950). *The Anglica Historia of Polydore Vergil A.D. 1485–1537.* Edited with a translation by Denys Hay, London.

Vives, J. (2000). *The Education of a Christian Woman: a Sixteenth Century Manual.* Edited and translated by Charles Fantazzi. Chicago and London.

Wakefield, Robert. (1528). *Roberti Wakfeldi sacrarum literaru[m] professoris eximij oratio de laudibus & vtilitate triu[m] linguar[um] Arabicae Chaldaicae & Hebraicae atq[ue] idiomatibus hebraicis quae in vtroq[ue] testame[n]to i[n]ueniu[n]tur.* London.

—— (n.d). *Kotser codicis R. Wakfeldi, quo praeter ecclesiae sacrosanctae decretum, probatur coniugium cum fratria carnaliter cognita, illicitum omnino, inhibitum, interdictumq[ue] effetum naturae iure, cum iure diuino legeq[ue] euangelica atq[ue] consuetudi[n]e catholica ecclesiae orthodoxe.* London.

Warnicke, R. M. (1998). *The Rise and Fall of Anne Boleyn.* Cambridge and New York.

Wood, M. A. (1846). *Letters of Royal and Illustrious Ladies of Great Britain.* 3 vols. London

Woodward, J. (1997). *The Theatre of Death: The Ritual Management of Royal Funerals in Renaissance England 1570–1625.* Woodbridge.

Wriothesley, Charles. (1875–77). *A Chronicle of England during the Reigns of the Tudors, from A.D. 1485 to 1559.* 2 vols. (Camden Society, New Series, vols. 11, 20). London.

Illustration credits

The Bridgeman Art Library

Portrait of Isabella I (1451–1504) 'The Catholic', Queen of Castile, c.1490–92 (oil on panel), Spanish School, Prado, Madrid, Spain.

Portrait of Ferdinand II (1452–1516) King of Spain (oil on panel), Master of the Legend of St Madeleine (fl.c.1500), Musée Sainte-Croix, Poitiers, France, Giraudon/The Bridgeman Art Library.

Portrait of a woman, possibly Katherine of Aragon (1485–1536), c.1503/4 (oil on panel), Michiel Sittow (1469–1525), Kunsthistorisches Museum, Vienna, Austria.

Portrait of Juana of Castile (1479–1555), c.1500 (oil on panel), Juan de Flandes (c.1465–1519), Kunsthistorisches Museum, Vienna, Austria.

Portrait of Joanna of Castile (1479–1555), Master of the Legend of St Madeleine (fl.c.1500), Kunsthistorisches Museum, Vienna, Austria.

Portrait of Philip I of Spain (1478–1506), son of Maximilian I (1459–1519) and Maria of Burgundy (1457–82), c.1500 (oil on panel), attrib. to Flandes, Juan de (c.1465–1519), Kunsthistorisches Musuem, Vienna, Austria.

Portrait of Henry VII (1457–1509), c.1500 (oil on panel), English School, Society of Antiquaries of London, UK.

Portrait of King Henry VIII (1491–1547), c.1536/7 (oil on oak panel), Hans Holbein the Younger (1497/8–1543), Thyssen-Bornemisza Collection, Madrid, Spain.

Portraits of the children of Philip the Handsome (1478–1506) and Juana of Castile (1479–1555), c.1510 (tempera on panel), Spanish School, Museo de Bellas Artes, Toledo, Spain.

Portrait of Anne Boleyn (c.1500–1536), c.1534 (oil on panel), English School, Hever Castle, Kent, UK.

Portrait of Philip II (1527–1598) and Mary I (1516–1558), c.1557/8, Hans Eworth (fl.1520–74), Trustees of the Bedford Estate, Woburn Abbey, UK.

Clare College, University of Cambridge, UK

The Alhambra and Granada (detail) from Georg Braun, *Civitates Orbis Terrarum*, Cologne and Antwerp, 1582. By courtesy of the Fellows' Librarian.

A map of Spain (detail) from Georg Braun, *Civitates Orbis Terrarum*, Cologne and Antwerp, 1582. By courtesy of the Fellows' Librarian.

St George's Chapel, Windsor Castle (detail) from Georg Braun, *Civitates Orbis Terrarum*, Cologne and Antwerp, 1582. By courtesy of the Fellows' Librarian.

Private Collection

The Emperor Maximilian I (1459–1519), from an 18th-century engraving, Private Collection.

Lady Margaret Beaufort (1443–1509), the King's Mother, Countess of Richmond and Derby, from a 19th-century engraving, Private Collection.

Baynard's Castle, London, from an 18th-century engraving, Private Collection.

Edward Stafford, Duke of Buckingham (1478–1521), from a 19th-century engraving by R. Ackermann, Private Collection.

William Warham (c.1450–1532), Archbishop of Canterbury, from a 19th-century engraving after Francesco Bartolozzi following Hans Holbein the Younger, Private Collection.

The Holy Roman Emperor Charles V (1500–1558), from a 19th-century engraving, Private Collection.

Prince Ferdinand (1503–1564), from a 17th-century engraving, Private Collection.

King Francis I of France (1494–1547), from a 17th-century engraving, Private Collection.

Sir Thomas More (1477/8–1535), from a 19th-century engraving, Private Collection.

John Fisher, Bishop of Rochester (c.1469–1535), from a 19th-century engraving after Francesco Bartolozzi following Hans Holbein the Younger, Private Collection.

Thomas Cromwell (c.1485–1540), from an 18th-century engraving, Private Collection.

Cardinal Wolsey surrenders the great seal in 1529 (pen and ink drawing), John Masey Wright (1777–1866), Private Collection.

Yale University, Beinecke Rare Book and Manuscript Library

Catholic Church Antiphonary, Castile, Spain, 16th century, MS 794.

Miniature of 5 falcons sitting on a perch in a niche, produced probably in Naples in the third quarter of the 15th century for Ferdinand II of Aragon, MS 446.

Jousters on horseback, wood engraving, part of Jost Amman (1539–1591), *Kunstbuechl[e]in/darinnen neben Fuerbildung vieler/ geistlicher vnnd weltlicher/ Hohes vnd Niderstands Personen/ so dann auch der tuerckischen Kaeyser/ vnnd derselben Obersten/ allerhandt kunstreiche Stueck vnnd Figuren ... begriffen*, Frankfurt am Main, 1599.

Other illustrations

Tomb of Philip the Handsome (1478–1506) and Juana of Castille (1479–1555), c.1519 (marble), Bartolomé Ordóñez (d.1520), Capilla Real, Granada, Spain © 2010 Photo SCALA, Florence.

The Royal Convent of St Clare, Tordesillas. By courtesy of José-Manuel Benito.

The Court of Myrtles, the Alhambra, Granada, Spain, photo © 2011, Julia Fox.

The gardens of the Generalife, the Alhambra, Granada, Spain, photo © 2011, Julia Fox.

The gatehouse at Ludlow Castle, Shropshire, UK, photo © 2011, Julia Fox.

The Round Chapel, Ludlow Castle, Shropshire, UK, photo © 2011, Julia Fox.

Prince Arthur (1486–1502), Prince of Wales, the Church of St Lawrence, Ludlow, Shropshire, UK, photo © 2011, Julia Fox.

Prince Arthur's tomb, Worcester Cathedral, UK, photo © 2011, Julia Fox.

Prince Arthur's Tudor rose and Katherine's pomegranate emblem from the carved tracery around Arthur's tomb in Worcester Cathedral, UK, photo © 2011, Julia Fox.

The first graves of Isabella of Castile and Ferdinand of Aragon, Monastery of San Francisco, the Alhambra, Granada, Spain, photo © 2011, Julia Fox.

The Royal Chapel, Granada, Spain, photo © 2011, Julia Fox.

Katherine of Aragon's tomb, Peterborough Cathedral, UK, photo © 2011, Julia Fox.

The tomb of Henry Fitzroy (1519–1536), Duke of Richmond and Somerset, the Church of St Michael, Framlingham, Suffolk, UK, photo © 2011, Julia Fox.

Framlingham Castle, Suffolk, UK, photo © 2011, Julia Fox.

Index